COMPULSIVE GAMBLING:
WHAT'S IT ALL ABOUT?

COMPULSIVE GAMBLING:
WHAT'S IT ALL ABOUT?

VALERIE C. LORENZ, Ph.D.

TATE PUBLISHING
AND ENTERPRISES, LLC

Published by Tate Publishing & Enterprises, LLC
127 E. Trade Center Terrace | Mustang, Oklahoma 73064 USA
1.888.361.9473 | www.tatepublishing.com

Tate Publishing is committed to excellence in the publishing industry. The company reflects the philosophy established by the founders, based on Psalm 68:11,
"The Lord gave the word and great was the company of those who published it."

Book design copyright © 2013 by Tate Publishing, LLC. All rights reserved.
Cover design by Rodrigo Adolfo
Interior design by Jomar Ouano

Published in the United States of America

ISBN: 978-1-62746-602-8
1. Psychology / Psychopathology / Addiction
2. Psychology / General
13.01.02

ACKNOWLEDGMENTS

It would have been very difficult, if not impossible, to write this book without the generous assistance from many others who believed in me and my urgency to get this book written without further procrastination. They gave suggestions, made corrections, reviewed, critiqued, and nudged when I needed to be nudged.

CLINICIANS AND RESEARCHERS

Ken Broghammer, CADC, retired, addictions counselor, who gave of his wisdom to many compulsive gamblers and other addicts

Robert Ladouceur, Ph.D., professor at Laval University, Quebec, respected for his many years of research on compulsive gambling and gamblers

Henry Lesieur, Psy.D., Ph.D., pioneer, founder of the *Journal of Gambling Behavior*, author, researcher and clinician on compulsive gambling

William Levin, Ph.D., clinical psychologist, member of the Maryland Psychological Association writers group

Kenneth Martz, Psy.D., clinical director and private practice, specialist in compulsive gambling treatment and research

Anita Solomon, Ph.D., clinical psychologist, member of the Maryland Psychological Association writers group

Thomas T. Truss, Ph.D., clinical psychologist, clinician, supervisor and director of compulsive gambling treatment programs since 1980.

Fred E. Waddell, Ph.D., prolific author and educator on financial matters, including *Solution-Focused Financial Counseling*

Robert Alan Yaffee, PhD, professor and researcher, New York University.

LAW ENFORCEMENT OFFICERS FOR THEIR INPUT ON ORGANIZED CRIME AND THE CRIMINAL JUSTICE SYSTEM

David Harvilak, MBus, Special Agent, FBI (retired) who specialized in Organized Crime/Gambling

William L. Holmes, M.F.Sc., Supervisory Special Agent, FBI (retired), who specialized in Organized Crime/Gambling

Honorable Judge Paul Wm. Ottinger. JD, various courts in Hagerstown, PA.

Robert L. Paul, B.A., Dauphin County, PA, Parole and Probation

Robert Snyder, Esq., LA County Sheriffs Department (retired)

COMPULSIVE GAMBLING PROGRAMS

Keith Whyte, Executive Director of the National Council on Problem Gambling

Thomas Grey, M. Div., Senior Consultant, Stop Predatory Gambling

Karen H., Executive Director of the International Service Office of Gamblers Anonymous

Regina K., Secretary, Gam-Anon International Service Office, Inc.

EDITING AND TECHNICAL ASSISTANCE

To Geoffrey Crawford, Ama Frimpong, and Jennifer Barnett, thank you for your technical support. I give my everlasting thanks also to the many men, women, and children who have walked the road of compulsive gambling and its effects. I am one of you and together we can heal.

Disclaimer: Opinions are based on my forty years of experiencing working in the field of compulsive gambling and obviously do not apply to every compulsive gambler or family member but rather to those in general.

TABLE CONTENTS

CHAPTER 1
COMPULSIVE GAMBLING AND MY STORY

It was February, 1972, Harrisburg, PA. After some dark moments in my life, the sun was beginning to shine. I was the single mom of three young children, studying for my master's degree in American Studies at The Pennsylvania State University, active in my community, and a member of the Junior League of Harrisburg. Little did I know that my Junior League service at Yoke Crest would be a turning point in my life.

Yoke Crest was a residential treatment program for adjudicated young offenders, a halfway house *before* prison instead of *after* prison. Its philosophy matched mine, prevention instead of addiction, treatment instead of jail. The director of Yoke Crest was Kenneth Mitchell Rigel – better known as Mitch Rigel, the mod ex-con, appointed by Pennsylvania Governor Milton J. Shapp to the newly-formed Governor's Council on Drug and Alcohol Abuse. How was that honor even remotely possible? Just a year earlier Mitch had been released from federal prison, having served two five-year terms for armed bank robbery. Robbed a bank, got $300, walked around the block, and returned it. Five years to feed his gambling addiction. Almost ten years on parole, then another desperate gambling indebtedness, another crime, another five years in prison.

I met Mitch at Yoke Crest and life as I had known it was no more. My prior life had been so different living on military bases, moving to Washington, DC, a fairy tale life of international friends and travel, of symphony concerts, art galleries, embassy galas, of academia with mixed career goals of international banking or museum curator, of the Smithsonian perhaps?

Mitch was highly respected for his innovative concepts of mental illness and prison reform. This mod ex-con—intelligent and motivated to achieve, loved his family, his community, and his service in the US Marine Corps. He was charismatic, once a bantam weight boxer while serving in the Corps, always whistling *Life is Just a Bowl of Cherries*. He was a kind and gentle man. He was also a compulsive gambler. And I didn't know.

We talked about his family and mine, his time in prison, his gambling, the pain in his life, his vulnerabilities, his distrust of people. "Then I met Newman Gaugler, of Yokefellow Prison Ministry. He taught me to trust. I don't have to be alone anymore, I don't need to gamble. Those days are over." And I believed him.

The foot of snow on the ground cast a stillness around us as Mitch Rigel and I were married. Driving to the airport we ran into a blizzard. Was that an omen? On our honeymoon in Florida, our car got stuck in the sand. Was that another omen?

Our first year together was a joyful one. Mitch was a loving husband and a loving dad, he made new friends, and work was rewarding. Then came the day before Christmas. Mitch suggested, "Instead of individual presents for everyone, let's have one big gift for the family. A new television." We agreed. The kids were excited. But as he was leaving the house to buy it, I noticed that he looked different – subdued, hunched over, no boxer's spring in his step, no quick good-by kiss, distracted. At ten, I was still looking out the window for him, at midnight I was calling local hospitals, at six on Christmas morning two of his staff members brought him home. He had been gambling all night at Jimmy G's Pool Hall, playing poker - no new TV and the money was gone. "It was just this once, to see if I could control it." I believed him. Again.

A few months later, after an on-site visit to a rehab in California, a staff member - a recovering drug addict - suggested they stop off at Las Vegas on the way home. After that, Mitch gambled more, disappeared often, lost more money. And he always had good excuses and promises. I had my doubts.

Thus began four years of hell – no longer the loving husband and father, instead life was arguments and threats, missing work, days of disappearances, no money, and always the lies. He was still on federal parole. What if his PO came over and Mitch was gone? Should I lie to protect Mitch, or should I tell the truth, risking a parole violation and back to jail? Even his staff didn't know what to do or say.

Life became a yo-yo - good moments for a few hours and the bad times for days. Mitch was accused of misappropriating federal funds. The district attorney and a legislator, both friends of ours, called for an investigation. The media loved it. They waited outside our house, wrote long articles, plastered pictures on the television news and in the newspapers. Eventually the FBI found him not guilty, but by then our friends were gone, Mitch was removed from the Governor's Council, told to resign from Yoke Crest, my children suffered and were afraid to go to school or church. And there was no help for us.

My committee at Penn State convinced me to change majors from American Studies to Community Psychology, with a focus on compulsive gambling. I did research and wrote my master's thesis on the impact of compulsive gambling on the family. I continued my studies and at the University of Pennsylvania, did more research, and wrote my doctorate dissertation on "soft signs of compulsive gambling. Dr. Robert Custer, pioneer in the field, served as my field supervisor for both. And for the next thirty-five years I "majored" in compulsive gambling – starting a Gam-Anon group, speaking to community organizations, providing expert witness testimony before state legislatures, Congressional committees, and courts, establishing an innovative residential treatment program that received international acclaim, and serving as advocate that compulsive gambling is a preventable and treatable psychiatric disorder.

In the 1970s I began my association with the National Council on Compulsive Gambling. We met many times, and we set new standards – is it Pathological Gambling or Compulsive Gambling; a disease or an addiction, is it hereditary or learned, what are the diagnostic criteria, is it preventable, does it require professional treatment, where can we find the needed funds? We started the path to understanding, but for Mitch and me our marriage was over. We divorced in 1976, but always remained the best of friends.

Nearly twenty years later, his new ex-wife wife and I convinced him to go to a VA hospital for treatment. He agreed, went on his last hurrah, drinking and gambling with his gambling buddies, went home, smoked a cigarette in bed, and died. This gentle man, this gentleman, lost his life to an insidious gambling addiction. Where was the help he needed all those years?

I hope this book will help others to get the help that was missing when my family and I were trying to survive the chaos created by compulsive gambling. I dedicate this book posthumously to Mitch. I dedicate it to other compulsive gamblers and their families. May this book help them to heal and to find Serenity in their own lives.

Valerie Lorenz, "Dr. Val"

CHAPTER 2
SOME WORDS ABOUT GAMBLING

UNIVERSALITY AND HISTORY OF GAMBLING

The antiquity and the pervasiveness of gambling are incontestable, so it is not surprising that the history of gambling throughout the world has been marked by controversy; nevertheless, virtually every society has incorporated wagering in its customs and lifestyles since prehistoric times. It is associated with many rituals, traditions, and legends, and within cultures, specific forms of gambling were ascribed to or preferred by certain social or economic classes, sex, or age groups.

Gambling tools and paintings of gambling scenes were found in tombs of pharaohs and unearthed in ruins in Egypt and Pompeii. Early Grecians and Romans used the knuckle bones of sheep and goats for dice. Dice are said to have been invented by Palamedes during the siege of Troy. Christians tolerated gambling but did not allow cursing. The Hindu code of India and the Koran denounced gambling. In AD 60, Tacitus, the Roman historian, commented, "The old Germans, after losing everything they possess at a dice game, then stake their freedom and even their life on the last throw."[1]

Other forms of gambling of antiquity were lotteries and cards. In Venice, lotteries first appeared some eight hundred years ago, in Holland, two hundred years later, followed by England in the 1500s. Cards were hand painted by the most famous of Italian artists, although England already forbade the importation of cards and dice. According to Cardano,[2] gambling is acceptable for "boys, young men, and soldiers... and disgraceful for a person of stature. The opponent should be of suitable station in life. You should play rarely and for short periods, in a suitable place, for small stakes, and on suitable occasions." He considered it a disgrace and dangerous to play with professionals gamblers. Galileo wrote a treatise on dice after he was approached with the problem of probability by a gambler. The knowledge of probabilities is of considerable advantage.[3] Sophocles wrote in 400 BC, "A wise gamester ought to take the dice even as they fall, and pay down quietly rather than grumble at his luck."[4]

Gambling was considered by the Chinese the greatest threat to family unity, above opium addiction, drunkenness, and sex irregularities, yet gambling was found prevalent among all ages and all social classes. Mahjong and dominoes were favored besides the usual dice and cards. According to the law, gambling was a criminal offense, yet paradoxically enough, it is also a New Year's custom. According to tradition, a small amount was acceptable; however, it did not end there nor did gambling end on New Year's Day.[5]

Montezuma and Cortes played a game called totoleque, using small gold balls and slabs. Gold and jewelry were used as stakes. Montezuma and Pizarro were known to share their winnings with their soldiers. For the Peruvian Indians, gambling was considered a violation unless permission was granted by the Inca. Punishment was fifty lashes on the arms and hands. A favorite form of activity on which to wager was racing, which were considered not only sports but also part of the social customs and traditions. Much of the racing, dice, or card playing was accompanied by rituals, with drums, songs, dances, and colorful costumes.[6]

In Jamaica, gambling appeared to be an almost continuous activity, and it was a means for men from a fishing community to gain quick access to large sums, changing the status of the village from a dependent to an independent economy. In the Hottentot culture, betting was part of a game for boys.

Gambling is found throughout literature, but perhaps in Shakespeare's *King Richard the Third*, the most desperate example is when King Richard laments, "Give me another horse! Bind up my wounds!"[7] and later, "A horse! A horse! My kingdom for a horse.[8] Interestingly, horse-racing gamblers also tend to gamble on casino games, and so it is found when once again King Richard proclaims, "I have set my life upon a cast and I will stand the hazard of the die..." (scene 4, line 7). In *The History of Gambling in England*, Ashton gives an anecdotal account of the pervasiveness of gambling and its vices, swindles, and victims. It includes *The Soldier's Prayer Book*, describing a deck of cards and their religious connotation from the perspective of a young soldier who gambled in church.[9] The *Gamesters* is a play in five acts depicting scenes of gaming, winning, and losing of estates and fortunes and magical thinking: "So, so, the Dice in two of three such nights will be out of my debt."[10] Victor Hugo wrote in *Marius*, "A creditor is worse than a master; for a master owns only your person, a creditor owns your dignity, and can belabour that."[11]

Brunner's *Treasury of Gambling Stories* is a selection of observations on gambling, such as *The Devil Invented the Dice* by St. Augustine and others such as Tolstoy, Charles Lamb, Daniel Defoe, O. Henry, Ring Lardner, Mark Twain, Bret Harte, and Somerset Maugham writing on various card games, chess, baccarat, faro, roulette, dice, billiards, and betting. Cunningham (1961) found that gambling flourished in boom towns such as Abilene, Dodge City, and Wichita and boasted well-known gamblers, including Wild Bill Hickock, Wyatt Earp, Bat Masterson, and Doc Holliday.[12]

HISTORICAL EVENTS OF GAMBLING IN THE UNITED STATES

Very little systematic research into problem gambling has been conducted in the United States, even though anti-gambling laws were enacted as early as 1624, when the Virginia Assembly passed a law against the playing of dice, cards, and unlawful games. Massachusetts considered gambling a great dishonor against God, but neither moral censure nor legislation dampened the American passion for gambling. By the 1700s, lotteries were well established in the Colonies and revenues from them were used to build roads, bridges, hospitals, a Harvard University building, a Rhode Island church, private industry, and for military defense. Lottery funds helped finance the war against England and were also used to erect buildings in the new federal town, Georgetown, Washington, DC. George Washington himself was an inveterate gambler who enjoyed betting on card games and horse races. He bought and he sold lottery tickets.

Gambling in the early days in this country had its own peculiar social distinctions. Wagering on horse races was the sole right of the gentry of the Colonial period. It was not unusual for Congress to lack a quorum during race weeks. Card games were played by the aristocrats in elegant surroundings, on plantations, or in posh casinos, which abounded in Washington. During the Civil War, the North profited from sales of cards to Rebel soldiers, and it was not unusual to see Abolitionists and Secessionists playing cards together. It was one of those rare occasions when officers and enlisted men mingled socially. The common folk played cards in taverns and at stage coach stops instead of posh casinos. Other games of chance that common folk engaged in were cockfights, dice, ninepins, and wrestling. The poor pitched pennies.[13]

Gambling has its sexual distinctions. Among the Crow Indians, plum seed and stick dice were strongly associated with women. A game of hiding an elk tooth in one hand while the opposing team had to guess was played by Indian men and women, although each sex by itself. Pony races and foot races by young braves were a favorite game among the Navahos and the Zuni, who staked ponies, blankets, and jewelry. Among the Tsimshan, "Men pass their time gambling...Some men play until they have lost all their property. They will gamble away even their wives."[14] The champion was the richest man in the tribe, the loser would have difficulty in finding a wife. In 1915, a gambling mania broke out among the Hopi Indians when virtually all the men on the Third Mesa were engaged in round-the-clock poker playing. It took complaints by the wives to government officials to break it up.[15] [16]

Poker is generally considered a man's game although the best come-on in any gambling house was the professional female gambler. There was Kitty the Schemer, who followed boom towns in the 1870s and '80s. Dona Tules, a coolheaded ruthless three-card monte player, earned enough one night to open her own place and soon had several gambling parlors in Santa Fe with wall-to-wall carpets, chandeliers, and musicians. Poker Alice was an English lady who was known as the smartest poker player around. Her eccentricities included smoking long black cigars and no drinking while playing. She never gambled on Sundays and breaking the bank was her greatest pleasure. At age seventy, she was charged with running a whorehouse, a gambling joint, and selling liquor illegally.[17]

Women gamblers, dependent upon their husbands for money, usually gambled for smaller stakes and preferred lotteries, raffles, punchboards, bingo, slot machines, and chain letters. Men then and today prefer gambling on sports, cards, dice, and horse races.[18]

In observing a number of gamblers about to bet on a horse race, a definite social order could be determined. Handicapping, based on a pragmatic system of analyzing information, such as past history of the horse and jockey, elicits the most respect. The "hot tip" was also positively valued because it was assumed that the informant had inside information on the race. The "hedge" is a subtype of the first two systems, with the gambler verbally betting on one horse while placing his money on another. This gives him a double chance for reward. At the bottom of the list is the hunch player, who receives no social reward at all from the group. Much of this has changed because today most bets on horse racing are made at off-track betting parlors, simulcasting on races from television screens, and at racinos singly, rather than with a group of gamblers.

The Mississippi River boat gambler, a poker player, is credited with creating the image of the gambler as a flashy dresser. His clothing was usually of the finest quality: black suits with white collared shirts, ties with magnificent diamond stickpins, expensive gold watch, jewels, a walking stick, and the inevitable stogie. His success depended on memory, scrutiny, quick deductions, sizing up the opponent, and mastery of facial expression, hence the term a *poker face*. Riverboat gamblers were generally honest gamblers, although frequently they had to jump ship just before reaching shore to avoid the authorities. The riverboat gambler, in his extreme way, reflected the contemporary temper of the country during the Gold Rush: each man for himself and the frenzied hope for quick financial gain.

During the nineteenth century, New Orleans was the queen of the gambling cities. At one time, there were over three thousand professional gamblers employed as housemen in the four to five hundred casinos. It was the city where craps, the most American of gambling events next to poker, was first introduced to whites and blacks alike. It also introduced the jazz players who added to the atmosphere of the gambling houses. New Orleans had its ups and downs for over half a century in the battle between moralists and legislation. It had its extremes of gambling and reform during the nineteenth century. At one time in its history, a section of New Orleans, Storeyville, had almost two thousand prostitutes and as many professional gamblers. Slot machines, invented in 1895, found great popularity here, being then and to this date a favorite among women.

Throughout the history of the United States, people have attempted to deal with the issues of gambling. Massachusetts tried to legislate morality and failed. Nellie Bly decried the moral decay of the affluent gamblers who whiled away their time and fortunes in Saratoga Springs, New York, the vacation spa for America's aristocrats of the nineteenth century. She succeeded in having the gaming houses closed down, although the horses raced on. Saratoga boasted a number of men of renown. The Honorable John Morrissey, a judge, member of Congress, and owner of a gambling casino, fought avidly against attempts to close down gaming houses, but eventually lost. Financier William C. Whitney's interests lay in horse racing, which throughout the history of the United States has been legal. Although Whitney survived the reform measures, the town no longer had the appeal and attraction it once enjoyed. Johnny Walker, Whitney's bookie, had the reputation of being an honest bookie. Upon Whitney's death, Walker paid off Whitney's gambling debt of over $150,000. There was no record of the debt.

There were other notables who gambled heavily. Senator Don Cameron, from Harrisburg, PA, played cards with President Cleveland and Speaker of the House, John Carlisle. There was Bet-A-Million Gates, who would bet $1,000 that a fly would land on a certain lump of sugar. Cornelius Vanderbilt amassed a fortune; his son gambled millions of it away. Louis Cohn, the Chicago importer, admitted that he and friends were shooting dice in Mrs. O'Leary's barn, which caught on fire. Arnold Rothstein, a New York financier, also trafficked in narcotics, ran gambling houses for gentlemen, was a banker to the underworld, and "owned" judges and politicians. The flamboyant included Lillian Russell, who was frequently in the company of Diamond Jim Brady, a notorious racketeer. The affluent aristocrats moved to the South, to Palm Beach where Henry Flagler built his fabulous hotel, with two wings, one a house of prayer and the other a house of chance. Women were not allowed in the latter.

In 1931, gambling was legalized in Nevada. Music, exotic revues, luscious chorus girls, and drinks added to the heady excitement of the gambling casinos in Las Vegas. The windowless, clockless casinos, then and now, are considered to be the heart and soul of any Las Vegas hotel. Today, one must walk past rows of slot machines, the dice tables, and roulette wheels in order to get to the shows, restaurants, McDonalds, and restrooms. Gambling is everywhere in Nevada, whether in a big casino, a local tavern, or at the airport.

In the 1930s, the Chicago Crime Commission stated that gambling was associated with swindlers, robbers, and murderers. Casino entrepreneur and mobster Bugsie Siegel bet thousands of dollars at a game, had society friends, a splashy house, and a beautiful wife. He bribed cops, got involved in mafia wars, and was murdered by the mafia. Bankruptcy and suicides are disproportionately high in Nevada compared to other states and among compulsive gamblers compared to non-gamblers.

Horace Greeley fought hard against crime and corruption in New York via his newspaper, the *Tribune*. Hank Greenspun did the same in Las Vegas, as did the Chicago Crime Commission and former US Attorney General, Robert Kennedy. Gambling continues in its movement of those in favor of increased legalized gambling, claiming revenues for the state and new jobs, while those opposed to gambling protest this escalation due to compulsive gambling, increased crime and bankruptcies, and impact on the quality of life. The expansion of gambling led the way of changes in social attitude toward gambling from illegal to legal gambling, from gambling to gaming, from immoral to family entertainment with fantasy-themed casinos, such as The Venetian, New York, New York, and Circus Circus, Wizard of Oz, and Pirate Ship, which appeal to children and families, and now its return to the former sex appeal shows of scantily clad chorus girls and dancing.

Currently, the US is in the midst of a strong pro-gambling movement, headed by the American Gaming Association, battling a weaker anti-gambling grassroots movement led by the National Coalition Against Legalized Gambling and the National Coalition Against Gambling Expansion, which in the early 2000s changed its name to Stop Predatory Gambling.

Today, gambling is universal and is strongly entrenched in the United States, with its customs and traditions, the love of it and the fear of it, the attempts to legalize it and repeal it, to corruption and investigations, and to investment by Wall Street, the financial benefits to support education, prevent tax increases, and protecting the horse race industry. Its opposition is based on the adverse impact on the individuals, family, and communities. Their view of the "normalized gambling community" is that of community and economic pathology. Gambling has become an opportunistic addiction.

Problem gambling was predictable, due to the increase of gambling, both legal and illegal, freedom of movement, access to money by women and minorities, advanced computer technology, and changing social attitudes. Problem gambling will continue to rise, especially given the lack of community awareness, training of mental health counselors, and funding for research and treatment.

In short, gambling is associated with many rituals, traditions, and legends in cultures throughout the world. Within cultures, specific forms of gambling were ascribed to or preferred by certain social or economic classes, sex, or age groups. Throughout history and to this day, gambling has had its zealous advocates and its bitter opponents. Adding to the complexity of the problem is the fact that practice is contradictory to societal and religious standards. In the religious arena, gambling is viewed as sin or as a sign of moral weakness, yet it is permitted at social functions, fund-raisers, or as part of traditional rites within the church building. In the judicial arena, some forms of gambling are illegal, yet they are either overlooked or protected by officials. Additionally, governments institutionalize gambling as a means of raising revenues for one segment of its citizenry while simultaneously increasing the incidence and severity of pathological gambling among other segments of its citizenry. Gambling has brought fame and riches to some, and destruction and loss of family and property to others. Yet gambling continues in spite of cultural, religious, moral, and legal sanctions.

WHAT IS GAMBLING?

By legal definition, gambling is risking something of value, on an activity that is predominantly chance, in the hopes of getting a larger reward. This is often confused with performing an activity that involves skill. Simply put, gambling may or may not involve skill—the defining rule is whether the activity is based on the predominant element of chance.

Take, for example, the video game of PacMan. This is a game that is based purely on skill. A coin is inserted and the game begins, always with one PacMan starting in the same position. The player can manipulate the PacMan in any direction as long as the PacMan is not gobbled up. The final score is based on length of play and credits. PacMan becomes gambling only when money is bet on the game or some other side bet.

In blackjack, each player is dealt a different hand. The skill factor comes into being with card counting, knowing when to bet and how much. The chance factor occurs when the player refuses to take another card, hoping to get as close to 21 without going over. Or the player may opt to take another card, again hoping to get as close to 21 as possible. It is a game based on chance, aiming to beat the dealer. The game is over as soon as all players at the table have bet their hand: some may win, others may lose, independent of the other players' strategies and monies bet.

Is bingo gambling? Yes, if the bingo card is purchased, because something of value has been given, on a chance activity, hoping for a reward. The fact that bingo is held in a church or bingo night is sponsored by a local charity does not eliminate the three elements of gambling: value, chance, and reward. Free bingo cards makes it a game rather than a gamble.

Tournaments with entry fees, such as the Internet Poker Tournaments, are also gambling because they meet the three criteria: value, chance, and reward. On the other hand, a threesome of youngsters playing a game of Crazy Eights for the fun of it or the final score is not gambling because it meets only two criteria of the three: chance and reward. There is no initial value bet on the game.

LEGAL GAMBLING

Gambling is legal if the courts or legislatures have deemed the activity, such as lotteries, racing, casinos, or slots, to be legal. Legal gambling ventures are typically owned or operated by profit-making enterprises and have only those limits as set by the laws or by the owners themselves. This does not mean, however, that every gambling game is run according to the law, without cheating or some other type of illegal activity taking place, i.e., internet gambling was once illegal in the US, now Delaware, Nevada, and New Jersey have legalized this form of gambling.

Legal charitable gambling, on the other hand, is typically time-limited, such as one day per week or month, operated by a not-for-profit group, such as a church, firehouse, or local festival, and all profits are distributed to a named charity, namely as support of its own organization, school bands or uniforms, a hospital, police athletic club equipment, or to purchase a fire truck.

Valerie C. Lorenz, Ph.D.

ILLEGAL GAMBLING

The most common form of illegal gambling is sports betting.

Most of the gambling is legal, but as in any enterprise, there is also illegal gambling, such as sports betting, pit bull dog fights, cockfights, or illegal numbers, most of which are favored by racial or ethnic minority groups. Numbers can be purchased for small amounts of cash, and wins are small, although they can add considerably to the household of a poverty-stricken family. Illegal numbers are associated with dreams, dream books, and socializing with friends and neighbors. Numbers dealers can earn over $100,000 a year, according to the FBI.

Other illegal gambling games are three-card monte, which is usually played on city streets involving a dealer, look-out and shill, and gullible people passing by conned into believing they can win. After-hours clubs with craps or card games are usually on a large scale, either in number of participants or with large amounts of money. A poker game held in a neighbor's house in which a certain amount of the money wagered goes to the owner is also illegal gambling.

Then there are the cheats and cheating methods. A deck of cards may be marked or shaved, dice may be weighted, rounded, or two-sided, a slot machine may be set below the state regulations, a horse may be doped, a football fumble may be deliberate in order to affect the outcome of the game. A card dealer may use slight-of-hand skills dealing from the bottom of the deck or two cheats may give each other signals. There are many ways of cheating or gambling illegally. Recognizing this, state lotteries or other government-run gambling activities and private for-profit gambling venues, such as casinos and race tracks, have their own security systems to prevent cheating and to apprehend cheaters.

In conclusion, gambling might be considered to be beneficial by some and harmful by others. Thus it was in the past, is in the present, and will be in the future.

ENDNOTES

1   Stekel, W. (1924). *Peculiarities of behavior.* New York: Liveright Publishing Co.

2   Cardano, G. (1961). *The book on games of chance, "Liber de Ludo Aleae.* Translated by S.H.Gould. New York: Rinehart and Winston.

3   Rouge et Noir. (1898). *The gambling world.* London: Hutchinson & Co.

4   Sophocles, 400 BC

5   Lamson, H.D. (1934). *Social pathology in China.* Shanghai: The Commercial Press.

6   Lopez-Rey. (1950). Gambling in the Latin American countries. *The Annals of the American Academy of Political and Social Studies,* May, *269,* 134-143.

7   King Richard, Scene 3, Line 12.

8   King Richard, Scene 3, Line 310.

9   Ashton, J. (1899). *The history of gambling in England.* London: Duckworth.

10 Shirly, J. *The gamesters.* London: John Norton.

11 Hugo, V. *Marius,* Book V, Chapter 1.

12 Brunner, R. K. (ed.) 1946. *Treasury of gambling stories.* Chicago: Ziff-Davis Publishing Company.

13 Chafetz, M. (1960) *Play the devil: A history of gambling in the United States from 1492-1955.* New York: Clarkson N. Potter, Inc.

14 Boas, F. (1916) *Tsimshan mythology*. Thirty-first Annual Report of the Bureau of American Ethnology. 1909-1910. Washington, DC: US Government Printing Office, p.72

15 Lowie, R.H. (1924*). Myths and traditions of the Crow Indians*. New York: American Museum Press.

16 Stevenson, M.D. (1902). *The Zuni Indians, their mythology, esoteric fraternities and ceremonies*. Bureau of Ethnology, Annual Report. Washington, DC: US Government Printing Office *of the Crow Indians*. New York: American Museum Press.

17 Waterton, E. (1969). *Gambling games of the West Coast*. Unpublished thesis. The University of British Columbia.

18 Cunningham, G.L. (1981). *Diversions of the storied West: An analysis of the preferred forms of gambling in the cattle towns of Kansas*. Paper presented at the Fifth National Conference of Gambling and Risk Taking. Lake Tahoe: University of Nevada/Reno.

CHAPTER 3
TYPES OF GAMBLERS

Not all gamblers are the same, nor do all gamblers become compulsive gamblers, nor do they gamble on everything or all the time. Some gamble on horses, others on slots; some are seniors, others are teenagers; some are Catholic, others are atheists; some are licensed professionals, others are factory workers; some are from South Africa, others were born in South Carolina—in other words, gambling is democratic, no one is exempt, except for those people who abide by their religious beliefs, which forbids them to gamble, or those who just plain don't want to gamble, seeing it as a frivolous waste of time and money. Not having much money to gamble with is not a deciding factor—betting on illegal numbers may cost a quarter, casinos have nickel slots, pitching pennies is just that, pennies. And there are other items of value with which one can gamble: incarcerated offenders gamble for services (do the laundry), tasks (do fifty push-ups), or food, a favorite being coffee or a can of tuna fish. In the past, Native Americans wagered their ponies or blankets, and of course, there was Macbeth, who wagered his kingdom ("A horse, a horse, a kingdom for a horse, my kingdom for a horse!" *King Richard III*).

While they all gamble, there are significant differences, identifiable in their reasons for gambling, their ability to control that gambling, and the damaging impact of problem gambling.

SOCIAL GAMBLERS

The social gambler is the person who gambles strictly for the fun of it and who will not let the gambling interfere with family, work, or health. Going to the casino or the race track, betting on the Penn State vs. Pitt football game, and playing bingo with the Ladies' Guild are opportunities to socialize with friends, have some fun, renew friendships, and simply take time off from the daily routine to do something different. Social gamblers enjoy what they are doing. They plan how much money to take along, hoping to win but accepting the fact that they might lose. They know how much time they want to spend, and they will stick to that schedule. They also know that if they're losing more than they had planned, their credit card is not to be used for more gambling; however, they may borrow a dollar or two that they will repay next day. Basically, their motto is "Have fun, but in moderation."

State lotteries, casinos, and other gambling venues also encourage having fun through their responsible gaming programs. "Gamble with your head, not over it." To make gambling more acceptable, they refer to it as "gaming."

Most gamblers are social gamblers, and their numbers are rapidly increasing ever since the unparalleled legalization of many forms of gambling, including state lotteries, bingo, simulcasting, slots, or video lottery terminals at race tracks (which are now termed "racinos"). It has been estimated that 80 percent of adults in the US gamble, and 85 percent of them are social gamblers.

Betting on sports is very popular with males, albeit becoming more so with females. Sports betting is without a doubt the largest illegal gambling in the United States. The Super Bowl and March Madness reign supreme among all illegal gambling.

Social gamblers have their own favorite forms of gambling. Some may buy a particular set of numbers, every day, from the state lottery. These are numbers associated with birthdays, anniversary, or other meaningful combinations. Gambling daily with a fairly steady amount of money is not necessarily an indication of problem gambling. There are also lottery players who may spend hundreds of dollars on Mega Millions or Powerball when the jackpot gets exceptionally large, hoping for better odds of winning.

At one time, it was thought that lottery gambling was too passive to be addictive. This concept was endorsed by state governments as they sought to legalize lotteries as a means of increasing revenues for their general fund budgets. However, if the lottery gambler starts drastically increasing the number of tickets, amount of money spent buying them, and *has* to gamble or becomes irritable when not gambling, then it is time to be on guard. These may be early indicators of a gambling problem. If it is no longer "fun," the social gambler will stop; the problem gambler will consider stopping, the compulsive gambler can't stop. For compulsive gamblers, buying lottery tickets, whether scratch-offs, Pick 3, or Pick 4, is not "I want to" but rather "I have to."

Most lottery gamblers appear to gamble regularly and for many years. Perhaps this is because lottery vendors are readily accessible—in supermarkets, airports, bowling alleys, bars, and there is little stigma to buying lottery tickets. After all, the lotteries are sponsored by state governments, which gives gambling the official stamp of approval. In addition, lottery funds are used for worthwhile causes, such as aid for the elderly and education. Buying lottery tickets is an act of fun, hoping to win, and an act of social responsibility by providing funds for those in need.

Lottery wins most frequently are for a free ticket, for $2, or a similarly small amount, while some are wins of several hundred or thousands of dollars. Do the winners quit when they are the lucky ones? Most don't; they continue in the same pattern of gambling. For the occasional lottery player, though, the Big Win may be a trigger toward gambling addiction. In March of 2012, an eighty-two-year-old woman won over $300 million on the lottery. The following day, she bought another eighty dollars worth of lottery tickets. Is she or will she become a compulsive gambler? The huge win will bring some joys and more stress, but not necessarily addiction, yet history has challenged that myth—lotteries, like any other form of gambling, can lead to gambling addiction, but there are several criteria toward becoming a gambling addict. The Big Win is just one of them.

PROFESSIONAL GAMBLERS

Then there are the gamblers who take their gambling much more seriously. These are the professional gamblers, whose gambling is planned and methodical and whose profits are the primary reason for taking calculated risks. They consider their risk-taking as their job and a major source of their earnings. An obvious example of this are the financiers, such as stock brokers or day traders. They view themselves as account executives who have conscientiously studied the market, watching stocks go up and down, why, the history of the stock, how many shares to buy or sell, for how much. They describe themselves as financiers who are speculating for their clients. Very dignified, socially accepted, yet the activity is the same, gambling: taking something of value, on a chance, with the expectation of a reward.

While gambling is fun and recreation for the social gambler, for the professional gambler it is all business, adhering to legal and ethical codes of conduct, usually long hours, and considerable stress. They, too, may go to the casino for social gambling or, less likely, buy lottery tickets; however, due to the nature of their business, the competitive nature of these individuals, and constant manipulation of monies, the professional gamblers are somewhat more at risk of becoming a problem or compulsive gambler than the social gambler. They may lose control over a different form of gambling, such as sports betting.

There are other examples of professional gamblers, the most popular one being the casino's nemesis, the card counter. Professor Kenny Huston gained fame not only by being the mathematician who could figure out the odds, but also because Vegas and Atlantic City casinos barred him from playing in their establishments.

Casino poker tournaments are a recent gambling phenomenon that has attracted over five thousand poker players. Many of them consider themselves to be professional gamblers.

State lottery operations are considered to be professional gamblers by offering a product that is placed at risk and uncertainty of outcome. The criteria are the same, running a gambling game, selling a product, which hopefully will be profitable, with carefully calculated odds of projected profits, yet not knowing exactly what the hoped-for outcome will be on any one game. State lotteries offer a variety of tickets, from a dollar ticket or a fifty-dollar ticket, hoping to attract new players and encouraging current gamblers to buy more. "Let yourself play to win" has been a popular and effective slogan. Most ticket buyers do so for a bit of anticipation or as gifts; however, there are also the lottery players who become addicted, and for them, the fun is gone and so is their money. While state lotteries supplement state budgets by millions of dollars every year, most often they acknowledge problem gambling with a meaningless slogan printed on tickets and some brochures, such as "Bet responsibly" and list a toll-free hotline number to call.

ANTISOCIAL GAMBLERS

Bookmakers in Nevada and the United Kingdom are considered professional gamblers because they operate within the law, whereas bookmakers who conduct the same business outside the law are operating a criminal activity. Legal bookmakers pay taxes. Illegal bookies do not. They take action on sports, parimutual games, numbers, cockfights, and dog fights. "Illegal appended enterprise" (coined by Henry Lesieur) is also conducted in bingo halls.

Illegal bookies may extend credit, but if a bettor's debt is not paid, the bookie may take the option of increasing the vigorish on the debt or using implied threats, such as "You don't want your employer to know, do you?" They may turn the debt over to a larger betting operation. The bookie may transfer the debt to a loan shark or the bookie may introduce the gambler to the loan shark. Loan sharks are known to use more coercive means, from damaging property to acting on threats of physical violence, inflicting personal harm.

Antisocial gamblers know they are operating outside the law and employ measures to protect themselves from arrest and legal charges. They may "buy" protection from a local politician, the police officer who patrols the neighborhood beat, or a prison guard who may operate as a bookie. While this is clearly illegal, the reasons for this are numerous: greed, coercion by a fellow officer, a desperate need for money, a sense of power or of being above the law, vindictiveness, to intimidate or control an inmate, or because this person, too, is suffering from a gambling addiction. These criminal gamblers put others at risk. They compromise the safety of other police officers, prison guards, and inmates.

Antisocial gamblers who have a history of criminal activities, with illegal gambling being just one of many such illegal acts, tend to be charged repeatedly for myriad illegal activities and sentenced to incarceration. Organized crime syndicates have their own ways of dealing with gambling cheats. Although most loan sharks are solo operations, large loan shark operations almost always are part of an organized crime syndicate. Asked what happens if the compulsive gambler can't repay the loan, one mafia loan shark informed a stunned group of high school students belonging to Students Against Gambling Addiction, "There's no such thing as not paying back."

It must be noted that some of these antisocial gamblers are also compulsive gamblers. Such is the case of Luigi, who was a cocaine addict, compulsive gambler, and hit man for the mob. He was sent to jail for a crime he committed to support his gambling and cocaine addiction.

Antisocial gamblers can also be compulsive gamblers who cheat customers as part of their antisocial activities. Using marked decks of cards, altered dice, sleight of hand tricks are some of the more common forms of cheating.

PROBLEM GAMBLERS

Problem gambling is to gambling what alcohol abuse is to alcoholism. It is that fine line between being in control and having lost control—that intermediate step where the gambler temporarily gambles beyond the initial intent. It is a subtle process usually developing after a few wins or perhaps even a big win. It gives the gambler that extra sense of excitement of the win and of having extra money with which to have fun, see a show, purchase something, or gamble some more. It is a temporary lift of emotions and gets attention from friends and other gamblers. It feels good.

It also gives the gambler that additional bit of confidence and daring and thus the willingness to increase the size of the bet. Of course, there will be some losses, but the problem gambler is more optimistic about winning rather than pessimistic about losing. "I can do it again" is the conviction instead of "I just got a lucky break." Their rationale is "I'm gambling with *their* money" and "I have to get back *my* money." If the gambler at this point decides to continue gambling, the bets become larger and more frequent—and so will the losses.

If the gambler has several of the personality traits of a compulsive gambler, such as being highly competitive and a need to be a winner, the gambler will try to recoup those losses.

This chasing may lead to the point of spending more time and money gambling, borrowing, or even lying about the gambling; however, at some point during this stage, the problem gambler will recognize that the gambling has become troublesome, that it is starting to interfere with family life and work and that it could lead to trouble. The problem gambler now may decide to cut down on the gambling or even stop gambling altogether.

On the other hand, the person who will become a compulsive gambler at this decisive time is no longer willing or able to stop gambling. The underlying factors and reasons for gambling have begun to surface, there is the additional heightening of emotional highs and lows, the stressors and discomforts, for which continued gambling offers a temporary intellectual and emotional escape. This problem gambler has lost control and has progressed to compulsive gambling.

The length of time of problem gambling varies with each individual and the type of gambling. The sensation-seeking gambler may advance from social gambling to problem and compulsive gambling within three or more years, given the expansion of simulcasting and the greater availability of high-action gambling opportunities. Slots players, on the other hand, report problem gambling for less than a year before becoming a gambling addict.

COMPULSIVE GAMBLERS

According to the Psychiatric Dictionary, seventh edition, "Compulsive is a repetitive motor action the need for whose performance insistently forces itself into consciousness even though the person does not wish to perform the act. Failure of the act generates increasing anxiety; completion of the act gives at least temporary surcease of tension. Compulsive behaviors are obsessions in action."

A more legal perspective is the volitional prong of diminished capacity—that the gambler acts intentionally but not voluntarily, and although he can perform the action, he cannot refrain from performing it even though there are many good reasons to so. This concept is difficult to understand, but criminal courts have ruled accordingly.

Since 1979, the American Psychiatric Association's *Diagnostic and Statistical Manual of Mental Disorders (DSM3)* has defined pathological gambling (the correct clinical term for "compulsive gambling") under impulse control disorders (Section 312.31) with its unique identifiable criteria. It is recognized as an emotional/behavioral response to psychologically intolerable life circumstances through the acts of gambling.

Compulsive gambling is considered a behavioral disorder or, more commonly, a psychological addiction that follows a progression in gambling frequency and amounts wagered, preoccupation with gambling, a continuous or periodic loss of control (binge gambling), and a continuation of gambling in spite of adverse consequences, such as serious and troublesome impacts on family, finances, loss of work productivity, health, and eventually the commission of criminal acts.

More specifically, the DSM4 listed ten criteria, requiring five or more to meet the diagnosis of pathological gambling. These criteria include:

1. Preoccupation with gambling: the gambler is constantly thinking about past or present gambling or fantasies about gambling;
2. Tolerance: the gambler needs to gamble more frequently and with larger amounts in order to experience the same "rush" (action gamblers) or relief (escape gamblers) from dysphoric moods;
3. Withdrawal: the gambler feels restless, irritable, and has other withdrawal symptoms associated with addictions during attempts to reduce or cease gambling;
4. Escape: the gambler has an intense need to escape or reduce external and emotional problems prior to and as a result of the gambling;

5. Chasing: the gambler tries to win back gambling losses by more gambling;
6. Lying: the gambler tries to hide the extent of gambling by lying repeatedly to family, friends, therapist, and/or others;
7. Loss of control: the gambler knows right from wrong, the intent is to cease gambling, but the gambler is unable to refrain from it in spite of potentially adverse consequences;
8. Illegal acts: the gambler thinks, plans, or commits illegal acts to acquire money for gambling in order to pay off debts, return misappropriated funds, and/or continue gambling;
9. Relationships: the gambler continues to gamble despite risking or losing relationships with family and others;
10. Bailout: family, friends, or others pay off the gambler's debts in an attempt to help the gambler refrain from further gambling, avoid getting hurt, or facing legal charges.

The DSM 5 excludes Criteria 8, Illegal acts, because it was not essential to making a diagnosis of gambling disorder. Whereas the DSM4 required 5 our of 10 criteria to meet the diagnosis of Pathologicl Gambling, the DSM5 requires only 4 out of 9 criteria for a diagnosis of Gambling Disorder.

ACTION AND ESCAPE COMPULSIVE GAMBLERS

There are two distinct styles of compulsive gambling, differentiated by the individual's personality, the form of gambling, and the sought-after emotional response. These are commonly referred to as Action gamblers or Escape gamblers. Action gamblers need excitement and admiration from others. They seek out those gambling activities that require skill, such as knowing the probability of the dice falling a certain way or the probability of a certain card being dealt. They count cards. They have their own system and adhere to a basic strategy of playing and betting. Similarly, the horse race bettors or sports bettors have a system of gambling, one they have studied and in which they firmly believe. Their goal is to win and they base their ability to win on the finely hued skills they have developed over the years. Gambling gives the action gamblers the attention from others, sought-after positive self-image, and the money to prove it.

The escape gamblers, in contrast, seek to avoid people and commotion and think more in terms of luck. Their goal is to escape reality and winning is secondary to that goal. Their gambling is passive and solitary: scratching off the lottery ticket, touching the slot machine screen, or daubing the bingo card. There is no communal shouting and cheering with others, it is quiet and solitary. They sit in front of a slot machine for hours, oblivious to their surroundings.

Another major difference between action gamblers and escape gamblers is reflected in the onset of their gambling experiences. Action gamblers report pitching pennies during childhood and buying packs of baseball cards in their teens, hoping to get that one special card they need for their collection. Horse race gamblers report that invariably they were introduced to horse racing in their midteens, usually by a close male family figure or friend. Escape gamblers, on the other hand, typically do not start gambling until they are in their thirties or forties. They were neither exposed to nor encouraged to gamble. Additionally, they did not have that competitive urge to take risks or be the best in whatever they undertook. Action gamblers are the controllers; escape gamblers are the nurturers. Action gamblers want excitement, escape gamblers want peace. Both consider themselves to be honest and honorable, yet in the course of their gambling addiction, they turn to lies, loans, and larceny, traits they do not condone in themselves and in others.

ACTION GAMBLERS

Action compulsive gamblers are individuals who typically, but not always, have been traumatized by life events, usually since early childhood, without receiving the emotional support to overcome the short- and long-term effects of these events. They hurt. They are angry. They are afraid. They begin to suffer from a low-grade or dysthymic depression, specific or generalized anxiety, or anger which often is suppressed rage. They have an underlying fear of disappointing a parent, usually the father, and need to get that parent's approval. They desperately seek acceptance.

Action gamblers spend their early childhood in the proverbial dysfunctional family. Many times, one of the parents, usually the father, is an active alcoholic. The mother is an enabler. Or she may be suffering from a serious medical or mental illness. Not infrequently the mother is described as being depressed, staying in bed for months.

Invariably, there is some form of abuse within these families, almost always verbal abuse and psychological abuse. "You'll never amount to anything" or "Why can't you be like your brother?" Psychological abuse is more in the form of being ignored or told not to bother someone. Physical abuse is common, especially if the father is an active alcoholic. Some of the physical abuse borders on monstrous behavior and today would be reported immediately to child welfare organizations or the police. On rare occasions, the mother has been reported as being physically abusive. Sexual molestation is also prevalent, from lecherous looks to homosexual rape, similarly as is reported in larger communities. However, it appears that being sexually molested as a child is more prevalent among gambling addicts, especially among male gamblers, than the community at large. It is an area of research that to date has been ignored.

Many action gamblers also come from broken homes, most often due to divorce, either in early childhood or when they were young adults. The younger ones feel abandoned and become fearful. The older ones become angry, feel they have been misled and cheated throughout their lives, and no longer trust their parents. Also occurring with regularity is the death of a loving grandparent, one who took over the role of parenting or who gave the child the love and guidance it did not get from its own parents. Often, the grandparent's death occurred when the compulsive gambler was a young teenager, and that love was not replaced by a parent. Another source of great loss and pain, especially in the male gambler, is the termination of a romance, typically occurring in late high school or early college years. In addition, the terminated romance was one of longstanding and ended in infidelity by the girlfriend, further resulting in a fear of relationships.

The parents lack effective parenting skills: they fail to guide their children, are unduly harsh in their disciplining, and inconsistent in teaching and adhering to basic rules. These future compulsive gamblers do not learn how to express their true feelings. They are fearful of saying the wrong thing and learn quite quickly how to skirt these potential injuries by manipulating a situation or person. Manipulation becomes their safety net in interacting with others. They are called con artists, yet often these gamblers are not even aware that they are manipulating. To them, this manner of speech is normal, just like everyone else's way of speaking.

Yet these psychologically injured children have become too vulnerable to seek guidance or support for fear of criticism or rejection. Through self-isolation and emotional distancing from others, they can prevent anticipated vulnerability and/or abuse. They have learned it is safer to be a loner. They have a low sense of self-esteem. When asked to describe their level of self-esteem between one and one hundred, many compulsive gamblers in professional treatment have responded, "minus twenty" or a similarly low level.

They also lack an emotional sense of safety. They fear rejection or even abandonment and turn to any means to be liked and accepted to gain the attention they so desperately need, the good attention. They seek perfection. One compulsive gambler described his coping as "To be the best in all things at all times." Thus, these future compulsive gamblers have poor coping skills and poor problem-solving skills and their emotional development has been truncated; chronologically, they may be forty, but their emotional maturity is closer to fourteen.

Action gamblers tend to be born into a family with a strong focus on money. Many grow up in homes of near poverty in which the talk about money is centered on meeting basic needs. One parent, usually the father, invariably works long hours to support the family, yet in that process the child is deprived of the father's attention. Asked to describe their parents, many compulsive gamblers respond with "My dad worked all the time and he was never home. He's hard." Mothers, on the other hand, are often described as "A saint, she'll do anything for you." Treatment, however, shows that these mothers are not always saints.

Gambling is universal. It is available and easily accessible. For future compulsive gamblers, it becomes the emotional salve and outlet. Paired with their competitive nature and their financial needs, they learn that gambling gives them that excitement and the attention when they win and money to spend. Gambling becomes the healer for their injured selves.

When action gamblers anticipate winning or when they do win, they experience a reduction of years of inner tensions. They feel good. They have learned that winning elevates them in the eyes of others, which they view as acceptance. It improves their sense of self-worth. Their low self-esteem is temporarily replaced by a sense of excitement rarely experienced before. They crave the rush, the euphoric states brought on by wins and excitement of gambling, the stimulation of the frontal cortex of the brain which sets off the pleasure syndrome, which has been compared to the high from cocaine.

Action gamblers are high-energy, constant motion people, who relish the shouting and backslapping associated with shooting craps or watching the races. They are the fast-moving, fast-thinking people who can't slow down and wait for others. Their minds are quick, their movements are quick, and they have little tolerance for those who don't measure up to their own speed. They are the type As of the gambling scene, convinced that their success reflects their superior skill rather than random chance or luck. Should they lose, which happens more frequently and with greater amounts of money as they are chasing their losses, they attribute these losses to their failure to follow their own system. They remember their wins and forget their losses. They succumb to "the gambler's fallacy": that they are due to win after a long streak of losing. As one horse racing bettor explained, "I had thirty losses in a row. I was convinced that the next bet would be the winning one. I was due. And then I lost again. I couldn't believe it. First, I ranted like a maniac, and then, I puked out my guts. That's when I realized how sick I was."

While rigorous research has yet to be conducted specifically on the action gambler, the sense from professionals and from members of Gamblers Anonymous themselves is that a large number of them might also be suffering from bipolar disorder, more often the manic form. This manic state is heightened during gambling. For them, dissociation and mania is preferred over depression and boredom.

Similarly, although the action gambler may have repeatedly studied the background and wins of the horse and the jockey, the randomness still occurs when the horse is sick or injured, the jockey falls off the horse or loses the whip, or the race itself might be rigged: the horse is doped or the jockey deliberately holds back the horse. Similar events can occur in dog racing or jai-alai. The same is true in other forms of gambling, i.e., the athlete may get sick or injured, the team makeup might change at the last minute, the throw or pitch may fall short, or again, the integrity of the game is compromised through shaving points or deliberately missing a throw. Yet the action gambler is convinced of beating the odds and winning.

In the past, most action compulsive gamblers were the narcissistic type A people. However, as gambling has expanded, these type As also tend to suffer from full scale or features of other personality disorders, including borderline and dependent disorders. In short, as a result of the vast expansion of gambling, the action gambler profile has changed to be one of greater complexity.

ESCAPE GAMBLERS

Escape gamblers function at the other end of the spectrum. They typically become compulsive gamblers later in life, in their thirties or forties or even in their seventies. They prefer to gamble on luck games, such as slots, poker machines, the lottery, or bingo. They more typically describe a family background of reasonable stability. Although there may be some anxiety or depression in their family, they consider themselves having grown up in a happy family and deny the severe and frequent emotional traumas as experienced by the action gamblers. They do, however, seem to have a strong concern about disappointing others. They fear confrontation: they do not confront others and they avoid any possibility of being confronted. They hide their true feelings. Just like the action gamblers, the escape gamblers strive to do well and present themselves in a positive image. They have learned to be cautious in interaction with others and especially fear disappointing an important family member, most often the father. They avoid calling attention to themselves. They strive to "fit in" and doing the best they can. They are described as nurturing and become the caregiver for family and friends.

Life for escape gamblers generally is satisfactory. They may have gambled socially for years; however, at some point in midlife or in their senior years, they, like action gamblers, experience a number of traumatic events. The stressor may be caused by a spouse with an alcohol problem. It may be the boss's unrelenting demands, financial pressures due to the economy, or the serious illness or death of someone close to them. Typically, there are five or more of these troubling events occurring within a two-year period. "I was overwhelmed, never knowing when the next shoe would drop. I was diagnosed with cancer, my best friend moved to another state, and I found out my husband was having an affair. And to top it off, my boss reduced my work hours, and it was tough paying the bills."

Gambling at a slots parlor takes on a different form. What once had been gambling for fun, now turns into gambling for hours, almost daily, hoping to overcome the financial pressures through the Big Win. It seemed to be the only or best way of escaping all the pressures and bad feelings. Playing penny slots was doable. "It doesn't cost much and I could just sit there and not think about anything." They ignored the fact that penny slots cost more than a penny. Most require twenty-five or fifty cents per play. The newest, more sophisticated ones have multiple game plays on one machine, and on some machines it is possible to play as many as fifty hands per play, every four seconds. They ignored their losses and recall only the wins. Their gambling to win becomes secondary to escaping from a troublesome reality. In the end, the goal of gambling now is no longer to have fun, rather, it is to escape from all those uncomfortable life situations, thoughts, and feelings.

Winning means they can gamble longer and thus escape into their own world longer. Although some slots players speak of being "in the zone" similar to action gamblers, most slots players speak of the hypnotic pull of "being drawn into the machine." They report being in a total state of oblivion, unaware of people or their surroundings. They seek solitude, not crowds. They seek quiet, not noise. They don't want to be interrupted. They are concentrating on playing not just one, but two or three machines. At one time.

No rigorous research has been conducted to date, but anecdotal accounts suggest that escape gamblers fit more into the role of passive or dependent roles rather than that of the highly competitive, narcissistic action gamblers. Perhaps that is one explanation why escape gamblers are more likely to seek treatment. Their family background is relatively stable and possibly they have more internal resources than their action counterparts

In summation, the mantra of the action gambler is to win, be the big shot and be admired by others, whereas the escape gambler prefers moderation and peace.

PROGRESSION OF COMPULSIVE GAMBLING

Compulsive gambling is considered to develop in four phases, of varying overall lengths of time of gambling, time elapsed between gambling, the type of gambling, access to gambling, money, and reasons for gambling. Many gamblers report having wagered at the race track for years before becoming addicted, when gambling at the track was interrupted between races and days of racing. This has changed since the introduction of simulcasting, OTBs, and racinos and is evidenced by membership in GA meetings. Not surprisingly, it appears these days that action gamblers turn to compulsive gambling much sooner than in the past. Whereas race track or casino gamblers, as well as sports bettors in the past may have been able to gamble socially for twenty years or more before succumbing to the addiction, spurred on by today's technology, quick access to monies, the vast expansion of legal gambling, and societal approval of gambling, these action gamblers are more likely to become compulsive gamblers within three or four years.

In contrast, gambling on slot machines is marked by continuous wagering, for hours on end, without interruption and even faster playing and paying. Many slots players are convinced they became addicted soon after they started playing the slots. Others report being able to play slots at a controlled level for five or more years until numerous adverse life events occurred. Their emotional discomfort was soothed only by rapidly increasing their gambling, succumbing to the addiction shortly thereafter. Equally, there may be interruptions between games of bingo, but these addicts can increase the speed by using fifteen or twenty cards, just as lottery addicts can gamble without interruption, buying long lists of scratch-off tickets.

Nevertheless, a general pattern of progression seems to hold true for most gambling addicts.

PHASES OF COMPULSIVE GAMBLING

In the past, the vast majority of compulsive gamblers were male action gamblers, gambling at the race tracks or casinos or with the bookie. A pattern of progression from social gambling to compulsive gambling was identified, which is still applicable today, with one major exception: action gamblers now can become addicted within three to five years instead of twenty or more years as in the past.

Another important distinction was made in 1992, when pioneer professor and clinical psychologist, Henry Lesieur, PhD, PsyD, coined the term "escape gambler."

Though the progression of the four phases is similar, there are distinct differences between action and escape gamblers.

WINNING PHASE AND THE BIG WIN

The winning phase may last a few weeks or several years. It starts as occasional social gambling, going to the casino two or three times a year, with friends and to have a good time. Social gamblers think about winning, but the more important reason for gambling is to have a good time with family and friends. Finding that this is indeed an enjoyable activity, they tend to go then more frequently than in the past.

As the gambling increases in frequency, so do the repeated wins. Even small wins are rewarding. Gambling becomes more fun, a good time for many and excitement for others. "That craps table was really hot. I couldn't lose." The pile of ten chips at the craps table now becomes twenty chips. The favored penny slot becomes a quarter slot. Losses are ignored; after all, losing ten dollars is not worth mentioning; winning a hundred dollars is worth some bragging. These social gamblers start to fantasize about gambling's rewards: winning, attention from others, feeling good.

Then the first of several major events occur, which start the road to problem gambling. First is a winning streak or the Big Win. This might be a monthly allowance for a student or a six-month salary for an employed adult. The gamblers start to believe that they are luckier than other gamblers and, of course, better gamblers. These wins also lead to a sense of anticipation that they hope to repeat by further gambling, using larger amounts to repeat the intensity of those feelings. Equally important for the action gamblers is the feeling of acceptance from their peers. "They all wanted to hang with me, the winner. Then when I started on a losing streak, they all disappeared. Now I became the loser."

How to counter that? The slots player starts to play more lines, and machines, increases the amount of money bet, or turns to dollar machines, and may win $1000 or more; a heavy action gambler playing blackjack may win $5,000. The amounts defining a Big Win are relative to the person's income and financial worth.

At some point, these heavy social gamblers, almost always action gamblers, may even convince themselves they can become professional gamblers. They spend more time gambling, going to various casinos, winning repeatedly, or hoping to have another Big Win. Some even give up their occupations. For some as yet unresearched reason, these pseudo-professional gamblers tend to have something in common. As one Las Vegas pit boss said, "Just go to any blackjack table and count the number of lawyers who think they are professional gamblers." These gamblers have already reached the level of problem or possibly compulsive gamblers.

LOSING PHASE AND CHASING

The wins cannot last forever. The bets become losses. There may be a number of smaller losses or several larger losses. These are viewed by the gamblers not just losses of money, but a temporary period of bad luck, loss of the excitement and big-shot image for the action gambler. Losses are a violation of compulsive gamblers' sense of competitiveness and their need to be winners in all aspects of their lives, not just gambling. It is a loss of self-esteem turning into an urgency to win back the money and thus avoid being viewed as a failure. The escape gamblers, on the other hand, have feelings of discomfort. They start playing a second machine to avoid those uncomfortable feeling while hoping to win. Both types start to gamble alone; they don't want to be bothered or distracted by others. Their losses continue, offset with occasional wins.

Their thinking becomes obsessive, constantly thinking about gambling, reliving past experiences. They plan on when to leave the work and what believable excuses to tell. "My grandmother died" or "I have to go to the dentist." A spouse or family member is told they have to attend a conference or stay at the office to finish an important report—whatever convincing lies can be made up to suit the occasion.

Gambling has what is termed the "near miss." These become triggers to more desperate gambling. "I had five numbers out of six." "The last reel was just one line away from the big one." "That horse lost by a nose." The gamblers chase their losses and begin to double up their bets, gambling more often, for longer periods. They convince themselves that their strategy and prior history of wins will assure them of reversing that losing streak. But they need money to do that. They start to borrow, but can't pay it back. They pawn or sell possessions, take out bank loans, refinance, and get a second mortgage. They apply for additional credit cards—five or six is typical. These are soon maxed out. They ignore family members and social functions. Relationships with coworkers become strained. Their work productivity fails: work is sloppy, late, or not done at all. Students fail courses, are suspended, or get kicked out of school. Yet these gamblers can't stop gambling. They need help from others but can't or don't want to ask for it. In their minds, all they need is money and they tell one lie after the other to get it.

Their lies become more creative as time continues. "I found a dead fish wrapped in a newspaper at my front door" was one lie told by a college student sports bettor to his parents, implying that the loan shark or the mobster were after him and that he desperately needed money to avoid being hurt. He needed a bail-out. This may be the first of many bail-outs from relatives or friends who see no alternative other than to continue paying the gambler's debts.

Social activities are avoided—the gambler's reputation is that of being "a liar and a stiff" and is no longer welcome. Family members are too embarrassed to be with friends or lack the money to pay for outings. Family trust, cohesion, and stability deteriorate. Phone calls and dunning letters from creditors are constant stressors. Family members themselves become the enablers of the gambling addiction without realizing it, although family life is disintegrating, marked by arguments, accusations, and threats of leaving. Lies have destroyed trust, financial disaster is looming. Family members are exhausted. "I was so overwhelmed. I was walking around with double pneumonia and never knew it. Even sleeping pills didn't help anymore." Family members, just like the gamblers, become depressed, anxious, or even suicidal.

DESPERATION PHASE

They know they are the cause of the debts, problem with work and relationship disasters. "I was drowning in guilt." The action gamblers seek "to zone out" and the escape gamblers want to maintain that state of numbness. They both want "to get away from it all."

Having used up all legal options to support their gambling, compulsive gamblers at this stage turn to stealing from the family first. They write checks that are returned insufficient funds, account closed, no such account. Responsible bank tellers or managers short-change customer accounts or write loans in phony names. Delivery men fail to turn in deposits. Business owners or executives launder money or submit false financial statements. Attorneys and accountants use clients' escrow accounts. These are just a few examples that occur with regular frequency when compulsive gamblers, either action or escape gamblers, are in desperate need of money to pay off debts, avoid discovery, and to continue gambling.

They are in an emotional tailspin. "It was a constant battle. I shouldn't go, but I did. I should quit, but just this once. I shouldn't, but I need to win. The *buts* won out over every *shouldn't*. It was torture." How to avoid this life of torture? Gamble more. For the action gambler: zone out, space out; for escape gamblers, to numb out, get into that hypnotic black hole.

They know what they are doing, know the difference between right and wrong, but (1) do not consider the seriousness and consequences of their actions, (2) are unable to stop these actions, and (3) do not steal with the intent to defraud or hurt anyone. Their intent is to repay these monies with the next bet, which is "sure to be a winner."

Family members face their own reactions to the gambling addiction. They may turn to their church leaders only to be told to pray. Doctors tend to prescribe antidepressants and sleeping pills; lawyers advocate divorce, relatives urge them to leave the gambler. Some may resort to drinking or abusing medication to ease the stress and anxiety. Even parents and grandparents of the gambler have reported thoughts of committing suicide because their life of stress and shame has become unbearable. They have mortgaged their home, which once had been paid for fully; they have spent all of their own assets to bail out the gambler and they see no hope for their own future.

Ironically, even at this period of chaos and desperation, many gamblers may appear to look normal, but in fact, they are wearing a mask, assuming a role of calm and self-control outwardly whereas in reality they experience multiple physical pains, such as chronic headaches, upper and lower back pain, muscle pain and tension, sleep irregularities, and being "sick at the stomach. I was either puking or doubling up in pain. I couldn't eat because I was too busy gambling or because everything tasted like cardboard." Others show clear signs of depression. They become irritable, argumentative, isolate themselves, and are unable to continue good hygiene.

HOPELESS PHASE (HITTING BOTTOM)

Approximately, one-third of compulsive gamblers have a prior history of alcohol dependency or are currently dependent on alcohol. If not, many compulsive gamblers in this phase turn to alcohol or drugs. Marijuana, amphetamines, and cocaine are the most common illegal drugs used. Other compulsive gamblers turn to prescription drugs such as Oxycotin, antidepressants, and sleeping pills. Death wishes are chronic. "I just wanted to go to bed and never wake up." "I thought about car accidents. I knew every curve on the road to Atlantic City where I could have flipped the car. People would say, 'What a tragedy.' The insurance money would pay off bills and my family would have money to live on."

Often, this first time of hitting bottom is when the marital relationship is threatened with separation or divorce. Unfortunately, though, without treatment and support, abstinence becomes too uncomfortable: they cannot escape the bad feelings from before, and now they are faced with the turmoil caused by the gambling.

Additionally, critical life events may occur, especially those concerning finances. What was hoped to be a final phase of gambling instead leads to a relapse back into gambling "and you start right back where you left off."

Compared to other bottoms, the relationship bottom is perhaps the easiest to repair because most parents and spouses want to keep the family intact. Their mantra for the gambler is still, "Just stop gambling and everything will get better."

Another bottom is the legal bottom, when the gambler has been arrested and is facing likelihood of incarceration. During the investigation, pretrial, trial, and sentencing period, the gambler is usually forthcoming, pleading guilty to all illegal transactions and abiding by the court stipulation to refrain from all further gambling. However, too many cases have been reported in which the gambler relapsed within a day or two of having resolved legal issues. "We were all watching the game at the bar, and I kept right on taking bets in front of my parole officer when he came in. I actually thought he wanted to take action from me. Instead, he clapped the handcuffs on me. Now I can see he didn't have a choice but to arrest me. How stupid can one get? I mean, how stupid?"

The final bottom of the hopeless phase comes only when the gambler is emotionally exhausted. Whereas the winning, losing, and desperations phases can last up to several years, the hopeless phase typically lasts for weeks or months. During this phase, the gambler may sit at a blackjack table for forty-eight to seventy-two hours, and the gambling becomes robotic, one hand after the other, without consideration for anything other than to sign markers and to knock for the next card.

Sports bettors recall sitting in front of the televisions set for hours, watching three games at a time, no longer yelling at the athletes for missing a play, barely listening to the game. They no longer care about the spread. Machine gamblers report playing the slots until their arms are numb, their pants soiled, and they have to be physically supported to their rooms or outside. Lottery addicts, too, talk of watching numbers roll in and out, buying dozens of scratch-off tickets, scratching until their hands are black, pain shooting up their arm, with upper back muscles tense and sore. Bingo addicts report playing twenty or or more cards, running their eyes over hundreds of numbers until their vision becomes blurry. The gamblers at this stage are physically and mentally exhausted and cannot continue any longer. They collapse.

When in a moment of clarity, they realize what they have done, they tend to break down in tears, crying for days, pleading for forgiveness while hoping to die. The weeks of suicidal thoughts and death wishes now become plans to commit suicide, unless someone intervenes and the gambler's actions are circumvented. This state represents total emotional exhaustion and is most often the point at which the gambler truly hits bottom. It is the point of final action. Some are successful in their suicide attempts. Action gamblers resort to car accidents or self-inflicted gunshot wounds. Escape gamblers tend to overdose on pills. For some, their final days are in a morgue and coffin. Others spend years in jail, typically two to five years in federal prison, more in state penitentiaries.

The more fortunate compulsive gamblers enter some form of therapy—either Gamblers Anonymous, emergency room treatment, psychotherapy, or are admitted into a professional rehabilitation program for compulsive gamblers. Each final option has its own dynamics, some more beneficial than others.

Unfortunately, there are few Gamblers Anonymous meetings in the United States. Only Nevada, New York, California, and New Jersey have meetings at all hours, every day. Many states have only four or five meetings per week, other states have none at all. There are fewer chapters of Gam-Anon, which is the 12-Step support group for the family and friends. Some states have allotted funds to support a hotline but not for community awareness. There is minimal funding available to train mental health counselors. Some states offer only outpatient care. Fewer have residential programs. There is less support for research. Most research conducted in the past decade has been privately funded, and these studies appear to focus more on prevalence and neurological factors or pharmaceutical support. Research on predisposing factors, family issues, personality characteristics, critical life events, emotional development, and related behaviors is needed as are treatment modalities and outcome studies. Literature is equally limited although the quarterly *International Journal of Gambling Studies* and the Canadian *Journal of Gambling Issues* publish many these gambling research studies.

Most people still believe that gambling is selfish and reckless behavior and scoff at the idea that compulsive gambling is an illness. Compulsive gamblers have many hurdles to overcome with little intervention or support.

STAGES OF RECOVERY

There are phases of the progression into compulsive gambling and phases of recovery. It takes many months or years to develop this addiction, and it takes many months or years to recover from it.

CRITICAL PHASE: IMMEDIATE AND GENERAL

The critical phase can be viewed in two parts: the immediate critical phase and the general critical phase, which follows thereafter. It starts once the gamblers have hit bottom, acknowledge the problems caused by their gambling, no longer want to gamble, and want to recover from this addiction. The compulsive gamblers at this stage typically face one or more immediate crises and the question becomes, "Which must be addressed first?"

Obviously, suicide prevention or intervention take priority over all else and response must be immediate. Finding a suicide note may be too late to prevent the act. In one particular case, a college student wrote a note on poster board paper, in red, designating personal items to his siblings. The note was viewed as a joke until his family found him unconscious.

Suicide by car is the most frequent method considered by compulsive gamblers, usually by running off the road, crashing into a tree, or similar action. "I didn't want to live until the water got up to the steering wheel. Then I thought of my kids." Gamblers who served in the military or who work in law enforcement, thus familiar with weapons, seem to prefer suicide by gun. It is quick and final, a desperate attempt to avoid further guilt and pain. There is less thought about the impact this will have on spouses, parents, or children.

Other than suicidal attempts, financial disasters are most often the immediate crisis: the family is facing eviction or their home is scheduled for foreclosure. Families of compulsive gamblers have been known to sleep in cars and even then being unable to go anywhere because they lack the money for gas.

Once the very immediate problems are resolved, other matters can be addressed: the gambler is facing arrest and criminal charges as a result of crimes committed due to their gambling. Legal problems can be addressed within a short period and virtually always require the services of a public defender. Once these critical situations have been addressed, the focus is on general crisis situations: restoring family unity, resolving work issues, improving health, treatment, and relapse prevention.

To begin, compulsive gamblers must have an honest and sincere desire to change.

They must accept that they have created many problems, need and want to have realistic attempts to overcoming these many problems. No longer can gambling serve as an escape from difficulties, no longer is it an option, but rather gamblers must begin to accept responsibility for their gambling and the impact this has caused.

In all cases, it is imperative that family members participate in a recovery program for the gambler and for themselves (more of this can be found in chapter 12, "The Family"). The gambler must have a sense of hope and conviction that the gambling and its impacts are reversible. This hope can lead to responsible thinking and responsible action. Without the ongoing turmoil and overwhelming feelings of guilt, depression, and anxiety, with the help of others, gamblers can learn to make realistic decisions and develop abilities for problem solving. The others at this time may be family members, Gamblers Anonymous, or staff of a professional treatment program. The gamblers are taught and become confident in making decisions with others rather than making unilateral decisions. They can learn to solve problems with the input from others, rather than once again using poor judgment and irrational efforts.

Because of the financial devastation, most often the first critical step beyond addressing the more immediate crisis situation is to return to work and develop a legal source of income. This can be difficult. Lawyers, accountants, and insurance agents may have lost a license to practice. Some may find it impossible to work in the same field if it entails handling money, such as bank tellers, delivery drivers, bookkeepers, and cashiers. Others may find there are limited opportunities for executive management positions. Thus, the gamblers may find it expedient to accept a lower-paying job or to change their occupation completely. One such gambler formerly had a highly successful real estate business. He accepted a sales job in medical equipment, in which he was able to utilize his experience in management in a more structured environment, without handling cash or other monies.

The growth phase can be indefinite. There is no time limit. Rather, it is a commitment by the gambler to think of others. "How can I become a better person? What good deeds can I do? What sacrifices can I make?" A frequent story heard from recovering compulsive gamblers is, "I'm good with numbers, so I help a kid who is about to flunk math class. It makes me feel good and it sure doesn't cost any money. Except for an occasional ice cream cone."

Life after abstinence from compulsive gambling can get better. Or, change is inevitable, recovery is voluntary.

See page 114 for the Chart of "A Chart of Compulsive Gambling and Recovery."

CHAPTER 4
MYTHS, FANCY STORIES,
AND OTHER (UN)BELIEVABLES

The propensity to gamble is by no means a modern invention, but rather something that has been passed down to cultures, traditions, and people from times predating written histories. Not surprisingly then, many myths and firmly entrenched beliefs have followed those same trails. Some of these myths and beliefs may have a smidgeon of fact and accuracy in them; nevertheless, they remain unproven according to adherence of scientific rigor. Some of the more common ones are shared here.

WHAT OTHERS SAY ABOUT
COMPULSIVE GAMBLERS

THEY EVEN BET ON WHEN THE
FLY LANDS ON THE SUGAR CUBE

Books can be written about the myths surrounding compulsive gamblers. The most frequent one is that compulsive gamblers will bet on anything, even when the fly will land on the sugar cube. Obviously, this myth is as old as America: when sugar cubes first came into common usage and could be found on everybody's table or cup of tea.

In reality, compulsive gamblers rarely bet on the hapless fly and the once ubiquitous sugar cube, although this is not to say that they didn't. However, more often, this tale turns out to be bravado when compulsive gamblers "are clean" and tell their story to add a bit of drama of their craziness to an enthralled audience. Most social gamblers have made a bet or two on some nonsense type of bet: "bet you he can't" type of momentary fun, including the sugar and fly bet. In real life, the compulsive gambler has one or two favorite forms of gambling and can't be bothered with something so inane and insignificant other than to be part of the boisterous crowd watching the football game.

THEY BET ON EVERYTHING

Not hardly, they wouldn't have the time, money, interest, or energy to gamble like that. More accurately, the full-fledged compulsive gambler typically favors two, sometimes three, forms of gambling: the horse bettor may also gamble at the casino, sports bettors also like the horses or the casinos. It is fairly common that horse race bettors, after having lost most of their money in one day of gambling, will then travel to the nearest casino in hopes of recouping their losses.

Another point to remember is that compulsive gamblers study the odds, regardless of the game. The horse bettors spend hours with the racing form, learning about the horse, its sire, the jocky, previous wins, the weather, the turf, the other horses, monies lost, and money needed to win. Card players are known to have many, many books, for instance, on blackjack or poker: how to play, how to bet, counting cards, developing their system, and of course, their own superstitions, sitting on the first chair around the blackjack table, the last chair, or having a favorite dealer. Anything to improve their odds using their knowledge and competitive drive to the maximum. Who can be bothered figuring out the odds of a winning bingo number?

Lottery players, too, prefer a second form of gambling, playing keno, bingo, or slots. They have their own system, their dreams, a dreambook, analyzing past winning numbers, buying the same numbers over and over again. One lottery addict would bet on the numbers on license plates, another said that he would watch the numbers "coming in and going out." Any magic wand to win the Big One will do.

THEY'RE ALL LIARS

True and not true. Certainly, they do lie when they believe it to be expedient or even necessary to cover up their gambling, where they were, their losses, or even their wins. They can come up with stories that defy the imagination, yet are told so convincingly that the targets of these stories accept them as true, at least initially. On second thought, how many teeth can the dentist pull, how many times can grandmothers die? Add up the numbers, and "it just ain't so."

During their gambling, the lies can become commonplace, even if the lies have nothing to do with gambling. "I didn't put the book there" is a quick example. Yet prior to becoming compulsive gamblers and after they are in recovery, they tend to be scrupulously honest, even with money. Find a wallet? They'll return it intact. Did the cashier give too much change? They'll return it.

THEY ARE ALL IRRESPONSIBLE

It certainly seems that compulsive gamblers are irresponsible: they show up late for work or not at all, they have excuses for everything, they borrow money and don't pay it back, they're always in arrears with their bills, they don't show up for social functions after they promised they would, their children are neglected, they are irritable and argue with their spouses, they sleep all day, they're never home, they'll lie about everything, now they look like bums…the litany goes on. The reality is, though, that these gamblers are caught in the midst of their addiction, they have gambled their lives into financial ruin and chaos. At this stage of their addiction, they are totally preoccupied with gambling, the world around them doesn't exist; they are what they call in The Zone. Their behaviors are aberrant from their previous behaviors, from their values and responsibilities. They know what they are doing is wrong, but their reasoning is impaired and they can't stop. When they are sick, they can do only what their sickness allows them to do.

THEY REALLY ARE SMARTER THAN OTHERS

High school senior Chuck went to the race track every day the horses ran. He always came early, bought the racing form, and pored over all the statistics and latest information on the turf, jockey, horse, the weather. He analyzed and strategized, and he won many times, including trifectas. He bragged about his wins and some of his classmates started going to the track with him. He showed them his system, and they were awed by his knowledge of horse racing. It became even more important for Chuck to keep on winning. He convinced himself that they would consider him one of the guys as long as he kept winning. That is called delusional thinking. When he started losing, which was inevitable, he lost not only the money but also his new "friends" and self-worth.

THEY'RE JUST WASTING ALL THAT MONEY

It is most difficult for compulsive gamblers to accept gambling as a waste of money. It was fun for so many years, they had winning lottery tickets of five thousand and ten thousand, hit the big jackpots on the slots, got all those free shows and gifts from the casinos. Compulsive gamblers look at the benefits without considering how much it cost them nor do they consider the consequences of those costs.

Tony, a compulsive gambler protested he knew exactly how much money he lost, but at the insistence of his family he agreed to meet with GA members and have a financial pressure relief group. He was stunned when he was shown his losses amounted to two million dollars. He was convinced he lost only one million. It was only after a period of abstinence that he realized the money was truly wasted on gambling.

THEY ARE SELFISH

Is there any spouse, family member, or friend who is not fully convinced that compulsive gamblers are selfish? Quite frankly, when it comes to addicted gambling, there is no world other than their own. They will use household money for themselves instead of on the family vacation, disappear for hours or days gambling at the track or sitting in front of a slot machine instead of going to the movie with friends or colleagues. "It's my time, my place, my money, what I want to do"; that is their mantra. They are self-centered during the crazy gambling, as are all addicts. It becomes part of their irrational thinking and behaviors. The addiction takes over and comes first, everyone and everything else is second. That is the nature of addiction.

THEY ARE BIG SPENDERS

What better way to earn respect and admiration than with generosity? It is virtually universal behavior among high rollers. When they win, they tip the dealer. When they win large, they tip the dealer, the waitresses, and buy gifts for friends and their family. They will buy an expensive car and fancy jewelry for themselves. It is part of the big shot image. When they've gambled and lost everything, they will put on the mask and walk away from the card table, giving the dealer the last bit of money they have left. "I had to pretend that losing meant nothing to me, that I could afford it. But inside, my stomach was in knots and the fear was overpowering. I could barely walk away. I wasn't generous, I was avoiding public humiliation." According to a poker-playing gambling addict, "You don't walk away with a pocketful of money. You give the others a chance to win back their money. That is proper gambling etiquette." His wife and probation officer disagreed.

THEY GAMBLE TO LOSE

Nothing, absolutely nothing, can be further from the truth. True, they lose, they lose often, and they lose a lot, but their goal is to win. They need the wins to "stay in action," or "to get away," to cover up earlier losses, pay the bills, or replace the money that they "borrowed" from the office bank account. About the only time that compulsive gamblers want to lose is at their very last betting spree. They want to lose every dime they have so that they cannot gamble anymore. They are broken in spirit and see this as the only way out of the tortured life they have led for so many months or years. It is their "last, painful hurrah."

THE GAMBLER'S DELUSIONS AND MAGICAL THINKING

Compulsive gamblers typically are above average in intelligence. They tend to ace courses in school, be the sharpest lawyers, and do well in sales. This would suggest rational, logical, and sequential thought processes, yet in reality, gambling leads to irrational beliefs and delusions. They survive on their magical thinking and denial.

COMPULSIVE GAMBLERS HAVE TO GAMBLE EVERY DAY

This is a belief shared by many people, but is not necessarily true. Some compulsive gamblers, indeed, do bet every day, but not all. Sports bettors have easy access to the bookie by way of phone, Internet, through a bookie's associates, or in person. But their sport may not be in season. Others may buy a lottery ticket at any nearby place, such as work or corner store. Some gamblers may go to the casino or OTB every day, especially if they are in the desperation phase, while others may go only two or three times a week, or only on weekends when they don't have to go to work. There are also binge gamblers, similar to binge drinkers, who gamble only every two or three months, but during that time, gamble without control. Compulsive gamblers have to gamble, but not every day. The problem with binge gamblers, unfortunately, is that they are convinced they are not addicted because "I bet only every two months. See? I can stop whenever I want." Sound familiar?

THE NEXT ONE WILL BE THE BiG ONE

One of the hallmarks of the progression from social gambling to problem and compulsive gambling is the Big Win. The first Big Win is truly a memorable event in the gambler's life. It is exhilarating, a high, a rush they have never experienced before. It creates an urge to gamble more and to have those good feelings again.

Once the gambler has become an addict, the Big Win becomes essential in order to get out of that desperation phase of gambling. There is no exhilarating joy in having the Big Win, only momentary relief and then the opportunity to continue gambling. Social gamblers would stop, compulsive gamblers can't. For social gamblers, the Big Win is fun, it is recreational; for compulsive gamblers, the Big Win is essential, it is part of the desperate bets of chasing.

THIS WILL BE MY LUCKY NIGHT

"This is my lucky night, Lady Luck is watching over me, I can feel it in my bones." All delusional, magical thinking. But many gamblers are firmly entrenched in their beliefs. Lottery players will buy the same birthday numbers each time. The bingo addicts use only a certain color of dauber, the little talisman in front of the cards, the right cards to pick, the place to sit. There is no skill or loving deity no matter how many cards are played or how many superstitions are followed. No one will really know if the night is going to be lucky until the next ball bounces up and the number is called. At the end of the day, the player may be ahead or more likely will have lost. It depends on the draw of the cards or the bounce of the ball, not on the mystical Lady Luck.

I SAW THE WINNING NUMBERS IN MY DREAM

It is not unusual to hear this, especially among illegal numbers gamblers. This is superstition of the purest form. There is no skill and no system involved in numbers gambling. It is based on pure chance. True, there is always the chance that the dream number will also be the winning number, but this is not a guarantee. Dream books can be very influential, but they cannot guarantee a win. It is still a gamble.

Dreams books are very much a part of the African-American culture. Illegal numbers and dream books allow for social interaction, a time to chat with friends, and hopes of winning some money to help out with finances. If the dream number turns out to be the winning number, it is still pure happenstance, but with the anticipated benefits.

THE BOOKIE IS MY BEST FRIEND

In the sports betting world, there are two types of bookies: the bookie who is my friend and the bookie who acts like my friend. The first bookie may have been a friend for several years, a childhood playmate, a college classmate, or a colleague at work, who may have turned to booking as a sideline, such as taking bets on the Super Bowl game.

But the real bookie only pretends to be the gambler's best friend. In other words, the bookie is to sports what hosts are to casinos. They will call, "How are you, John? I haven't heard from you in a couple of weeks." The bookie appears to show a concerned interest, the gambler feels important, but the bookie's real intent is to entice the gambler to bet and then to take the degenerate's money.

I'M DUE TO WIN

One hapless horse race gambler lost fifty races in a row until he threw down his handful of losing tickets and yelled out in pure frustration. His "I'm due to win" belief kept him betting one race after another, losing more and more money on the unending chase until he had used up all his cash, wrote check after check until his account was overdrawn, and maxed out his credit cards, all three of them. And he still lost.

I DIDN'T STEAL THE MONEY, I JUST BORROWED IT

Many years ago, Jerry Fulcher, founder of the Delaware Council on Compulsive Gambling, coined the phrase "Lies, Loans, and Larceny" in describing the actions of desperate compulsive gamblers. Gambling addicts will lie. They will follow the downward spiral of options for acquiring money legally, according to Henry Lesieur, author of *The Chase*.

Compulsive gamblers need money to feed their addiction. Where to get it? Cashiers will submit fraudulent transactions or the daily bank deposit is short, lawyers will borrow from a client's escrow account, owners of the family business may take it from their own company, salesmen tend to use the company credit card. In the compulsive gambler's mind, these acts are not crimes; they are simply loans to be repaid the next day after their Big Win. The first one is easy, but after many of these "borrowed" monies, unable to replace what was stolen, they realize the quandary they are in. They cannot simply stop their addiction because they are out of money; they will steal more, again and again, and getting deeper and deeper into debt and fraudulent "loans."

Question 16 of the Twenty Questions of Gamblers Anonymous is "Have you ever committed or thought of committing an illegal act to support your gambling?" The thefts are real, but compulsive gamblers think they are "just borrowing."

I CAN WIN WITH MY SYSTEM

The Las Vegas Bookstore has a table covered with systems developed by horse race gamblers, blackjack and poker players, lottery gamblers, sports bettors, slots players, all winners or losers. The systems abound, so do the losers. Only the house: the state lottery, casino, bookie, have the winning systems because the odds are legislated by state government or set by the gambling venue, and the odds are always in favor of the house. How many losers does it take to have a million dollar lottery jackpot?

I CAN WIN BECAUSE I KNOW

Many compulsive gamblers are active in sports since early school days. Whether they are playing sports, following the games, or collecting baseball cards, they know sports, the players, the teams, their wins and losses. They tend to be the sports bettors, believing they have that edge; however, whereas they may have a slight advantage by knowing the odds, it is no guarantee, anything can happen, and in the long run, the bookie is more likely to be the winner taking money from that degenerate.

SOME OF THE GAMBLERS' FAVORITES: I GAMBLE BECAUSE...

I CAN AFFORD IT, SO IT'S NOT A PROBLEM

Compulsive gambling is not just about the money, it is also the impact on the family, losing friends, doing poorly at work or in school, and compromised health. It leads to ongoing loss of self-esteem, together with a multitude of bad feelings, especially guilt. Lying is also part of compulsive gambling: lying to others as well as lying to oneself. Can the gambler really afford it? After all, in the end it is not just the money that is lost, it is all the related losses.

IT'S FUN

Of course, it is fun. That is the favorite slogan for the two major gaming industries, casinos and state lotteries. "Gamble for fun and recreation" is their theme song. It is especially fun when the wins include free tickets to shows, invitations to special events, and gifts for family members. "Gamble responsibly, don't play more than you can afford." It is geared to social gamblers, compulsive gamblers are way beyond that warning. The irony is not lost though. Some twenty years ago, the Illinois State lottery even had a second prize on a winning lottery ticket: an all-expense trip to Las Vegas.

I LIKE IT

Social gamblers will say, "It's fun" and "I like it." But social gamblers also set limits on gambling. They determine how much money they are willing to lose. It is the cost of recreation, no different than going to a ball game or movie. Another consideration is how much time to spend on the gambling. Who would deny the friends from watching and betting on the Monday night football game, with potato chips and beer, or the five old-timers and their Friday night poker game? However, when these social gamblers find that the gambling interferes with family life or work, they will turn to another form of recreation. Recreation is just that, it is supposed to be fun and not something that causes chaos and unhappiness.

Compulsive gamblers, on the other hand, will use any and all excuses they can come up with: "I like it, it's fun, I've earned it, I need time off" and more, but this has a greater force, entitlement, demand, and challenge behind it. In the world of addictions, this is called denial.

I'M NOT GAMBLING

Mike was a casino high roller when he lost his entire business due to gambling. He joined Gamblers Anonymous and was an active member. "I was clean for eight years." His wife bought daily lottery tickets, but that didn't bother him, it was just the lottery and not "real" gambling. Then one day, his wife asked him to pick up her tickets. He looked at her numbers, thought there was a smarter way of choosing them, and bought her tickets with the numbers he thought were better. Once again he rationalized that he wasn't gambling, he was simply buying the tickets for her. Two years later, he lost his second business and was sentenced to jail for money laundering. "I wasn't gambling. I was just buying tickets for her" was his rationale, but Gamblers Anonymous states that even buying a lottery ticket is gambling.

IT'S HER FAULT I GAMBLE, SHE MAKES ME SO ANGRY

Any excuse is better than none, but this one is used fairly often. Blaming someone else for compulsive gambling is much easier than accepting one's own addiction. There is an inkling of truth in this, however. The gambler's spouse may have been critical of something; the gambler becomes angry and rushes off to the gambling haven of safety rather than resolving the conflict. Often, there is guilt associated with this kind of rationale, especially if the gambler recognizes that the spouse's criticism is valid.

IT MAKES ME FEEL LIKE A WINNER
(BUT WITH AN INFERIORITY COMPLEX)

Action gamblers have a long history of low self-esteem. They may be outstanding employees or own a successful business, coach the most winning Little League, but that matters little in how they think of themselves as a person. They think they don't measure up to others. Many casino gamblers have acknowledged feeling important and the envy of others after a Big Win. They tip the dealer, they buy gifts for the family, they look and act generous. Yet more often, they think, "I'm a king with an inferiority complex." Winning was just an illusion, just paper. It didn't change their reality back home.

"Good player, yes. Good person, no. Look at all the things that are wrong with me, or better yet, don't look at them. Let me put on my mask so that no one will know who I really am because if they knew, they wouldn't want anything to do with me. They think I'm a show-off or big shot because I wear expensive clothes and have the biggest house on the street, but all I really want is to wear blue jeans, mow my own lawn, and be one of the guys."

Being accepted by others was very important for a farmer in Midwest America. His family farm was one of the largest in the state, he served on community boards, was on the board of judges for 4-H contests, and people respected him. But always in the back of his mind were the days when his dad would criticize him or when he got those beatings. One day, a friend introduced him to a bookie. "Why gamble on sports? I'd rather be the bookie." He loved the action at the track and the excitement of going to Vegas, looking the part with his silk shirt, black suit and tie, diamond rings and gold chains. Mr. Big. The relief he felt when he was in rehab and didn't have to wear those identifiers made him realize who he really was: a good farmer, an active community leader, and most of all, a good person. He didn't need gambling to measure his worth against others.

THERE'S NOTHING LIKE IT

This statement requires some scrutiny and understanding of the different types of gambling. Rarely will a slots addict talk about the sense of exhilaration or rush. They think of their gambling as a total escape from reality, of blotting out the world. The more action-oriented gamblers speak of being in the zone, a state of dissociation from reality. One gambler said the minute he drove over the bridge to Atlantic City, he felt safe. Another one said the moment he stepped through the turnstile at the track, he left the world behind.

Craps shooters and horse race gamblers talk about the fast action of the game while "I'm spacing out." The sense of euphoria of a win can be overpowering—"Better than sex"—but lasts for only a few seconds and the gambler is already making the next bet. The "Nothing Like It" is more akin to a momentary state of mania, when the impulsive mind and body outrace each other without thought of plan or consequences.

ALL ABOUT MONEY

Obviously, gambling is about money, but compulsive gamblers have some unique beliefs and understanding with respect to money. True, they abuse money in the course of their addiction, which is based on gambling something of value in the hopes of winning, thus a greater return, but the item of value is something that is predetermined by the gamblers. Boys gamble when they pay for the packet of baseball cards, hoping to win that special one they need. This is different from actually trading or buying the card they desire. Until they had their own casinos, Native Americans bet on ponies or horse blankets; others wager their jewelry, land, or anything of value. The actual medium may be different, but it is still something of value.

I QUIT REAL GAMBLING, NOW I JUST BET A DOLLAR

Gambling has become such an integral part of these addicts' life that they will resort to any means of convincing others and themselves that some gambling is okay. "I'm a sports bettor, I don't play bingo" or "I need the action I get from craps, lotteries are much too slow." But the most frequent one espoused while attempting to gain abstinence, thus some control over their lives again, is to put in a dollar, hoping to win more. Lottery tickets can be bought for a dollar, slots can be played for a quarter. It is all gambling.

The comparison might be made with beer, wine, and whiskey—they are all alcoholic beverages. There are distinctions, and there are similarities. Some people drink wine, others use whiskey to feed their dependence on alcohol. The same is true of gambling; it can be for a nickel or it can be for a thousand dollars. The amount of money does not matter; it is the fact that gambling requires something of value on an activity, hoping to win, with the predominant element of chance.

IF I ADMIT HOW MUCH I REALLY OWE. . .

Fearing dad's disapproval or that a spouse may leave are the most common reasons among compulsive gamblers for minimizing the amount of money lost or owed. The same is true when they are being bailed out. Consider one such case: a Chicago banker owed his bookie $50,000. Chicago has an organized crime family among its midst. The son/banker admitted to his parents of owing only $45,000, somehow that would be more forgivable, but then he was left with the extra $5,000 owed to the bookie. The parents were terrified the bookie might harm their son, and thus agreed to pay the bookie with the understanding that the father would manage the son's income. The only way he could repay the bookie without the parents' knowledge was to set up phony loans at the bank, which he did, except now he had to bet and win so that the phony loans could be repaid. He lost and then started chasing those losses. Nearly one million dollars later in phony loans, he was arrested and went to federal prison, all because he couldn't bring himself to admit to his parents that he owed the extra $5,000.

The irony of this is that while dads and spouses may in fact become quite angry, they rarely abandon the gambler. As one spouse said, "Just tell me the whole story, then I know what I'm dealing with."

SO I CAN PAY BACK WHAT I OWE

There is the old adage of "Good intentions pave the road to hell." It seems to have been coined (pardon the pun) for compulsive gamblers, who have all good intentions to pay back what they have borrowed legally, to replace what they have taken illegally, or "borrowed" as they see it, and to pay the bills that have been ignored, often for many months, even leading to threats of foreclosure. Unfortunately, two things stand in the way of fulfilling their good intentions: (1) the big win doesn't come, and (2) when they do get the Big One, they are more likely to pay back what they lost most recently, to chase those losses, get close to that figure, and then lose it all before reaching their goal. Their good intentions are based on a prediction of outcome; unfortunately, there is no certainty with gambling, other than it results in many wins and even many more losses.

I CAN ALWAYS GET BAILED OUT BY SOMEBODY

Well, just about anybody. Compulsive gamblers, also referred to as con artists, are most adept at manipulating others in their desperate quest for gambling money. Actually, they use these skills in their jobs, which is one reason they become the best of the best in sales and other business endeavors which entail money. Their manipulative techniques are finely honed and used in their everyday speech. Interestingly, one such manipulative expert, when confronted on this, was astonished to learn that not everybody spoke like him and that he was described as a manipulative person. Another compulsive gambler, in recovery, was giving a talk on just this topic to a group of bankers and other financiers, almost bragging to them, "I can get money out of one of you before I leave this meeting." And sure enough, he did, much to the consternation of the lender and the rest of the audience.

It is only when compulsive gamblers have been discovered by a spouse or family member, now fully aware of the gamblers' manipulations, that these efforts are less than successful.

I ALWAYS WIN

If gamblers always win, they would not become compulsive gamblers. They would be considered heavy social gamblers or high rollers. The only way gamblers could always win is if they are cheats: they might use marked cards, shaved dice, crooked wheels, weighted balls, tightened springs in the carnival peach basket, by using shills, or any of the many other methods of cheating. Law enforcement agencies have vice squads to uncover these cheats. Casinos spend millions of dollars each year to apprehend them, constantly checking their machines for accuracy and using eight decks of cards in the shoe instead of dealing by hand.

Compulsive gamblers might win many times in a row, which gives the illusion of being luckier or smarter, but these can also be offset by the losses. Gambling is based on chance, not skill, cheating, on the other hand, can increase the chance to win.

I GAMBLE BECAUSE I NEED THE MONEY

There are many options to overcome the need for money: set a budget, negotiate for reduced monthly payments or interest, work longer hours, spend less, consolidate bills, sell something. The least effective way of overcoming the need for money is to gamble. Statistically, the odds are against the gambler. A quick example illustrates the point: casinos depend on the many losses from gamblers in order to sparkle with magnificent chandeliers, send the limos, and give out those comps.

PEOPLE WILL THINK I'M A BUM
IF I DON'T HAVE MONEY IN MY POCKET

In cognitive therapy, this statement would be considered mind reading. No one really knows (1) what others are thinking and (2) knows how much money the gamblers may have in their pockets. Gamblers tend to believe that others will consider them to be a bum but don't stop to analyze this misconception whereas a moment of reflection would verify that even presidents can walk around with empty pockets and not be considered bums. Nevertheless, this is one reason why so many gamblers have relatively large amounts of money in their pockets. To be caught shorthanded would be the epitome of being considered a failure and a bum.

PEOPLE WILL ACCEPT ME IF I HAVE MONEY

Action gamblers are raised in families in which there is an emphasis on money: working long hours to support a family, valuing items or behaviors in terms of money, or measuring up to others in their social environment. Gambling is all about money. Money is also a social indicator of one's station in life; thus, certain gamblers with a strong need to be liked or accepted will pursue those needs through gambling.

GAMBLERS' ATTITUDES TOWARD OTHER FORMS OF GAMBLING

Most compulsive gamblers tend to have firm convictions about different forms of gambling, and they rationalize their form of gambling is somehow superior to other forms. Having determined a hierarchy of types of gambling, they tend to have two or three favorite forms: the casino gambler also prefers sports betting and race tracks, lottery players also like to gamble on slots and bingo, while Asians tend to view pai gow and other Asian games as superior to craps or blackjack.

BINGO IS FOR OLD LADIES

Before equal rights, it was unheard of for a grandma type of gambler to go into a casino. It just wasn't proper etiquette. By the same token, grannies did not want to be involved with any kind of illegal activities, much less associate with bookies or loan sharks. Lotteries were a fairly new form of legal gambling, but playing bingo inside their church to raise money for the church or school was not only socially acceptable but also an act of stewardship. Bingo is still a predominantly elderly ladies' game, but on Indian reservation bingo halls, there are as many males as females and many younger gamblers. Times have changed and so has gambling and the gamblers.

THE CASINO HOST REALLY LIKES ME

For compulsive gamblers suffering from low-esteem, the attention they get from the casino host is a far cry from their fears of rejection or disappointing others. The casino host will not reject; rather, the host will shower the gambler with attention and comps and act as someone who cares. These perks increase as the gambler makes larger bets and comes to the casino more frequently. In the needy compulsive gambler's eyes, the host becomes the best friend. Who else would be so kind and generous? It is not because the host is truly interested in friendship, but rather because the gambler represents an income for the host. For the host, it is all about good business and income, not friendship.

RACE TRACK GAMBLERS ARE THE MOST INTELLIGENT OF ALL GAMBLERS

There may be an element of truth in this, for who can figure out a racing form or remember all the statistics, past performances of horse or jockey, weather conditions, and knows how to wager on a winning trifecta? On the other hand, maybe the most intelligent gambler is the sports bettor, who has the same uncanny memory of players and games, who can make large bets and win more. This attitude more often is a prejudice.

LOTTERIES ARE TOO PASSIVE TO BE ADDICTIVE

This statement is precisely what a former leader in the field of compulsive gambling proclaimed at a gambling conference in the 1980s. He said the same thing about slots. Unfortunately, the speaker had worked and met only the "high action" type of gamblers because race tracks, casinos, and cards were legal and accessible only to specific groups of gamblers, and secondly, state lottery tickets were of small denominations: fifty cents, a dollar, rarely ten dollars, and therefore were not recognized as potentially leading to gambling addiction, and thirdly because the speaker hoped to ally himself with the gaming industry on the expectation of getting funds for treatment and research. Instead, it was soon learned that lotteries, bingo, and slots can, indeed, lead to compulsive gambling and all the consequences of other forms of gambling.

LOTTERIES HAVE HOT NUMBERS

Some lottery addicts are convinced that certain numbers are drawn more often than others. The fact, however, is that lottery numbers are drawn at random, thus each number has an equal chance of being drawn, and each number has an equal chance of being the winning number. Yet as one lottery addict vehemently insisted, "I watch them coming in and coming out, and I know when the winning number will come up." Unfortunately, he ended up stealing to support his lottery addiction, still convinced he could predict the hot number coming in.

VENDORS KNOW WHICH TICKETS ARE THE WINNERS

Many people are convinced that the vendors have secret information about lottery tickets and therefore sell these tickets to their friends or family. However, state lotteries have strict security procedures, which must be followed by anyone associated with the lottery operation, including ticket designers, manufacturers, distributors, and retailers. A caveat: the holes in punch boards must be opened and a small slip with a number is pulled out. The board has one larger winning prize. The owner of the punchboard will know when the high winning number is drawn, but may continue selling the numbers to others. Since punchboards are illegal and therefore not subject to state regulation, this is not an unusual practice. The owners will cheat and the gamblers will cheat. It is fast, but not the fastest. (Note: A Maryland State Lottery sales representative was recently charged with several counts of theft, having stolen lottery tickets from 2008-2012.)

CRAPS IS THE FASTEST ACTION

This belief is common among craps shooters and observers of gamblers at a dice table. It is a fast game; it takes only the throw of the dice and exchange of chips to have constant fast activity. On the other hand, there is always the few seconds of down time, when chips are raked in and bets are placed. Instant action is also obtained through scratch-offs and the high or excitement of gambling at the OTB with simulcasting: twelve races at a time, from one machine to the next, from noon to midnight. Is there anything faster or more exhausting? Scratch-off lottery tickets have instant plays. What is faster, for longer hours, than playing the slots, not just one, but two or three at a time? Craps being the fastest form of gambling is a misperception.

SLOTS IS ESCAPE GAMBLING, SO IT IS NOT REAL GAMBLING

All gambling addiction serves as an escape from the gambler's reality of pain, fear, and stress. True, shooting craps involves much more active and faster body movement than that which occurs while sitting in front of a slot machine or at a bingo table, yet the emotional escape that occurs while "being pulled into the machine" or "being in the zone" is true for all forms of gambling.

ONLY THE POOR PLAY THE SLOTS OR LOTTERIES

This was actually true at one time. Men and women who were less educated and with lower incomes could afford to buy only fifty-cent lottery tickets, play the nickel slot machines, or the illegal poker machines. However, as lottery promotion and jackpots increased, so did the diversity of players. Now the high income earners can also be seen sitting in front of a slot machine for hours, while those preferring lotteries or keno have been known to lose their businesses or end up in great debt, just like compulsive gamblers who prefer other forms of gambling. An example of this is Judge Paul W. Ottinger, 68, from Hagerstown, MD, a lottery addict who was found guilty of theft in state and federal court and sentenced to five years of incarceration (see Appendix 4).

GAMBLERS' VIEWS OF THEMSELVES

Compulsive gamblers are often described by themselves and others as Dr. Jekyll and Mr. Hyde. How can someone have been so friendly, responsible, and dependable in the past and now act like a madman, lying, arguing, and being irresponsible? That is what others say about compulsive gamblers. This is what compulsive gamblers also say about themselves. They are caught in the whirlpool of self-deception and self-demeaning.

I TELL MYSELF I CAN WIN, BUT I REALLY CAN'T

One of the irrational beliefs held by virtually all compulsive gamblers is "I won in the past, I know I can win again." Chances are the gambler will win again, but at what costs, financial and otherwise? These competitive gamblers will chase that elusive dream of the Big Win, forever optimistic, until they have a moment of clarity in which they realize they can't win, that gambling is a losing game, that gambling rules are always set in favor of the house. Being a winner can be determined only after carefully analyzing all past plays, wins and losses, and when they have stopped gambling and begin to see the facts.

I'M A BIG SHOT, BUT WITH AN INFERIORITY COMPLEX

Compulsive gamblers have a poor self-image. They may or may not know how intelligent they are, yet they still feel inferior to others. They work hard and become achievers, the best of the best in the work field, yet they still struggle with the fear of failure. Thus when they have a big win and other gamblers applaud, they cherish the moment of exhilaration and acceptance. This is a grand moment for them, one which they try to extend with a smile of nonchalance and another bet. But they know it's phony.

I CAN ALWAYS GET THE MONEY, BUT I CAN'T HOLD ON TO IT

So true, gamblers get their money through hard work, manipulations, and thievery. Compulsive gamblers are also known as con men, and through their expertise with words, they are able to convince others to lend them money on the promise of repayment or to avoid being harmed by a bookie. When legal options are no longer viable, they will steal. Some way or another, they will get the money: of course, they just as quickly will make the next bet and lose it. Ironically, many compulsive gamblers work in a financial arena, such as bookkeepers or accountants, and know how to set up budgets and financial statements and they can continue to do this with other people's money; however, their own budgets have fallen by the wayside during their out-of-control gambling.

I KNOW I'M A NICE GUY, BUT I DON'T ACT LIKE IT

Compulsive gamblers talk about guilt, the all-encompassing guilt that they feel about the damage they have caused. They know that at one time they were caring and honest people, yet when the gambling addiction took over, they changed from the intelligent and respectful person of Dr. Jekyll to the monster of Mr. Hyde. One compulsive gambler said, "My son was pleading with me to stay home and I was dying with guilt, but I had to get to the track. I went. The rest of my life I have to live with the look on his face and my guilt."

I HAVE MONEY FOR THE BILLS,
BUT I SPEND IT ON GAMBLING

Gamblers are often heard to say, "I have two pockets of money, one for the bills and the other one for gambling." At some level in their confused state of mind, they know that bills have to be paid. They use all kinds of devious means to hide them from a spouse, yet they keep a portion of the bill money for gambling, hoping to win enough to pay all the bills, with some left over for the next gambling spree. To them, gambling money is gambling money, no matter what. One compulsive gambler admitted that he owed a New York loan shark a large sum of money. The loan shark stuck a gun to the gambler's head, demanding his money, yet the gambler insisted he didn't have it, even though the money was in his pocket. For this degenerate, gambling had greater value than his life.

I'M SMART, BUT SO STUPID

Being smart does not mean an individual has good insight, uses good judgment, or is immune from addictions. This is a difficult concept to understand, yet intelligence does not mean using good judgment. In fact, gamblers have a history of using poor judgment. Relating it to money, gamblers know how to earn it, yet they rarely abide by a budget. Their thinking is, "Let's spend it today, I can always earn more tomorrow."

It is equally poor judgment from others to expect addicts to act responsibly while in the throes of their addiction. A responsible addict? It is an oxymoron.

No doubt there are other myths and beliefs that defy reality, but these are the more common ones held dear by compulsive gamblers and the general public today.

CHAPTER 5
TERMS AND DIAGNOSTIC TOOLS

There are various terms and criteria used in diagnosing a compulsive gambler. These differences depend on clinical diagnostic criteria as well as clinical versus popular terminology. Numerous criteria are used to make the diagnosis of compulsive gambling, some based on official nomenclature, another from Gamblers Anonymous, various short assessments, some geared to specific populations, others for making a clinical evaluation. Some refer to "problem, compulsive, or pathological gambling" or to terms coming into usage more recently: or gambling disorder." "Problem" gambling may not meet the criteria for a diagnosis of pathological gambling, although all five terms represent problematic gambling.

There are various screens used to make the diagnosis of pathological gambling, which also cull out those gamblers who abuse gambling but do not meet the full criteria required for a diagnosis of pathological gambling. There are well over three dozen screens, but the ones discussed in this chapter are those most commonly used at this time in the United States.

TERMS AND DESCRIPTORS

Historically, the British favored the terms "hazarder" and "gamester," but these were more frequently found in the 1800s and in literature. Although used occasionally, neither term was popular in the United States. Other terms used in Britain and the United States are "inveterate" gambler, "habitual" gambler, or "bettor." The British also use the term "punter," but all of these terms are used sparingly in the United States today. The term "wagering" is used on occasion, referring to individuals who make wagers or bets.

In today's society, the preferred use is "compulsive" gambler. Second to that is a term that has come into favor in the last thirty years, namely, "problem" gambler. It was introduced initially to encompass the larger number of gamblers, including those on welfare or with minimal funds, who used that money for gambling instead of meeting basic needs. Since then, problem gambling has defined those individuals who have encountered more serious difficulties or problems as a result of their gambling and are faced with making a choice: continue at their present rate of gambling, which possibly could develop into compulsive gambling, or conversely, limit their gambling to social gambling or cease gambling altogether. Problem gamblers cannot be diagnosed as compulsive gamblers, those who have lost control over their gambling.

Bookmakers, loan sharks, and others often associated with illegal sports betting tend to use the term "degenerate" gambler. Nevertheless, the clinically correct term for this disorder, as listed by the American Psychiatric Association in its *Diagnostic and Statistical Manual of Mental Disorders* and the World Health Organization's *International Classification of Diseases* since 1979, is "pathological" gambling and in the DSM5 "gambling disorder".

Over a half century ago, anyone with an alcohol problem was commonly referred to as a "drunk," albeit more recently a distinction was made, especially by clinicians and the mental health community, between someone who *abuses alcohol* in contrast to someone who is *alcohol dependent.* By comparison, "problem" gambling is the equivalent of substance "abuse" while compulsive gambling is the equivalent of substance dependency. Both are considered to be addictions by the general community and those serving in the clinical arena; thus, whereas pathological gambling was first categorized as a disorder of impulsive control, the DSM5 refers to pathological gambling as a gambling disorder, and under a general category of addictions. This is due to the similarities and links between gambling and substance abuse, the progression of these disorders, co- and cross addictions, their impacts and recoveries.

During the 1800s, the word "gaming" became popular in England, which had many forms of gambling, and referred to the process of gambling rather than referring to individuals who gamble. More recently, however, the Las Vegas casino industry was instrumental in introducing the word "gaming" to mean "gambling" in an attempt to rid itself of the association with illegal gambling and the organized crime syndicates of Las Vegas gambling of the 1930s. Further, recognizing the profit potential of its industry, it sought to expand through attaining corporate status and trading in the financial fields. This was accomplished most successfully by the American Gaming Association, which represents Vegas-type casinos. The Association, while in the forefront of this goal, does not represent the entire industry, such as Native American casinos, horse racing, state lotteries, slots, and other forms of legal gambling, although these forms of gambling benefit directly and indirectly from the work and efforts of the Association.

The American Gaming Association draws a clear distinction between "gaming," which is the gambling industry, and the word "gambling," which represents the individual who places bets. The industry in more recent years has also established "responsible gaming" programs as a reminder that gambling should be fun and a social event, rather than an activity in which the outcome can result in emotional and financial damage to the gambler and others. In contrast to their earlier definition, however, the Association itself now uses the term *gaming* for those who gamble instead of *gambling* in referring to the gamblers.

Similarly, an attempt was made by researchers, supported by casino funds, to use the term "disordered" gambling. This again is confusing in that it refers to the process of gambling rather than a psychiatric disorder or individuals who have lost control over their gambling.

Gamblers are also referred to by the casino industry as "high rollers" and "whales"—depending on the high stakes gambled, usually in the hundred thousands of dollars or higher, although these gamblers could be considered to be heavy social gamblers who may or may not meet the criteria of problem or compulsive gambling.

DIAGNOSTIC CRITERIA

Various measures are used for quick assessments or precise clinical evaluations. Each has its own functions for specific purposes and in specific settings. Most also have inherent weaknesses, which are discussed briefly.

THE DIAGNOSTIC AND STATISTICAL MANUAL OF MENTAL DISORDERS

Categorized gambling as a *disorder of impulse control*, and listed as *pathological gambling (Section 312.31)*, the DSM first included pathological gambling in its third edition in 1980, and subsequently also in the fourth edition, and later revisions. In the fifth edition, it is listed under the general term of addictions. The weakness of the current definition lies in its focus on money and its failure to make a distinction between problem gambling and pathological gambling. Further, it does not distinguish between types of gamblers, such as the action gambler and the escape gambler. Nevertheless, the DSM5 criteria are currently used in the United States as the official definition of compulsive gambling.

The DSM5 lists nine criteria for the diagnosis of gambling disorder, of which four or more are necessary for the diagnosis, based on:

1. Preoccupation (obsessions about gambling and money);
2. Tolerance (gambling with increasing amounts of money to achieve the desired emotional response);
3. Loss of Control (repeated unsuccessful attempts to control, reduce, or stop gambling);
4. Withdrawal (becoming restless or irritable when attempting to cut down or reduce gambling);
5. Escape (escaping from problems or to escape a dysphoric mood);
6. Chasing (gambling to recoup losses, to get even);
7. Lying (lying to conceal the extent of gambling);
8. Risked Relationships (jeopardizing personal relationships, a job, career, or education); or
9. Bail-out (relying on others to provide money for or due to gambling).

A comment must be made about the deletion of Criteria 8, from the DSM4R criteria — "Illegal Activities (committing illegal acts to finance the gambling)." This is a reflection of the committee's desire for consistency in determining criteria for all addictions rather than considering one the the three most critical factors in gambling addiction — Big Win, Chasing, and Criminal acts. These factors define the uniqueness of gambling addiction. Telephone research studies tend to result in low figures with questions of illegal activities.

Interestingly, these DSM5 criteria, with the exception of chasing and bail-out, are consistent with the criteria for diagnosing substance dependency as well as process addictions, such as compulsive spending or workaholism.

Another of the criteria most likely these addicts have in common is that of illegal activities. Alcoholics may injure someone while in their inebriated state, drug addicts often turn to violence to obtain their substance of abuse, and compulsive gamblers will need more money "to feed their addiction." Chasing is an essential feature of compulsive gambling. As money is spent and lost, compulsive gamblers first turn to family, friends, and legal sources of money, but invariably will turn to illegal acquisition of funds to pay off debts and to continue gambling. They may steal, falsify records, commit fraud, or resort to other illegal activities to acquire the money to support their addiction. In other words, these once honest individuals become compulsive gamblers who commit crimes.

SOGS (SOUTH OAKS GAMBLING SCREEN)

The SOGS was developed in 1987 by Professor Henry Lesieur, PhD, PsyD, and South Oaks Hospital psychiatrist Nora Blume (*American Journal of Psychiatry*, September 1987, 144(9):1183-8), and was revised by them in 1993. It has found great favor among clinicians and researchers in the United States and world wide.

The SOGS is a twenty-item questionnaire that can be self-administered or can be administered by nonprofessional or professional interviewers. It is based on some of the DSM criteria of pathological gambling and was administered to over 1,600 subjects, including members of Gamblers Anonymous and nearly 900 patients diagnosed with substance abuse and pathological gambling. It is used to screen for pathological gambling among substance abusers and general populations.

South Oaks Gambling Screen (SOGS)

Please check one answer for each statement:	Not at all	Less than once a week	Once a week or more
a. Played cards for money			
b. Bet on horses, dogs, or other animals (at OTB, the track, or with a bookie)			
c. Bet on sports (parlay cards, with bookie, at Jai Alai)			
d. Played dice games, including craps, over and under or other dice games			
e. Went to casino (legal or otherwise)			
f. Played the numbers or bet on lotteries			
g. Played bingo			
h. Played the stock and/or commodities market			
i. Played slot machines, poker machines, or other gambling machines			

j. Bowled, shot pool, played golf, or some other game of skill for money			
k. Played pull tabs or "paper" games other than lotteries			
l. Some form of gambling not listed above (please specify):			

2. What is the largest amount of money you have ever gambled with on any one day?

_____Never gambled

_____$1.00 or less

_____More than $1.00 up

_____More than $10.00 up to $100.00

_____ More than $100.00 up to $1,000

_____ More than $1,000 up to $10,000

_____ More than $10,000

3. Check which of the following people in your life has (or had) a gambling problem.

_____Father _____Mother

_____Brother/Sister _____My spouse/partner

_____My child(ren) _____Another relative

_____A friend or someone important in my life

4. When you gamble, how often do you go back another day to win back money you have lost?

   _____Never _____Most of the time

   _____Some of the time

   _____Every time that I lose (less than half of time I lose).

5. Have you ever claimed to be winning money gambling, but weren't really? In fact you lost?

   _____Never

   _____Yes, less than half the time I lost

   _____Yes, most of the time

6. Do you feel you have ever had a problem with betting on money gambling?

   _____No _____Yes _____Yes, in the past, but not now.

7. Did you ever gamble more than you intended to?

   _____Yes _____No

8. Have people criticized your betting or told you that you had a problem, regardless of whether or not you thought it was true?

   _____Yes _____No

9. Have you ever felt guilty about the way you gamble, or what happens when you gamble?

   _____Yes _____No

10. Have you ever felt like you would like to stop betting money on gambling, but did not think that you could?

____Yes ____No

11. Have you ever hidden betting slips, lottery tickets, gambling money, IOUs, or other signs of betting or gambling from your spouse, children or other important people in your life?

____Yes ____No

12. Have you ever argued with people you live with over how you handle money?

____Yes ____No

13. (If you answered "yes" to question 12) Have money arguments ever centered on your gambling?

____Yes ____No

14. Have you ever borrowed from someone and not paid them back as a result of your gambling?

____Yes ____No

15. Have you ever lost time from work (or school) due to betting money or gambling?

____Yes ____No

16. If you borrowed money to gamble or to pay gambling debts, who or where did you borrow from (check "Yes" or "No" for each):

    1. From household money ___Yes ___No

    2. From your spouse/partner ___Yes ___No

3. From other relatives or in-laws ___Yes ___No

4. From banks, loan companies, or credit unions ___Yes ___No

5. From credit cards ___Yes ___No

6. From loan sharks ___Yes ___No

7. You cashed in stocks, bonds or other securities ___Yes ___No

8. You sold personal or family property ___Yes ___No

9. You borrowed on your checking accounts (passed bad checks) ___Yes ___No

10. You have (had) a credit line with a bookie ___Yes ___No

11. You have (had) a credit line with a casino ___Yes ___No

Score Sheet

Scores on the SOGS are determined by scoring one point for each question that shows the "at risk" response indicated and adding the total point.

Question 1	X	Not counted
Question 2	X	Not counted
Question 3	X	Not counted
Question 4	_____	Most of the time I lose **or** Yes, most of the time
Question 5	_____	Yes, less than half the time I lose **or** Yes, most of the time

Question 6   _____   Yes, in the past **or** Yes

Question 7   _____   Yes

Question 8   _____   Yes

Question 9   _____   Yes

Question 10   _____   Yes

Question 11   _____   Yes

Question 12   X   Not counted

Question 13   _____   Yes

Question 14   _____   Yes

Question 15   _____   Yes

Question 16a   _____   Yes

Question 16b   _____   Yes

Question 16c   _____   Yes

Question 16d   _____   Yes

Question 16e   _____   Yes

Question 16f   _____   Yes

Question 16g   _____   Yes

Question 16h   _____   Yes

Question 16i   _____   Yes

Question 16j   X   Not counted

Question 16k   X   Not counted

TOTAL POINTS _____

(Maximum Score = 20)

INTERPRETING THE SCORE

0-2 No problem with gambling

3-4 Some problems with gambling

5 or more – Probable pathological gambling

The SOGS may be reproduced as long as the language is used as printed and the scored items are not revised without permission of the author. Revised 01/06/2003

TWENTY QUESTIONS OF GAMBLERS ANONYMOUS

This is the questionnaire used by Gamblers Anonymous to screen newcomers. Typically, a member of the GA group will take the newcomer aside and ask these questions of this man or woman who wishes to join the group. If the person answers yes to seven or more of the twenty questions, the individual is invited to join the group (See appendix 2 for the complete questionnaire.) A bit of information about GA groups: many GA meetings are closed, for gamblers only, some are open to the public at large, others for GA and Gam-Anon members only, for women only, under thirties, step meetings, Spanish-speaking, or other preferences.

TWO-QUESTION LIE TEST

The Lie-Bet Questionnaire for Screening Pathological Gamblers (Johnson, E.E., Hamer, R., Nora, R., Tan, B., Eisenstein, N., & Englehart, C. in *Psychological Reports*, 1988, 80, 83-88,) is a tool used in clinical settings to rule out those individuals who are not pathological gamblers. It has gained in popularity and is used as a quick screen when a considerable amount of information must be collected about an individual or when it becomes necessary to use a quick screen for groups of individuals.

The test consists of two questions:

1. Have you felt the need to bet more and more money?
2. Have you ever had to lie to people important to you about how much you gambled?

Admittedly, this is only a quick screen, but the vagueness of the questions is likely to lead to an unacceptable rate of false positives; nevertheless, these false positives can be screened out once more specific information is obtained.

Briefly, question 1 refers to tolerance of certain behaviors. Tolerance is one of several criteria in determining addictions. In gambling, betting more and more money could refer to the excitement of action gamblers for whom the initial goal is "the rush" and to win money; in contrast, escape gamblers' primary goal is to avoid emotional stress, which requires money so that they are able to continue gambling. Betting more and more money could also refer to "chasing," which is an all-important criterion of pathological gambling. Nevertheless, the content of the question is consistent with the intent of the question.

Similarly, the wording of "have you ever had to lie" is sure to result in false positives. Admittedly, compulsive gamblers are given to considerable lying in their "losing" and "desperation" phases of gambling as they continue in the downward spiral of their addiction. However, even occasional social gamblers may be embarrassed about how much they gambled and lost and thus deny or distort their answers.

Nevertheless, the Lie-Bet screen does what it purports to do: identify those individuals in a large number of participants who may or may not admit to some questionable gambling behaviors. It is not used for comprehensive clinical assessments or evaluations.

BRIEF BIOSOCIAL GAMBLING SCREEN

This screen was first published in February 2010, under the title "Optimizing DSM-IV-TR Classification Accuracy: A Brief Biosocial Screen for Detecting Current Gambling Disorders Among Gamblers in the General Household Population (Gebaurer, L., LaBrie, R. & Shaffer, H., in *Canadian Journal of Psychiatry, 2010, 55(2): 82-90*)." Its purpose was to develop a brief screen that could be used by mental health clinicians and epidemiologists to consider current pathological gambling along with other psychiatric disorders, such as alcoholism, mood disorders, addictive behaviors, and personality disorders.

It established three questions and stated that "A 'yes' answer to any of the questions means the person is at risk for developing a gambling problem." These three questions are:

1. During the past twelve months, have you become restless, irritable, or anxious when trying to stop/cut down on gambling?

2. During the past twelve months, have you tried to keep your family or friends from knowing how much you gambled?
3. During the past twelve months, did you have such financial trouble as a result of your gambling that you had to get help with living expenses from family, friends, or welfare?

Unfortunately, the research study used the term "pathological gambling" whereas the Brief Biosocial Gambling Screen itself makes reference to "the person at risk for developing a gambling problem." This discrepancy should be corrected thus reducing the potential for false positives.

The three questions are somewhat vague, as well. Question 1, for instance, is more consistent with out-of-control or compulsive gambling. These emotional reactions are not likely to occur with those individuals who merely abuse gambling, the problem gamblers; rather, they are more consistent with withdrawal symptoms suffered by those gamblers who can be diagnosed as pathological or compulsive gamblers, instead of those who may only be at risk of developing a gambling problem.

Question 2, also, is somewhat vague. Does "how much you gambled" refer to length of time, frequency, money spent on gambling, money lost due to gambling? Is keeping gambling hidden limited to family and friends, or might the question also include others, such as an employer within the financial arena, especially someone who would want to know about an employee's gambling habits and the potential for misappropriating funds.

Question 3 might better serve the purpose of being a gambling screen for "someone who is at risk for developing a gambling problem" by eliminating the source of funds from "welfare." Clearly, a gambler who has resorted to seeking welfare is beyond the definition of "at risk of developing a gambling problem" and more likely is in the desperation phase of compulsive gambling. In addition, someone at this level of gambling typically will first resort to legal loans, selling valuables, illegal acquisition of funds, and loans from sources such as bookies and loan sharks. The incidence of problem gamblers seeking welfare is virtually nonexistent, and for compulsive gamblers is rare. Compulsive gamblers are more likely to steal, vanish, or commit suicide.

Further, if the word "welfare" is removed, then the question of "getting help" could also be true of the problem gambler who has overextended gambling but is not yet out of control of the gambling.

Another short-fall of the Brief Biosocial Gambling Screen is its time frame. The screen limits the gambling to the "past twelve months"; it does not include those individuals who are in a temporary stage of abstinence or those who have suffered from the disorder for many years prior to the twelve-month time frame and are temporarily reduced to gambling for a can of tuna fish while incarcerated, who may suffer from medical incapacitation, or are otherwise restricted during this time frame.

While this biosocial screen has merit, it would be more useful if a clear distinction is made for those "at risk" and questions which are more likely to refer to pathological gambling. Time restrictions and elimination of words such as "welfare" and substituting it for "others" could be beneficial.

DIAGNOSTIC INTERVIEW
FOR GAMBLING SCHEDULE (DIGS-DSM)

The Diagnostic Interview for Gambling Schedule (DIGS-DSM) (Winters, K.C., Specker, S. & Stinchfield, R. (2002). "Measuring pathological gambling with the Diagnostic Interview for Gambling Severity. In J.J. Marotta, J.A.Cornelius, & W.R. Eadington (Eds.). *The downside: Problem and pathological gambling* (pp143-148). Reno: University of Nevada, Reno.) is a twenty-item structured interview administered by clinicians and trained interviewers, based on DSM-IV criteria, with True, Somewhat True, and False responses, based on gambling within the past twelve months and over the lifetime of the individual gambler. It includes different modules: demographics and background, DSM-IV criteria, gambling problems severity, other behavioral disorders, and psychological functioning in work and interpersonal relationships. It is not widely used.

GAMBLING BEHAVIOR INTERVIEW (GBI)

The Gambling Behavior Interview (GBI) was developed in 2005 (Stinchfield, R.M, Govoni, R., & Frisch, G.R. "DSM-IV diagnostic criteria for pathological gambling: Reliability, validity, and classification accuracy." *The American Journal on Addictions, 14, 73-82)*. It is a 106-item standardized interview done over the phone and takes approximately fifteen minutes to complete. No training is required to interview the subject.

While its utility for prevalence surveys could potentially be good, it is not widely used, most likely due to the large number of items and additional shortcomings typical of telephone interviews.

NORC DIAGNOSTIC SCREEN FOR GAMBLING PROBLEMS: SELF-ADMINISTERED (NODS-SA)

Disclaimer: The NORC Diagnostic Screen for Gambling Problems-Self Administered (NODS-SA) was developed by the staff from the National Opinion Research Center at the University of Chicago. The instrument is a modification of the NODS, a diagnostic instrument based on the American Psychiatric Association's DSM-IV criteria for Pathological Gambling. Please note that while the NODS has been tested and shown to be reliable and valid for use in the general population, the NODS-SA has not yet been fully validated.

The NODS-SA admonishes, "This screen below provides a simple self-test to evaluate your gambling behavior. It is important to note that this self-test is not a diagnosis and DOES NOT replace a face to face evaluation with a trained clinical professional." It suggests that "self-administered tests can help you determine if it is likely that you have a problem." The respondent is asked to answer the ten questions honestly.

1. Have there ever been periods lasting 2 weeks or longer when you spent a lot of time thinking about your gambling experiences, planning out future gambling ventures or bets, or thinking about ways of getting money to gamble with?

    Yes_____ No_____

2. Have there ever been periods when you needed to gamble with increasing amounts of money or with larger bets than before in order to get the same feeling of excitement?

    Yes_____ No_____

3. Have you ever felt restless or irritable when trying to stop, cut down, or control your gambling?

    Yes_____ No_____

4. Have you tried and not succeeded in stopping, cutting down, or controlling your gambling three or more times in your life?

    Yes_____ No_____

5. Have you ever gambled to escape from personal problems, or to relieve uncomfortable feelings such as guilt, anxiety, helplessness, or depression?

    Yes_____ No_____

6. Has there ever been a period when, if you lost money gambling one day, you would often return another day to get even?

   Yes_____ No_____

7. Have you lied to family members, friends, or others about how much you gamble, and/or how much money you lost on gambling, on at least three occasions?

   Yes_____ No_____

8. Have you ever written a bad check or taken money that didn't belong to you from family members, friends, or anyone else in order to pay for your gambling?

   Yes_____ No_____

9. Has your gambling ever caused serious or repeated problems in your relationships with any of your family members or friends? Or, has your gambling ever caused you problems at work or at school?

   Yes_____ No_____

10. Have you needed to ask family members, friends, a lending institution, or anyone else to loan you money or otherwise bail you out of a desperate money situation that was largely caused by your gambling?

    Yes_____ No_____

If your score is:

0: You probably do not have a problem

1-2: Your results indicate you are at risk of developing a problem

3-4 times: You may currently have, or have had in the past, a gambling problem

5+ times: You may currently have, or have had in the past, a serious gambling problem.

FINANCIAL MARKETS GAMBLING QUESTIONNAIRE

This questionnaire was developed by clinical psychologist Marvin Steinberg, PhD, Executive Director of the Connecticut Council on Problem Gambling. It is a self-administered screen.

1. On a daily basis I have been preoccupied with seeking information about the status of my investments or trades or have been preoccupied with thoughts of past and future investments or trades.

    Yes_____ No_____

2. A major reason I have invested or traded is to change an unhappy mood, for example, escape worries, pressures, anxiety, depression, etc.

    Yes_____ No_____

3. I have experienced extreme highs when I win and extreme lows when I lose in the markets.

    Yes_____ No_____

4. I have felt uncomfortable when any cash accumulated in my brokerage account and have needed to quickly find a way to keep it in action.

    Yes_____ No_____

5. I have been restless or irritable when unable to be active in the markets, for example, when short of money, away on vacation, trying to cut back on trades.

    Yes_____ No_____

6. I have needed to increase the amount invested or traded to maintain the high or excitement of being in action.

Yes_____ No_____

7. My investments or trades have become increasingly speculative or risky over time.

Yes_____ No_____

8. I have had more money at risk in the markets than I could afford to lose.

Yes_____ No_____

9. I have often engaged in high volume investing or trading, for example, to outguess the direction of the market.

Yes_____ No_____

10. My investments or trades have been highly leveraged.

Yes_____ No_____

11. I have not opened brokerage statements to avoid having to think about my losses.

Yes_____ No_____

12. I have borrowed money from family, friends, credit cards or other sources to invest or trade.

Yes_____ No_____

13. I have borrowed money to invest or trade and have not paid it back.

   Yes_____ No_____

14. I have had to have someone else provide money to relieve a crisis caused by my investing or trading.

   Yes_____ No_____

15. I have lied to people in order to hide that I was investing or trading or to hide how much money was involved

   Yes_____ No_____

16. When losses have piled up, I continued the same investments and trades or increased the amount, in hopes my strategy would work, or my luck would change and I would regain the losses.

   Yes_____ No_____

17. I have wanted to stop investing or trading but did not think I could or I have been unsuccessful when I have tried to control, back or stop investing or trading.

   Yes_____ No_____

18. I have risked losing or lost important work, family, or other commitments due to the amount of time and money taken up by my trading or investing.

   Yes_____ No_____

19. I have committed an illegal act to get money to continue to invest or trade or to pay back a loan for my investment activity.

    Yes_____ No_____

20. I have wondered whether I was gambling excessively in the markets.

    Yes_____ No_____

    Totals: Yes_____ No_____

    Score Key

    0 = No gambling problem

    1 or 2 = Possible future problem

    3 or 4 = Mild current problem

    5 or 6 = Moderate current problem

    7+ = Severe current problem

YOUTH SELF-ASSESSMENT

This assessment was developed by clinical psychologist Durand F. Jacobs, PhD (Redlands, California), an early pioneer in the field of pathological gambling.

1. Do your friends gamble a lot?

    Yes_____ No_____

2. Have you ever gambled at school?

   Yes_____ No_____

3. Have you ever stayed away from school or work to gamble?

   Yes_____ No_____

4. Is gambling more important than school or work?

   Yes_____ No_____

5. Do you often spend your free time involved in gambling activities such as poker or sports betting?

   Yes_____ No_____

6. Do you find gambling to be the most exciting activity you do?

   Yes_____ No_____

7. When you are gambling, do you tend to lose track of the time and forget about everything else?

   Yes_____ No_____

8. Do you often daydream about gambling?

   Yes_____ No_____

9. Do you feel your friends are envious of you when you win money at gambling, and that you get extra attention from them?

   Yes_____ No_____

10. When you win, do you want to gamble more because you believe that you will continue the winning streak?

    Yes_____ No_____

11. When you lose, do you feel you must bet as soon as possible to win back your losses?

    Yes_____ No_____

12. Do you often gamble with money you originally intended to use for other things... like lunch money, gas money, clothing money, money for CDs, MP3s, etc.?

    Yes_____ No_____

13. Do you ever "borrow" money from parents or friends to gamble?

    Yes_____ No_____

14. Have you ever sold a favorite possession or something very special to you to get money to gamble or pay a gambling debt?

    Yes_____ No_____

15. Do you try to prevent your family and friends from knowing how much and how often you gamble?

    Yes_____ No_____

16. Do you ever lie about your gambling? For example, do you ever tell people that you did not gamble or that you won money gambling when in fact you had lost money or possessions?

    Yes_____ No_____

17. Do you get into arguments with your parents because of gambling or with your friends over a gambling activity?

Yes_____ No_____

18. Do you feel depressed or lose sleep or feel guilty because you lost money gambling?

Yes_____ No_____

19. Have you ever thought about suicide as a way of solving your problems?

Yes_____ No_____

20. Does one or both of your parents do a lot of gambling?

Yes_____ No_____

Score Key

A score of 7 or more suggests problem gambling.

V-CHART OF PROGRESSION OF COMPULSIVE GAMBLING AND RECOVERY

A less specific assessment is the V-Chart of Progression of Compulsive Gambling and Recovery. It was developed in 1973 by Robert L. Custer, at that time Chief of Psychiatry at the Brecksville VA Medical Center in Cleveland, Ohio, based on military patients suffering from alcoholism and compulsive gambling, a high percentage of who were also suicidal. Thus, began a new field of a psychiatric disorder, pathological gambling, which was classified in the DSM3 under impulsive control disorders.

The V-Chart divides the progression of compulsive gambling into four phases, the winning phase, losing phase, desperation phase, ending with the hopeless phase or that of "hitting the bottom." The time between phases varies with each individual.

WINNING PHASE

In this phase, the gambling starts as social, controlled gambling, marked by frequent small wins or even some large wins, leading to increased gambling and optimism prior to and with gambling. Eventually, the gambler has a "Big Win," which is considered by those in the field as the start of the losing phase.

LOSING PHASE

The Big Win gives the gambler a sense of unrealistic optimism, of future Big Wins, and also the attention that action gamblers favor and the avoidance of discomfort that escape gamblers seek. Increased bets, losses, and debts lead to larger losses, repeated bail-outs from others, and then chasing the ever-growing losses.

DESPERATION PHASE

At this point, the gambler uses any means to pay bills, make restitution, and continue gambling, accompanied by lies, escalating losses and illegal activities, with failed attempts to stop gambling.

HOPELESS PHASE

At this phase the gambler has lost control and is unable to refrain from further gambling. The compulsive gambler, with threats of divorce, financial ruin, being fired from a job, poor physical health, and fears of arrest, leading to death wishes and suicidal intents and "hits bottom." The V-Chart also indicates a typical path of recovery, from the critical phase to the rebuilding phase, and leading to the growth phase.

The V-Chart helps in identifying the point of progression of compulsive gambling and the recovery. It is useful in clinical treatment sessions, especially those involving the family.

FOREIGN OR LESS-USED SCREENS

There are many other gambling screens, most of which are developed by researchers and clinicians in the United Kingdom, Australia, and Canada. Although they may be popularly used in those countries, they are rarely used in the United States.

The Victorian Gambling Screen was developed in 2001. It originally had twenty-one items on it and was used to determine adult gambling in a time frame of the past twelve months. The Canadian Problem Gambling Index is a gambling severity measure, which contains items from the DSM 3 and 4. The Pathological Gambling Modifications of the Yale-Brown Obsessive Compulsive Scale (PG-YABOCS) is used to determine gambling problems among adults.

SUMMARY

There are many gambling-specific screens, but only those mentioned above are commonly used for clinical or forensic diagnostic purposes. The DSM criteria, the SOGS, and the Twenty Questions of Gamblers Anonymous are the most widely used and most definitive whether or not someone who gambles could be considered a social, problem, or pathological gambler.

A CHART OF COMPULSIVE GAMBLING AND RECOVERY

WINNING PHASE

Occasional Gambling
Excitement Prior to & With Gambling
Increased Amount Bet
Big Win
Frequent Winning
More Frequent Gambling
Fantasies About Winning/Bigshot
Unreasonable Optimism
Bragging About Wins

LOSING PHASE

Gambling Alone
Thinking Only About Gambling
Can't Stop Gambling/Borrowing Legally
Careless About Spouse/Family
Prolonged Losing Episodes
Covering Up, Lying
Losing Time From Work
Personality Changes
Irritable, Restless, Withdrawn
Delays Paying Debts
Home Life Unhappy
Heavy Borrowing/Legal & Illegal
Unable to Pay Debts
Bailouts
Reputation Affected
Marked Increases In Amount & Time Spent Gambling
Alienation From Family & Friends
Blaming Others
Remorse

DESPERATION PHASE

Legal Acts
Panic

Hopelessness
Suicide Thoughts & Attempts
Arrests
Divorce
Alcohol
Emotional Breakdown
Withdrawal Symptoms

CRITICAL PHASE

Hopeful
Responsible Thinking
Spiritual Needs Examined
Decision Making
Return to Work
Personal Stock
Thinking Clearer
Problem Solving
Realistic, Stops Gambling
Honest Desire For Help

REBUILDING PHASE

Restitution Plans
Accept Self-Weaknesses & Strengths
Self Respect Returning
Family & Friends Begin to Trust
More Family Time
Less Irritating Behavior
New Interests
Develop Goals
Resolve Legal Problems
Improved Spouse & Family Relationships
Paying Bills, Budget
Less Impatience
More Family Time
More Relaxed

GROWTH PHASE

NEW WAY OF LIFE
Sacrificing For Others
Giving Affection To Others
Insight Into Self
Understanding Self & Others
Facing Problems Promptly
Preoccupation With Gambling Decreases

Robert L. Custer, M.D.

114

CHAPTER 6
CONTRIBUTING FACTORS

Numerous factors contribute to the development of compulsive gambling. Some of these are external, found in the culture or environment, others within the gambler, and yet others in the process and progression from social gambling to compulsive gambling.

ENVIRONMENTAL FACTORS

If gambling exists, some people will gamble. If gambling is expanded, more people will gamble. If more people gamble, it is predictable that more will become compulsive gamblers. And compulsive gambling can lead to serious environmental, community, and personal consequences.

SOCIAL ATTITUDES TOWARD GAMBLING

Both legal and illegal gambling is tolerated, welcomed, or despaired by American society. In the latter part of the 1900s, state legislators were influenced by gaming industry lobbyists to increase legal gambling and are responsible for the national acceptance of gambling by virtue of legalizing state lotteries.

They needed funds to balance their budgets and recognized the tremendous boons to general funds in this approach. Lotteries took gambling a step further: by marketing themselves through campaigns directed at specific groups, especially the poor and lower income citizens, the elderly, females, and people of color. "You have to play to win" and "Kiss your boss good-bye" are popular slogans, along with promises of aid for education and social services for the elderly. Legislators and lottery officials touted, erroneously, that lotteries were "too passive" to be addictive.

At the same time, the Las Vegas casino industry wanted to expand to Atlantic City and other metropolitan areas. They saw a lucrative opportunity to change the Las Vegas image set up by Bugsie Siegel and organized crime syndicates and turn their industry into a legal, viable one, complete with lobbyists and corporate recognition. Billions of dollars were at stake.

This was in stark contrast to social attitudes in the past, when gambling was considered to be sinful, a violation of the teachings of the Bible or immoral because gambling preyed on the poor and the less fortunate, reducing the quality of life especially among those populations already disenfranchised or marginalized.

Today, two groups are battling each other, akin to David and Goliath. The Goliath is the powerful, well-financed, and well-connected gaming industry, which championed itself as bringing in revenues for depleted state government budgets, salvation for the horse racing industry, and creating thousands of new jobs. Gaming itself included not just the gambling sites, but also the manufacturers of machines, gaming tables, tickets, computer programs, etc. Gaming became a legitimate business, with large corporations, stocks, and shareholders.

In 1964 New Hampshire started the trend for state legislatures to establish lotteries, both state-wide and multi-state, with prizes of multi-million dollars. Most often these lotteries were formed to support education and to aid specific groups of populations among its citizenry.

Fighting Goliath was David. Local communities began to object. In 1994 they formed a grassroots organization, the 501(c)3 not-for-profit educational agency, and then the 501(c)4 non-profit political action committee, National Coalition Against Gambling Expansion, National Coalition Against Legalized Gambling, which was renamed Stop Predatory Gambling, a 501©3 not-for-profit agency. It now has local chapters throughout the United States, all supported by volunteers and with little funds to challenge the spread of gambling. They gathered evidence of the breakdown in quality of life of local communities and how historic towns were turned into local gambling meccas. They warned of the increase of gambling addiction, which brings broken homes, loss of work productivity, bankruptcies, and crime. Academic researchers identified economic destruction of the loss of income and forced closings of small businesses within a fifty-mile radius of casinos and racinos. While these groups have had mixed success in their efforts, they have been successful in alerting legislators of the by-fall of legal gambling and escalation of gambling addiction. Currently, twelve states have allocated funds from their General Fund to support gambling education, prevention, research, and treatment.

AVAILABILITY OF GAMBLING

"Gaming" is universal, historically and today. Children play cards and table games for fun with friends and family. Boys learn to shoot marbles to get the biggest one, others pitch pennies, and before long, they collect baseball cards, buying a pack of cards and hoping to get that special one they need for their collection. There was little parental objection; it was considered an innocent form of spending money and shooting marbles was just a game. It was not considered to be gambling because so little money was involved.

Boys played poker with friends at school or at home, with chips. How could that be considered gambling when it was for chips and not for cash? Besides, it was deemed that poker was a game of skill. The gambling rule, however, applied: wagering something of value, on chance, for a reward. Neither the value nor the reward had to be currency. Something of value could be "my kingdom for a horse" as lamented by King Richard, for financial stocks, a business, Native American ponies or blankets, services or food.

Girls recount accompanying their grandmothers to church to play bingo. Church-held bingo was viewed as a social event for fund-raising, not gambling because, after all, it was done by the church, in the church, and for the church. How could it possibly be sinful and contrary to the teachings in the Bible or be considered immoral because it preyed on the losers if the money went for a good cause? In fact, who ever heard of bingo addicts?

Monte Carlo and Las Vegas casinos are world renowned, elegant, expensive, and limited to those who could afford to travel. In contrast, mobster Bugsy Siegel saw an opportunity to turn a desert into a thriving casino gambling metropolis. This rapidly expanded with the federal and state legislation, leading to land-based and riverboat casinos, and Indian reservation casinos in small towns and in large cities. Thirty-seven states currently allow casino gambling.

The Irish Sweepstakes was a cultural model for later state and multi-state lotteries and served as a source of revenues for belabored government coffers. The horse racing industry lobbied successfully to legalize slot machines in order to save the dying racing industry. With the legalization of gambling, church groups overcame their objections to gambling on bingo. Bingo was no longer charitable gambling on special days in church or school; it now became a business accommodating over one thousand players at any one time, throughout the day. In short, American gambling sites were available to anyone, young and old.

ILLEGAL GAMBLING

Legal gambling, intended to reduce or eliminate illegal gambling, instead accelerated it, according to the FBI and local law enforcement. After-hours clubs and illegal casinos continued to operate and expanded into sites across the country. Illegal gambling brought its own profits and had the added attraction that winners and operators did not need to pay income taxes.

Twenty-some years ago, sports betting via the Internet became the fastest growing illegal gambling industry. Referred to as off-shore gambling, these sites were operated by individuals and organizations headquartered in the various Caribbean Islands, beyond the geographic and legal boundaries of the United States. Payments for gambling were made through credit card or wire funds to these off-shore sites. Internet gambling offers sports betting, card and other casino games, horse racing, and bingo. It appealed to a huge number of gamblers. One highly regarded Maryland police officer was admired for constantly working on his computer writing up crime reports when, in fact, he was gambling over the Internet and had stolen over one hundred thousand dollars from the Police Officers Benevolent Fund to support his gambling addiction.

The highly promoted Las Vegas poker tournaments started a new trend in gambling. Marketed as a tournament rather than as gambling, it was promoted as a game of skill and attracted thousands of players, especially young adults, who considered themselves to be exceptionally good at playing poker. Nevertheless, regardless of the name or description, poker tournaments still meet the legal criteria of gambling: value, chance, and reward. Playing tournament poker in Las Vegas or betting on sports over the Internet is just a variation of format and location, one that simply makes gambling more available and readily accessible.

EASY ACCESS TO GAMBLING

Not only is the plethora of legal and illegal gambling readily available at any hour of the day, but access to the gambling sites is equally possible with ease. State lottery vendors and vending machines are ubiquitous and can be found in almost any location except in federal government buildings. Lottery tickets can be purchased in malls, supermarkets, convenience stores, bars, restaurants, fraternal clubs, airports, and other businesses. Many also sell keno tickets. Today, a lottery player can walk or drive a short distance to the nearest lottery vendor and buy lottery tickets within a few minutes of making the decision to do so.

Adolescents and young adults have virtually immediate access to gambling. They can gamble in their schools, at home with their families, or at friends' homes, with and without a computer. Adults can go to their fraternal clubs that offer charitable gambling, using tip jars or pulltabs legally or illegally, and grey area poker machines, mostly illegal. Churches, schools, firehouses, and neighborhood groups sponsor charitable casino games and raffles, all within a short distance from home or work. Indeed, some high schools in recent years sponsored casino night for its graduating class, using "fun money" and games operated by teachers and parents. Casino nights for graduates were viewed as being less harmful than drinking and driving. In addition, it was not considered gambling because "play money" was used instead of legal currency, nor was it viewed as an entry to possible gambling addiction.

Horse racing was expanded by simulcasting races from across the country from noon until midnight. Wagering on horses could take place at race tracks, off-track betting parlors, and in casinos. Since the 1990s, race tracks also began to offer slot machines or video lottery terminals, thus becoming racinos, all of which are a short driving distance for most gamblers.

Although gambling is illegal and prohibited in American penal institutions, it does exist among inmates and guards. The medium of exchange varies—between inmates, the prize may be for food or personal services, such as doing the other inmate's laundry. The wins for gambling between inmates and guards could be for a service, the guard passing contraband to the inmate. Inmates have access to telephones, making it simple to phone their bookie, place a bet and arrange for a money transfer, either directly or through a visitor.

In short, if someone wants to gamble, it can be done in person, through others, over the phone, or over the Internet. Both legal and illegal gambling are readily available and accessible to anyone who wants to gamble, whether it is social gamblers, professional gamblers, or problem gamblers.

EASY ACCESS TO MONEY

Gambling requires something of value to be wagered. Although the options are virtually limitless, in most instances the medium is money: money in the form of cash, checks, credit cards, markers, or personal property, including, stocks and bonds, real estate, or anything else of value.

This access to money and something of value has changed rather dramatically in the past fifty years. In the past, women were dependent upon their husbands for financial support. They were not expected to have careers or to be financially independent. Today's women more often have a job or a career and have their own savings and checking accounts, credit cards, and financial assets. In addition, funds are readily transferable through the Internet. Money transfers are a matter of simple computer-based procedures, allowing for millions of dollars to be transferred from one account to another within minutes. Customers can access their checking account funds through the use of debit cards or ATM machines to get cash during hours when banks are closed.

ADVERTISING AND MARKETING

It is virtually impossible to avoid exposure to lottery ads indoors on television, on the radio, in newspapers and magazines, outdoors on billboards and road signs, and ads in stores, gas stations, buses, and elsewhere. Lotteries have displays at conferences and generously pass out pencils, key chains, and T-shirts with the lottery logo. Who can resist buying a lottery ticket when the billboard displays a $377 million jackpot prize? A big lottery winner is front-page and television news.

Casino and racinos spend even more money on advertising and marketing. The industry knows quite well: "Advertising sells." Ads for casinos and casino boats are like lottery ads—everywhere. Casinos also have the marketing extras of compts: free shows, inexpensive meals, limousine service, charter flights, expensive gifts—all of which appeal to the social gambler and the compulsive gambler. For the competitive gambler with low-self-esteem, plagued by bad history and bad feelings, these excursions into gambling are a first-rate attraction, impossible to ignore with the onslaught of mailed promotions of special events, birthday cards, and season's greetings and phone calls from their hosts.

In sum, today legal and illegal gambling are available everywhere, both are easily accessible, and both the action and escape gamblers have access to something of value that is needed for gambling.

PERSONAL FACTORS

Environmental factors are not uniquely responsible for social gambling to develop into problem gambling and compulsive gambling. Other equally important factors are the gambler's family of origin, critical life events, personality characteristics, and underlying affective disorders from which the gambler seeks emotional relief. Gambling for the social gambler is fun; for the compulsive gambler, it is self-medication.

FAMILY OF ORIGIN

It is common knowledge among addiction therapists that addictions are rooted in troubled relationships. Exposure to dysfunctional families starts in early life when the potential addict is an infant or young toddler. Most common among these troubled families is the presence of alcoholism, with all its dynamics of loud arguments, abuse, violence, and child neglect. This is true in families of the action gamblers, whereas escape gamblers more often describe their childhood as happy and uneventful. Yet both action and escape gamblers suffer from low self-esteem, have a need for approval, fear disappointing others, and are non-assertive or emotionally distant in interpersonal relationships.

THE TROUBLED PARENTS

Perhaps two out of three action gamblers have a parent, most often the father, who suffers from active alcoholism during the early years of their life. Alcoholism is associated with outbursts of anger, violence, and other behaviors that impact on the emotional development of young children. More recently, it became apparent that some of the parents may have other disturbing influences: one may be incarcerated and the other may be a drug addict or suffer from other psychiatric disorders. In other cases, the mother may have a long-term major depression, barely able to function. Gamblers have reported that their mother was bedridden for several years. Others report that either the gambler or a sibling suffered from a serious physical impairment.

In any circumstance, there is disproportionate attention given to the member of the family or lack of attention to other members. The gambler from early childhood on faces vulnerability or rejection or both.

ABSENT PARENTS

Many action compulsive gamblers describe their father as "a hard man" who works long hours and shows little emotion. Often, these gamblers also come from broken homes, in which the parents are divorced, absent due to military deployment, incarcerated, or deceased. The child feels neglected and fears abandonment.

Escape gamblers appear to be raised in an intact family, with fewer divorces, illnesses, or other long-term absences, yet, they too feel vulnerable in relationships with significant others. They learn not to trust personal relationships.

DEATH OF LOVING CARETAKER

Early research seemed to indicate that compulsive gamblers lost a parent through death before the age of fifteen, and in fact, this was one of the features discussed in the earlier versions of the DSM. Later studies found that in more cases it is the caretaker, usually a grandfather or grandmother, who takes on the parental role of the loving, supportive parent and served as the gambler's emotional support. The death of this substitute parent generally occurred during the gambler's childhood or early teens. The future compulsive gambler would be told to "go play outside" on the belief the child was then spared the emotional upheaval of this sad time. In reality, however, the child was grief-stricken, received no emotional comfort, felt rejected and abandoned, and was not given guidance or taught how to cope with life issues, to communicate at a feeling level, or to solve personal problems. The child became the loner, a description associated with a compulsive gambler, especially the action gambler. Escape gamblers more often fell into the role of self-imposed isolation and becoming emotionally distant, thus refusing emotional support from well-meaning friends and relatives and surviving as a loner.

VERBAL AND PSYCHOLOGICAL ABUSE

Verbal abuse, and at times also physical abuse, is virtually universal among families of action gamblers since early childhood. "You'll never amount to anything." "You never do anything right." "Why can't you be like your brother?" This can lead to self-imposed pressure to high achievement goals and perfectionism, to be "the best of the best." Psychological abuse is also present since early childhood: being ignored or rejected by a parent, not protected from the abusive parent. Seen less often is the gambler's need to please the parents, whereas the parents insist that they "just want my child to be happy." In contrast, the outer community admires rising to a certain level, such as "my son, the doctor" or being able to attain the same financial level as the parent or sibling. "I was always the black sheep, the poor one, because I didn't earn as much as my brother or father." This leads to a strong motive to achieve, in terms of financial worth, to be loved and accepted. Gambling is a means of gaining quick access to money.

AFFECTIVE DISORDERS

DEPRESSION

As stated earlier, addictions are rooted in bad relationships and life circumstances. Many action gamblers have a history of not fitting in, feeling different from others, and needing to be loved and accepted. Many suffer from a steady, long-term low level of depression called dysthymia. On a Beck Depression Inventory, their scores typically are in the lower range, 15 to 20. This level, however, can be exacerbated with later-life critical incidents, which may lead to a major depression, single episode or chronic. Gambling becomes a temporary relief. However, the gambling addiction itself leads to greater stressors; thus, a chronic major depression can also turn into an onset of death wishes and contemplation or attempt at suicide.

Too little research has been conducted to suggest that escape gamblers equally suffer early onset of depression, although anecdotal experience would suggest that they do not. More often, the depression begins in adult life, after having experienced a number of adverse life incidents, such as serious marital problems, major illness, death, loss of job, and therefore reduced income, becoming overwhelmed with strong emotional discomfort, for which gambling offers relief from these traumatic experiences. "When I'm drawn into the tunnel, hypnotized by the slots, I don't have to think or feel anything. I just numb out and the rest of the world doesn't exist." These are strong motivators to continue gambling. The serious consequences of problematic gambling also leads to tremendous feelings of guilt; "it was always 100 percent guilt. The only way I could avoid it was to gamble some more. I didn't know how to stop and fix the problems I had created or how to fix the problems that led to my gambling."

ANXIETY

The turbulent, chaotic life circumstances in the home of a dysfunctional family can result in various forms of anxiety, which, like depression, are also exacerbated with critical life events in childhood, continuing into adulthood and senior years. The critical life events might be natural disasters: floods, tornadoes, hurricanes, military combat, fires; or man-made disasters: growing up in poverty, violent neighborhoods, or political acts of terror. Anxiety, like depression, can be avoided through long hours of gambling.

Nevertheless, compulsive gamblers become extremely anxious during the desperation phase of their gambling and depressed when gambling ceases for the moment and beyond that time. "I was always worrying about them finding out about my gambling." "I never knew when she was going to throw me out." "I was always scared the bookie would not take my action anymore or hurt me or my family." "The casinos had all my markers that I couldn't pay off." These are some of the more frequent admissions of anxiety.

ANGER

Many compulsive gamblers have a long history of controlling their emotions, especially feelings of anger, which are rarely expressed verbally or through violent behavior. Instead, they will resort to passive-aggressive behaviors and manipulation as an excuse to gamble. "You nag, nag, nag. I'm out of here." This blaming is their rationalization and excuse for going to the track or casino.

PERSONALITY CHARACTERISTICS OF THE COMPULSIVE GAMBLER

Why is it that one person becomes addicted to alcohol or drugs and another one to gambling, some to excessive eating or smoking, others to shopping or playing games on the Internet? Some facts relating to gambling have already been mentioned—the vast expansion of legal gambling, changing societal attitudes toward gambling, easy access to gambling sites, and easy access to money. These in of themselves are not the only distinguishing factors; rather, it is the personality characteristics of the gambler, both positive and negative, that figure significantly in becoming a gambling addict.

POSITIVE CHARACTERISTICS OF COMPULSIVE GAMBLERS

Some of the characteristics of the compulsive gambler are present in both the action gambler and the escape gambler. These differences became evident in the past two decades as more forms of gambling were legalized, became more readily available, and attracted different type of gamblers. Nevertheless, some factors apply to all compulsive gamblers.

FOCUS ON MONEY

Compulsive gamblers apply unique meanings to money; it is necessary for gambling, to pay the bills, and to gamble some more. Action gamblers specifically gamble "for the action and for the money" and to present themselves as a person of success. Money is the measure of their worthiness. This focus on gambling for money is an extension of family emphasis on money during the gambler's childhood. Escape gamblers are more likely to consider the importance of money in terms of financial stability, getting bills paid on time, and not as a defining factor of themselves as a person.

COMPETITIVENESS

Gambling is a competitive activity: the gambler against the dealer, the gambler against the house, one gambler versus another gambler. There are two outcomes, one is the winner, the other is the loser. The action gamblers have a fear of being a loser; being a loser means being seen as a failure, not just in one area, but as a total person. The escape gamblers tend to put somewhat less importance on competitiveness and more emphasis on doing their best. Both types admit their competitiveness to be a long-standing and useful personality characteristic, something which helped them achieve their occupational goals. This also applies to their gambling. "You can't be a gambler expecting to win and not be competitive."

INTELLIGENCE

Above average intelligence is a fact among race track gamblers, card players, sports bettors, and other gamblers, which require quickness of mind, facility with numbers and gambling systems. It requires intelligence to understand a racing form, to count cards, and to figure the odds in craps and sports. This is not a requirement for escape gamblers playing the slots or bingo or buying lottery tickets. Nor is intelligence a requirement with other addictions: alcohol, drugs, food, shopping, smoking, or sex, for example. Nevertheless, impressions seem to bear out that both action and escape gamblers have a level of intelligence that is above average.

MOTIVATION TO ACHIEVE

For action gamblers, failure to be the best is viewed as having failed as a person. That leads to other irrational beliefs such as, "I must be accepted, I must be respected, I need positive attention," which is easily achieved when winning at the craps table or sitting with piles of black chips at the blackjack table. Winning big at a casino offers the gambler the opportunity to be the big shot. Thus, these gamblers are not only the highest ranked among sales associates in their company, but they also achieve the highest rank in their district or regional territories and many also at the national level. "I was always the number 1 salesman in my company. And my biggest goal in gambling was to break the casino." Escape gamblers are also highly motivated in their occupational and educational pursuits and gamble to win so they may continue to gamble or avoid emotional discomforts. Either goal begets recognition and acceptance, at least while they are still winning and before they have created financial havoc or committed crimes to support their gambling.

EXCELLENCE IN MATH AND NUMBERS

Both action and escape gamblers are skilled in their mathematical abilities and in using numbers. They work in occupations that involve complex numbers, such as accountants drawing up financial statements, or owners of profitable businesses. Academically, most often they major in accounting, law, or business administration. Escape gamblers, who usually have lower incomes, tend to work in occupations with less emphasis on numbers and complicated mathematics; instead, more often they work as bookkeepers, cashiers, bank tellers, or delivery truck drivers. Most often, they are high school graduates, with technical or service training. Both action and escape gamblers manage finances in their jobs.

MEMORY

Mention sports gamblers and one can hear, "He is awesome. He can remember every game, every inning and even who was up at bat in games of fifteen years ago. He remembers the score and the player who made the score. Unbelievable." Sports bettors do appear to have these abilities; however, it is not yet known if this extraordinary memory is true of all gamblers and of all forms of gambling or only with sports bettors.

Ironically, many compulsive gamblers do not recall the exact amount of money they have lost due to their gambling. This may be for several reasons: losing the money that they won earlier instead of losing their own money, the fast pace and long hours of gambling, sleep deprivation, dissociation while gambling, or repression. Many gamblers are shocked when confronted with the total amount that was "borrowed" or misspent. It is only when they see actual records of withdrawals that they are convinced of the magnitude of their losses or thefts. This is true of both action and escape gamblers.

BUSINESS SENSE

It appears that the action gamblers are more likely to start up their own manufacturing/service business, legal or accounting firms, or serve in a similar business venture at the upper level of management. They are the type A casino, racetrack, and sports bettors. The escape gamblers also figure prominently in businesses, handling bank accounts, and performing the bookkeeping duties. It is extremely rare for either action or escape gamblers to serve in the creative arts field, other than as an officer of a not-for-profit foundation, which gives grants to museums, theatres, or other artistic ventures.

NEGATIVE CHARACTERISTICS
OF ACTION AND ESCAPE GAMBLERS

The emotional development of compulsive gamblers was truncated in early childhood, resulting in immaturity, low sense of esteem, and confusion. This leaves them with a host of painful feelings, often reinforced by critical life events from which they seek relief through gambling. They wear a mask to hide their inadequacies and to be accepted by others. These negative qualities are present in most compulsive gamblers. They seek acceptance and fear disappointing others. Confident in work, they feel equally confident in their gambling and their system.

IMPULSIVITY

Compulsive gamblers are impulsive people, at least in the area of their gambling, if not in others as well. They act before they think. They know right from wrong but do not consider the consequences of their actions. The gambling industry acknowledges this personality trait and therefore encourages fast-action plays. Craps is fast. Simulcasting is fast. Playing five-line slots or fifteen bingo cards at a time is fast. This does not allow for studying odds, evaluating, or strategy.

LONELINESS

A lack of healthy interpersonal relationships leads to isolation. Compulsive gamblers are viewed as loners, and whether they are alone or with others, they still feel lonely. They have no close friends with whom they feel safe, to share their secrets and concerns, their bad times, their dreams and hopes. The loneliness can become overpowering and painful; they don't know how to change. They have learned that through gambling, they get attention, especially from a casino, racino, or bingo host. These hosts or bookies are thought of as friends, someone who "really cares about me."

Although compulsive gamblers speak of their loneliness, this is particularly true of elderly seniors who have lost their friends through death or whose children no longer live with them or near them.

BOREDOM

Compulsive gamblers are both lonely and bored. They have no friends other than their coworkers or classmates, and when the day is over, they are alone. What to do? Prior to their gambling, they had hobbies, such as collecting baseball cards, and interests, such as coaching Little League baseball (a favorite with male action gamblers) or going to social events. Gambling gives them friendships, albeit superficial, so they are no longer bored when they associate with others. The gambling gives them a temporary relief from boredom, something to do, but that boredom returns with abstinence from gambling.

Being an external person, with little insight into themselves, they are at a loss how to overcome that boredom. Once again, gambling offers that temporary escape.

SENIORS AND THEIR UNIQUE PROBLEMS

Aging brings with it poor health, such as impaired vision, loss of hearing, and slowed reflexes. They can no longer drive their own cars. Their income has been reduced to pensions and Social Security benefits, yet their medical expenses rise. Their spouse may have passed on, friends move, and they are left alone. They have lost their independence and can no longer participate in their past hobbies and activities. They become depressed and anxious. Gambling is a brief escape from their misery. They can catch a bus at their local mall, which will take them on a day's excursion to a racino and with the added benefit of twenty dollars in gambling money. Seniors face the additional problem: the spouse may also have an addiction or encourages and enables the gambler.

FRUSTRATION

Compulsive gamblers have a rather low frustration level. They get upset, they get angry, but most of all, they get frustrated if things don't go their way. They have not learned how to cope with difficult events or how to express themselves on an intimate or effective level. Those gamblers who are exceptionally intelligent and quick thinking are frustrated with the slow pace of others. They become impatient, so they will push the slow ones to move faster. Or they do the job themselves. Their frustration level can peak up to 100 percent at which time their tempers flare or they walk away and mutter about the stupidity of others. Therefore, they carefully select their position on a craps table or ignore persons who interrupt or slow down the game.

LOW SELF-ESTEEM

If their frustration level is low, their self-esteem is lower yet. Asked to rate themselves on a scale of one to one hundred, "Where would you put your level of self-esteem?" "Minus twenty." "The scale is from one to one hundred." "It's still minus twenty. I have no self-esteem." Self-esteem is a measure against others and gamblers tend to have a long history of low self-esteem. In addition, they tend to confuse confidence, such as doing a good job, with self-esteem. The Serenity Prayer of Gamblers Anonymous to turn low self-esteem into acceptance of who they are, what they can change, and accept what they can't is something gamblers learn after the fact.

MAGICAL THINKING

"The next one will be the Big Win and all my problems will go away." Such is the magical thinking of the compulsive gambler, especially during the desperation phase of the addiction. Along with that is the delusional thinking, expressed in "I know I won because of my system" or "I know Lady Luck is watching over me." These are not idle verbalizations of their thoughts, but rather firm convictions, which are reinforced by the gambling industry's rewards of a free lottery ticket or many small wins on slots.

NEUROLOGICAL AND GENETIC ROLES

Some research studies have been conducted exploring the possibility of neurobiological influences, which contribute to compulsive gambling or which might maintain this disorder. Unfortunately, what little research has been conducted has some significant flaws: the research is conducted on very small samples, 10, 16, 24, or 45 cases, or tested various pharmaceuticals, including placebos, with an even smaller sample of subjects. In a gambling population of several million compulsive gamblers, these studies can be acknowledged but cannot be generalized to the gambling addicts at large. Frontal cortex, limbic system, serotonin levels, dopamine, and other areas of the brain require intensive and extensive research under rigorous standards.

A second factor to consider is the source of funding for some of these research studies, namely the gaming industry. The industry has a vested interest in promoting the concept that compulsive gamblers are inherently and genetically flawed prior to the increase of casino and other forms of gambling, thus the industry cannot be held responsible for the increase of gambling addicts. Economic studies tend to find this to be less than accurate. In response to criticism, the industry, mostly casinos and state lotteries, on their own initiative or in accordance with state laws, have developed a responsible gaming initiative. This program is directed toward social gamblers and problem gamblers. It does not address issues of treatment and treatment outcome studies.

Additionally, virtually, no research has been conducted to determine the strength and influence of the environment. Studies on twins and adopted children might prove helpful, yet whatever studies that have been conducted to date used small subject samples and were inconclusive. Comparison studies with alcoholics did not suggest a genetic component among compulsive gamblers. More likely, action gamblers grow up in an alcoholic home, are psychologically injured, and subjected to societal influences. The family also fails to respond effectively, if at all, to the gambler's early critical life incidents, the gambler's unique personality characteristics, and poor coping, problem-solving and communication skills. In short, it begs the question: "Is it nature or nurture, or both?"

CRITICAL LIFE EVENTS AND TRAUMAS

It has been this author's experience in over thirty years of researching, treating, and knowing compulsive gamblers that they suffer psychological injuries in childhood and/or adulthood, which remain emotionally unresolved and disturbing to them. Not only do these early life critical incidents lead to affective disorders such as dysthymia and anxiety, but they can also lead to later addiction and relapses.

Everyone experiences critical and adverse life incidents throughout their life from early age on. If the emotional impact is addressed, the incidents can be understood, accepted, and will no longer be troubling. If there is no acknowledgement and emotional support, the individual is very likely to develop weakened coping skills, suffer from low self-esteem, and is more subject to developing addictions or other psychiatric disorders.

Current knowledge suggests that there is a difference in the occurrence of critical life events between action and escape gamblers. Action gamblers typically suffer two clusters of such events, one in childhood and another in adulthood. These clusters consist of five or more troubling events usually within a two-year period. Escape gamblers more typically experience a cluster of five or more adverse events within a two-year period in adulthood, but not childhood.

Escape gamblers state that they, like the action gamblers, have a strong need to measure up to parental expectations and not disappoint them. This left them feeling vulnerable and resulted in guarded personal interactions, and in finding a sponsor to help them through the difficulty in recovery.

Both action and escape gamblers experienced a cluster of critical life events and traumas in adult years. Some of these adult events include a broken romance, an alcoholic spouse, termination of a close relationship, serious work or school problems, accidents or natural disasters, severe illness or death of a close friend or family member, and unexpected financial changes and thus lower income.

These occur in a cluster of five or more, typically within a two-to-three year period, during which time the gambling escalates from occasional or social gambling to excessive, problem gambling. An escape gambler recounted a number of troublesome and painful events: "My husband retired, so he had nothing to do all day. Then he'd go to the Legion and come home drunk. Every day. My best friend was hit by a car and killed. My sister was diagnosed with cancer, and then I found out my teenage son was skipping school. I had no one to turn to, so instead of going to the racino once a month, I started going once a week, then every weekend, and then almost every day. I lost a whole year's salary in one month, and when I didn't have the money for the mortgage, I took some from the office escrow account."

Many therapy clients and members of Gamblers Anonymous admit that the last three months of their gambling were the worst. As another gambler lamented, "I went totally crazy, I didn't know what I was doing, money and everything else had no meaning or importance, and all I did was gamble, nonstop, without thinking or feeling. You get sucked into the machine and you numb out, nothing exists." Action gamblers recount similar experiences. "I was drowning in depression and anxiety, couldn't eat or sleep, barely moved or talked, and just sat at that blackjack table hour after hour. It didn't matter whether I won or lost. I just needed to keep on gambling. I signed so many markers that in the end, I didn't even recognize my own signature. The last few weeks, I was obsessed with death wishes. The month before I hit bottom, the death wish turned into thoughts of suicide and how to kill myself. I was convinced that everyone would be glad to be rid of me."

Another event that seems to happen with regularity to male compulsive gamblers is that of a broken romance. "We were together since high school and we were going to get married as soon as we graduated from college. Then I found out she was cheating on me. That was twenty years ago and it still hurts." These broken romances are a critical influence in future relationships. "I became the nice guy, but I never let anyone know how I was really feeling. My wife used to tell me 'Don't shut me out,' but I just couldn't open up." Many action and escape gamblers seem to suffer these broken romances in early adulthood, although there is no hard data on it.

CRITICAL FEATURES IN DEVELOPMENT OF COMPULSIVE GAMBLING

The gambling progression is from occasional social gambling, to heavy social gambling, gambling abuse, and finally, compulsive gambling. In the final stages, the gambling becomes progressive in frequency and amount of monies lost, reaching tolerance levels, attempts to abstain leading to uncomfortable feelings, urges and cravings, relapses, until the bottom is reached reached, at which time the gambler is emotionally, physically, and spiritually exhausted, on the verge of suicide. At some point during this progression, the gambler could have reversed the process. However, there are several events that are consistent and necessary in becoming a compulsive gambler and remaining in the active period of gambling.

THE BIG WIN

Invariably, the trigger from social gambling to problem gambling and then compulsive gambling is the variable ratio principle of repeated small wins. It gives the illusion of winning all the time. Then comes the Big Win. The dollar amount of the Big Win is relative to the gambler's income—repeated free tickets or small lottery wins and suddenly a Big Win of $1,000 or $5,000 or $50,000. Similarly, the small wins, repeated over time, and then the big win are major factors in gambling frequencies and larger bets. If a $2 lottery ticket can lead to a $1,000 jackpot, then why not buy a $20 ticket for a $100,000 jackpot? After all, how does the lottery promote itself? "You've got to play to win."

THE NEAR MISS

Nothing is more disturbing to the competitive gambler than to be one digit off on the interstate Mega lottery: having five winning numbers out of six. And the sixth number is 64 while the gambler selected number 65. "Every time I lost, I bet again. I was determined to play until I won." Race track gamblers call this "the tough beat." This near miss is most blatant in slot machines. Supposedly, there is only one space between symbols, but upon closer inspection, there are many degrees of separations between symbols, thus leading to a higher number of near misses. The designers and owners of the slot machines know that, but the losing gambler does not.

CHASING

Perhaps the most critical behavior in compulsive gambling is that of chasing one's losses. "It's putting good money after bad, and I did a lot of it. I lost a thousand dollars, convinced myself I had to and could win it back. I got up to 950, and instead of quitting, I lost that and another two hundred. Chasing is the worst thing you can do. You're just kidding yourself."

GAMBLING REINFORCEMENTS

In addition to modeling gambling and second-order conditioning, gambling is also reinforced by the immediacy of wins and payments. The repeated wins experienced by a slots gambler, and in particular the person who plays two or three machines simultaneously, give the impression and firm belief that the gambler is winning constantly while ignoring the losses. How can anyone go wrong with gambling if there are constant wins? The casino industry has capitalized on this psychological pattern of behavior by placing dozens of slots in row after row and with a multitude of popular themes, sounds, types of plays, and machines with initial bets, from a penny to one hundred dollars, on three or five reels.

ENABLERS

The gaming industry constantly seeks to enlarge its player base—more gamblers means higher profits. Thus casinos, racinos, and bingo parlors have hosts, send notices of upcoming events, and offer assistance, gifts, or other rewards to gamblers and their families. These enticements are difficult to ignore for the gambler in early stages of recovery, who wants to abstain from further gambling. Family and friends also enable because of their own needs and lack of understanding.

DENIAL

As in other addictions, gamblers deny the seriousness of their gambling and the impact this leaves on others. Too often, the denial is expressed in phrases such as "It's only a little, I can afford it." "I don't do it very often. I can quit any time" and similar irrational thinking. Too often this denial contains elements of control by the gambler or by enablers, leading to the thinking of "Just this one time, just with fifty dollars" or similar self-deception. It is an axiom that "No addict has access to logic."

SUMMARY

There is no one reason or two why someone becomes addicted to gambling. Insurance companies, the courts, state governments, and the mental health professions acknowledge that this is a psychiatric/behavioral disorder of monumental impact, affecting the individual, family, small and large businesses, financial fields, law enforcement and the legal profession, medical and mental health fields, local and larger communities and governments, in the United States and worldwide. Health insurance companies today are more inclined to include gambling disorders among their covered benefits.

Why does someone suffer from pathological gambling and not from other substance or process disorders? Why is the onset early for some and late for others? It appears at this time that there are a number of contributing factors, which lead an individual to compulsive gambling, with or without another addiction. They are exposed to revolving social attitudes toward gambling, from gambling to gaming to family entertainment. They are also exposed to the availability of gambling, easy access to gambling, easy access to money, and emphasis on money by the family of origin and marital families as well as the community.

What is the impact of the family of origin and the marital family? What other factors must be considered: possibly neurological responses, genetic determinants, critical life events, personality characteristics, personality disorders, co- and cross morbidities? To what extent are these factors compounded by the general lack of awareness and understanding of compulsive gambling by the larger community? What education and prevention programs are effective?

How large is the population of gambling addicts? Who is more at risk? Can compulsive gambling be treated? What treatment approaches lead to long-term abstinence and recovery? Only large-scale, rigorous research will find answers to these unknowns.

CHAPTER 7
CO-OCCURRING DISORDERS

Compulsive gamblers, just like many other addicts, suffer from one or more co-occurring disorders, whether this might be any of the affective disorders, such as anxiety or depression, any personality disorders, or medical illnesses. For instance, compulsive gambling, a behavioral disorder, has also been associated in recent years with Parkinson's Disease and depression. It begs the question, which came first: the gambling addiction, Parkinson's Disease, or depression? Is it a coincidence that they occurred within the same period, or is compulsive gambling a reaction to various medications prescribed to treat a medical disorder? Might action gamblers have self-medicated with additional gambling to temporarily ease their loss of control and depression or might any combination of these three be a consequence of flawed research?

Similarly, in the 1970s, early research suggested that most active duty military personnel and veterans being treated for their gambling addiction at the Brecksville VA Medical Center in Cleveland, virtually all action gamblers, were also found to rank high on the narcissistic personality disorder scale. Does this still hold true, could this restricted sample be generalized to all military compulsive gamblers, or all action gamblers?

Could some other dynamics, not subjected to rigorous research, especially in view of the vast expansion of legalized gambling, be equally responsible? Without a doubt, much more research is required to answer these and many other questions particularly with personality disorders.

Even limited research of gamblers in professional treatment settings and also from members of Gamblers Anonymous, suggest that invariably one or more co-occurring disorders are found among all compulsive gamblers, young or old, early onset or late onset of compulsive gambling, type of gambling, differences between action and escape gamblers, and complexities of impacts of this addiction. Most prominent among these disorders is that of various forms of depression, anxiety, other addictions, and personality disorders. Unfortunately, the information provided below is based on limited research studies, anecdotal accounts, experiences within treatment settings, Gamblers Anonymous, and literature, rather than on robust, rigorous research with samples from all types of gamblers and gambling experiences. Thus, it cannot be applied with certainty and is not generalizable to all compulsive gamblers.

DEPRESSIVE DISORDERS

DYSTHYMIC DISORDER

It appears that an early onset of dysthymic disorder is the most frequent form of depression among action gamblers. Almost always, they are raised in dysfunctional families of origin, families in which there is much emphasis on money. They are subjected to various forms of abuse, suffer other adverse incidents in their young lives, and do not receive the emotional support and guidance required to help them cope with everyday life stressors and overcome the effects of these events. They are psychologically injured and learn from early age on it is better to refrain from confronting or asking for help and to keep their feelings to themselves rather than subjecting themselves to further distress and vulnerability. They have learned to isolate themselves emotionally and to internalize their emotions. They are the proverbial loners.

On a Beck Depression Inventory, their typical score is in the teens. They acknowledge having felt this way since childhood. "I never quite fit in. I always felt a little sad but never really knew why. It was just there." Thus, their depressions are situational and externally caused, rather than from clinical factors, such as a low serotonin level.

MAJOR DEPRESSIVE DISORDER

Major depression, whether single or chronic, is diagnosable in virtually all compulsive gamblers as they have passed from the desperation phase and succumb to the exhaustion phase. They have endured weeks or months of desperation, frantically seeking to recoup gambling losses, realizing they have depleted family funds, may have lost their jobs, witnessed the deterioration of their families, and themselves suffer from a number of physical pains and illnesses. They have emotional mood swings. "Win, I'm happy, lose, I'm depressed" seems to be their emotional existence. As their losses and the disorder progresses, there are greater losses and fewer wins, thus longer and deeper periods of depression.

During these latter stages of their gambling, realizing the seriousness of the impact of their gambling and their repeated failures at correcting them, they turn to desperate measures. Casino gamblers, for some as yet unknown reason, have strong urges "to disappear. I just wanted to get away from it all. From the gambling, my family, from everything. Instead, I went right back to the casino and stayed there until they found me."

A lottery addict who was facing legal charges disappeared for three months, buying lottery tickets from vendor to vendor across several states, before he was apprehended. He hoped to win enough money for restitution and to pay for an attorney. Instead, he lost more and sought legal services from a public defender.

The major depression can become chronic, especially when the compulsive gambler is incarcerated, receives no psychiatric support, and has to come to grips with the reality of facing a hostile situation alone. Major depressions can also occur immediately prior to their compulsive gambling, such as the death of a close friend, but which will then contribute to the greater need for emotional escape. This is true of both the action gambler and the escape gambler.

ADJUSTMENT DISORDER WITH DEPRESSED MOOD

This level of depression is common in escape gamblers, who tend to have experienced a relatively short period of compulsive gambling. They have caused less financial damage and less damage to family members and others. It does not meet the criteria of a dysthymia or major depression and is therefore also readily treatable on an outpatient basis.

Note: Some clinicians have found it advantageous to submit a diagnosis of adjustment disorder, even though another level of depression is more accurate. This tends to improve the likelihood of insurance reimbursement, which can be difficult with some insurance benefits and managed care companies.

BIPOLAR DISORDER

Manic-depressive or bipolar disorder appears to have been diagnosed considerably more often in the past ten years. It begs the question: is this realistically a recent phenomenon, perhaps through the ready availability and accessibility to gambling, is it true of the general population as well, or does it suggest a failure in the past to fully or accurately diagnose the gambling addict? The out-of-control phase of compulsive gambling mimics the manic behaviors: does that therefore meet the diagnosis of obsessive compulsive disorder or bipolar disorder? Whatever the reasons, bipolar disorder occurs more frequently now, particularly with action gamblers who are also diagnosed with various levels of a narcissistic personality disorder. In addition, it seems that more often the bipolar disorder is not the classic manic-depressive disorder, but rather is "bipolar disorder, manic."

UNRESOLVED GRIEF

Vulnerable action gamblers, and less frequently, escape gamblers, and usually males, have endured a paralyzing emotional pain, that of a broken romance. Typically, the gambler and his girlfriend were in an exclusive relationship, often since high school, and expected to marry as young adults when, for one reason or another, the relationship is suddenly and unexpectedly ended. "I never knew what happened. One day, we're making marriage plans, the next day, she's dating someone else." The pain of unresolved grief can last for many years and usually is not treated until the gambler is participating in professional therapy and issues other than the gambling are identified and addressed. As stated before, addictions are rooted in poor relationships.

ANXIETY DISORDERS

Just like depressive disorders, anxiety disorders can have an early onset, from childhood on, or a later onset, in early or late adult life. Considering the disastrous effects of compulsive gambling, it is not surprising that gambling addicts invariably live in a state of emotional anxiety and often also in physical fear during the losing, desperation, and exhaustion phase of their illness. Some of these anxiety disorders may be mild, or generalized, or acute, even to the point of physical impairment and contemplation of suicide.

GENERALIZED ANXIETY DISORDER

Those compulsive gambler growing up in a dysfunctional home are more likely to suffer from a generalized anxiety disorder. This may be compounded with anxiety-provoking natural events, i.e., surviving the Katrina hurricane, or who have been exposed to man-made disasters, living in a violent community, or with a physically abusive parent, once again without the benefit of emotional support or physical protection. Lamented one compulsive gambler, "My wife's so negative, always criticizing me, worrying and predicting disasters. It drove me nuts. My battery went bad, I was convinced the car couldn't be fixed. Sales were down, I expected to get laid off. We had a blizzard, I just knew the roof was going to fly off. Always something bad was going to happen."

ACUTE STRESS DISORDER

Not surprisingly, the level of anxiety will rise to the level of acute anxiety as the gambler desperately seeks money to continue gambling to pay off debts, return stolen monies, or to avoid discovery of other illegal activities. Their anxiety then leads to "chasing," which is a critical component in the progression of compulsive gambling. With every throw of the dice, turn of the card, scratch of the lottery ticket, or spin of the slot reels, the gambler is in a state of anxiety and tension, praying for the Big Win, but losing instead. This level of anxiety can lead to constant headaches, gastro-intestinal distress, and muscle tension as well as various sleep disorders. "I couldn't fall asleep, I couldn't stay asleep, and on top of that, I had one nightmare after the other. I was always exhausted, work piled up, my boss was yelling at me, and it got from bad to worse. Now I have to worry about getting fired or being kicked out of my house." One college student, betting on sports, became so afraid of physical harm from the bookie's enforcers, "I used to puke as soon as I got back to the dorm. That trash can was always right next to the door."

ADJUSTMENT DISORDER WITH ANXIETY

This level of anxiety occurs more often when the compulsive gambling is of a relatively short period, such as within a year or two among slots players. The amounts of money gambled away tend to be within the range of an annual salary. Family members are more inclined to seek help for the gambler. Various states now also have gambling prevention programs; thus, there is growing availability of treatment opportunities than in the past. Adjustment disorder with anxiety is readily treated on an outpatient basis and does not require anti-anxiety medication or inpatient treatment.

Often escape gamblers have an underlying anxiety about disappointing family members or others close to them. While this is not more generalized or acute anxiety, nevertheless, it exists and becomes pronounced under stressful situations, especially when the gambler is responsible for the situation.

ADJUSTMENT DISORDER WITH MIXED ANXIETY AND DEPRESSED MOOD

At times, this diagnosis is appropriate, although it can rise to the level of a more serious level of depression or anxiety. It generally does not require medication.

POSTTRAUMATIC STRESS DISORDER

Considering the number of critical life events experienced by many compulsive gamblers, it is curious or unfortunate that the diagnosis of posttraumatic stress disorder is not made more frequently. Conceivably, this may be attributable to confusion with other disorders associated more directly with compulsive gambling, i.e., anxiety or depression. Nevertheless, the high incidence of sexual molestation and physical abuse would suggest that a diagnosis of posttraumatic stress might also be appropriate. More likely, this diagnosis will increase in the near future, not because of gambling alone, but rather from trauma experienced by Katrina victims, the recent super storm on the East Coast, especially in New York and New Jersey, and warriors returning from Iraq and Afghanistan. Katrina victims are especially at risk due to the close vicinity of the Louisiana and Mississippi riverboats, combined with their desperate need for financial relief after having lost everything to the hurricane.

ATTENTION DEFICIT DISORDER AND ATTENTION DEFICIT/HYPERACTIVITY DISORDER

Both of these disorders are being diagnosed more frequently in conjunction with compulsive gambling; again, is this a function of improved clinical evaluations, of new research findings, or is it a function of a broader population of gamblers? Interestingly, studies on compulsive gamblers show high rates of ADD and ADHD, and children with ADD and ADHD are more likely to become problem gamblers than those without these diagnoses.

BEHAVIORAL AND SUBSTANCE ABUSE AND DEPENDENCY

Co-addictions and cross-addictions are common in the general field of addictions.

ALCOHOL ABUSE OR DEPENDENCY

Research and experience indicate that at least two-thirds of action gamblers are either raised in an alcoholic home whereas escape gamblers more often are married to an alcoholic. Approximately, one-third of compulsive gamblers themselves abuse alcohol. In most instances, the alcohol abuse or dependency occurs prior to the onset of compulsive gambling. If later, typically, the alcohol is ingested after a gambling spree in order to remain focused on the game and be in control of their behavior. In the past, casinos tended to provide free drinks to gamblers, although now in most casinos or racinos, the gambler must purchase a drink. More often, the gambler will drink after a losing gambling episode. Nevertheless, in the course of treatment, alcohol-related issues stemming from the gambler, the family of origin, and the marital family become a focus for therapeutic intervention, family support, and 12-Step programs, such as Alcoholics Anonymous, Al-Anon, and Adult Children of Alcoholics.

In far fewer instances, the gambler cross-addicts to alcohol dependency. Thus, while several alcohol issues exist, most typically, the gambler is raised in an alcoholic home or is married to an alcoholic. Further, the gambler may first be an alcoholic, cross over to gambling or have a co-dependency on alcohol and gambling; finally, the gambler may develop an alcohol dependency after abstaining from gambling or jointly with the gambling although this is seen less frequently.

DRUG ABUSE AND DEPENDENCY

Although compulsive gamblers may have developed a substance addiction in the course of their adulthood, in the majority of cases, the compulsive gambler has refrained from using drugs during teen years. Drinking and drugging become issues of control for them—the gamblers want and insist on being in control of themselves, their thought processes, and of situations. This does not allow for mind-altering drugs. If in adulthood, they turn to using drugs, typically they smoke marijuana, perhaps one or two joints several times a week, as a relief from an underlying depression, stress, or anxiety. Action gamblers tend to prefer using cocaine during their gambling. On occasion, a compulsive gambler will use methamphetamines, but again, this tends to be considerably less frequent. They rarely, if ever, use drugs such as heroin, LSD, or any of the other major mind- and mood-altering substances.

NICOTINE-RELATED DISORDER

The use of nicotine, i.e., cigarettes, can increase dramatically during the out-of-control stage of gambling. "I used to smoke one pack of cigarettes a day. When I was gambling, I smoked nonstop, up to three packs at a time. I'm down to half a pack a day since I stopped gambling. I hope to stop completely. Who needs it? Not me." When they are in treatment, they will often protest that they cannot work on more than one addiction at a time. In reality, however, they have virtually stopped smoking by the end of a four- or six-week residential treatment program, without any special treatment emphasis on smoking cessation.

EATING COMPLICATIONS

Few incidents of anorexia and bulimia have been reported; however, diagnosis of eating disorders, NOS, does seem appropriate. The eating habits during the latter phases of compulsive gambling reflect poor nutritional intake. Escape gamblers will play their slot machines for eight or ten hours without a break, even to relieve themselves or to eat. Casino action gamblers will play blackjack for two or three days, occasionally quickly relieving themselves, grabbing a bite to eat or to sleep for two or three hours. "I couldn't take time out for eating. I was convinced I would hit the Big Win the next time. I was glued to the chair. Time didn't exist." Conversely, Gamblers Anonymous seems to have an inordinately high number of overweight members, both men and women. "I felt so empty without gambling. I always felt better when I was eating, so that's what I'm addicted to now."

WORK DEPENDENCY

Compulsive gamblers are noted for being workaholics. They work to excess, to the extent of not being with their families or spending quality time with them. They no longer participate in social or leisure pursuits. This can be attributed to a number of their beliefs and self-imposed pressures. They are driven to succeed, to be the best of the best, to be any less than that is the equivalent to being a failure. Hard work is socially accepted, and results in praise rather than criticism. There is the benefit of a higher income. Working long hours serves another purpose: they fear close relationships and can therefore avoid emotional intimacy. They are protecting themselves against potential discomfort while also gaining praise through excessive work.

Once they have achieved abstinence, this pattern of working hard and long hours continues. The reason now is, "How else am I going to pay off all these debts?"

SLEEP DISORDERS

Almost without fail, compulsive gamblers suffer from a variety of sleep complications during the losing, desperate, and/or exhaustion phase of their gambling addiction. These sleep disorders most likely are a function of their depression and/or anxiety and include insomnia, hypersomnia, early morning awakening, or intermittent sleep disruption. "I kept thinking, how am I going to get the money? It went round and round in my head all night. And when I finally fell asleep, I would wake up with the same thoughts, over and over again. I was always stressed and tired."

The sleep disorders tend to be temporary conditions and are a function of the compulsive gambling and its many impacts.

During the withdrawal period, it may be necessary to use prescribed medications briefly. Without some mild medication, many will suffer withdrawal symptoms. "When I first quit, I was climbing the walls, I was so agitated and restless. I got sick to the stomach, I couldn't sleep, and the headaches, they were really bad. It felt like someone was pounding me with a hammer. Sleep was impossible. Then the psychiatrist gave me something for sleep, it was mild, but I sure started feeling better."

After a brief period of abstinence, typically within the first month, compulsive gamblers will become confused and distressed. Although committed to refrain from all further gambling, they may suddenly have dreams of casinos, excitement, and the Big Wins. They tend to fear them as triggers to an imminent relapse. Through counseling, they learn that these dreams are part of the "letting go" process and are able to resist temptations for further gambling. Who would believe that you can have fantastic gambling dreams that turn to nightmares when you wake up?

PERSONALITY DISORDERS

Compulsive gamblers, virtually without exception, can be diagnosed with a personality disorder or with features or traits of a personality disorder. The Brecksville VA Medical Center determined in 1972 that their patients were more likely to have a full narcissistic personality disorder. More recent studies and a broader subject sample negates this finding in today's compulsive gamblers. Indeed, only traits or features of a personality disorder tend to be more prevalent.

The personality disorders that appear to be most prevalent are avoidant, borderline, dependent, and narcissistic. Those gamblers with a lengthy history of compulsive gambling, thus also a long history of violations of the law, also tend to have features of antisocial personality disorder. A personality disorder, NOS, that merits further research and treatment is that of self-defeating disorder. This disorder shows up prominently in test results of the Millon Clinical Multi-axial Inventory, but is not yet included in the DSM. This disorder may be a contributing factor in relapses.

MEDICAL AND DENTAL DISORDERS

Ask a compulsive gambler, "When was your last physical exam?" and the answer will be "I don't remember, maybe when I got discharged from the service?" This may have occurred fifteen years ago or longer. A similar answer is given when asked about the last dental examination. If there were any hospitalizations, most likely these were due to injuries suffered during high school or college sports activities.

Warriors returning from combat with temporary or permanent injuries, finding themselves without jobs or being able to return to former activities, have shown evidence of alcohol and drug abuse to alleviate physical pain, and also gambling, to alleviate financial pressures and emotional trauma.

Generally speaking, though, one might be tempted to say that compulsive gamblers, prior to their gambling addiction, are healthier than the general population; however, there is no research to prove or disprove that assumption. Nevertheless, the medical problems occurring consistently among compulsive gamblers during the latter stages of their disorder are gastrointestinal disorders, upper and lower back pains, muscle tension, headaches, sleep disorders, and dental disorders. Similarly, during the withdrawal period, they may experience severe headaches, upset stomachs, nightmares, agitation, irritability, and "I felt I was climbing the walls."

CHAPTER 8
EARLY WARNING SIGNS

Compulsive gambling has been described as a "hidden" illness. "You can't see it, or smell it, hear it or touch it." In contrast, one can see an active alcoholic stumbling against a wall or smell the alcohol on the person's breath. The active drug addict can be seen nodding after a dose of heroin, unaware of the danger of oncoming traffic. But not so with compulsive gambling.

To the casual observer, the person walking down the street or working hard at the computer seems perfectly "normal." There is nothing to identify this person as a compulsive gambler. However, observe a sports bettor watching a football game, or two and three games at one time, yelling at the players and expecting a different play, then that would be a likely sign of being a bit over-involved, a behavior which is typical of a problem gambler. Observe a casino player sitting at the blackjack table for forty-eight hours or more, without sleeping or eating, without facial expressions and signing one marker after the other, then one might readily say, "That's a compulsive gambler."

Strangers watching a slots player, feeding twenty dollar bills into a machine every few minutes or playing two or three machines at one time for many hours, may wonder if that player is a problem gambler. Most likely, yes. Compulsive gamblers who are lottery addicts can be seen buying long lists of numbers, scratching off one after the other, and then buying more. One might see that same person again the next day, doing the same thing. A Maryland judge did exactly that, except he would buy only twenty dollars' worth of lottery tickets from one vendor and then go to another vendor and another. Asked why he would do that instead of buying one hundred dollars' worth of tickets from the same vendor, he responded, "For a number of reasons. I didn't want to hold up the line and inconvenience others. It gave me a chance to walk a bit instead and I didn't want to call attention to myself. It really is not good form for a judge to buy dozens of lottery tickets. It is not dignified." This judge was sentenced to five years in prison for using clients' escrow accounts to support his lottery habit.

A family member, friend, close neighbor, or coworker would or should be able to see changes in the gambler's moods and behaviors, which would suggest a gambling problem rather than social or professional gambling. Some of these signs are obvious, others are deceptive. Some are verbalized, others are kept unspoken, but nevertheless, the signs are there. One must know what the signs are and to be suspicious or concerned about a possible problem. These signs can be found across many areas.

GAMBLING

Social gamblers go to the casino to shoot craps or play the slots, bet on sports, or buy a ten-dollar MegaBucks lottery ticket with a hundred million dollar jackpot. A group of coworkers together may buy a ticket, and this is a diversion from everyday routine. They will brag about their wins and share the good news with others. This poses no problem; this is the way gambling is intended to be.

But then there are the signs that may be suggestive of problem gambling. These gamblers will talk more than usual about their bets, their systems, they brag about their wins and flash their winning money around. They get involved and then over-involved in gambling activities, such as starting a weekly lottery pool at work.

Sports bettors will use gambling lingo, such as "juice," or "vig" which refers to the interest charged by the bookie. Their betting strategy may be over-and-under, and they speak in terms of nickels and dimes, instead of five hundred or one thousand dollars. When they buy a newspaper, they flip first to the sports section. They may make or receive an unusually high number of phone calls at work, more than is normally required to do the job, and seem to get more agitated with each call. In most cases, they are not doing their job: they are calling the sports lines to get the latest odds, place a bet, or to get money to support their gambling activities. At home, they may watch the sports channel on television for hours on end and have two or three screens on at a time. "At night, I used to hide my radio under the pillow so I could listen to the game without waking up my wife."

Casino gamblers tend to favor one or two casinos over the others, speak in terms of comps, which are gifts from the casino based on the gambling patterns and amount of money wagered, of limos and jets, hosts or hostesses, and regular mailings of future events. The occasional, casual gambler does not get this kind of generous attention from the casinos.

Addicted race track bettors can be observed intently studying the racing form, talking about favorite horses, leaving their office to gamble at off-track betting parlors, and eventually preferring sites that offer simulcasting from noon to midnight, watching all races from across the country. "I was racing from one machine to the next, watching the races on television and didn't even have my glasses on. I couldn't see a thing. But I placed those bets. Crazy." This gambling is neither hidden nor is it social gambling.

Gambling-addicted card players will spend hours studying the odds of certain plays, read how-to books, and develop their own betting system. Losses are attributed to not following their own system. Like bingo players, they have their own superstitions—sitting at a table with their favorite dealer, in the same chair location, preferably alone without noise and delays from other players so they can count cards even if only four decks out of eight are dealt.

Gamblers addicted to playing slot machines are readily differentiated from occasional or social slots players. These gamblers have their favorite type of machines, do not want to be bothered by others around them, typically play two or three machines, for many hours, punch the numbers on the machine without deliberation, and appear to be in a trance. They have a host or hostess who will reserve the machines if the gambler needs to leave to visit the rest room. These casino hosts will use the same techniques as other casino hosts to entice the gambler to return by sending greeting cards, making phone calls, sending literature about special events, and even offering limos and comps.

Lottery addicts have their own betting strategies. They typically have long lists of numbers, carefully study past wins or prefer the more complex betting, such as trifectas, prefer Pick Three and Pick Four, and have their favorite lottery vendors, where on occasion they can also bet on credit instead of paying for their tickets at the time of purchase. Some are more impulsive, see a license number they like, and bet those numbers. Numbers players buy dream books, bet smaller amounts thus have smaller wins, and consider this a form of socializing. However, they often also turn to lotteries and can become addicted.

Bingo players may play at their church or grandchildren's school, socializing with friends and neighbors, and play at most three or four cards. However, once they are addicted, they prefer to play in bingo parlors, which may be open for twelve hours or in casinos which are open twenty-four hours a day. They have their favorite cards and play twelve or more at one time. They often play until they have no more money and can no longer see their numbers as vision becomes blurry.

These formerly social gamblers used to brag about winning and flash their money around, but no longer. Regardless of the form of gambling, their styles and behaviors when gambling have changed. Even a stranger can notice that something is amiss.

MONEY

As the gambling progresses, the wagers become larger. Pocket money is spent first, then quick loans from colleagues and family, which are paid back as promised. As access to ready cash becomes scarce, the gambler typically will pawn baseball card or other collections or use personal items, such as laptops and jewelry, as collateral when borrowing from a friend. Jewelry or other items of value belonging to family members are likely to be pawned or sold as well. Family and friends may wonder about disappearances and start to mention it, but are likely to get "I don't know" answers.

For compulsive gamblers, an almost guaranteed source of money for gambling is from credit cards. If they gamble at casinos, they will charge travel costs, rooms, and food and get cash advances. Once one card is maxed out, they tend to get more credit cards, and it is not at all unusual for a compulsive gambler to have five or more credit cards, all charged to the maximum limit. If the gamblers have department store credit cards, then an easy source of money is to charge items of value, such as an expensive laptop, and sell it for less to get immediate cash. After some time, family members will notice return addresses from banks and credit card companies that they don't use. An alert bookkeeper at a business may note something unusual and start monitoring credit card charges. Most often, early signs of compulsive gambling are related in one fashion or another to property or money. Money, after all, is the substance needed for gambling.

Compulsive gamblers use their paychecks for gambling. Once the gambling has become more problematic, the gamblers resort to a host of explanations for not bringing home a full paycheck: the company is using a new payment system so paychecks are late, personnel made a mistake, sales were slow thus there are no commissions, promised pay increases were not granted, the company is losing business due to the economy, or the gambler lent money to a coworker who was in desperate need for medical care. Then there are stories such as having lost the paycheck or having been robbed. All these stories are signs relating to money that something is amiss.

They will withdraw monies from savings accounts and replace it whenever possible to avoid discovery by a spouse. If there are designated funds or accounts, such as college tuition, it is taken surreptitiously with the intent of replacing it, but more often, it has been gambled away. If they have life insurance, they will get a loan against it or take out the cash value. Premiums for home liability, auto and health insurance are paid late or not at all. Stocks, bonds, and other investments are sold. Another favorite method of getting quick cash is to take out personal bank loans and home equity loans or refinance mortgages without the knowledge of the spouse or cosigner. Bankers know they need both signatories present to authorize a loan, but they can be convinced by the con artist compulsive gambler that the spouse is out of state or sick and signed the forms at home.

They may borrow from one family member and whisper, "Don't tell Mom, it's for her birthday gift," or inveigle up some similar promise of secrecy and then borrow from another family member with the same warnings. Initially, they will borrow from friends or coworkers and pay back on time, but then borrow larger amounts and are unable to pay back as promised or not at all.

As the debts increase, the gamblers cannot make required monthly payments on utility bills and credit cards. They are threatened with cut-offs and hounded by bill collectors. By this time, usually spouses and family members are aware of the financial manipulations and lies, especially when they receive continuous calls or threatening letters from bill collectors.

Gamblers may finally acknowledge that the money has been lost gambling and plead for a bail-out and promise to abstain from all further gambling. Bail-outs invariably occur, particularly if the gambler talks of potential harm from the bookie or if the gambler may be facing legal charges. "He'll go to jail if I don't make good on his bad checks. He's my son, I can't do that to him." These lenders understand the debt and threat but not their role of enabling. The money signs are everywhere.

Yet compulsive gamblers continue to gamble, hoping for the Big One. If they do win a large amount or hit the jackpot, their intention is to catch up on bills, and indeed, often, they pay the most urgent bills, but invariably, the wins are used for more gambling as they chase their losses.

Compulsive gamblers are adept at hiding their activities. A favorite method is to open a post office box and use that address for secret credit cards and bank loans. They intercept the mail carrier, offer to take the bills to be paid to the mail box, or convince a spouse, "I'll take care of the checking account and bills at the office. You're too busy with the kids." The stories sound kind and believable, but compulsive gamblers know how to convince others. They try their utmost to keep their money manipulations hidden, but at some point, their shenanigans are discovered.

WORK OR SCHOOL

Signs of problem gambling are readily discernable if the gambler is a student or an employee.

STUDENTS

The once outstanding student who becomes increasingly involved with gambling will eventually do poorly. Adolescents and young adults typically start betting on sports, starting with football games and eventually betting on all sports throughout the year.

They win but lose more and get desperate. They spend less time on their studies and homework assignments and more time on gambling or getting the money for it. They find it difficult to concentrate or they may fall asleep in class, having spent the night on Internet sports betting and worrying about parents finding out. Grades start plummeting, the former A-students now will miss classes, submit incomplete assignments or none at all, do poorly on tests, and eventually they are suspended or they drop out. There has been a plethora of studies on college students gambling (including the 1983 doctoral dissertation by the author); thus many state affiliates of the National Council on Problem Gambling and the NCAA have implemented prevention programs. The warning signs are there, but who challenges the excuses?

WORK

Prior to becoming a gambling addict, an employee is recognized for outstanding work performance, often becoming Employee of the Month. But then coworkers realize that the gambler is asking for larger loans, which are not repaid. The lenders and gambler avoid one another at work and no longer associate socially.

The employee/gamblers start coming in late for work, fall asleep at their desk, leave early, complain of being treated unfairly, being sick, needing to go to a family member's funeral, or have a tooth pulled. Assignments are not completed, are sloppy, full of errors, late, or not done at all. The gamblers usually start working many hours overtime, either for the money or to manipulate financial ledgers because they have "borrowed" from the company and desperately want to avoid detection. Company morale sinks. The gambler is suspended or might even be terminated. As one employer lamented, "I never knew anyone who could have so many dying grandmothers or bad toothaches." Not surprisingly, company EAPs now also refer employers and employees to gambling treatment programs.

HEALTH

The gamblers' appearance and health turn for the worse. Once neat in their dress and grooming, now they may come to work or be seen in rumpled clothes, smelly and with stains. Their hair may be uncombed or disheveled; they haven't shaved or put on their makeup. They may have bad body odor. They appear to have lost their energy, seem lethargic, and move about slowly.

They may complain about various bodily pains, especially frequent and severe headaches. They are bent over with a possible lower back injury or upper back muscle tension. Do they have carpal tunnel from working on the computer for long stretches of time or is it from hours of playing slot machines? They may complain about chest pains. They may feel nauseous or that their stomach is tied in knots. They have trouble breathing, have panic attacks, or break out in a rash. They nod off at work, show up late, and have many sick days. At home, they sleep many hours, not at all, can't fall asleep or stay asleep. They can't eat, they vomit, and seem to take more and more pain pills and sleeping pills. They may even start to drink or smoke more than usual. Their health is suffering, yet they won't see a doctor; they don't have the copay or health insurance. The signs of deteriorating health are there, but others need to be able to associate them with gambling.

ABUSE OR DEPENDENCIES

An obvious warning sign is the dramatic escalation of smoking. Whereas in the past casino gamblers may have smoked very little or not at all, during the midst of their out of control gambling, they smoke two or three packs of cigarettes per day. Much of the smoking takes place wherever the person is gambling and lasts until the gambler is in GA or in professional counseling, but their smoking is also observable at home.

Some gamblers may start abusing alcohol, especially during the desperation phase of gambling when they have incurred major losses. This is rationalized by them as needing to relax, to avoid feelings of guilt and anxiety, or easing stress and tension. The alcohol intake tends to be minimal during the actual gambling in order to keep a clear focus, but more typically, it results in alcohol abuse or dependency after the gambling spree has ended.

They may also start using drugs, something which they adamantly avoided during high school days because of their personal emphasis on physical health, sports-related need for fitness and control, and their own sense of morality. After years of problem gambling, however, they may smoke marijuana in the evening to feel better or use their supply of medications for depression, anxiety, sleep or pain. Visits to the family doctor tend to be brief and focus on the presenting problem, real or imagined, instead of the whole person, noting the changes in appearance and behaviors.

Other gamblers, females more than men, turn to prescription drugs to the point of abuse or dependency to mellow out or fall asleep. Again, these signs are visible; it is just a matter of becoming aware of them and associating them with gambling.

BEHAVIORS

There is a noticeable change in the behavioral patterns of social gamblers as they progress to compulsive gambling. The once-honest person becomes a chronic liar, eventually lying not just about the gambling but also about insignificant matters, such as denying they placed a book on a table when, in fact, they did. Is this deliberate in order to avoid a reprimand or forgetfulness because of their general confusion? Nevertheless, the lying about their gambling becomes routine: wins are exaggerated, losses are denied or minimized, and the gambling itself may be denied. They will lie about absences from work, missing money, reduced paychecks, unpaid bills, bank loans, credit cards. The excuses become more fanciful or bizarre, yet are told convincingly and accepted as the truth. Co-dependents don't question. They believe.

The compulsive gamblers stop socializing with others, including family members and close friends, they no longer attend school functions, and they themselves no longer participate in sports or physical work-outs. They no longer are interested in their hobbies nor do they participate in them. What they once cherished has now been exchanged for gambling. Why?

Their manner of speaking changes: their speech may be rapid, less focused, sound garbled, or is slow and without inflection, and are noted for their monosyllabic responses. The pitch and volume change. Often, there is an undertone of anger and responses tend to be defensive.

Invariably, there is a noticeable change in driving patterns as the addiction progresses. Speeding is the most common concern, driving at 80 or 90 mph while in a rush to get to the track or casino. "I couldn't get there fast enough." One state trooper admitted, "I put my sirens on and drove on the berm. When I got to the casino, I used a tarp to cover my vehicle. I didn't want anyone to see an out-of-state police car on the parking lot." Others drive recklessly. "I was all over the road because I was too tired or couldn't concentrate." Some admit to driving recklessly deliberately. "I just didn't care anymore. About anything." They tend to deny that an accident was, in fact, a failed suicide attempt.

In the acute desperation phase, they may disappear for days or weeks. "I slept in my car in front of my house in the dead of winter. I just didn't feel worthy of living in my own house. My wife finally dragged me in, and then she dragged me to GA." When casino gamblers disappear for weeks or longer from home and work, without disclosing their whereabouts to anyone, most often they can be found gambling at their favorite casinos. Signs?

One casino gambler, single and in his early thirties, would go to work in the morning, keeping a strict 9-5 schedule, and return to the casino at night. "I ate and slept at the casino for a whole year. I knew the pit bosses and the cocktail waitresses even though I don't drink. From work to the casino, for one whole year. Can you believe it? I still can't." His parents never asked. Why not?

It is not unusual for compulsive gamblers to disappear because they prefer committing suicide over going to jail. One wife reported how she "looked all day for him. Then I found him sitting at the edge of the river, crying." Another gambler, a lawyer, recalls walking into the courtroom and waking up in a strange city. "I still don't know how I got there." Clinically, this is severe dissociation leading to amnesiac fugue. Their behaviors are "hidden," some only temporarily. In one unusual case, the compulsive gambler was deep in debt, had stolen huge amounts of money, owed thousands to his bookies and loan shark, feared for his life, and staged an accidental death by drowning while fishing. His body was never found. He was discovered several years later, he faced criminal charges, and was sent to jail. Compulsive gamblers can fool people who ignore or deny the obvious.

CRIMINAL ACTIVITY

Once taking pride in their rigorous honesty, during their compulsive gambling they start to commit civil or criminal violations. Most of these are fairly transparent: motor vehicle violations typically consist of a large number of unpaid parking tickets, failing to abide by motor vehicle codes, driving a car without insurance, and not keeping licenses and registration current. More signs.

In most instances, the family becomes the victim of the gambler's criminal acts. They may find that the gambler has stolen their money, used credit cards without their knowledge or permission, forged a spouse's signature, stole items of value belonging to them, to name the more common acts. Family, friends, neighbors, and coworkers—no one is safe, but they can be alert and confront the behavior rather than ignoring them.

Almost without fail, compulsive gamblers will eventually resort to writing any number and types of bad checks: checks, which are returned NSF, checks against a closed account, change the value of the checks, or they may float checks from one bank to another, forge a signature, or make unauthorized withdrawals from a savings account requiring two signatures.

They frequently fail to file income taxes, file fraudulent income taxes, or submit fraudulent financial statements. Some of these financial crimes can be kept hidden for some time before discovery. Spouses may sign tax returns without first reviewing them, trusting them to be accurate and complete. Or spouses may sign financial forms in blank. The warning signs are everywhere, tend to be ignored, and the gambling continues. Who challenges the gambler?

VIOLENT CRIMES

Historically, compulsive gamblers are nonviolent by nature. However, there is some evidence that this profile is changing as the gambling population becomes larger and more diversified and more gambling is available. Perhaps the most troubling warning signs of compulsive gambling, which are considered violent crimes, are those of child endangerment and domestic violence. Fortunately the numbers are small, and early intervention can keep those numbers low. Yet it is a new phenomenon. Fathers who were described as a doting parent or a mother as "a good mother" before becoming gambling addicts now leave their infant or toddler locked in their car, for many hours, without food or physical care, often in extreme hot weather or on the coldest days of winter. These children died while Mom or Dad were playing the slots, unaware of the many hours they spent at gambling. Gambling sites now employ parking lot security personnel to inspect cars in an effort to prevent such tragedies.

Other compulsive gamblers have left their infants or toddlers at home alone, again for many hours, only to be found hungry and without sanitation or health care. One young mother proclaimed, in tears, "I would never abandon my baby. I just thought I could go for an hour while she was sleeping." The mother was located by police in a nearby casino the following day when her parents reported her missing and discovered the infant home alone. Casino personnel had seen the young mother there, knew she had a baby, was a single mom, had gambled there for almost two full days, and did nothing. Even strangers could tell.

Such cases are not isolated events: they tend to be repeated, often with unfortunate consequences.

The incidence of domestic violence has increased; most often, it is a husband verbally threatening or physically abusing the wife. One case was especially troubling: the wife was the compulsive gambler who had lost the couple's entire savings account. Their son was a police officer. He felt torn: "I wanted to protect my mom from dad's beatings, but to do that I had to arrest my dad for domestic violence. I finally told my partner and he took over."

Other crimes that often defy early detection, such as selling, but not using, illegal drugs or bookmaking are aberrant behaviors of the compulsive gambler, and these secret behaviors eventually come to the attention of people more closely associated with the gambler. They see, but don't associate it with gambling addiction.

MOODS

As the gambling escalates so do the moods. Statements of "People think gambling's fun and entertainment. It was, a long, long time ago. Now it's plain torture" are often heard in treatment centers and Gamblers Anonymous meetings. They speak of mood swings, from being withdrawn and nonresponsive to being irritable and angry. "I feel like I'm being pulled on a yo-yo string. I'm nervous one minute and depressed the next. I can't concentrate and then I get frustrated and yell at everybody to keep quiet. It's not them, I was the problem."

Typically, at this point in their addiction, they are severely labile: their moods swing from depression to anxiety, from frustration to anger, and rarely, do they feel relaxed or comfortable with their emotional state of mind. "My mind's always running, obsessing about the money, figuring how to get there. I get excited, then desperate. Even booze and sleeping pills don't help."

In their manic state, they want to run away from it all. In their depressed state, they just want to go to sleep and never wake up. Family and friends don't recognize this new person, don't understand the connection between gambling, and don't know what to do or where to go for help. Their solution is to get annoyed with the gambler. "Get off the couch and go to work." Family members tend to know about the gambling, the warning signs are there, but they avoid confrontation until the obvious can no longer be ignored or a crisis has occurred. This is called Denial.

DANGER TO SELF OR OTHERS

To say the signs that something is very wrong with the gambler is one thing, but it is another to understand the significance of them. The gambler may have been the cause of a major single-vehicle accident, having driven off the road or hitting a tree. Was it an accident or was it a deliberate attempt to commit suicide? Suicide by vehicle is the Number One method used by these addicts. "That way my family gets the insurance money and the bills can get paid." Casino gamblers tend to have two preferences while they are still at the casino: jumping off the roof when they are by themselves or overdosing on pills in front of others. "She was playing blackjack for the last two days, taking maybe two or three hours off to sleep. She was popping pills for half an hour in front of the dealer, the pit boss and other gamblers at the blackjack table. No one interfered until she fell to the floor and had to be rushed to the hospital. She nearly died." In this particular case, she was back at the casino the following day. Casino personnel failed to take any action to protect her.

On rare occasions, a gambler who has lost a significant amount of money will set up a confrontation with the police, hoping for a "suicide by cop" solution. Law enforcement personnel and military members, both trained and accustomed to using guns, later use them in suicide attempts. Other methods used include hanging or drowning. The method depends on the person's life experiences. Almost always, the gambler may have made statements of "I might as well shoot myself" or similar implied warnings. Ignoring or scoffing at these threats can lead to painful consequences.

Less visible warning signs occur when a compulsive gambler plans and carries out a homicide in order to collect insurance money. One compulsive gambler admitted knowing that the car tires were bad, but did nothing. The bad tires were threadbare and obviously dangerous. Homicides are rare, so far, but what will the future hold as more compulsive gamblers become desperate for money? Only time and research can provide answers. But the hints are there. "I was hoping she would have an accident."

SUMMARY

Compulsive gambling behavior is not hidden; instead, it is not noticed, not acknowledged and not challenged. It is ignored, misunderstood or not understood at all, or it is not associated with the gambling. Acknowledging or responding to warning signs can prevent gambling from being "a hidden illness."

CHAPTER 9
THE COMPULSIVE GAMBLING *'ACTION'* INVENTORY: A PSYCHOLOGICAL DAY IN THE LIFE OF THE COMPULSIVE GAMBLER

Valerie Lorenz, author of this book, developed the *Compulsive Gambling 'Action' Inventory* in 1995 as a research instrument. The purpose was to learn when this moment of "action" or "in action" first occurred and also to arrive at a clearer understanding of this process and events relating to it. There appeared to be two oft-used phrases of the terms: "I'm looking for the action" or "When I'm gambling, I'm in action." When did this "action" occur: just prior to the bet, while making the bet, or during the play? The results were surprising and unexpected. It was discovered that the extreme mood changes which led to the feeling of "action" could occur at any point during the gambling: this might be as early as leaving the house or office to gamble or during an actual gambling episode.

For some, it occurred when a certain road was reached or bridge was crossed or while driving to the race track. For others, this sense of being "in action" came about as they were considerably closer to the gambling site, such as going through the turnstiles at the race track or going through the revolving doors of a casino. For some lottery addicts, making up lists of numbers for Pick 3 or Pick 4 lottery games was the high point of their gambling, and for others, it was deciding which bingo cards to purchase or which slot machine to play.

It was found that the feelings of excitement or euphoria were more likely to occur during the winning phase, when gambling was still a social activity, or during a period of problem gambling, as described in earlier studies. Nevertheless, for some action gamblers, it was not the excitement that was sought, but rather that brief moment of euphoria lasting only as long as the next throw of the dice or turn of the card, six or eight seconds, followed at once by the need to win and to continue gambling.

A lack of precise definition of the term "anticipation" could account for this confusion. For some, this meant a sense of eagerness, for others "anticipation" meant a state of anxiety, and for almost all, "anticipation" described strong feelings of turmoil, vacillating between the two conflicting moods of euphoria and anxiety. During the Desperation Phase of gambling, however, the very brief euphoric state experienced by action gamblers was immediately followed by a longer period of anxiety.

Compulsive gamblers described as action gamblers prefer that form of gambling that involves speed of play, rapid body movements, loud verbalizations, such as cheering on the horses at the race track, yelling at the quarterback while watching a football game on television, or shouting at the dice at the craps table. They also sought the attention from other gamblers around them. However, a caveat must be noted: in the final stage of compulsive gambling, when the gambler is "in the zone" and dissociates from reality, none of these factors apply. The gambler resembles a robot, an automaton in a state of stupor and mindlessness.

This sense of action is not shared by escape gamblers who sit in front of slot machines or video poker machines, oblivious to others around them. Nor does it apply to lottery addicts who silently scratch away the film covering the numbers, one after the other, over and over again. Yet both types of gamblers reach a mood state in their gambling in which the action is too slow. The slots player increases the speed of play by using not just one machine, but two and then three machines. The bingo addict may start with eight cards and play fifteen or twenty cards by the end of the night. The lottery gambler may have long lists of numbers, buy dozens of tickets, and in larger denominations, such as twenty-dollar tickets.

For all, though, being "in action" or being "in the zone" in the desperation phase, is that of "chasing" their losses in the hopes of recouping enough money to pay off debts.

More importantly, though, is the goal to be able to continue their gambling. They eventually reach that stage of gambling and dissociation, betting repeatedly, until all their money is lost and they have reached a state of physical, mental, and emotional exhaustion. It is the ultimate state of "spacing out" or "being in the zone" for action gamblers and "numbing out" for the escape gamblers. Through gambling, they are able to escape all the painful events and feelings of the world in which they live.

DESCRIPTION OF THE COMPULSIVE GAMBLING *'ACTION'* INVENTORY

The *Inventory* itself (see end of chapter) is a 16-question, one-page instrument that follows the gambler's thoughts, feelings, behaviors, and physical impact during one specific day of gambling within the recent past. The gambler's family members participate in the session, which takes two hours or more to administer.

Before it is implemented, the therapist meets with the family members who will participate to prepare them for the session, cautioning that it may be quite emotional for all of them: they may be shocked by what they hear, become angry or cry, or want to help or comfort the gambler. They are instructed to refrain from speaking or acting out during the interview, that it is important not to interrupt the flow of the gambler's thoughts.

The therapist informs the family they may want to ask many questions, such as, "Why do you gamble? Why don't you just stop? Did you know how we felt? Did you care? How long have you gambled? Where did you get the money? How much have you lost? How much do you owe?" The therapist must be supportive, "Those are good questions, but let's not ask them until we're finished with 'The Day.'" It is wise to have a box of facial tissues handy.

The therapist then meets briefly with the gambler to answer any immediate questions or address any concerns the gambler may have. The family is brought into the room and the therapist makes sure everyone is physically comfortable, sitting in a triangle or circle, facing each other.

> "Let's take a minute first to describe what we will be doing. Think of one day of your gambling, perhaps one or two months ago. Where are you gambling and on what? We want to follow you throughout that day, from the moment you wake up until you go to sleep at the end of the day. What are your thoughts, feelings and behaviors during this day? Where do you experience any kind of physical response? How strong are these emotional and physical feelings?"

The family initially may want to ask questions, but are reminded that many of their questions will be answered in the course of the interview or afterwards. This should be done in a supportive manner, so that both the family and the gambler will feel their needs are being met. The therapist then hands the

Action Inventory to the gambler and to all others in the room. The form is given to the gambler first, thus subtly keeping the focus on the gambler's role and the therapist's support of the gambler.

> "I want you to focus on one typical day of your gambling within the past month or two. Take a minute to look at the Inventory. It lists a number of feelings often associated with compulsive gambling. Look at the ones listed and feel free to add any others as we speak. The form also lists sixteen steps related to this one day of your desperate gambling. I will ask you questions about each of the sixteen steps as they come up. Sometimes you may respond to two or three steps ahead. I will guide you through that and bring you back to the earlier question. OK?
>
> For each of the questions I want you to tell me what you are thinking, how you are feeling, how strong is that feeling on a scale of one to a hundred percent, what are you doing, what part of your body is affected by these feelings, and how strong is that physical reaction. For instance, if you feel anxious, what were your thoughts that led to your anxiety and where do you feel that anxiety – in your head, your back, your stomach, or where? How strong is that feeling of anxiety, again from zero to a hundred, and and where does that feeling impact on your body?

The therapist informs the family they may keep their copy of the Inventory to follow along, but retrieves the one from the gambler. This prevents the gambler from reading ahead and from other distractions. The family is again reminded to refrain from commenting until the gambler has responded to all questions of the Inventory. In addition, family members are reminded to refrain from giving off any kind of physical cues. This becomes a gentle but firm reminder to keep emotions in check. The therapist has a notepad and is prepared to write down all of the gambler's specific responses, to be discussed when the Inventory is completed.

In this instance, the gambler, Laura, is a 45-year-old woman, married to Jim and they have two teenage children. Five years ago, she, her husband, and their friends started going to a nearby racino, which had opened at that time. They would go monthly, enjoying the outing, having dinner together, and playing the slots. They all won and lost some money. They could afford it.

Laura had worked full-time for twelve years as a bookkeeper in a small company. She was highly regarded by her employer and coworkers. Two years ago, her work hours were reduced because the company was experiencing financial difficulties and on top of that, Jim retired without first discussing it with her. She was not prepared for this sudden loss of incomes. Bored with the sudden free time and anxious about the lowered income, she started going to the racino more frequently, first with Jim, then alone. Her goal was to win money, just as she had in the past, and to pay off some of their bills.

During that time, a number of other serious life events occurred. Her best friend was killed in an auto accident. They had been friends since kindergarten. Then her sister was diagnosed with cancer. Jim's drinking increased, and they learned that their son was also developing a drinking problem. Then the brakes on her car needed to be replaced. Jim's answer was to get drunk "at least four times a week."

Her gambling increased during those two years. She was going to the racino nearly every day, usually without Jim, and with larger amounts of money. He never knew how much she took or lost. After all, she was handling all the household finances, and it appeared the bills were being paid. Her gambling increased over time, and she believes she lost control over her gambling one year ago. Since then she has "borrowed" over $20,000 from her company and was recently fired. The therapist starts:

Question #1 (T=therapist, G=Gambler)

T: What are your first thoughts when you wake up?

G: I wake up thinking the same thing I did when I went to bed, the same thoughts, over and over, I've got to get the money.

T: How does that make you feel, having to get the money?

G: Sick. Sick at the stomach, it starts to sour, I feel anxious, like 65%.

T: What are you thinking to feel so sick at the stomach?

G: What if they find out I took the money? Will I go to jail? What will others think of me? They won't want anything to do with me.

T: That's a lot of thoughts. Can you tell me what feelings go with these thoughts?

G: Disgust with myself, I should have known better, 75%; anxiety, 80%. How could I have done that? I betrayed all of them. The guilt keeps building up.

T: Do you feel this physically anywhere?

G: My shoulders and muscles, they're all tense. My head, I keep on shaking it, like I want to shake it off. I'm tired all the time.

T: Is there anything else you are thinking or feeling when you first wake up?

G: Well, I already know I'm going to play the slots. And it's always about money.

Question #2

T. Let's go on to the next step. At what point then do you decide to gamble?

G: When I'm still in bed I know I'm going to the racino.

T: How do you feel at that moment?

G: It's a lot of anticipation.

T: That anticipation, is it a good feeling or a bad one?

G: It's good, because I know I'm going. My whole body feels light, 45%. Well, no, it's also a bad feeling. Will I get there in time, how do I get the money, all of those kinds of thoughts. It becomes anxiety overload. Now my whole body is tense, muscles are tight, stomach hurts. I need the money.

T: Anything else, when you decide to gamble?"

G: I decide to dress casual. Maybe I should wear work clothes, then Jim won't find out I went to the racino. He finds out anyway, but I don't tell him about the money I lost. He's always trying to control me with money.

T: What are you feeling when you say 'He finds out anyway'?

G: Angry and disgusted with him, 50% in the neck. So what if I go to the racino, I'm an adult, not a kid. I feel 80% resentful. It's mostly in my head.

T: You said you don't tell him about the money you lost. Can you tell me what that's all about?

G: If I tell him, he goes off on me and I feel lousy. If I don't tell him, I've pulled one over on him, I feel great, all over, 65%. Or I might just tell him I broke even. Anything's better than telling him the truth.

T: Is there anything else when you decide to gamble?

G: Well, I need money.

Question #3

T: How much money will you need for gambling and how long do you plan on staying at the racino?

G: That all depends on what happened the last time, if I won or if I lost. If I won, I use that or maybe some more. I need at least $200. I didn't win too often in the end.

T: Two hundred dollars. Is that what you usually take with you?

G: Well, it's the least I take, but I take more now, too. I triple up, play three machines, play the dollar slots. I don't plan for how long, I just go. I used to think I'll just go for two or three hours, and then it's ten hours later.

T: Let's side step a bit here. What are you trying to get away from?

G: Everything. Jim and his drinking, my friend being killed in an auto crash, my sister with cancer, finding out my son is drinking, all the money problems, everything, and always feeling angry, or scared, or sad, or bad, just everything.

T: I know, we've talked about some of these events, and we will talk more about them later. Maybe it will be helpful if Jim and others could participate in those sessions.

G: It would be but...we'll see (indicates doubt, shrugs shoulders).

Question #4

T: Let's go back to the money. Tell me how you get the money.

G: First I go the ATM and draw out what I need.

T: How do you feel at that time?

G: Anxious, 45%, and my hands get sweaty. I hope I have enough money in my checking account. I usually don't. I already took everything out of savings. He doesn't know about that.

T: So Jim doesn't know about the savings account or the credit cards?

G: There's a lot of stuff I don't tell him. He always tries to control me with money, ever since we got married. I'm sick of it. It makes me really mad just thinking about it (85%). My shoulders and neck tense up, my arm muscles get tense, I feel like smacking him one (85%). I worked throughout our marriage. I always paid my share. (Laura looks really angry now.)

T: You told me you need at least $200 for each trip, but have nothing in the bank, so how do you get the money for gambling at the racino?

G: I always get the money from somewhere. I wouldn't pay a bill, or I borrow from friends if I can, I already owe them a lot. I used the mortgage money, then I got a second mortgage, and then another credit card. I sold my rings and Jim didn't even notice I wasn't wearing them. And a few months ago I started doing things with the company books. I borrowed some money. I didn't make a deposit and took the money to pay my mortgage. I paid it back, at first. That's when the headaches got really bad, (85%). Non-stop, nothing helped. My doctor gave me pain pills. It was anxiety (85%), and guilt (100%).

T: You borrowed? From your job?

G: That's how it started. I won enough and paid it back. But I still owed on the other bills. Then I started losing, again and again, and couldn't put it back. I don't know what happened to me. I never lied or stole before this crazy gambling.

Question #5

T: Now you have your money. How do you get to the racino?

G: I call my host to let him know I'm coming. He makes me feel good, I am 75% happy, I feel it in my face, I smile for the first time that day. But I can't drive my car, my brakes are bad, and Jim wouldn't give me the money, said I lost it all gambling.

T: So how does that make you feel?

G: Angry, 75%. He does that all the time, try to control me with money. So I take the bus. I outsmarted him. But I've got to hurry, I can't miss it. There comes the anxiety again. What if I miss it? I grab my things and can't get to the bus fast enough. I feel rushed, my whole body is running at 90 mph. I always try to get a seat up front, so I can get off first. I even pushed one of the passengers, I was in such a hurry to get off. That was bad. I felt disgusted with myself, 85%. I couldn't even look her in the eyes. It just isn't like me to do something like that. Wow, I never realized I was acting like such a maniac.

Question #6

T: Now you're in the racino. What's next?

G: I have my favorite machines, the fruits, so I head for my favorite slots area, in the middle of a row. That way I can play one on both sides. I talk to them, "You're so pretty, so colorful, you sing to me, you let me win." I feel alive. In the beginning when someone came up to me and asked me a question, I would answer, play it cool, let them see my credits, like I was good. But now I get really annoyed (75%, neck muscles). I feel like telling them "Leave me alone, mind your own business. Don't bother me." I give them a dirty look or I just ignore them. It breaks my concentration, but I pull myself back. Now I have to play two machines.

T: Two machines?

G: I always start with one machine. the penny slots, but sometimes the quarter slots. If I feel lucky, I play two. Or if I lose, I play two, then three. Just hit the buttons as fast as I can. My host holds them for me if I have to go to the bathroom, but I rarely go. What if they get cold? I'm worried (head, 85%). I try to hold it in, but one time I had an accident.

Question #7

T: Do you watch the reels when they spin?

G: I used to, but now I never watch the reels spin. I play the second slot while the reels are spinning on the first one. Now I just hit the buttons when they stop. I'm pretty good, I can hit real fast, about every six seconds. If the credits are used up, I buy more. If I'm broke, I try to borrow or sign a marker.

T: So what would you be feeling?

G: At first I would feel excited, I could feel it all over, then I kind of got used to it. About a year ago I started to zone in. I don't hear anybody, I just sit and play. It's total escape, oblivion. No problems, no worries, no bad feelings. Just me in my machine, in my zone.

T: Can you tell me more about your "zone"?

G: It's a big, black blank. You feel like you're being pulled into the machine, like you're hypnotized. It's quiet and safe. You don't hear anything, you don't see anything, you don't feel anything. You're 100% at peace. Winning or losing doesn't matter, just as long as you can keep hitting those buttons and stay in the zone. It's total escape. 100% total escape. I don't feel anything.

Question #8

T: Tell me what it's like for you in the beginning, when you first start playing, when you're either winning or losing.

G: When I win, I know I'm going to have a good night (relief and excited, 65%, shoulder muscles relax). The slots are hot, my hands move faster. I bet more, maybe pick a second slot or third. I'm excited at first (65%, head) but later on it's just another win, it lets me play longer.

T: And if you lost at the beginning of the night?

G: I swallow hard and then get angry at the machine, it let me down (80%, shoulders).I was supposed to win, I was due. I hit the buttons faster. So I get a second slot then, too. Now I bet more each time, to get back what I lost. After a while, win, lose, it's all the same.

Question #9

T: Assume you've been playing for several hours. How are you feeling now?

G: I don't feel. I'm zoned, everything's quiet, I'm in it. I'm part of it. I'm in total escape mode, no worries, no husband, no problems. It's just me and my slots. It pulls you in, like being hypnotized. I'm numb. As long as I'm playing, I'm numb, 100% numb, relaxed. Except my arm and hand really hurt, and my back from sitting so long. I feel the pain later.

T: Anything else that you can think of you can tell me?

G: The machines fool you. You think the penny machine is the cheapest, but you have to put in fifty credits (50 cents) minimum for each play. And the machines are so fast, with many small wins, that you think you're winning all the time. You don't realize you've lost until your players card is used up, it's so frustrating (95%). Then I have to get more credits. If I don't have the money, my host lets me sign a marker.

T: What are markers?

G: They're IOUs. You give them a blank check when they set up your credit information. When it's too high, they tell you to pay. You have forty five days to pay it. If you don't, they fill it in and take it to the bank. If it bounces, they file bad check charges against you and you have to go to court.

Question #10

T: Let's say you've been playing now for several hours. When do you stop gambling and why?

G: I hate to stop, 100%. I feel stunned (80%), my head jerks up, but I'm out of money. That's the main reason I stop. I have to. Who wants to go home? Jim puts me down all the time, says I'm destroying the family, blah, blah, blah. He's drunk and flies into rages. He's never supportive. When Janey died two years ago he didn't even go to her funeral. She was my best friend. And all those other things happened – my sister, my job, Jim retiring, the car. So I go back to the racino, I don't have to deal with things there.

T: But you stopped.

G: I tried, I felt more miserable, more than ever. I need money. I was doubling up, chasing. I was broke. I started to borrow from the office. I knew then that I was stealing, but it didn't matter. I can't believe I did that, not just once but over and over again. Hoping each time I would win big and put it all back. A few months ago I won $7,000, almost enough to put the money back, but lost it all a few days later. Now I owe my boss over $20,000.

T: I know that the past years have been very difficult for you, but maybe your husband and family will participate in future sessions with you.

G: Hah.

T: You look upset. Do you feel OK enough to continue?

G: It's a lot I'm feeling and remembering, I know without a doubt that he won't come, but I'm OK.

T: Alright, let's continue then.

Question #11

T: You're done for the day and going home with money.

G: That's a good one. It doesn't happen too often now. Gambling's not about the money, it's to get away from it all, and for that you need money, and you'll do whatever you have to in order to get it. The slots are my salvation. Jim doesn't understand that. He doesn't get it. My family didn't either.

T: And how do you feel about that?

G: I'm not angry anymore. I just don't care. I feel kind of limp.

Question #12

T: Let's try to continue. Now you're going home after a big loss and you're broke.

G: That happens all the time. I'm sick at the stomach, my head hurts, my arm is killing me, my back hurts, I have to vomit. I'm 100% miserable and in pain. I beat myself up, over and over. Why do I do this? Why don't I quit? I know I'm going to lose. I've tried to quit, but I always go back.

T: What happens when you try to quit?

G: The misery in life comes back and knocks me down. I just want to get in the car and drive to the end of the world, but I don't even have a car. It's hell, pure hell. One thousand percent hell.

T: Is there anything else you're thinking or feeling at this time, on the way home?

G: Disgusted with people, too. People think gambling is fun. They have no clue what it's like. It's torture, sheer torture. And you can't stop. You have to go back.

Question #13

T: You've arrived home. Now what happens and how do you feel?

G: I don't know what's worse, the ride home or getting there. I already beat myself up the whole way back (guilt 100%). I hurt all over, emotionally and physically. I just want to die. Go to bed and not wake up.

T: Is there anything else going on at that time?

G: I try to sneak into the house, hoping he's asleep, but he's either awake or drunk. Lately he's been giving me the silent treatment, for days. I'm always afraid he's going to leave or kick me out of the house (scared,

90%). I know I don't deserve to stay in the house (guilt 100%).

Question #14

T: Now you're in bed, ready to fall asleep.

G: Sleep? I haven't slept in weeks. I toss and turn, I can't fall asleep or stay asleep. Even sleeping pills don't help. I keep thinking I've got to get the money and go back tomorrow (desperate 100%), but how? I know I can win, I did before. Then I wish this night would end. I have the sleeping pills and pain killers. I can end this torture. Maybe I should. One time I sat in the bathroom holding the pill bottles for I don't know how long. I kept wanting to do it, but I didn't because I didn't want to hurt the kids. That went on for days. Then I couldn't handle it anymore. I took them.

T: You took them?

G: Yes, but I didn't have enough. Can you beat that? And nobody knew about it.

Question #15

T: This gambling has caused you and others so much misery. Who could have stopped you and when?

G: Stopped me? I thought nobody even knew how bad it was, but they did. Jim yells, my boss threatened to tell the police, the kids cry and started to skip school, my father is disgusted and says 'Just stop" and wants nothing to do with me. Mom keeps asking what did she do wrong? Was it her fault? My pastor says to pray and my doctor gave me more pills. They all tried in their own way. Who could have stopped me? Nobody.

Question #16

T: At what point could you have stopped yourself?
G: I couldn't. Oh, I tried. It was always go, don't go, go, don't go. The "go" always won out. I finally ended up totally exhausted in every way – physically, mentally, emotionally. I couldn't go on anymore. The last week, I couldn't stop crying. That's when I took the pills the second time. All of them. Jim found me on the floor and called 911.

Discussion

As stated earlier, conducting the *Compulsive Gambling 'Action' Inventory* is not only highly emotional for both the gambler and others participating in the session, but it also provides the therapist with considerably more information in a very brief period of time.

At the end of the session, there is typically a period of stunned silence, followed by family members making statements such as "I had no idea" or "I'm so sorry you suffered so much. I thought you just didn't care." Their emotions come out: painful tears, wanting to comfort the gambler, recognition of the impact of their own behaviors, the many problems that have existed in the family, and a consensus of "we can work together." Very rarely is anger expressed, although occasionally it does. As one wife said, "I've heard all of this before." She filed for divorce.

By revealing to the family all of the emotions and reasons for gambling, the family is now in a better position to follow through with family therapy. Jim is encouraged to participate in couple's sessions, during which time the therapist can also encourage Jim to seek counseling for his alcoholism.

Question #1

During this session, the therapist has more exposure to Laura's strongly held irrational beliefs and cognitive distortions and can counsel her how thoughts lead to feelings, which then lead to behaviors and how these impact on the physical body. Various cognitive/behavioral techniques can be used for future sessions, including biofeedback, yoga, muscle relaxation, deep breathing, or some other method. Hypnosis has been tried in the past five years and appears to be an effective tool. Cognitive therapy is essential to dispute irrational beliefs and to teach the gambler to think rationally.

Question #2

It is an axiom that all addictions are rooted in troubled relationships. The client is already identifying some problems. More will be identified as sessions continue. These are targeted in treatment and relapse prevention therapy.

Question #3

The substance abused in compulsive gambling is money. Debts and financial ruin require a solid budget, one that is meaningful and practical. The therapist can assist or refer the client and significant others to a financial consultant to develop a financial management plan, which can be monitored until stability is achieved (see chapter 18). Gamblers Anonymous offers a Financial Pressure Relief group, which is exceptionally helpful in financial recovery. These sessions also help the gambler understand how emotional stressors lead to gambling and use this information in relapse prevention training.

Question #4

The gambler says she took everything out of her checking and savings account. Using cash on hand and monies in checking and savings accounts and paychecks are the first source of money for gambling. Money taken out of a savings account and other sources is kept secret, and eventual discovery brings about family fracas.

She goes on to say that "there's a lot of stuff I don't tell him." This should be explored at first in individual therapy sessions and at some point in couple's sessions. What is kept secret, why, how serious are the problems, how can they be resolved? Rigorous honesty and learning to trust each other must be stressed if marital and family relations are to improve.

She states she began to "borrow" from her job. No doubt, initially, she viewed taking company money as borrowing, with all intentions of returning it the next day. However, in the eyes of the law, and in her own eyes, once she is calm enough to look at her behaviors objectively, this is stealing. Stealing and lying repeatedly are virtually essential to maintaining a gambling addiction. These behaviors lead to the intense feelings of guilt and eventual conviction that suicide is the only option left for them.

Question #5

She states that her whole body is running at "90 mph." This sense of rushing, of racing thoughts and bodily effects, is true mostly in action gamblers but can also occur with escape gamblers. Their thoughts and behaviors become manic, and this is heightened by the rushing sense in the body. They have difficulty focusing. They drive at excessive speeds in order to get to the gambling site as quickly as possible. Notice also her mood swings.

She mentions her host. Casinos and racinos employ individuals, known as hosts or hostesses, who serve as liaisons between the gambler and the gambling venue. The host establishes a friendly relationship with the gambler, sends holiday and birthday cards, and stays in constant contact. The host will offer comps such as free shows or dinners, and as the gambling escalates, will offer free limousine service, shows and dinners for the gambler's friends and family, and ultimately even give expensive gifts, such as diamond jewelry, for the gambler's spouse or friend. The gambler relishes this preferential treatment and is manipulated into gambling more frequently and with more money. The bigger the high roller, the larger the comps.

Even bingo parlors have hosts and comps.

Question #6

Compulsive gamblers not only have their preference for a particular type of gambling, i.e., cards, lottery, or sports, but slots players have additional preferences. They gravitate toward certain areas of the room, select the money value of the machine, often starting with penny slots, and play slot machines which have certain sounds and themes. Wheel of Fortune is the most popular of all slot machines. Slots with symbols of cherries, plums, and bells appeal more to female or social gamblers. Poker machines or eight-liners tend to be preferred by males, although the preferences are not mutually exclusive.

Note that she says she had an accident one time. In other words, she could not hold her urine. Casinos and racinos have employees whose sole job is to change slot machine seats, dozens per day, and clean up the area. Slots addicts are also known to wear diapers.

Question #7

Many slots players state they became compulsive gamblers with their very first bet. This phenomenon has not been scientifically researched; however, it is heard often enough to give it credibility and to merit further investigation. Additionally, while no rigorous research has been conducted on the length of play before becoming addicted to gambling, anecdotally, the last two years of gambling suggest a serious state of addiction, while the last four or five months represent a totally out of control state of mind and, thus, gambling and other behaviors.

Both action and escape gamblers talk about the state of oblivion, which they refer to as "spacing out" or "being in the zone." The action gamblers describe periods of time when they have out-of-body experiences, looking down on themselves while gambling; escape gamblers describe this time period as being more akin to a state of dissociation from reality to numbness: no thinking, no feeling, just doing. Like a robot.

Compulsive gamblers insist that gambling "is not about the money." Yes, they need money to gamble, but the greater need is to escape into a state of dissociation, when they are able to separate themselves from a reality which is beyond their endurance or ability to change or tolerate. Thus, winning is important to continue to gamble and to pay bills.

Question #8

In this question, she "knows" she is going to win. She does not recognize that this is delusional or magical thinking. She wants to win, but there is no guarantee that she will. She believes "the slots are hot" and thus they will pay off because she is "due to win," which is yet another irrational belief that what happened in the past will occur again in the future or also that strong beliefs will result in the desired outcome. They do not consider that the slots pay-off is based on randomness and that the slot machine is programmed for a percentage number of wins.

Question #9

She talks about being "in a total escape mode, no worries, no husband, no problems." Throughout the implementation of the Inventory, clients will allude to certain difficulties in their lives. In this case, Laura's relationship with her husband appears to be paramount and couples therapy is clearly indicated. Other critical life events must also be addressed.

She further describes the complete isolation from the world, "it's just me and my slot" and the power of the slot as she feels being pulled in and hypnotized. She is acknowledging a complete loss of control, a state of numbness, in which she feels safe. How else might she feel safe, become assertive, and improve her sense of self-esteem?

The treatment goal is to find other ways of coping and resolving the issues besides gambling.

Question #10

At some time during the interview, it is best to let the gambler talk on and on, without interruption. It is an opportunity for the family to hear the obsessive, delusional, and magical thoughts, disregard for factual issues, illegal activities, the multitude of the gambler's painful and unresolved emotional issues, and the irrationality of it all. The timing for this uninterrupted talking varies from gambler to gambler, thus the therapist needs to be keenly aware and relate to the gambler's emotions throughout the interview.

Why did she stop gambling at various times? She was out of money. Research does show that this is the Number One reason for stopping at a particular time. It is of necessity and is not necessarily the moment of "hitting bottom" and wanting to abstain from all further gambling.

Throughout this *Inventory*, compulsive gambler will make references to incidents which are emotionally painful. She has already mentioned her troubled relationship with her husband, Jim, but now other painful events are brought to everyone's attention and for which she desperately wants some resolution and comfort: her friend's untimely death, her sister's medical diagnoses, the reduction in work time and Jim's retirement, and her teenage son's drinking, especially in view of Jim's alcoholism and his poor parenting. All of these issues represent potential triggers for future relapses. This is an opportune moment for the therapist to set the stage for future individual, marital, and family therapy.

Question #11

This client is asked if she has given up hope and her response is she wants to go to bed and never wake up. Again, this is a typical progression of the end stage of compulsive gambling. At this time, they usually have two themes: one is to disappear and the other is the death wish. The idea of driving away, forever, is common with casino gamblers. Many are found only after the police have been notified. Both action and escape gamblers have death wishes which last for weeks.

Question #12

The client acknowledges she has tried to quit gambling several times. While gambling, she was able to escape the emotional and factual turmoil in her life, yet she has no hope of relief without gambling.

Compulsive gamblers attempting to stop gambling experience a number of withdrawal symptoms: severe headaches, nausea, irritability, sleep disturbances, restlessness, and agitation are the more common ones. The emotional conflicts are more severe: guilt, depression, anger, anxiety, fear; all of them lead to physical and emotional misery and relapse, no matter how determined the gambler may be to refrain from further gambling. Even though they know the difference between right and wrong, they do not consider the consequences of their actions. They lack the ability to refrain from their gambling and gambling-related actions. In the eyes of the law, this is diminished capacity.

Notably, she talks about the torture of compulsive gambling, being 1,000% hell, not 100% but rather 1,000% hell. Compulsive gambling is not fun and games and excitement, it is torture.

This *'Action' Inventory* helps the family get a better sense of compulsive gambling and to differentiate between the fun of social gambling and the turmoil of compulsive gambling.

Question #13

She recognizes her own aberrant behaviors and the impact her behaviors have on others. It is also apparent that Jim follows the traditional pattern of enabling and codependency and failure to understanding her addiction.

Neither of them recognize that she is suffering from a "mental" illness: she thinks all she needs is money, he is convinced all she needs to do is to slow down and stop.

Question #14

The death wish at this stage of loss of control has grown into suicidal ideation.

Gamblers think repeatedly of the benefits of suicide, viewing it as their only option, and thus they begin to decide on the best method. Certain trends have been noted: gamblers who drive to the gambling location will drive at high speeds to get there and will drive even more recklessly on their return trip. They develop a plan for suicide. The therapist must know about these methods, as it is often believed to be an accident rather than an actual suicide attempt. The gambler will deny the intent, but as trust develops with the therapist, the gambler will admit that the accident was not an accident, but rather a failed suicide attempt.

A second form of suicide attempt especially by females and seniors, is that of overdosing on pills. Adolescents are more likely to use a combination of alcohol and drugs. Other young males on occasion precipitate a "suicide by cop." Pills are usually prescription medication, which they have received from their family doctor because of insomnia, anxiety, depression, headaches, or other physical pains.

Gamblers accustomed to handling weapons, such as law enforcement personnel, military members, and hunters, are more likely to commit suicide with lethal weapons. Thus, in this suicide intervention, it is paramount to convince the gambler to turn over the weapon.

Adolescents are more likely to use a combination of alcohol and drugs. Other young males on occasion precipitate a "suicide by cop."

Question #15

This time period is akin to "all hell broke loose," and denial is no longer possible.

The boss threatens jail, but more often just wants his money back. Everyone affected by the gambling addiction wants the gambler to stop, yet no threat or tears seem to work. They've tried.

There are several bottoms, and each one brings the compulsive gambler closer to the final bottom. In the meantime, family members can protect themselves from financial disasters by limiting the gambler's access to money and dishonest practices.

Question #16

Hitting bottom is a phenomenon of all addictions, but equally true is the fact that there is not one bottom, but many bottoms for most addicts. With compulsive gamblers, the first may be a financial bottom, which all-too-often is quickly reversed with a bail-out. A major bottom is the threat of separation or divorce, but usually, this remains a perceived threat rather than an actual threat. Another bottom may be due to legal charges and fear of imprisonment, but being first-time offenders with no prior criminal history, they are not likely to be incarcerated. It may be actual incarceration, but this is a matter of geography: gambling is available in prison. It appears that only after all bottoms have failed, and the gambler is physically, mentally, and emotionally exhausted, that the "final bottom" has been reached. This is often accompanied with an actual suicide attempt.

SUMMARY

This *Compulsive Gambling 'Action' Inventory* is a powerful tool in treating compulsive gambling. It is equally powerful as a research instrument.

The *Inventory* requires for the therapist to know the rudiments of gambling dynamics, of gambling sites and peculiarities of each form of gambling, the involvement of the family, the reference to money, the labile emotions and community cultures. The many marital and family problems emerge in the course of treatment.

Very importantly, the therapist treating a slot machine addict should know as much as possible about the appeal of certain slots. Common sense would dictate that the money gambled on a one-cent slot results in lower losses than on a nickel machine. In reality, these penny slots are programmed to accept a minimum amount, many times twenty-five or fifty cents per play. Some slots are as much as $100 per reel, with up to five reels per machine. The client in this interview for the most part played penny slots, but as her desperation increased, so did her gambling. She attributes her stealing of over $20,000 to losses on the slots with larger minimums, longer hours, and playing three machines at a time.

A LATER QUESTION

It is folly to believe that once the compulsive gambler has "hit bottom" and has made long-term strides in recovery, that there will be incentive to refrain from all further gambling. In reality, most gambling addicts, even those who have been treated by professionals and are active in the Gamblers Anonymous program, will relapse within the first or second year of abstinence. A session with a compulsive gambler in professional therapy is illustrative:

T: Now that you've stopped playing the slots, what are your hopes and intentions for the future concerning gambling?

G: I can't gamble anymore. I know that and I don't want to. I'm done. I have a full-time job to pay off my debts and the money I stole from my former boss. I want to pay them all off in one year. Counseling and GA are helping me. No, I don't ever want to gamble again, not ever. Well, maybe just once, after all the debts are paid off, just to make sure I'm OK. And I can be a social gambler again.

Note: She did, in fact gamble at the racino several months after being discharged from professional therapy. Jim insisted she was cured, so there was no problem with them "going and having a good time." He convinced her she could "play the slots for a couple of hours, while I have a few beers." She agreed and had several losses before she recognized the seriousness and seduction of her addiction, called the therapist for some aftercare sessions, and is now committed to remaining abstinent "with the help of others and my higher power."

COMPULSIVE GAMBLING "ACTION" INVENTORY©

This inventory is administered by the clinician to the gambler. It should be done in the presence of family members and significant others, who have been prepared for this session, being reminded to be non-participant observers until the interview with the gambler is completed. This session will help in understanding the gambler's thoughts, feelings and behaviors throughout one day of out-of-control gambling. The clinician is keeping notes of the gambler's statements and also identifies issues to be clarified and possibly requiring further therapy.

Name _____ Sex _____ Age _____ # Years Gambled _____ # Years out of control _____

Type of gambling described during this interview _____ *Where* _____ *Today's date* _____

Participants

"This interview is to determine how you think, feel, and act from the moment you wake up in the morning until you go to bed at night, during the out-of-control period of your gambling. We will go from step to step. Tell me all of your thoughts during each of the various time periods. Then tell me what feelings you are experiencing, how strong each feeling is, from 0% to 100%, and then in what part of your body you experience that feeling or sensation – in your head, back, stomach, etc. Please look at the form to familiarize yourself with this inventory. Add any feelings or sensations you experience."

Accepted	Anticipation	Desperate	Euphoric	Frustrated	Important	Panicked	Sedated	Tense
Action	Anxious	Disgusted	Excited	Guilty	Lost	Relaxed	Shocked	Uptight
Alive	Ashamed	Empty	Exhausted	Hypnotized	Mind racing	Relieved	Spaced out	Watching myself
Angry	Depressed	Escape	Fearful	Impatient	Numb	Rushed	Stressed	Other

Gambling or Related Acts	All Thoughts All Behaviors	All Feelings Sensations	% how Strong	Body Parts Affected
1. First thoughts on waking up				
2. Deciding to gamble				
3. How much $, for how long				
4. Getting the money				
5. Getting to site, computer, fone				
6. Which slots, seat, bookie				
7. Watch the race, game, spin, card				
8. Winning early on				
9. Losing in the beginning				
10. Reason for Stopping				
11. Going home with a win				
12. Going home after a big loss				
13. Face to face, confrontation				
14. Thoughts & type of sleep				

15. Who could have stopped you, when, how?

16. At what point could you have stopped yourself?

This clinical/research instrument was developed by Valerie C. Lorenz, Ph.D., Forensic Center on Compulsive Gambling, 651 Washington Boulevard, Baltimore, MD 21230. Administration requires brief training. The author encourages users of this instrument to collect data and present findings to the field. The Author and Inventory must be referenced in all writings.
© 1995, R2003, R2008, R2013

CHAPTER 10
SCRAMBLED COGNITIONS

Why do some people appear to maintain balance and calm during an event or incidence and others flounder under any form of stress? It could be their way of thinking, which leads to feelings, which then lead to behaviors. These behaviors may be inappropriate or destructive, while other ways of thinking can lead to effective coping and problem-solving. Ineffective ways of thinking becomes a treatment issue, and psychiatrist David Burns has written a book called *Feeling Good*, which is considered a bible on cognitive behavior therapy. It explores cognitive distortions, and presents chapters on various issues which are particularly helpful for compulsive gamblers. Most significantly is one titled Your Work is Not Your Worth, and the other focuses on feelings of guilt. Another chapter identifies several cognitive distortions which are commonly germane to compulsive gamblers (and others), which are discussed in this chapter.

Psychologist Albert Ellis is equally important to the field of mental health treatment. He identified a number of irrational beliefs, which again, are found with regular frequency in compulsive gamblers. An important aspect, then, in treating compulsive gamblers is to identify these cognitive distortions and irrational beliefs, allowing the gambler to cope and communicate in a manner which allows the gambler to improve problem-solving skills and establish healthy and meaningful relationships.

Gamblers Anonymous is without the most effective support group for compulsive gamblers. However, its program is based on fellowship, which is an alien concept for the gambler who is a loner. It also teaches to adhere to the twelve steps of the recovery program— gamblers like to be the master of their own universe.

Another area of resistance to Gamblers Anonymous is the gambler's inability or unwillingness to accept the basic steps of the recovery program. The First Step is the most difficult one. It requires the gambler to admit to being "powerless over gambling," which is in direct conflict with the gambler's irrational belief of: *I must be in control of all things at all times.* It is equally difficult for the gambler to admit to defects of character when the irrational belief is *I must be fully competent in all things at all times.* Both underscore a basic fear of rejection.

Irrational beliefs are firm convictions of certain ideas that are held over time and become part of a person's emotional defense mechanism and daily functioning. They differ from automatic, distorted thoughts, which are the quick intellectual responses to any given event. For instance, Joe can't find his car keys. His immediate response to that realization is:

> "Darn it, I did it again, I am such an idiot" (Labeling, I must be Perfect, I should not…) and he feels angry and disgusted with himself;
>
> "Now I can't drive to work, I'll be late, I'll get suspended…" (Negative fortune telling, Catastrophizing, Mind reading, and feels terrified, angry, frustrated, etc.;
>
> "Now I can't get to Atlantic City. I have to win my money back or else…" (All or Nothing thinking, Should statements)
>
> "Let's see, I used the key chain to get in the house, walked over to the chair, and ah, ha, there they are" (Acceptance).

Compulsive gamblers tend to use myriad distorted thoughts and irrational beliefs which lead to ineffective problem-solving and poor coping skills, low frustration levels, and ineffective communication, to name some of their more consistent troubling emotions. This way of thinking and believing was started in very early childhood, reinforced by poor parenting, and eventually leading to emotional immaturity and impulsivity, which are the hallmarks of compulsive gamblers. Lacking these skills, they invariably use poor judgment in everyday activities and have little insight into their internal and external realities.

DISTORTED THOUGHTS

Some of the more frequent distorted thoughts expressed by compulsive gamblers are listed below. There are more, of course, but these seem to be the prevailing ones:

SHOULD STATEMENT

"You shouldn't have told my wife I was at the track. Now I have to lie" places the gambler's demand and blame on another person and leads to feelings of anger. The *should* statement directed against himself about having to lie, once again, lead to intense feelings of guilt. Without exception, compulsive gamblers speak of the intense guilt they feel during and after their gambling sprees.

Indeed, gamblers virtually always will admit that guilt weighed on them so much and for such a long time, even after they stopped gambling. Guilt can lead to additional pressures and is very likely to lead to relapse. A more productive response is "I know I lied, repeatedly. I can't take it back, but I can apologize and work toward being rigorously honest." Learning to be rigorously honest is difficult, especially since it encompasses many areas of the gambler's life and communication style, but the message can be incorporated in teaching the GA step of removing one's "character defects" or during therapy sessions. *Should* statements are the Number One style of distorted communication and belief and reveals an underlying and ongoing feeling of anger, resentment, guilt, and with some even rage.

MAGICAL THOUGHTS

"I know this will be the Big One. I'm due." The gambler doesn't *know* the next bet will be the big one, he *hopes* it will be. Magical thoughts are delusions and convictions, they are not based on reality, yet they are very much a part of the compulsive gambler's beliefs and coping mechanism, especially during the desperation and exhaustion phase of compulsive gambling. More accurate is, "I hope I will win. I've studied the odds, I've practiced but in reality I have no guarantee I will win, whether I'm due or not."

NEGATIVE MIND-READING

"I just know that my wife will leave me. She's sick and tired of my gambling." This creates intense anxiety but is not necessarily true of the wife's feelings or goals. In fact, most wives prefer to stay in the marriage if there is some hope that things will change, that the gambling is a thing of the past, and that bills will be paid. Unfortunately, the fear of separation is acutely uncomfortable for the gambler, and the quickest way to ease that discomfort is through focusing on something else: gambling, winning money, then paying off the bills.

NEGATIVE FORTUNE-TELLING

"I know they'll throw me in jail." The gambler *believes* this, but in the meantime, the anxiety is severe enough to lead to intense stomach problems and other physical feelings of discomfort.

In reality, the gambler *does not know* what will happen. He may get bailed out by a family member, the judge may give him a suspended sentence, the probation officer may recommend community service, etc. In contrast, acceptance would be, "I don't like the situation I'm in, I've done the best I can to show remorse and make restitution, and now it's up to the my attorney, the prosecution, probation officer, and the judge to decide my fate. I will deal with it when I know what it will be." So logical yet it is so difficult for most compulsive gamblers to think in terms of logic; it is something that must be taught and learned.

LABELING

"I'm such a loser." This represents a common belief among gamblers and and how others feel towards them. Labeling implies the whole person is something, whereas doing something good or bad is an act and not a person. A more accurate way of thinking is to say, "I lost a lot due to my gambling. I'm a good person, but I've done some very hurtful things."

MAGNIFYING

"I stole more than anyone" is a form of exaggerating or lying favored by compulsive gamblers, whether the act is commendable or if it is unacceptable. It plays on the gambler's competitive nature. Magnifying good or bad takes things out of proportion and is not factual. Magnifying among compulsive gamblers is not limited to self-praise, it is also typical of the "war stories" heard in GA meetings. The one Big Win of $50,000 becomes two wins or three wins of that amount. It is almost better to be "worser." It begets a reaction from others. Better that than to be ignored.

MINIMIZING

"I only lost a little bit." How many times have gamblers said that when in fact they lost a considerable amount of money? In their minds, minimizing the problem will result in a less severe reaction from a significant other from the gambler's circle of contacts. It also leads to self-deception of the total amount of money gambled away. Nevertheless, in most instances the truth will come out eventually.

ALL-OR-NOTHING

"I need money and I have two choices, gamble or not gamble." All-or-nothing thinking is a concrete style of response and limits the possibility of finding other options in solving problems. For instance, the gambler's response to meet the need for money is to gamble; other options could be working longer or taking on a part-time job, borrowing, selling something, spending less, consolidating expenses, negotiating a lower interest rate, or not gambling at all. *All-or-nothing* thinking leaves them few options, thus resulting in poor judgment in their decision-making.

DISCOUNTING THE POSITIVE

"She says I'm intelligent, but she's saying that only because she's the therapist and is trying to make me feel better." Is the therapist lying? Many compulsive gamblers believe that they are of average intelligence, when in fact most often they are above average. This is not a matter of being shy or humble; instead, they have a limited perception of their own qualities and talents.

OVERGENERALIZING

What is true for one event becomes an always or never conviction. "My car is always giving me trouble." There is no acknowledgement that the car is several years old and that tires get flat or that cold weather can prevent the batteries from turning over. This response style leads to frustration and self-contempt, feelings that can be diminished or avoided by a few hours of gambling or conversely, more accurate thinking.

YES, BUT

"I'll try, but I know it won't work." Why even bother trying since the obstacles are so great? This is self-defeating behavior and serves no good purpose, yet is a frequent response by gamblers who, for instance, have been found guilty of criminal charges. "I'll look for a job but who is going to hire a felon?" Gamblers need to learn that "if plan A doesn't work, go to plan B." In work situations, often one solution in filling out a job application is to leave blank the question regarding criminal charges or write that the question is best answered in person.

SELECTIVE NEGATIVE THINKING

"You could have won if you had done…" A person can do well in 99 things out of 100, but the focus is the one negative act. This is Sissyphus in action. Compulsive gamblers are often the recipient of this kind of psychological abuse, especially from a father figure, thus the gambler is constantly trying to excel, in the hopes of getting the desired approval.

Every one of these thought processes have unfortunate consequences, but they can be disputed by the therapist and replaced with more accurate views and understanding. This can lead to more productive outcomes and can drastically reduce the uncomfortable feelings and desperate needs which are triggers to relapses. Cognitive therapy should always be part of a comprehensive treatment approach with compulsive gamblers if recovery and an improved quality of life are the goals.

IRRATIONAL BELIEFS

Compulsive gamblers have developed a thinking style that is composed of myriad distortions. They have also encompassed a belief system that cannot be proven. The difference between distorted thoughts and irrational beliefs tend to overlap; for instance, the automatic response to a situation may be, "Oh, he will criticize me" whereas the more long-term ingrained belief is that "criticism is awful and therefore must be avoided." Compulsive gamblers invariably adhere to a number of irrational beliefs, which must be challenged and corrected so that the gambler can avoid potential relapses and improve chances of recovery. Some of more salient irrational beliefs are:

MONEY WILL SOLVE MY PROBLEMS

This belief is true of virtually every compulsive gambler. Gambling is about money. Money solves problems; it is the gateway to acceptance. The action gamblers' focus on gambling is to win that money. In their pursuit of money, the casino gambler's goal is to "break the bank." Once accomplished, they want to do the same thing at the next casino and the next. It is a goal that cannot be met, but they will continue to pursue it, without any need for the money other than to gain acceptance. Many compulsive gamblers have made statements like "I want to be a millionaire by the time I'm thirty." Asked by a therapist, "And then what?"

they will respond with a shrug of the head with an "I don't know. I guess I'll get the second million."

Compulsive gamblers have difficulty distinguishing between money that is essential for living and having money for the sake of having money. They do not consider themselves to be greedy or miserly, yet some of their behaviors reflect precisely those attributes.

Escape gamblers turn to focus on money, usually in adult life, due to a number of recent critical or traumatic life events, which require quick access to money which they do not routinely possess. These critical life events always seem to include one or two events revolving around unexpected financial burdens. Gambling is seen as a means of resolving this dilemma.

NOT HAVING MONEY CAUSED MANY PROBLEMS

The lack of money and the emphasis on money caused many problems in the action gambler's childhood. The lack of money meant living in a poor neighborhood, being rejected and being without a dad because Dad was working long hours to support the family, thus rarely spending time with them. These gamblers miss out on having a close relationship with their father, who does not attend school functions, sports and the gamblers' other activities because he's too busy or too tired. They feel rejected because of their circumstances, and should their financial circumstances improve and they move to a better neighborhood, they will feel inadequate and fear they will not be accepted by the new group. These gamblers seek money to give their children a better life and to feel more secure in their own life.

I MUST BE IN CONTROL OF ALL THINGS AT ALL TIMES

This is a statement that can be heard again and again from compulsive gamblers. Control means being in charge and never being rejected. Thus they will con and manipulate those around them, especially family members, no matter what the issue may be that is being confronted. They manipulate others in order to control with money. They must be liked, cannot be rejected or abandoned, cannot tolerate criticism, so they will use any means and manipulations to obtain and maintain control over others. Ask gamblers what would happen if they did not have control over a spouse, they would immediately respond with a conviction and anxiety that the spouse will leave. Control means they are the master of their universe.

They are convinced of their ability to control, all things at all times, but lack the insight on the reality of such a goal. They will manipulate until they get what they want, even without the gambling. It is a lifestyle, based on fear of rejection.

CRITICISM IS AWFUL AND MUST BE AVOIDED AT ALL COSTS

This puts an enormous self-imposed burden on the gambler: having to measure up to the expectation of others. A boss's comments on the gambler's work is not viewed as being constructive and helpful, but rather as an indication of being a failure. Being a failure translates into rejection as a person, not as an employee working on a particular project. Criticism was the hallmark for action compulsive gamblers in early childhood. It caused hurt feelings and at times also led to beatings; therefore, it must be avoided at all costs. It is the impetus for compulsive gamblers to become workaholics and the motivation to do the best and be the best.

REJECTION IS AWFUL AND MUST BE AVOIDED AT ALL COSTS

This irrational belief leads to many other irrational beliefs, such as needing to be competent, in control, avoiding criticism, etc. A classic case is when an invitation to the school prom is refused by the recipient. The gambler almost always sees this as a rejection of himself, rather than considering that the other person may have a previous commitment, is involved in a relationship, or does not feel well. Rejection leads to depression, anxiety, and despair, and is rarely viewed with a sense of understanding and acceptance. This fear of rejection is indicative of a lack of insight and necessary life skills.

I MUST BE COMPETENT IN ALL THINGS AT ALL TIMES

This is closely associated with the fear of criticism, which forces the compulsive gambler to work better and to be better. To be less than competent means having failed. To be less competent in one area and competent in another simply is not allowed. Competence means in all things at all times and does not allow for illness or any other inadequacy. To be competent in gambling means to be the best; therefore, they read books and study systems and develop their own system. Their system may improve the odds of winning, but it is not a guarantee for winning. It forces them to chase after their losses to salve their injured ego, in spite of the odds being against them. Compulsive gamblers see themselves as winners, thus they resort to magical thinking that they can beat the odds.

I MUST BE LOVED, LIKED, RESPECTED, ETC. BY ALL PEOPLE AT ALL TIMES

Once again, to be ignored or criticized or being viewed as second best is intolerable, thus they put forth all efforts to be accepted, loved, and liked. Asked to name one person who meets all those criteria, many have answered, "Jesus." They believe this at face value and do not consider that Jesus was hated by many, was betrayed, and nailed to the cross.

I WON IN THE PAST SO I WILL WIN AGAIN

There is a certain amount of truth to this belief, but obviously no guarantee. Experience and knowledge can improve the chances of winning on certain forms of gambling, i.e., cards, sports betting, horse racing, but still is not a guarantee. The future win is dictated by a number of circumstances: the deal of the cards, amount of money bet, number of players, money lost in previous bets, etc. Perception is not reality and a prime example of that is gambling on slots: the fast action and the number of wins gives the impression of winning all the time, yet compulsive gamblers are shocked upon learning how much and how many times they have lost or that the losses far exceed the wins.

I MUST AVOID DISCOMFORT AT ANY COST

All bad feelings must be avoided and one way to avoid feeling this way is through diversion. Prior to their addiction, compulsive gamblers were involved in sports, hobbies, family, and had many interests and outlets. However, during their progression from social gambling to compulsive gambling, they no longer sought comfort in these activities and instead sought relief through gambling. The gambling then led to more feelings of guilt, anxiety, anger, depression, frustration, which they then hoped to avoid through more gambling. Ultimately, many seek avoidance through suicide.

OTHERS MAKE ME FEEL ANGRY

This is a classic example of the defense mechanism of blaming, and one that is used with abandon by compulsive gamblers when they are thinking of excuses that allow them to gamble. "You make me so angry, it's no wonder I have to get out of here." And of course, the silent statement is that the "out of here" means "going to the track" or gambling in some other manner.

WRONGDOERS MUST BE PUNISHED

This irrational belief is firmly entrenched in the gambler's belief system. It leads to guilt, often extreme guilt, and to a further sense of unworthiness. Ironically, this reinforces their other irrational beliefs, which can lead to depression or anxiety, and then thoughts of suicide. Action gamblers rarely think of having brought shame to the family and others. They think in terms of themselves and what they have done wrong and obsess on self-punitive thoughts. Their sense of wrongdoing and self-centered behaviors leads them to an overpowering sense of guilt. Compulsive gamblers put it in numbers, 100% guilt. Their self-punitive attitude leads to constant self-criticism, anger at self, or feeling inadequate and unworthy to the point of sleeping in their car rather than impose on a spouse or significant other person.

Early indications suggest that escape gamblers have similar intense feelings of guilt during their gambling and after abstinence. As one compulsive gambler stated, "I haven't made a bet in five years, all the bills are paid, things are going well, but I can't get over the tremendous guilt that I feel for having put my family through hell." This gambler has not learned the difference between *guilt*, which requires punishment, and *remorse*, which is learning from one's mistakes and taking the appropriate steps to make amends and avoiding similar wrongdoings.

Guilt is the overpowering emotion among compulsive gamblers, which underscores the high incidence of suicide among them. The suicide rate among gamblers is higher than any other addiction or psychiatric disorder.

DISCUSSION OF GAMBLERS ANONYMOUS AND COMPULSIVE GAMBLER

These irrational beliefs interact with one another and also with their distorted thoughts. Some are stronger or more prevailing than others, but basically, all are based on the fear of rejection and abandonment. It happened in early childhood, continued into adulthood, and is too painful to bear now. Compulsive gamblers will do whatever they must to avoid these situations.

They constantly struggle with their ingrained beliefs and later with the GA program, thus they tend to rationalize "*I'm not as bad as them*" or "*I can't relate to them*" or pose similar objections to acceptance and recovery. Since their fear of giving up control and fear of failure lead to the ultimate burden of criticism and rejection, it is only a matter of time until good intentions of abstinence are replaced by stronger needs to avoid these feelings.

The case of one compulsive gambler's personal story reflects some of the distorted thoughts and irrational beliefs, which would lead to a more stable and satisfactory life if they were challenged and revised. The gambler is Caucasian, 41, married, businessman, who bet on race horses, sports, and casinos. He was in a professional treatment program for two weeks and during a group sessions was instructed to "tell us how you got here."

> "When I first went to GA, I thought, "Those guys are f...
> ing sick. I don't belong here." I quit after the first meeting.
> It gave me an excuse to go back to gambling."

This is classic denial, a truism of all addictions. He quite obviously did not want to be there and thus projected that others may need GA but not he. Most likely, this gambler was also turned off to the GA program after hearing the First Step of Powerlessness. Cognitively, this is *overgeneralizing*, that one or a few compulsive gamblers are representative of all compulsive gamblers, which therefore includes him. It also indirectly labels him as sick and therefore having failed. His *all-or-nothing* thinking limits him to two options, either staying or leaving, instead of considering other options, such as going to a different meeting, finding a sponsor, learning the Twelve Steps, or seeking professional help. He is *avoiding* uncomfortable feelings and situations, to which he readily admits.

Most importantly, however, is the concept of powerlessness. Powerlessness means losing a competitive activity. Change leads to anxiety. It means uncertainty and lack of predictability. It is uncomfortable. The gambler feels lost and helpless.

> "The basic reason and thinking in my gambling is money, the big score. If I couldn't bet on football or baseball, I would bet on Wimbledon tennis. I never even saw a tennis match and I would bet on it."

This happens with regular frequency with sports bettors during the final and exhaustion phase of their gambling. Bets become desperate and automatic, a necessity to "stay in action." This betting without forethought and study is seen in all forms of gambling, whether staying in action or escaping bad feelings. They are on the proverbially "run-away train, going downhill, unable to stop, until they hit bottom." At this point, the "basic thing" in a gambler's life is money because that is the medium necessary to feed their addiction.

> "It's self-torture. It is never enough. It is the challenge, you're there to beat them, and when you do, it still isn't enough. My dream used to be to beak the bank and that the casino boss would say, "Sir, we can no longer handle your bet." You know what a thrill that would have been? It doesn't happen in real life, but if it had, I would have gone to the casino next door and start all over again, winning and losing."

This is the ultimate goal of the very competitive action compulsive gambler. "It is the challenge." However, this challenge is not limited to gambling, but rather is pervasive in the gambler's total lifestyle and functioning. The "self-torture" is common in the desperate and exhaustion phases, during which time they also tend to dissociate, being out of touch with reality, "living in the zone" and spacing out as though they were looking down on themselves. The self-torture consists of the desperate need to win and to avoid the horror of losing.

> "You think your good time is gambling, that one good day is worth twenty bad days. You remember the good days and ignore the bad."

In gambling, the numerous smaller wins give the illusion of constant wins, whereas losses are ignored or not even recognized. By ignoring the "bad days," the gambler is also reinforcing his own superiority over the losers in a game that has only winners and losers. It is selective memory and self-delusion.

> "If I had money in my pocket, I would go to the track. If I had a check bounce, I never thought the guy would charge me with theft. I only thought, 'Now I can't borrow from him anymore.' I'm a lawyer, you'd think I would know better."

Compulsive gamblers in the course of having lost control will resort to acquiring monies illegally, in many different forms but usually starting with a variety of bad check charges. This gambler clearly knows that he has written a bad check but naively is convinced that he would not be prosecuted. This may have been true in the earlier stages, but if the amount of the "loan" is large or there are a number of bad checks, more often they will be charged. Gamblers know they have taken money illegally, but rationalize this as "borrowing" with full intent of replacing the money. They do not fully consider the consequences of even one act of illegal acquisition of money or items of value or misdeeds. Although knowing the difference between right and wrong, they lack the ability to conform their actions to the requirements of the law.

> "My last fling made me realize that I needed help. I took a large wad of money and put $500 in one pocket, the rest in the other. I wanted to prove to myself I could play with just $500. I bet four races, $20 or $50, and thought this is ridiculous. So I spent the whole wad from the other pocket on the next race and lost it all. I knew then that I couldn't just keep to the $500. I knew I had a problem."

This is a classic example of *all-or-nothing thinking, money solves all problems, magical thinking, delusional thinking,* and impulsiveness. He is making a decision to stop, namely, gambling away all money available and being unable to sign any more markers, and the final realization that winning and recouping lost monies is not possible. The "chasing" has ended. Typical also is using remaining money on one large bet, just to be done with gambling, once and forever. There is no real desire for gambling, the only desperate wish now is to stop the nightmare, the torture.

This was his final realization of "hitting bottom." The gambler throughout this time also has very little awareness of the impact of his gambling on others and of the reality around him. Compulsive gamblers refer to this exhaustion state as "being in a fog" or spacing out. This is symptomatic of a state of dissociation.

This seemingly is the final bottom, but without learning how to confront triggers and overcoming them, he is still at risk of relapsing. Good intentions do not equate to the ability to control his actions or his seemingly irreversible commitment to abstinence.

> "I wish I had known about compulsive gambling a lot sooner. I never would have started."

Compulsive gambling is considered by many to be an act of selfishness and greed. More accurately, it is a form of self-medication to escape an underlying depression or anxiety, often present for many years or even since early childhood in action gamblers. It may also be a form of self-medication in response to some more current horrific life experiences over which neither action nor escape gamblers had control.

> "Now that I haven't gambled in two weeks my head is starting to clear. I can actually see things, like I never noticed that tree before. I'm beginning to think. I used to believe that my first thought was the only way. Now I know there are different ways of thinking and many options, not just one or the first. It's amazing, I had to be 41 years old and go through hell before I learned to think. And to think before acting."

For some, Gamblers Anonymous is the hallmark of recovery. For others, a combination of professional help together with Gamblers Anonymous gives continued strength for recovery. Professional help without Gamblers Anonymous may be helpful in early stages of recovery, but no research has supported findings of long-term recovery of professional treatment without Gamblers Anonymous.

CHAPTER 11
GAMBLING: IT *IS* ALL ABOUT
THE MONEY

In gambling, the substance used and abused is money. Typically, the social gambler starts by placing small bets, which become larger simply because larger bets can lead to larger wins. For instance, a one-dollar lottery ticket may have a potential win of $500, whereas a ten-dollar lottery ticket may have a potential win of $5,000. Social gamblers say, "It's more fun, besides, I can afford it." State lotteries are well aware of this type of reasoning and were quick to capitalize on it, expanding from fifty cent tickets to multi-dollar tickets, and from weekly drawings to daily drawings and then to twice-daily drawings. State lotteries today also offer many more games, designed to appeal to all groups of players, from college-age males with interests in sports to little old ladies who prefer slot symbols like cherries and Lucky Sevens.

The old-time penny slots required one, a nickel or a quarter per pull of the handle for each play, but advances in technology and the casino's escalating efforts to increase the profit-margin, have expanded slots which now have multiple plays for each pull of the handle or push of a button, with three or five reels at a time. Thus a penny machine may cost a penny, fifty or even ninety cents per play, every four seconds. Casino slots can easily cost as much as $500 per play for a fifteen second bet or up to $2,000 per minute. To make this form of gambling even simpler, today's casino slots no longer are slowed down by inserting coins or dollar bills; rather, now the slots player simply needs to insert a plastic "fun card" and play off the credits, typically twenty-five cents per credit. But no matter whether a gambler plays a slot machine or buys a lottery ticket, the result is an instant outcome, either a win or a loss, with a push on the button, or a scratch on a lottery ticket, the outcome is an instant reward or an instant loss.

Of course, all of this use and abuse of money begs a question or two. One might ask, what is this whole emphasis on *money,* what are the money *influences* or *needs* that lead the gambler from social and occasional gambling to out-of-control, devastating gambling, from occasional wins to 20- or 30-game losses of increasing amounts? One might also wonder, Why does someone become addicted to gambling, a money addiction, instead of to compulsive shopping?

FAMILY EMPHASIS ON MONEY

Parental influence on money is distinguishing factor between gambling and other addictions. Many compulsive gamblers grow up in families in which one parent, usually the father, places a strong emphasis on money. This emphasis on money is exhibited in a number of ways in different families, imprinting on the young child/future compulsive gambler during its formative years the importance and impact of money.

There is also another emphasis on money within the family that leaves a strong impression on the child and that establishes the meaning and importance of money; namely, when the child grows up in an affluent, usually highly respected or visible family, and the child feels the self-imposed pressure to live up to the family's social and economic standard of living. Yet invariably, these parents will protest, "We never wanted or demanded that our child be a financial success, we just wanted our child to be healthy and happy."

Nevertheless, there are a number of factors relating to money in the compulsive gambler's family of origin, in the marital family, and in the community, which are a driving force in developing a gambling addiction, rather than another form of addiction.

FAMILY POVERTY

Many compulsive gamblers recount growing up poor, some even in extreme poverty. This forced Dad to work long hours simply to provide basic needs, such as food and housing, and coming home tired or after children were in bed. "I lived in the hills of Tennessee. It wasn't until my high school graduation that I got my first store-bought clothes." Even when the family's financial circumstances improved, and they moved to a better neighborhood, the gambler had difficulty adjusting to the new environment and strangers. "I felt that I was never accepted by the other kids."

PARENTAL ALCOHOLISM

Many compulsive gamblers report having an active alcoholic father when they were growing up. The father often has an unstable work history, getting fired, arrested for alcohol-related incidents, or suffering poor health. What are the consequences? Lack of income, increased expenses, and ongoing financial instability.

PARENTAL GAMBLING

When Dad is the compulsive gambler, household finances suffer: no money for rent, food, clothes, school activities, utilities, but also many dunning letters and phone calls from bill collectors. In addition, Dad may also be facing legal charges and jail for stealing money to support his gambling addiction. As one child of a compulsive gambler stated, "The worst part was hearing my friends talk about my dead-beat dad."

MONEY RULES

Many of the income-producing fathers define their love for the family by "working hard and supporting them." In low income families, Dad was forced to work, thus also became the absent parent. The child soon learned that not having money means Dad was not at home. The child also learned that Dad being a workaholic also meant that Dad was not home. One son reported that he felt the impact of money from both parents: "My dad was always working to support us and he would come home exhausted. He never had time for me. Mom just bitched at him to clean out the garage, so one day I did it for him, I spent all day cleaning it and then I painted the walls with some paint that was there. I figured Dad would have more time for us. When he came home, he just hugged and hugged me. When Mom saw it, she yelled at me because I should have used the cheaper paint. It was always about money with her and with Dad."

MONEY EQUALS SELF-WORTH

Many compulsive gamblers believe that "net-worth equals self-worth." Stated negatively, "Lack of financial success equals lack of self-worth or being a failure." Especially in the United States, the person who appears to be rich is treated with greater respect than the person on welfare or standing in the food line. Unfortunately, the poor person then might himself ascribe to the belief that "I am what I *don't* have. I'm a bum."

MONEY EQUALS SECURITY

This dependency on money can lead to an underlying fear of depending on others or ending up in poverty. "I'd rather do anything than risk being rejected by others or constantly living in fear. Gambling offered me that security. At least when I was winning."

MONEY EQUALS POWER

Having money for many people means "I can do what I want and buy what I want." As some children of compulsive gamblers have admitted, "My dad used to say he'd rather be guilty and rich than not guilty and poor. I learned early on that having money means you can get away with things. He'd tell me to be honest, to do the right thing, and then he got the cops to throw away his parking tickets. It was very confusing, especially when he bragged about it. He also bragged about buying votes on election day. Money was power and gambling is all about money."

MONEY EQUALS PRICE

With this type of thinking, an object is viewed as costing xxx number of dollars instead of being seen as an object of beauty or talent. So many times, children in these families hear, "How much did that jacket cost?" instead of "That jacket is beautiful and you look stunning in it."

MONEY EQUALS LOVE

"My mom always preached to my dad that a friend of theirs lavished his wife with expensive gifts. She'd tell dad that 'Joe really loves his wife. Look what he's always buying her.' So that's why he was always working, and I never had a dad. I would never do that to my kids." But he did when he became a compulsive gambler. He learned to love Lady Luck and ignored his children during those gambling periods.

THE VALUE OF MONEY

"My parents always gave me anything I wanted. Cost didn't matter. I never had a savings account, and I didn't understand the value of money until I was broke. I'm an accountant. I developed and worked million-dollar budgets for companies, but never had my own budget. I always knew the price of items, instead of the joy that item might bring. I would brag about owning a ten thousand dollar painting but never noticed the beauty of the painting."

SPENDING OF MONEY

It is fairly typical of gamblers, at least of action gamblers, to have the attitude of "Buy today, pay tomorrow." This attitude seems to carry over in all forms of spending, not just on gambling, in which credit cards are charged to the maximum or above.

Is it then surprising that gambling, or quick money, appeals to these sons and daughters? Later in life, these compulsive gamblers almost universally will say, "It's not about the money" and that certainly has some truth to it at a conscious level, but subconsciously, their early childhood influences contribute to the development of an underlying emotional vulnerability or the emotional attachment to money. "The absence of money caused the problems and having money will prevent them," becomes an ingrained part of their belief system. Gambling wins ease those tensions and bad feelings. Being without money just isn't an option for them.

THE COMMUNITY, GAMBLING AND MONEY

In our capitalistic society, the emphasis on money for prestige and social acceptance is also expressed in individual communities. Some of these communities are noteworthy for their influence and impact. While financial goals or "bottom line" are not necessarily disreputable or undesirable, they do contribute to the compulsive gambler's conviction that money is essential for acceptance. There are several of the more common ones which bear scrutiny.

ACCEPTANCE OF GAMBLING IN THE UNITED STATES

Gambling has had its proponents and its opponents since the founding of this country. At the present time, the emphasis is on legalizing more and more gambling opportunities. This trend was started with the implementation of state lotteries in the 1960s, followed by the expansion of Las Vegas casinos, Native American casinos, slots at race tracks which are now termed racinos card clubs, and slots in other locations not associated with casinos or race tracks. The reasons for this expansion are rationalized as new sources of revenues for declining state coffers, new jobs to local communities, and prevention of the demise of the horse racing industry. These newly established casinos and racinos are privately owned and listed on stock exchanges, marketed as legitimate businesses rather than the organized crime syndicates of Vegas casinos in the past. The legalization of casinos in 1976 led to the newest gambling haven, Atlantic City.

Lotteries, on the other hand, were operated by state governments. The argument for establishing them was that anticipated income would provide funds for social services and education. Government-sponsored gambling gave state lotteries "the Good Housekeeping stamp of approval." Buying lottery tickets was promoted as fun and recreation while serving as an act of civic responsibility. Those who objected to state lotteries protested that it turned state government into a bookie.

The concern by the gaming industry and state governments regarding compulsive gambling to this day remains rather minimal. The current trend of the gaming industry is to encourage gamblers to "gamble responsibly." This does not equate to financially supporting a community service, such as a local business might offer, nor does it address the need for education, prevention, treatment, and research into compulsive gambling.

In more recent years, state lotteries have acknowledged this concern by allocating funds from lottery profits or from their general budget. Nevertheless, this funding may at the maximum be four or five million dollars a year in a few states with large populations, while many more states allocate either minimal amounts, perhaps $100,000 for a hotline, or none at all. Most state lotteries publish an 800 helpline number on their tickets and some literature; unfortunately, these hotlines for the most part are limited to making referrals to Gamblers Anonymous because of the lack of treatment centers and trained therapists who are knowledgeable about compulsive gambling.

This cultural acceptance of myriad forms of legal gambling has dramatically increased the number of gamblers and thus also compulsive gamblers. Funded research indicates that the number of gambling addicts ranges from two to four percent of the adult population in the United States, or between three and five million addicts, while Gamblers Anonymous suggests that the number of compulsive gamblers more likely is closer to ten million.

ACCEPTANCE OF GAMBLING BY ASIAN CULTURES IN THE UNITED STATES

Gambling is more culturally accepted in some Asian countries than in other countries throughout the world. Japan at the present appears to be in the forefront. Notable is the high number of Japanese gamblers at Hawaiian casinos, and although this may be a consequence of geography, Japanese are also the largest number among Asian gamblers seen in Las Vegas casinos. One hypothesis is that as a thriving nation, Japanese citizens have more money to spend. Whereas this is merely an observation rather than based on rigorous or any research, it does appear to be true at least at the present time. This may change in the future, as casinos become more prevalent in other Asian communities: Singapore, China, Vietnam, for example, and in American states with Asian populations.

EDUCATION AND INCOME

The commitment to higher education and hard work is a personal standard. Whereas most assuredly there are many businessmen who lack extensive formal education, more often the road to financial success is through education. State lotteries are cognizant of this fact, thus proceeds of lottery sales are designated for education; however, often there is no increase of monies for education, but rather a diversion of funds from one budget item to another.

COMPETITION FOR FINANCIAL GAIN

Along with education and occupation in the American mind-set is the promotion of competition and winning, which in the financial arena brings its monetary rewards. Thus a competitive person is more likely to seek out competitive activities in which the end result is money. Not surprisingly, competitiveness is an essential personality component required to be a compulsive gambler.

JEWISH COMMUNITIES

Gamblers Anonymous has a disproportionately high number of Jewish members. Whereas the Jewish population in the

United States accounts for approximately three percent of all Americans, within Gamblers Anonymous, it is more likely to be twenty to thirty percent. This may be due to the emphasis on financial success expressed in the Jewish culture in statements such as "My son the doctor" or "My son the lawyer." Notably, is the observation that a disproportionate number of lawyers gambling in Vegas casinos consider themselves to be professional gamblers. In contrast, physicians and dentists rarely tend to become compulsive gamblers. Again, this may be due to personality characteristics, competitiveness being essential, whereas excellence or skill are not. A caveat must be mentioned: the high percentage of Jewish members in the past and currently were action gamblers; today approximately half of all compulsive gamblers are escape gamblers. This does not necessarily suggest a preponderance of Jewish gamblers. It could suggest that Jewish gamblers are more likely to seek psychological treatment sooner than non-Jewish gamblers.

FINANCIAL OCCUPATIONS

In the United States and most advanced communities, as opposed to third world countries, the object of value in gambling is something of monetary value. Again, research has not been conducted in this specific arena, yet it seems that a higher number of individuals working with finances, in which the goal is also the bottom line, become compulsive gamblers. Among businesses, these are the owners of automobile dealerships or manufactured products. These are also the super salespersons, usually males, who distinguish themselves not only by being the company's highest producer, but also the regional and national standard bearers of successful sales, and consequently higher income and bonuses. This higher income is a leading contributing factor to gambling higher amounts of money – the high rollers and whales of casino customers.

Other larger groups of compulsive gamblers include accountants, bankers, stock brokers, and financiers. Their occupation centers around earning profits for themselves or for their clients. In order to rank among the more successful, they also need to be highly motivated, competitive, and have a talent for understanding numbers. These are qualities seen universally among compulsive gamblers. They may not reach the level of a Bernie Madoff, but members in these groups are greater than those of other occupations and professions seen in GA and professional treatment programs.

The implementation of state lotteries led to many new gamblers, especially blue collar workers and minorities who now could afford the lower cost and who also had easy access to gambling. This led to an increase of compulsive gamblers, particularly delivery personnel, cashiers, or office managers in which the individual handles money.

SOURCES OF MONEY FROM PERSONAL ASSETS

What, then, are the gamblers' sources of funds to support their gambling? Some basic generalizations and patterns have been identified over the years, based on research, hotline data, treatment program statistics, media reports, gamblers' anecdotal accounts, cultural histories, literature, and personal experiences. These can be grouped into general categories, with the caveat that the onset of gambling and access to money to support this gambling varies with age, sex, and other determinants.

PERSONAL FUNDS

Most gamblers initially use their own funds for gambling. Of course, there are always exceptions, such as when a child purchases a lottery ticket out of a vending machine with money given to it by a parent. This is illegal because the child is a minor;

nevertheless, the child is gambling, whether with its own money or someone else's money. Another frequent occurrence is that a father or grandfather, uncle or family friend will take the teenage son to the race track and give him money to pick a horse and then place the bet for that teenager, usually a boy around the age of 15 or 16. Ask any man addicted to race track gambling and he will acknowledge that a close male figure introduced him to horse racing when he was in his teens. This introduction to gambling appears to be universally true among race track addicts and not of those gamblers who prefer some other form of gambling.

ALLOWANCE

This source of funds is virtually universal: it is pocket money that the gambler may spend without too much supervision from parents. Young boys typically start their gambling on pitching pennies and purchasing packets of baseball cards or Pokemon cards, hoping for the winning one. They use their allowance for this. It is conceivable, that with the changes in society's view of gambling and the ubiquitous forms of gambling, girls will start gambling at an earlier age than before and also use their allowance for the purpose of gambling.

NEIGHBORHOOD JOB EARNINGS

Many male gamblers report having had their own paper route and lawn care jobs, using that money for gambling. Teenage girls use their earnings from babysitting.

CHURCH DUTIES

Others, usually boys rather than girls, report taking jobs as acolytes, officiating at weddings and at funerals to earn extra money which they use for gambling, even at that early age.

PART-TIME JOBS

As they get older, they get more permanent part-time jobs after school and during summer vacations. Many compulsive gamblers report working long hours after school to help support the family and then also using the money for their own gambling, hoping to win more and thus work less. A particularly troubling example is that of a father insisting that the son forego any activities after school and instead work in the father's grocery store, resulting in poor social awareness and development. The son turned to gambling, protected himself from a loan shark, and now is serving a life sentence in a Michigan prison.

SAVINGS ACCOUNTS

Having a savings account during childhood or adolescence is the exception rather than the norm for compulsive gamblers; nevertheless, those that do have a savings account very quickly tap into their piggy banks and savings stored at home, and later in savings accounts held by their parents or a bank.

Teenage girls going to play bingo in their church with Mom or Grandma might use their own pocket money and allowance, but more often are treated to a "Ladies Night Out" evening with the family. Bingo under these circumstances tends to be viewed as an acceptable social church activity and fund-raiser, rather than in a more legalistic view of "Bingo is gambling." Today, bingo is associated more with gambling on Indian reservations and in huge bingo halls, all day, every day, which are operated by professionals, instead of members of the church for three hours on a Friday evening, with cakes and pies donated by church members.

Adult gamblers follow a similar route, using pocket money first, then taking money out of the household entertainment budget, or using some money out of the paycheck. The gambling is controlled, and money used for this social gambling is extra, available, and not designated for bills or other commitments initially.

TEMPORARY QUICK FIXES

Temporary fixes are funds that a gambler is able to get quickly through a variety of means, but usually with the intent for timely repayments. If this social gambling increases and becomes problematic, the gambler may seek other forms of funding that are less risky or may take a step closer to becoming addicted. In that case, there are more options for getting the money rather than the ones listed previously.

BORROWING

Social gamblers may borrow small amounts of money from a friend, family member, or gambling partner. Typically, this starts toward the end of a gambling spree, when it is at closing time, the time to go home. Or a desire to gamble "just one more time." It is repaid the following day or as agreed upon between them. Compulsive gamblers, though, eventually are unable to repay loans.

BETTING WINS

Whereas initially betting wins were saved or used for a special purpose, the monies won now are used to place more and larger wagers. Wins of money or a free lottery ticket can lead to increased frequency of gambling, from one day a week to several days per week, and from one dollar tickets to five or ten dollar tickets.

PAWNING OWN BELONGINGS

Finding themselves in need for more wagering money, adolescent or adult gamblers may pawn their own items of value: the first edition comic book, rare baseball card, Gameboy, or Kindle.

SELLING BELONGINGS

Interests and hobbies change as a youngster becomes an adolescent or adult. Collecting comic books or Barbie dolls may no longer have the appeal it once had, so the gambler is willing to sell off all or part of the collection, at times keeping the more valuable and scarce comic books or dolls. In advanced stages of problem gambling, selling possessions can include also selling jewelry, computers, antiques, or other items of greater value.

CREDIT CARDS

College students receive many solicitations to open a credit card account. One eighteen-year-old college freshman opened a small charge account at a local department store, which enabled him to get a charge account in two other stores in his own name and thus establish a good credit rating by the time he was nineteen years old. He accepted the solicitations from Visa and Master Card and was able to get cash advances. Within one year, he owed ten thousand dollars. Thus by the age of nineteen he had a poor credit rating, which lasted well into his twenties.

ADVANCE ON PAYCHECK

Getting a paycheck in advance is generally quite simple for an employee who is single and without family expenses or obligations. It just means tightening the budget a bit and spending less, watching TV instead of going out for dinner or to the game. However, if the income earner is married, the excuses will start: "The boss put in a new payroll system, the boss was out, I lent some money to my partner" or similar seemingly good reasons and acceptable excuses. Of course, by this time, the gambling and the debts have escalated.

LONG-TERM FIXES

In addition to quick fixes, the gambler is adept at finding many other sources for gambling money, such as second mortgages, home equity loans, demand notes, or cash value on insurance policies and when these are no longer possible, turning to illegal activities. It can be said that virtually every compulsive gambler eventually has used up legal access to money and has turned to illegal acquisitions of money.

SUMMARY

Concepts of the meaning of money and its power are developed in early childhood based on family of origin attitudes and behaviors and the influences of the community. Money becomes the substance of abuse during compulsive gambling, resulting in severe financial strain and indebtedness. These debts may hinder the gambler's recovery if others in the family help pay them, as this is yet another form of bail-out in which responsibility for the financial chaos is "shared" with others rather than the gambler taking full responsibility for the financial impoverishment. Financial planning and adhering to budgets is difficult for the gambler whose mind-set is often, "Let's spend it now, I can earn more tomorrow." Thus, financial stability becomes an important ingredient in abstinence and recovery from gambling addiction.

However, faced with legal and illegal debts, without access to money, and confronted with continuing negative impact on the family, poor work or school performance, co-morbidity and other health problems, legal issues, and without emotional support or professional treatment, it is predicable that the gambler will suffer emotional and physical collapse, leading to jail or death, often by committing suicide. Money made gambling possible, lack of money led to addiction and devastation.

CHAPTER 12
IMPACT ON THE FAMILY

A Wife's Story

She stood there stunned, clutching the certified letter, her hands trembling. The letter from the bank was a foreclosure notice on their house. Foreclosure? How could that be? *Our bills are always paid on time, never late*, she thought.

The phone rang. She saw it was from the bank and was too scared to answer it. Should she call David at work or wait until he came home? Should she let David take care of it? No, he would just give her another story, like in the past. She became aware of his lying about a year ago when the trouble with the paychecks started. They were different almost every time: smaller amounts, late, extra taxes withdrawn. And David always had good reasons for it: a new payroll clerk, new computer system, holidays, revised work schedules, the economy. It was always something, but David sounded sincere. He told her to cut down on expenses. But she didn't trust his excuses anymore; she knew some of them were lies. Why the lies? What on earth was happening?

She decided to call the bank. "I received this foreclosure notice today. Can you explain it to me? What, no payments in seven months? Monthly overdue notices unanswered. Are you sure? We always pay our bills on time."

She couldn't believe what she was hearing. Up until a few months ago, she paid the bills as soon as she got them and David mailed them on his way to work. He even picked up the mail from the post office on the way home and he never mentioned that they were behind in any bills. She went to get the checkbook, but remembered that David was paying the bills now at the office. "So you can spend more time with the babies," he had told her. That was so considerate of him. At the time, she never had any suspicions that something might be amiss.

But were the bills being paid on time? When the credit card company called a few months ago about an overdue payment, she thought it was a mistake. She didn't even bother to tell David and he was so tired all the time, working extra hours. When several credit card companies called, she was convinced it was a case of identity theft. They had only two credit cards, one for her and one for David in case of emergencies. She didn't like credit cards. Use cash and pay the bills before they become due, that was her way. Now five different credit card companies were calling about chronic late payments, no payments, charging over the limit, and threatening to cut off their accounts. It had to be identity theft.

David came home late and got really angry when she told him about the foreclosure notice. "Can't anyone do anything right anymore?" He was going to speak to the bank manager and take care of it since she obviously didn't know how. By now, she was feeling more confused and scared. What was going on?

What happened to their life? They were married five years ago, bought the perfect house near her parents, had their little girl a year later, agreed she would be a stay-at-home mom to take care of both their daughter and the new baby. They had good friends, good health, they used to go on exciting vacations, and occasionally, they went to the casino for dinner and a show, invited by David's host. A host? Comps? What's that?

David loved his job: he was the top salesman in the company, earning good money, was well-liked, and worked hard. He was even promised a promotion to regional manager. Nothing could have been better, that is, until about a year ago when the boss decided to give the promotion to someone else. David took it hard, but she knew he would get over it, he always did, he was an achiever.

But instead, David felt cheated and betrayed. He was angry at first, then became more and more withdrawn. He lost interest in his job and his accounts went down. Gone were the bonuses, but now they had two babies and house payments. On top of that, the car broke down and the roof needed to be repaired. Their savings account was down to zero.

The bank called about a bad check. Her mom and dad lent them money; it was hard but David promised them, "Just until I get over this slump." He even took a part-time job and came home late. She lied for him when he was too tired to go to work and told his boss that "David is sick."

"Talk to me, David. Tell me what is going on?" She pleaded, got angry, tried to lure him to bed, cried, but nothing helped. He had this huge wall around him. He was yelling at her constantly, "Can't you stop your nagging?" And then he would go out, sometimes for hours and even overnight. For the past several months, he was gone almost every weekend. Was he having an affair? That had to be it. He was good-looking, easy to get along with, women were attracted to him, and maybe that accounted for the missing monies. How dare he? They didn't have time or money to be with friends or to go places like they used to. That had to be it: he had a girlfriend.

The phone kept ringing and ringing, all day long. Not again. Should she answer it? It was probably another bill collector. Stop ringing! She covered her ears, her heart was pounding, she couldn't breathe. The doorbell rang. It was the man from the gas company to turn off the gas. "No, no, no, you can't do that. It's winter, we need gas for heat. We have two babies. Please don't shut it off, please don't. Call my husband, he'll take care of it." The man phoned the gas company and got a one-week extension. After he left, she just hunched up on the couch and sobbed for hours. What happened? Her life was totally out of control. It was a nightmare.

She knew they needed help so she called her parents. She was shocked when she learned that they had lent David another five thousand dollars. "He never repaid us one dime. David asked us not to tell you. He didn't want you to be upset." They were fed up with his lies and gambling. "Get rid of that bum." She couldn't. She loved him and the children needed their dad. Her pastor said the congregation would pray for her and her family. She needed money, not prayers. Her doctor prescribed tranquilizers, but how could she take them when she was responsible for their two little ones? She went to a lawyer, but he wanted a three thousand dollar retainer "to protect yourself." How was she to find three thousand dollars? Maybe she should get a job, but she could barely earn enough to pay for day care.

She felt like she was going in circles, she had constant headaches, couldn't sleep at night, and was always too tired to do anything. She finally told her closest friend, Susie, feeling embarrassed but so desperate for help.

Susie listened. "Let's call Gam-Anon. It's a support group for friends and families of compulsive gamblers." "Compulsive gamblers?" "Yes, I think David is a compulsive gambler. He sounds just like my husband did, except Bill likes to drink and David likes to gamble." That night, they went to Gam-Anon, the 12-Step group meeting for family and friends of compulsive gamblers. And life began to change.

Is this exaggerated? No, this is a fairly typical story of the wife of a gambler whose occasional social gambling, occasional trips to the casino with their friends, or the occasional company conventions to Vegas were fun and part of their life. That is, in the beginning, before gambling took over David's life. How could she have been so blind?

In Gam-Anon, she learned that she was an enabler. She learned that as an enabler, she was not responsible for David's gambling; nevertheless, unwittingly she had contributed to it in many ways:

- By fooling herself, convinced that it was just pressures from David's job;
- By ignoring the problems, it wasn't really a problem, at least not at first;
- Letting him take the money out of their savings account;
- Covering up for him by keeping the problems to herself and not telling her parents or friends. It was too embarrassing;
- Covering up for him about missing work and lying to his boss;
- Believing his lies about his absences from work and home;
- Not confronting him about the real money issues and believing his excuses;
- Avoiding their friends because David owed them money;

- Hiding money from him but always giving in when he became too demanding;
- Threatening to leave him, but never following through.

Yes, she was an enabler but never knew it. She had no experience with addictions or money problems, with overdue bills, and lies, but she was learning, and most importantly to her, she was happy that it was only a gambling addiction, a mental illness and not an affair. But how dare they tell her that she was sick too!

She learned that Gam-Anon was for people like her, wives of the compulsive gambler. But there were also other family members in the group: parents, husbands, boyfriend and girlfriends, siblings, even adult children. She learned that compulsive gambling hurts everyone. She realized that David's gambling had affected all aspects of their life: their relationship, their parents, his job, their financial disaster, her health and David's health, David's moods, no more social life or community involvement. Now even possibly, legal charges against David by his boss for using the company credit card. Her story was not very different from those of other Gam-Anon members.

Yes, David's gambling had seriously affected her; she still loved him but it was hard to trust him. At times, she really did not like him, well, at least not his behaviors. She resented that he put his gambling first over the family.

Gam-Anon told her to work on her own issues, get strong and healthy again, one day at a time. "If you change, he will change. Addictions can survive only with enablers and codependents." She felt herself fortunate because David agreed to attend Gamblers Anonymous. Some of gamblers thought they just had a temporary problem and did not attend GA or seek professional help. "That's called denial." She learned that the road to recovery was difficult, but with the help of Gam-Anon, life could be better than before. "You can trust him in everything except with money. Money is the substance of his addiction, he needs money to gamble. So don't trust him with money." She felt bad about that, but on the other hand…?

THE PATH TO THE BOTTOM

(While the non-gamblers can be male spouses, parents, siblings, etc., the phases in this section will speak in terms of the wife of the gambler.)

In the past, spouses stayed in the marriage. Fifty years ago, many of the husbands went to race tracks or flew to Vegas to gamble. There were breaks between gambling sprees, and it took years before they became compulsive gamblers. There were many good days and some bad days. The wives stayed in the marriage because they feared being alone, not having money to support themselves, were too embarrassed to let others know, but always hoping that he would stop, that her love would win over his desire to gamble, or that he would come to his senses about the money it was costing them. This would go on for many years, they could barely make ends meet, there were more and more bad checks, constant arguing, feeling sick, divorce was out of the question, they felt trapped. Some started drinking, others thought of suicide. There was no help. There was no hope.

Today's younger spouses are less tolerant. They have careers to support themselves. They are accustomed to being independent and making their own decisions; they are familiar with addictions; they are more willing to reach out to others for support; and attitudes toward divorce have changed. They aren't willing to stay in a bad marriage. Yes, they will try to make the marriage work, they will insist that the gambler go for counseling, they will set up budgets, but if the gambler hasn't hit bottom, these attempts are futile.

Many of the wives, young and old, do not want to break up their family, despite the turmoil and chaos of compulsive gambling. It is also true that in many instances the gambler is able to hide the gambling. Spending hours on the computer may be mistaken as being hard at work instead of gambling. Staying out late means he is at work. Business owners can manipulate company funds and not use family money. Gambling can, indeed, be a "hidden illness," at least for a little while.

DENIAL PHASE

Once they are aware of the gambling, wives will worry about the husband's absences. "Where is he? Is he at the casino? Maybe he is visiting a friend and forgot to tell me. I can call his office. Was he in an accident?" They wait up, look out the window for his car, pace back and forth. But they always worry. They know he is gambling but try not to think about it. They start to rationalize and make excuses for his gambling: he works so hard, he needs time to relax. So what if he goes to the track or the casino without her? His gambling is only a temporary escape from the pressures, he'll stop.

They question him about the gambling and the unpaid bills, but are easily assured and accepting of his explanations. They become aware of his increased gambling, going to the casino more frequently, or finding losing lottery tickets. "I was cleaning his closet after we separated and got the shock of my life. I found seven shoe boxes filled with losing lottery tickets. I checked the dates and even started putting them in piles according to dates and the amounts. The oldest ones were for fifty cents. Later, he was buying more tickets, sometimes as many as thirty or forty a day. The dollar amounts got bigger. Before he left, he was buying nothing but five and ten dollar tickets. I never knew about it, but now I understand why we were in such a financial jam."

Typically, a wife will start making excuses to his boss for his absences, telling him "David is sick" when in fact he was out gambling the entire weekend. She believes David when he tells her "things cost more these days," like getting the car repaired.

Is that why the mortgage wasn't paid? She tells herself things aren't really that bad financially. Whatever works. But why were the stocks and bonds sold? She is in the classic denial phase.

STRESS PHASE

The denials cannot continue forever. They now have frequent arguments about unpaid bills and his absences. She pays off the money he borrowed from their friends. She doesn't know about the effects of a bail-out. She accepts his apologies and remorse, yet the gambling, lies, and absences continue. She tries to control his gambling, bargaining that he can go to the casino on Saturdays and gamble only a certain amount of money. She went with him to make sure he followed their plan. It worked exactly one hour. He made a scene in front of everyone when she refused to give him any more money. She gave it to him and fled to her room.

She feels humiliated and angry. Instead of trying to help him cut down on the gambling, now she demands that he stop. "This is the last time. You quit or get out." The bills pile up; they get turn-off notices and constant calls from collection agencies. She gets more and more stressed out, angry, and resentful. She finds out that he hasn't been showing up at work. She is too embarrassed to socialize because they don't have the money for it. Friends avoid them because money they lent him hasn't been paid back.

EXHAUSTION PHASE

The gambling and problems don't stop, in fact, everything seems to escalate. She is more confused about bills and can't think straight. "I always seem to get things mixed up. I put grocery money on the kitchen counter, and then, I can't find it. At times, I think I'm going crazy." She starts having physical problems, chronic headaches, sleepless nights and constantly being tired, sick at the stomach and unable to eat, and at times she is too sick to get out of bed. But there is no money for doctors, the dentist, not even for health insurance or house repairs.

This is not what marriage is supposed to be. She gets increasingly angry and resentful.

The gambler yells at her, she yells at the kids. It is total bedlam and she sees no way out. She has no hopes of saving the marriage. Sex? That stopped over two years ago. Neither one even mentions it. It is too late for divorce. Nothing is left, nothing except suicide. She looks at bottles of sleeping pills in her hands. She is exhausted and has "hit bottom." If she is fortunate, someone will notice and step in.

What are the effects of compulsive gambling on the spouse? Family turmoil, financial ruin, divorce, suicide. The lucky ones find Gam-Anon and professional help. There are very few Gam-Anon meetings in the United States. Maryland, for instance, has eighteen chapters of Gamblers Anonymous, but two chapters of Gam-Anon. Some states have two or three chapters of Gamblers Anonymous, others have none; many states have no chapters of Gam-Anon. For many family members and friends of the compulsive gamblers, the best or only option is to find guidance and comfort through AlAnon. In short, in spite of the unparalleled escalation of legal gambling in the United States today, help for families of compulsive gamblers is very limited, both in 12-Step meetings and professional therapy.

THE ROLES TAKEN BY THE FAMILY

The terms "codependent" and "enabler" swept across the field of substance abuse, in large part due to the efforts of Melody Beattie and her classic book *Co-Dependent No More*. Many of Beattie's wisdoms about alcoholism can also be applied to compulsive gambling. (Note: while the non-gamblers can be male spouses, parents, siblings, etc., for purposes of simplicity, the phases of this section we will use the term "the wife" of the gambler.)

Addictions are based on troubled relationships. Addictions survive because they have the support of codependents and enablers. These typically are the persons closest to the gambler: a spouse, parent, friend, or other loved one. Then there are the people who will sabotage the gambler's efforts at recovery. The road to the bottom is hard. The road to recovery can be just as hard, indeed, harder because of all the damage caused by the gambling addict.

Some of the more common roles taken on by the wife (and others) of an alcoholic are those frequently also seen in families of compulsive gamblers. The wife benefits from these roles, often unknowingly or without deliberate intent.

ENABLERS

Money, or the lack of money, is usually the first sign of problem gambling and ultimately the most prominent feature of this addiction. Not surprisingly, then, the wife will attempt to step in to confront or control the situation. Unfortunately, the wife has unwittingly assumed the role of the enabler, making it possible for the gambler to outwit the efforts of the spouse. Addictions can survive only with the help of enablers. The spouse may also be codependent, fearing dissolution of the marriage and the family.

THE FINANCIER

By far the worst of all roles of the enabler is that of the financier, the person who takes control of the finances. These enablers believe they are doing what is necessary for a multitude of reasons and the most damaging one, the acts that will enable the gambler to continue acting out the addiction, is that of the "bail-out." "The bookie will hurt Jim if he doesn't pay off" or "I can't let Jim go to jail because of the bad checks." So the enabler bails out the gambler on the seemingly sincere promise of "I'll never gamble again." More accurately, the gambler has been absolved of the responsibility and still has access to more money and the bookie. Financial enablers are convinced that the gambler has learned his lesson, there will be no more gambling, no more debts, and life can get back to normal. Bailouts to compulsive gamblers is like giving a bottle of whiskey to the alcoholic. They temporarily relieve the gambler of the pressure of debts and guilt.

THE BUDGETER

The financial enabler of the family takes on other duties, desperately trying to set up and maintain a budget, to pay the bills before utilities are shut off, and to avoid late fees, interest charges, and other penalties of unpaid bills. They strive to make a budget and to adhere to the budget, repeatedly, by paying the gambler's debts, cutting back on expenses, cosigning for loans, selling items of value. They may take on a part-time or full-time job. They soon recognize the futility of setting up a budget. It is a losing battle because the money required for these budget items has been lost on the slots or the horses, casino, lottery, or bookie.

THE COMPTROLLER

The financial enabler may take on an additional role—that of the comptroller. This enabler seeks to reduce the financial damage by predetermining how much money can be used for gambling. The intentions by both may be sincere, but as soon as the gambler has lost that money, he more often will make a scene or use other manipulations until she gives him additional money. There is no rigorous research to prove that compulsive gamblers are capable of long-term controlled gambling even though that is their dream and goal when confronted but before hitting bottom.

THE BENEFICIARY

Another role of the financial enabler in the earlier stages of compulsive gambling is when the wife herself seeks to benefit from the gambling. "Look at what the casino is offering us. Free dinners, free shows, gifts: we might as well take advantage of it. After all, we paid for this through his gambling." Unfortunately, this sends a message to the gambler that she has no objections to his gambling, and the addiction continues.

THE LIAR

In most instances, the wife is described as honest and responsible, but as the gambling increases, she will resort to covering up for the gambler. She informs the boss that the gambler is late for work or absent due to "illness" or a death in the family. Late or non-payments of loans or other debts are explained because of unexpected and high financial costs. They resent having to lie but feel trapped into it.

CODEPENDENTS

Whereas the enablers focus on the gambler and the gambling, the codependents are the people who have emotional needs and seek support from the gambling addict to meet these needs. Thus while they may appear to be strong, in fact they tend to seek support for themselves. "I love him and I need him, it's as simple as that." For the compulsive gambler who has been a loner all his life and now feels guilt-ridden by his gambling, this "clinging" only serves as an extra weight for him to bear.

ESCAPE FROM BOREDOM

Many spouses admit that a major attraction to the gambler was the excitement the gambler had to offer. "He was bright, knowledgeable, personable, liked by others, fun to be with. It was easy to fall in love with him." The gambler offered her the means to escape boredom and the routine of daily life.

ESCAPE FROM RESPONSIBILITIES

Most gamblers, whether action or escape, want a normal life. This means the gambler works, the wife becomes a stay-at-home mom. The gambler makes major decisions, manages the finances, handles the checkbook, prepares the income tax statements. The wife's responsibilities lie in taking care of the children and the home. It is something they both want. It is not until the gambling has become out of control that the wife recognizes the need to step in and take over some of these responsibilities.

MOTHER SUPERIOR

Compulsive gamblers like to be in control. They will do whatever is necessary to avoid being controlled. They do not like to give it up. "First, I was controlled by the nuns at school, and now I have Mother Superior trying to control me at home. You should see the looks she gives me. She didn't have to say anything, I got the message." Taking on the role of Mother Superior may serve the wife's needs but even minor incidents turn into demands and emotional upheavals.

THE MARTYR

"You poor thing, I am so sorry you have to put up with him." Such are the comments from others, reinforcing the wife's martyrdom.

She complains about the gambling, the debts, the nasty calls from collectors. "I have to do everything, poor me" is her mantra. "I should have never married him. Now we have kids, now it's too late."

THE HEROINE

This wife sees herself as the heroine who gallantly tries to save the family from falling apart. She takes over, handles financial disasters or whatever other problems as they come along, and puts up a good front. However, who takes care of the heroine? No one, at least not until the heroine herself is exhausted from all the burdens, so she bravely carries on, perhaps even to the point of taking desperate actions.

THE NEED TO BE NEEDED

Conversely, this wife sees herself more in the role of weakness and inabilities. She needs someone to take care of her. She needs to take care of him. They are dependent upon each other. She must stay in the marriage, how else can she help him, the man she loves who is so dependent upon her? So she subjugates her own needs to serve others. Where would he be without her? Where would she be without him?

MAINTAINING DISTANCE

There are many ways of controlling others: the gambler's choice is through money and verbal manipulations. The wife uses other means, the most frequent one being to withhold sexual intimacy. While this may satisfy her needs of getting even or to protect herself emotionally, in fact, it only serves to reinforce the gambler's sense of being rejected.

The wife can also maintain emotional distancing through silence, psychological abuse, and through threats of separation.

The gambler seeks to please and what better way to accomplish that than through the Big Win and hand her the money, or at least part of the money? Or she may glare at him, without speaking. The message is clear: "I don't like what you're doing, I am angry, very angry." One gambler said he felt "completely confused when I came home after three days at the casino. I expected a verbal lashing, temper, and tears. Instead, she just looked at me and smiled. She smiled the whole night. I had no idea what was going on. That was worse than the fights and tears."

Or the wife may actually take advantage of the gambler's fear of separation: she may carry out those threats. "I was always afraid she would kick me out of the house. Sometimes, I stayed at a friend's house, because I didn't feel good enough about myself, she deserved better. But I really fell apart when she left."

THE PROTECTOR

Enablers are also protectors. They cover up or deny the gambling and the financial mess it has created. Why do they cover up? Because money is the basis of our society. How can a banker who is a gambler be trusted with money? How can a gambler be trusted with company funds or clients' escrow accounts? The gamblers either get fired or they don't get hired once their addiction is discovered. So enablers cover up. These enablers are convinced they are being protective of the gambler and the family; in reality, their actions extend the period of compulsive gambling. "He's under so much pressure from work."

THE SABOTAGERS

Being a compulsive gambler or living with a compulsive gambler is like war and "war is hell." So why would anyone want to return to hell? Why would anyone interfere with the gambler's attempts at recovery? It doesn't make sense, yet sabotaging the gambler's attempts at abstinence and recovery to a healthier way of life may be innocent and unknowingly, but this is not always true. This wife's sabotaging has a very definite purpose. "I was afraid for him to get a clear head and see me for who I really was. What if he decided I wasn't good enough or I had too many of my own problems? What if he decided our marriage would never work out? I couldn't let that happen. As long as he was gambling, I was safe." The many stories heard in Gamblers Anonymous and Gam-Anon meetings are testimony to that.

THE REWARD

"He was really doing well. The bills were getting paid off. He went to GA, I went to Gam-Anon. He made new friends, we were doing things together instead of yelling at each other. I was so proud of him. So for his first year anniversary of abstinence, I bought him a beautiful recliner with heat and massage and I could hardly wait to see his surprised face. I was stunned when I saw his reaction. Instead of being happy, he was drowning in guilt. He kept saying he didn't deserve it, he had put us through so much misery."

Another wife bought the gambler a new computer. "It never occurred to me that he would go back to gambling in order to pay for it." And now he gambles with it over the Internet.

THE SCAPEGOAT

"As long as we could focus on the gambling, we didn't have to look at our own shortcomings. It was bad even before the gambling and got worse with the gambling. He was always messing up – late for appointment or forget about them, lousy driver, lousy at fixing things around the house." This marriage didn't have much chance for surviving, as long as the gambler was blamed for all the ills in the family. Blaming others is as much fodder for a relapse as the ongoing pressure of meeting financial needs.

Addictions continue to thrive as long as there are enablers, codependents, and sabotagers. To remain abstinent and to attain recovery requires outside help, whether this is professional therapy, 12-Step programs, or both.

THE CHILDREN

The adults, spouses, parents, other relatives are hurt by the addict's gambling, but the young children, growing up in a gambling family, may bear the brunt and the scars of a parent's gambling addiction for many years. These are the stories of children of compulsive gamblers who were in therapy when asked to describe their family as an object, a plant, or an animal:

Dad, who has been a gambling addict for several years. His choice of gambling is shooting craps at the casinos:

> *My family is a tree. Mom is the trunk, I am the branches, my baby sister is the leaves, and Dad? He's the wind that flies through the tree.* (Daughter, 10)

Dad, who has gambled on horse races for many years, going to the track, off-track betting parlors, and racinos:

> *My family is a rose. Mom is the long stem, my brother and I are the flowers, and Dad is the thorns.* (Daughter, 12)

Mom, who has been buying lottery tickets for the past three years:

> *My family is a yo-yo. Mom is the string and we are the yo-yo, going up and down.* (Daughter, 10)

Both parents are addicted to slot machine gambling. The family has been in turmoil for five years:

My family is a closet. Empty. (Son, 17)

Both parents are addicted, the father to alcohol and the mother to bingo and keno:

My family is a vine; we all go in different directions. (Daughter, 16)

Dad gambled on blackjack at the casinos and poker in illegal card clubs:

My family is like a couch. I am the couch, my brothers are the cushions, and Mom is the pillow. (Son, 13)

Dad has been a sports gambling addict for seven years:

My family is us. Mom's the caretaker, Sis is the friend, I'm a nice kid, and Dad? He's a cold-hearted, sinister jerk. He's not in the family. (Son, 12, parents are recently separated)

THE PATH TO RECOVERY

(Again, whereas the non-gamblers can be male spouses, parents, siblings, etc., for purposes of clarifying the phases of recovery this section will speak in terms of the wife of the gambler.)

Just as there are phases in the downward effects of compulsive gambling on the spouse, so there are paths of recovery for her. Recovery depends on many factors: her motivation, her ability, support from family and friends and Gam-Anon, and professional treatment for guidance for her and the family. There will be slips and relapses, but with each step, the gambler and the family can learn and get stronger on their road to recovery.

CRITICAL PHASE

This is the beginning and often the most turbulent. Although the wife may feel hopeful and encouraged by the gambler's efforts, they are now facing the reality of their financial situation. She has come to accept the fact that compulsive gambling is an illness and that he was not in control of his ability to reason and use good judgment, but the bills and debts are real. They will try to work out a budget, but he wants all gambling bills paid off in one year (this is very typical of compulsive gamblers' goals). They struggle setting priorities, and it is hard not to argue or blame. She has learned to stand her ground and refuse to give any more bail-outs in spite of his efforts and demands.

He no longer feels the pressure of his gambling, indeed, he feels good about not gambling. He wants to get closer to his wife, and the very last thing she wants is sex. "How dare he, after all the torture he put me through? It may be good for him, but for me, it is misery." It will take time to restore the sexual relationship.

She struggles with her feelings of resentment and guilt, but they learn to communicate openly and together they resolve issues between them. Slowly. As much as she wants everything to be "cured," she knows that is not a realistic goal. Getting the finances straightened out is realistic. Facing and resolving legal problems is realistic. She wants to be assertive but finds herself "walking on eggs," fearing she might say the wrong thing that will be trigger a relapse. They know it will be difficult, but now they are willing to talk things out and solve problems together.

REBUILDING PHASE

They no longer avoid the subject of gambling and instead talk about the triggers that lead to relapses and how to combat them.

There may be a slip, but they can learn from it: what happened, why, what can each of them do to prevent the next one? They review their budget, is it realistic? Who will handle the money, and how can she be assured that all income will go to her without the gambler feeling angry or demeaned by it? She gets a sense of security instead of disaster.

She feels stronger, becomes assertive, and gains in self-confidence. She relishes being able to make decisions without fear, and solving problems alone and together. She is able to focus on being a family again, working and playing together.

She has learned to overcome the biggest hurdle of all: to talk about compulsive gambling instead of hiding it or covering up. They agree to tell their family and their friends, together, and ask for their support in combating the addiction and in their efforts at recovery from it.

GROWING PHASE

Having faced the damage of the husband's gambling, they have learned to work together on confronting the many challenges rather than making unilateral decisions. She visits her friends and enjoys her hobbies. She is no longer stressed out, afraid, or depressed; instead, she feels relaxed and optimistic. She volunteers at church and once again becomes active in her community. She is able to "smell the roses" and has found serenity.

Addictions hurt the entire family, and the entire family needs help, especially the children. Compulsive gamblers can to Gamblers Anonymous for help. Family and friends have Gam-Anon for support, but there are few, if any, 12-step meetings for adult or young children of compulsive gamblers. Professional counseling can help with individual, group, and family counseling. Some members of the family may need to see a psychiatrist for medical support to overcome depression or intense anxiety. Psychologists focus on addressing the feelings and relationships.

Counselors can teach communication and coping skills and provide training for relaxation and anger management.

Being the spouse of a compulsive gambler is painful, but she and the gambler can restore their lives to one of stability and closeness within the family. They can achieve serenity.

My special thanks to Sheila Wexler for her permission to include the V-Chart of the Effects of Compulsive Gambling on the Wife/Family

A Chart on the Effects of Compulsive Gambling on the Wife

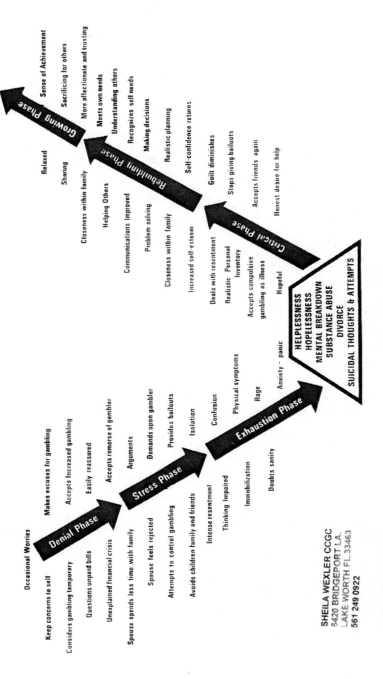

Denial Phase

Occasional Worries
Keep concerns to self
Considers gambling temporary
Questions unpaid bills
Unexplained financial crisis
Spouse spends less time with family
Makes excuses for gambling
Accepts Increased gambling
Easily reassured
Accepts remorse of gambler
Spouse feels rejected
Attempts to control gambling
Avoids children family and friends

Stress Phase

Arguments
Demands upon gambler
Provides bailouts
Isolation
Intense resentment
Thinking Impaired
Immobilization
Doubts sanity

Exhaustion Phase

Confusion
Physical symptoms
Rage
Anxiety - panic

HELPLESSNESS
HOPELESSNESS
MENTAL BREAKDOWN
SUBSTANCE ABUSE
DIVORCE
SUICIDAL THOUGHTS & ATTEMPTS

Critical Phase

Deals with resentment
Realistic Personal Inventory
Accepts compulsive gambling as illness
Hopeful
Closeness within family
Increased self-esteem
Problem solving
Communications Improved
Helping Others
Closeness within family

Rebuilding Phase

Guilt diminishes
Stops giving bailouts
Accepts friends again
Honest desire for help
Self-confidence returns
Realistic planning
Making decisions
Recognizes self needs
Understanding others
Meets own needs

Growing Phase

Relaxed
Sharing
More affectionate and trusting
Sense of Achievement
Sacrificing for others

SHEILA WEXLER CCGC
6420 BRIDGEPORT LA.
LAKE WORTH FL 33463
561 249 0922

© 1981 Sheila Wexler

CHAPTER 13
COMPULSIVE GAMBLING'S
SPECIAL POPULATIONS

Gambling has been part of the American scene since its founding, starting with state-authorized lotteries supporting worthwhile causes, such as education, roads, and the military. It quickly expanded to horse racing, long an English pastime, which became so popular that at times Congress lacked the quorum to carry out its functions. These Congressmen were the genteel gamblers, men who made a social event out of an afternoon at the race tracks. Gambling quickly developed a hierarchy of who was allowed to gamble: Harvard upper classmen could indulge, lower classmen were deemed too immature.

There were other gamblers, the colored men, as they were called then, and they would throw dice in the backfield or gambled outside the race track. They and their ladies also played the numbers. Though illegal, numbers was a part of their culture, in which the colored men and women were allowed to participate. Dream book and socialization, inexpensive and with good odds of winning, were a pleasant diversion from their everyday life.

In 1890, the first slot machine found its way to the local gambling halls, many of them located in New Orleans. They were an instant attraction for entrepreneurs who opened slots parlors, offered drinks and call girls, and who weren't above offering a bribe or two to the local sheriff and politicians. Slots players attracted men and women and were very much a part of the social scene.

Life was very different in the nineteen fifties. There was a strict code of conduct for women. Gambling for women was socially unacceptable, except for bingo, which was usually held in churches or at local events. It was not viewed as "real" gambling. Gambling was for men, young and old, rich and poor. Fifty years ago, the typical compulsive gambler was a middle-aged, middle-class, white male. He had the money, time, and freedom to gamble in Vegas or go to the race track. That image has changed. Now the definition of a gambler and compulsive gambler is male or female, of any race, religion, nationality, or ethnic group, teenager or senior, highly educated or illiterate, wealthy or indigent, whatever the distinction.

At the same time, the Women's Liberation and Civil Rights movements were in full swing: women began to work and have careers, they could travel without husbands, and their social world expanded to allow them to gamble where they chose and with their own monies. Minorities and the less educated had access to gambling and could afford the lower-priced lottery tickets. Computer-savvy teens and young adults could gamble over the Internet.

Playing the lotteries was now a woman's game; it was legal and it was socially encouraged by state lotteries as supporting, as usual, education, health, and social services. Lottery tickets were sold in convenient locations, throughout the day, without restrictions other than selling on credit. Lottery tickets had to be paid for at the time of purchase, not later, although some vendors ignored the rule and accommodated the lottery addicts who would purchase long lists of numbers and in larger denominations. The changes were also observed in slots players. Slots were now available, legally and illegally (gray area machines) at casinos and racinos, a combination of race track and casino.

It's all there: easy to get to, comfortable, attractive surroundings, good food, polite waitresses, friendly staff, and even a host or hostess who sends Christmas and birthday cards. Lose a little, that's to be expected, it is the price for a good time, away from life's drudgeries.

As gambling continued to expand on land and sea, so did the Internet and these thousands of new gambling sites were quick to offer many of the same forms of gambling, betting on sports, horse racing, bingo, card games, and slots. Today's female gamblers had a choice they never had before: should they gamble on land, on boats, or over the Internet? They could choose between physical slots and virtual slots, between games of skill and games of luck, alone or with others, every day or once a week. The question is, who does what and why? What are the differences and what are the similarities between gamblers? Not surprisingly, those at greatest risk were the marginally poor, females, older adults, teens, and people of ethnic or racial minorities.

GENERAL DIFFERENCES

Today, women make up the majority of slot machine players, and in some areas, like Las Vegas, there are more women attending Gamblers Anonymous meetings than men. Why? What attracted women of all social levels and ages to play slots? Why didn't they limit their gambling to bingo and lotteries, which were, considered social gambling and "too passive" to lead anyone to addiction? What are some of these differences?

AGE DIFFERENCES

Men started gambling in their teens, betting on sports and cards. *Women* were in their forties, buying lottery tickets, playing slots or bingo.

LOCATION OF GAMBLING SITE

Older adults gambled in casinos, race tracks, or legal sites.
Younger adults were familiar with computers and gambled over the Internet.

FAMILY ROLES

Homemakers can go shopping, buy lottery tickets at the nearby store.
Working mothers can plan time away from jobs, go to gambling sites.

CONFIDENTIALITY

Internet gambling can be disguised as games, job, or school assignments.
Gambling sites were observable, could not be disguised.

AMBIANCE

Internet gamblers can choose their own gambling sites and comforts.
Land-based gamblers are dependent on the site's activities and players.

LEARNING TO PLAY

Races, games, and sports *require knowledge* of the game, the odds, and experience.
Slots, lotteries, bingo are *purely random*, do not require any skill.

TYPE OF GAMBLER

Action gamblers want excitement, high tension, play for the money.
Escape gamblers want peace, quiet.

GAMBLING PREFERANCE

Sports, cards, dice were *preferred by males* (this is now changing). Bingo, lotteries, slots were *preferred by females* (this is also changing).

MONEY EMPHASIS

Dysfunctional families stress the need for and importance of money. *Healthy* families stress financial stability.

SOME EXAMPLES

Action gamblers grow up in dysfunctional families, with emphasis on money. They convince themselves they need to earn as much as other family members or their peers in order to be accepted. Still others indicate they dropped out of school to help support the family. Escape gamblers more often describe their families as loving and supportive, in which emphasis on money was limited to financial stability, paying bills on time rather than being used as a vehicle to control family members or insist that money was the value of their worth. Spending was within their means and without external pressures.

MALE AND FEMALE SENIORS

It is estimated that three out of four adults live within a thirty mile radius of the nearest casino. Seniors, both male and female, are considered to be most at risk of becoming compulsive gamblers. There are many reasons for this, and unfortunately, these are virtually impossible to overcome with any degree of success.

HEALTH

Seniors tend to suffer from a multitude of aches and pains. Their vision and hearing are impaired, they are more prone to broken bones, may have heart or lung problems, are forgetful, and overall have lost their former state of well-being. They no longer face health and opportunities; instead they face illness, fear, and death.

MEDICAL COSTS

Seniors visit their physician and specialists frequently and take a variety of medicines. They may require costly prescription drugs, new glasses, hearings aids, wheelchairs, walkers, nursing care, or other health needs. Even with Medicare and health insurance, the deductibles and copays costs add up. These costs are even greater if the seniors are a couple, especially if one spouse is disabled or unable to be self-sufficient.

INCOME

Seniors generally do not have the earning capacity they had before. The former aggressive award-winning salesman who would travel across the country is now limited due to health, stamina, and energy. Cost of living goes up, income goes down.

LOSS OF MOBILITY AND INDEPENDENCE

Americans are accustomed to freedom of travel: by air, train, bus, and most of all, by car. Americans are accustomed to getting into their cars at a whim's notice, drive to the nearby supermarket and church, visit friends, and get together with their families. As they reach their senior years, they find that driving at night has become a visual problem, losing their sense of direction, tiring more easily, or being too nervous to drive in the dark or on roads with fast speeds. The cost of buying or maintaining a car may be too high, gas in unaffordable, and they need to depend on others, yet do not want to be a burden. The free bus trip to a casino is most welcome, and the casino floor can accommodate their wheelchairs and walkers. Seniors get special attention from casino hosts.

CHANGE OF SOCIETAL VALUES

Since early childhood seniors were taught that gambling was sinful and immoral, besides being a waste of time and money. Instead they spent time with the family. Today, gambling is promoted as fun and entertainment in a safe and pleasant environment. Senior citizens centers schedule free trips to casinos, with free slots coupons and an opportunity to mingle with others on the bus; churches, firehouses, and other non-profits offer bingo, giving seniors more opportunities to socialize and perhaps win money to supplement their income.

BOREDOM AND LONELINESS

Compulsive gamblers repeatedly admit they are bored and lonely. For seniors, this is an even greater reality, having lost a spouse or closest friend and being limited in former hobbies, interests, and social activities due to poor health, limited funds, and dependence on others. They don't have the options to overcome their boredom and loneliness that they once had. Gambling offers them temporary respite.

FEAR OF DEATH

Young adults are ready to face life's challenges, they feel invincible. Seniors, on the other hand, are faced daily with the likelihood of the death of someone they know or love or of their own death. It prevents them from making an emotional investment in a new friendship. They are leery instead of eager for new challenges.

COUPLES

A more recent phenomenon is that of husband and wife, or partners, both taking trips to casinos and similar gambling venues. As one partner gambles and eventually becomes addicted, the other partner may spend the time sitting in the lounge, having a drink or two, or too many. This can have poor outcomes: developing either a drinking problem or perhaps also a gambling problem. One wife felt she gambled out of loneliness and boredom. "The only time we're together and even talking is when we're driving to the racino." That was their recreation for nearly six years. It led to her gambling addiction and his alcoholism. Neither was willing to help the other because it meant having to stop, which they couldn't without the support and encouragement from the other spouse. They became dependent upon one another, reinforcing the other's behaviors and addiction.

SUICIDE

Statistics have proven that more seniors commit suicide than any other age group. Depression, anxiety, loneliness, boredom, fear of death, poor health, cost of living, all of these seem insurmountable. They are burdened with guilt for their irresponsible behavior and for having lost their children's inheritance. They may not know about Gamblers Anonymous, be too ashamed to attend a meeting, afraid to go out at night, or may lack the means to get to a meeting, which may be too far away from home. They are overcome with a growing sense of helplessness and hopelessness. No one knows, no one understands, and no one is there to help. Suicide may be their only option, and they have more than enough prescription pills, more than any other group of gamblers, to quietly escape, forever.

TEEN GAMBLING

States vary in their definition of illegal gambling based on the person's age, usually 18 or 21. Each year, Atlantic City casinos refuse admission to thousands of minors. Parents have been known to purchase lottery tickets for their child or let the child redeem a winning number at a bank or vendor. This is illegal. It is also illegal for a student to bet with the bookie (bookmaking is illegal), or to be part of a bookie's operation, i.e., a senior taking bets from a student, paying the bookie or the student.

Not too many years ago, high schools in various states conducted casino nights at school, sponsored by parents and teachers, in lieu of the more traditional proms, rationalizing this would reduce drunk driving and accidents. Proms at school with casino nights were deemed safe and acceptable and were not viewed as gambling or illegal, since "funny money" was used instead of legal currency. Teachers and parents operated the games, suggesting casino proms were legal; nevertheless, it was illegal and complaints by parents objecting to casino nights were heard, ending this practice.

WHY DO TEENS GAMBLE?

Young people have limited life experiences to help them make mature decisions. They are repeatedly taught to stay away from drugs and alcohol, but this is not true of gambling. Instead, there are TV announcements, billboards, and Internet ads espousing the fun of gambling and monies to be won. Today's youngsters grow up in communities in which gambling is "normal" behavior.

GET RICH QUICK

Many young people are impulsive and do not consider all their options when having to make a decision. They need money for clothes, dates, and spending money to hang out. What quicker way to get it than through gambling, even if it is illegal?

AVAILABILITY OF GAMBLING

Today's youth know how to use computers. They play games on them, do their homework on them, and use them at school or home. The Internet has hundreds of gaming sites where teens can play for free or for points, leading up to playing for money. They don't have to be 21 to gamble on a computer.

EXCITEMENT

Adolescents like excitement and attention. What better way than to brag about a Big Win, have money in hand, go on spending sprees, buy a new computer, go to concerts with friends, and just have a jolly good time? Life is fun.

ACCEPTANCE

Puberty and teen years are difficult. This is the age when teens want independence while at the same time they want the support of their family. Winning the trifecta at the race track is exhilarating, a time to get the attention and admiration from their peers, to fit in with the crowd. Wins become a chance to brag and flash their money around. Money won is a step towards independence.

POKER TOURNAMENTS

Teen action gamblers study books on gambling strategies and soon develop their own system. They are highly competitive and intelligent, able to focus and concentrate. Poker tournaments appeal to them, and often younger gamblers are the top winners.

There are currently six television networks which carry poker tournaments.

SPORTS BETTING

Sports betting may be illegal, but it is also part of the American character. Once primarily wagering on professional and collegiate sports such as football, baseball, and basketball, today's sports gambling includes betting on the many other sports, including tennis, hockey, and girls basketball. There is no limit on what types of sports are available for betting. Today's adolescent girls participate in sports and bet on sports.

PARENTS WITH PROBLEMS

No one is exempt from illness or disease. It can be frightening to live with a father who is an alcoholic, having to bring him home from the bar, or being beaten by him. A mother may be severely depressed, unable to function for weeks or months, the other parent may be incapacitated, incarcerated, deceased, deployed, or have abandoned the family. Gambling for a few hours on the computer becomes a temporary escape, but dependency on escaping through gambling can also lead to a gambling addiction.

PARENTS WHO DON'T KNOW

Gambling is often referred to as a "hidden" addiction, but in reality, there are many signs of gambling addiction. Similar to alcohol or drug abuse, parents may not be observant of their teen's behaviors and moods, or the parents may rationalize the gambling is part of growing up, thereby becoming enablers to the youth in denial. Teens and parents, more than ever before, face pressures within the family and externally from the community. Gambling is just one of them.

DEPRESSION AND SUICIDE

Depression is common among adolescents and teen suicide ranks high among all age groups. Suicide ideation and attempt is higher among compulsive gamblers than any other addiction. Teens are second only to seniors in their suicidality, partly due to their inexperience with life.

SPECIFIC SIGNS OF AT-RISK YOUTHFUL GAMBLERS

Contrary to popular beliefs, there are many signs that a young person may have a gambling problem. These include:

- Showing an intense interest in gambling and gambling conversations
- Gambling with others or over the Internet
- Bragging about winnings, but minimizing or denying losses
- Using gambling lingo: point spread, bookie, jackpot, vig, or frequent use of "bet"
- Having extra money, or no money at all
- Borrowing money, being slow to repay it, or not repay it at all
- Pawning or selling personal items of value
- Appearing to be listless, sleeping more, eating poorly
- Skipping classes, incomplete study assignments, poor grades, being suspended or kicked out of school
- Dropping out of sports, social activities, avoiding friends and others
- Stealing from friends, classmates, parents, school, or job
- Lying about gambling and non-gambling
- Spending excessive time on the Internet, often in secret
- Disappearing and being unable to account for time, absences
- Being moody, depressed, hyper-anxious, argumentative, irritable

- Making subtle death comments: "I wish I could go to sleep and never wake up"
- Making overt suicidal comments and giving clear indicators of suicidal intent.

In sum, youthful gamblers are at greater risk of becoming gambling addicts than ever before and over other age groups. Unfortunately, there are very few education and prevention programs geared specifically to adolescents.

WHALES: THE ULTIMATE CASINO GAMBLERS

Casino high rollers gamble thousands of dollars. Whales bet in hundreds of thousands or millions of dollars. Being a whale has many benefits; the ultimate of accommodations, gifts, offers, and playing in the millionaires golf course in Vegas.

"Breaking the casino" becomes the goal. When that no longer satisfies, they may turn to gambling on investments and businesses—buying and selling one business after another in order to stay in action and to chase the losses. One such gambler started, bought, and sold over one hundred businesses in two years without realizing that his behaviors were out of control. He was in a virtual continuous state of dissociation and did not cease until he was arrested.

An investment broker's gambling similarly spun out of control after casino games and sports betting could no longer assuage his need to stay action. He turned to day trading and hedging his bets. Chasing led him to ultimately embezzle over two hundred fifty million dollars.

Escape gamblers are unlikely to escalate their gambling into the extraordinarily high wagers, wins, losses and thefts of the excitement, seeking action gambler. Gambling with businesses is a high roller's or whaler's form of gambling. It is too stressful or not desired by the escape gambler who prefers the escape into oblivion. A word of caution: some escape gamblers may also seek the "rush" that is more typically seen in action gamblers.

CULTURALLY DIVERSE GAMBLING AND GAMBLERS

Gambling is as diverse as its gamblers. Who, what, where, when, why, and how of the basic journalistic queries can also be applied to gambling and gamblers. In many cultures gambling is part of rites of passage. This is true of tribal societies, in which sticks, stones, and races are competitive forms of gambling and items of value were determined by the players. Winners were held in high esteem, losers were scorned.

Native American bingo halls and casinos on reservations are a means of economic advancement. Native Americans are also more likely to suffer cross-addiction from alcohol and coaddiction of alcohol and gambling. Treating Native American compulsive gamblers requires knowledge of cultural and historical differences, respecting and including teachings and methods used by medicine men, turning to sweat lodges to cleanse the body and spirit. Although a number of Native American casinos contribute funds for state affiliates of the National Council, their own treatment programs vary, some reservations providing for prevention and treatment programs of Native Americans while others do not.

The Irish: Irish Sweepstakes are as much a part of the Irish culture as breathing. It is the forerunner of today's state and national lotteries, imbedded in everyday life, available everywhere, to everyone.

Hispanics: Demographic studies report high rates of problem gambling among Hispanics in the US. The diversity of populations among Spanish-speaking gamblers requires familiarity with the uniqueness of each country, whether this be Mexican, Puerto Rican, or Cuban, for example. Cock fights are favored by Puerto Ricans, whereas Cubans favor casino games. Generally speaking, Hispanics are more amenable to treatment than other minority groups, i.e., Koreans, which favor resolving such issues as gambling problems within their own, closed societies. Hispanics appear to be amenable to treatment by non-Hispanic therapists, and the language barrier is less among Spanish-speaking gamblers than among Asian gamblers.

Violent or bloody sports: Cock fights, dog fights, and boxing are found in many societies, more accepted among some groups than others. Hispanics in the US and elsewhere favor cock fights. They, along with dog fights, are almost universally a male form of gambling, illegal, and usually held in secret locations. Boxing is equally bloody, wins are equated with conquering rather than outsmarting an animal or person. Compulsive gamblers tend to avoid bloody, violent forms of gambling.

Gambling with friends: The same group of friends may get together to gamble daily or weekly for many hours each time. Their games of choice suggest differences between sexes and forms. Greek men may sit in a tavern for hours playing cards. Caribbean island males can be seen playing dominoes on sidewalks under the sun.

Church gambling: In the United States, church bingo was and still is preferred by elderly women. Bingo was viewed as a fund-raiser for church needs and functions, while also being an opportunity to socialize with other "church ladies." A treatment focus becomes in finding alternative means of socialization for these compulsive gamblers, while still remaining active in church functions.

Among *African-American* men and women "playing the numbers" was associated with dream books and a chance to socialize, while also supplementing their meager funds. Numbers are illegal lotteries; they can be bought for lower amounts, often based on numbers seen in dreams, and offer a better opportunity for winning, without paying taxes on the wins. However, in more recent years there has been an upsurge of compulsive gamblers in this population, especially elderly females. Unfortunately, very little research has been conducted on this specific population;

thus, anecdotal information may suggest an increase in compulsive gamblers among African-Americans, but rigorous research is required to get a better understanding of their gambling habits.

Asian games: Asian gamblers, especially Chinese, Japanese, and Koreans, favor gambling games of superior intellect, cunning, and swift decision-making. Wins can be substantial, but losing is associated more with loss of stature rather than money. Asian casino gamblers in the United States tend to be more affluent and thus these compulsive gamblers also tend to lose large amounts of money.

A particular difficulty challenging professional treatment providers is being aware and understanding individual behavioral differences among cultures—in some societies it is considered disrespectful to look an adult in the eye, or to speak instead of listening. In the "closed society" of certain cultures, such as in Asian communities, it would be unthinkable to "lose face" by not paying off debts. Illegal acts are handled within their societies whenever possible. Similarly, in Orthodox Jewish communities, it is the cultural norm for the family and community to pay off a gambler's debts.

Unwittingly, these families and communities are providing bail-outs and thus are enabling the compulsive gambling to continue.

SUMMATION

Gambling is universal, with culturally and socially defined standards of behaviors. Compulsive gambling is found in all groups and sub-groups, historically, currently, and in the future. Neither gambling, compulsive gambling, nor treatment are static. This suggests that a whole array of treatment modalities are necessary to provide the appropriate care to the compulsive gambler and family members, using both verbal and non-verbal methods, not the least of which is to be able to communicate in the client's language. Thus, a treatment team approach is considerably more desirable.

1972—Husband Mitch Rigel and I at our engagement

The Governor's Council on Drug & Alcohol Abuse

Chairman of the Council
THE HONORABLE MILTON J. SHAPP

Executive Director
DR. RICHARD E. HORMAN

Brochure, Governor's Council on Drug & Alcohol Abuse,

The original Commissioners
appointed by Governor Milton Shapp

The Honorable Milton Berkes
House of Representatives

Mitch Rigel
Yoke Crest, Harrisburg

Rabbi Abraham Twerski
St. Francis Hospital, Pittsburgh

Judy Vicary
Erie County Drug Council

The Honorable Paul Dandridge
Municipal Court, Philadelphia

Mildred Gordon, PhD
Reading Hospital, Reading

Pennsylvania Governor Milton Shapp, Mitch and
I at the opening of the White
Hill Penitentiary therapeutic program in 1974

Mitch and I with my son, Bobby

Our first Christmas together, the day before Mitch's big relapse

1975 Co-founders of the National Council on Compulsive Gambling

Dr. Robert L. Custer, M.D. who started the Brecksville VA gambling treatment program

Monsignor Joseph Dunne, the beloved New York City Police Department Chaplain

Board members of the National Council on Compulsive
Gambling at a 1976 Strategy meeting

Robert L. Wagner, board member of the National Council and
Board Chairman of the Compulsive Gambling Center

Friend and colleague Dr. Alida Glen, Director of Brecksville VA
gambling treatment unit who graciously let me use her library

Chatting with Monsignor Joseph Dunne

Special friends and colleagues—Dr. Tor Meeland, member of
my doctorate dissertation committee, and mentor Dr. Julian
Taber of the Brecksville VA gambling treatment program

1980 opening ceremony of the first residential gambling treatment
center, funded by the MD Department of Health and Mental Hygiene.
Msgr. Joseph Dunne, Lillian Custer, Ruth S. and I

With Jack O, member of the Chicago GA, at a GA conference

At a GA Conference with Robert Wagner, and Cris C, my guardian
angel who introduced me to GA and Gam-Anon, and who spent
many hours with me on the phone during those dark days in 1972

Ruth S., Founder of Gam-Anon and dear friend

Two very special men – Arnie Wexler of the Compulsive
Gambling Council of New Jersey, and Bill B., the only member
in the world to have been a member of GA for fifty years

Mark and Pat Andrews of St. Louis, who started a grass-roots community organization to fight casino expansion

With Robert Walgate, Vice President of the American Policy Roundtable at NCALG and NCAGE-gambling conference

With Rev. Tom Grey, Director, and board member and JoDean Joy
of the National Coalition Against Legalized Gambling (NCALG)
National Coalition Against Gambling Expansion

Speaking at the Annual Conference of NCALG and NCAGE-
National Coalition Against Gambling Expansion

Irving Sacher, Treasurer, National Council and Baltimore GA member,
Lee P. front row, and me with Lillian and Bob Custer, back row, who
testified on casino gambling before a Pennsylvania legislative committee

Attending the national Gambling and Risk-Taking Conference
in Las Vegas, with prolific author Prof. William Thompson,
University of Nevada, Las Vegas and Psychologist Frank Quinn

VALERIE C. LORENZ, Ph.D.

Executive Director

and the staff

are pleased to announce

the opening of

HARBOUR CENTER

the nation's first residential

treatment program for

compulsive gamblers and

their families

Located in downtown Baltimore, Harbour Center consists of two turn-of-the-century red brick buildings, rehabbed and converted into one facility. The first floor is used for administrative offices, classrooms, self-help group meetings, library and a brainstore. The second floor consists of clinical offices, including special rooms for biofeedback, art therapy, and groups. The resident counselor's apartment is on the third floor, as are patients' bedrooms, kitchen, meditation room, and an intern's study.

The

NATIONAL CENTER for

PATHOLOGICAL GAMBLING, INC.

announces its

relocation to

924-26 East Baltimore Street
Baltimore, Maryland 21202

Phone (301) 332-1111

FAX (301) 685-2307

COMPULSIVE GAMBLING HOTLINE

National 1-800-332-0402

The National Center for Pathological Gambling, Inc. is a 501(c)(3) not-for-profit agency. Contributions are tax-deductible.

The Hotline is funded in part by the
Maryland Department of Health and Mental Hygiene.

Announcing the opening of Harbour Center, the country's first privately funded residential treatment center for gamblers and families

Compulsive Gambling Center Founded 1986

Harbour Center opened 1991

Michelle Todd, administrative assistant, with Bill Holmes, Compulsive Gambling Center treasurer

Guests of Dr. James Dobson, Director of Focus on the Family, during a documentary on gambling—with FF staff, psychologist Frank Quinn, South Carolina, Tom Coates of Consumer Credit Counseling, Prof. John Kindt, Esq. University of Illinois, me, FF staff, and Dr. Dobson

Four students from Pikesville Senior High School, Pikesville, MD, who started the Students Against Gambling Addiction, SAGA, with a mom, after filming the Walter Cronkite, Show

SSA William L. Holmes, FBI, Organized Crime Unit, who helped
many of our patients who were in trouble with bookies and shylocks

'A Special Issue of

**JOURNAL
OF
GAMBLING
BEHAVIOR**

Sponsored by the National Council on Compulsive Gambling, Inc.

COMPULSIVE GAMBLING AND THE LAW

Edited by

I. Nelson Rose, J.D. &

Valerie C. Lorenz, Ph.D.

Volume 4
Number 4
Winter 1988

ISSN 0742-0714
JGBE 4(4)293-332(1988)

SSA William L. Holmes, FBI retired, cofounder and strong supporter of the Compulsive Gambling Center, and Harbour Center, its residential treatment program—My professional and personal partner since 1981

Journal of Gambling Behavior

Listing of members of the Editorial Board, including Dr. Lorenz

Henry Lesieur, Founder and Editor of the
Journal of "Gambling Behavior

Department of Sociology and Anthropology
St. John's University
Jamaica, New York 11439

The Pennsylvania State University
Penn State Alumni Association
with sincere appreciation, confer upon

Valerie Lorenz
the permanent title of
ALUMNI FELLOW
for exceptional contribution and personal interest
in the University's Academic Community.

_____
President of the University

_____
Executive Director, Alumni Association

The Pennsylvannia State University Alumni Association
conferred upon me its most prestigious award, Alumni Fellow.
I am #398 of thousands alumni

CHAPTER 14
THE BAD GUYS:
BOOKIES AND LOAN SHARKS

Sports betting has always been a man's form of gambling. The reasons are simple: males were encouraged to play sports since they were young children, they play in Little Leagues or neighborhood teams, they are considered heroes in high school and earn sports scholarships to college. True, in more recent years, girls are also encouraged to participate in sports, have their own teams, and may also win sports scholarships. Nevertheless, betting on sports is still a predominantly man's choice. They play sports, they know sports, they socialize through sports, and they bet on sports. They know it is illegal but rationalize sports betting is okay because "everybody bets on sports." (The bettor in this chapter is considered to be a male.)

Mr. Joey Our Neighbor

Mr. Joey is our neighbor,
he lives in the middle of the block
He calls my dad a lot, my dad calls him a lot.

They talk in secret talks about numbers and nickels and dimes.
I wave to Mr. Joey on my way to school. He's nice.
But my mom doesn't like him.

THE BOOKIES

Bookies are everywhere. They can be the gambler's relative, friend, neighbor, teacher, or boss. They might also have a working relationship with loan sharks. Bookies and loan sharks are the gaming authority of sports betting. Without a bookie, there simply would be no sports betting because it takes two people to make a wager, and without the loan shark, many gamblers would not be able to pay off the bookie to continue gambling. The bookmaker (or bookie, in common usage) calls the line source in Vegas for the betting line. Many bookies use that same line, while others use the line and adjust it to the action taken. "Action" in this case refers to the number of bets and amount wagered that are accepted by the bookie.

Bookmaking is based on credit. Assume a bet is made for one thousand dollars, known as "a dime." If the *gambler* wins, the bookie pays one thousand dollars. If the *bookie* wins, the gambler pays one thousand and one hundred dollars to the bookie. The extra hundred dollars paid to the bookie is the "vigorish" or interest. That's the rule. Payments are made weekly, either directly to the bookie or by the bookie, or through an intermediary, a "runner" for the bookmaking operation.

Bookmaking is illegal (except in Nevada); therefore, it is done mostly in secret. To protect the gambler and the bookie, they use surreptitious means. The bookie may be known as "Joe" and the gambler is known by a number, such as "23," by the gambler's occupation, "the doctor" or an arbitrary designation.

Bookmaking can be highly profitable, especially since this is income that is not declared on income tax returns. Bookies will threaten, cajole, and intimidate through subtle hints at violence in order to collect the money they are owed. Bookies know that they are limited in the use of violence against the gambler; therefore, they use a more subtle approach in collecting their money. An intimidating technique is to make frequent calls to the gambler's workplace, or they may use a guilt-inducing approach, such as "Be fair. I always paid you." Some may commit violent acts, not against the person, but rather acts such as smashing the gambler's windshield, cutting tires, or setting the gambler's mailbox on fire.

Every so often, the bettor needs to rely on a loan shark for a quick loan to bail him out of a desperate financial situation, usually a debt owed to the bookie, or to prevent discovery by a spouse or employer for non-payment of a major debt or a theft. Loan sharks are more likely to be "connected" and more prone to committing violence. They not only threaten, but they act on those threats. One might say that an interest in sports and money, increased through gambling, leads to an unholy trinity, one against the other: the gambler, the bookie, and the loan shark. The bookie's mantra is "I'm your friend" while the loan shark's mantra is "Pay off or else."

Bookies pretend to be the gambler's best friend while in reality wanting to outsmart the bettor and take his money; thus, not surprisingly, there are many different types of bookies. It may be someone at work who organizes and gets a percentage of a betting pool during college and NFL playoffs. It is estimated that more bets are made on the Super Bowl than on any other game or form of gambling. For these bookies, it is more a social activity than a business, a part-time activity, while for others it is a full-time business, to the exclusion of any other type of work. One bookie may be a college classmate while another may be part of an organized crime syndicate.

According to the FBI, bookmaking is a multi-billion dollar industry, warranting special investigative units such as the Organized Crime section within the FBI and vice squad units in local police departments. So why is bookmaking so tempting when it is clearly illegal? The answer is money. Yes, there clearly is some social aspect to betting on sports with a bookie, especially on the Super Bowl game and March Madness, whereas taking action by the Pepsi cola deliveryman is a minor but lucrative activity: quick cash without giving a share of it to the IRS. So why not do a little booking for fun with guys who want to bet?

WHAT DOES THE BOOKIE LOOK LIKE?

Mention the word "gambler" or "bookie" and it conjures up an image of a cigar-puffing man dressed in black with a gold tiepin and loaded down with a pinky ring and fancy pocket watch. That is somewhat reminiscent of the 1800's riverboat gambler: the dandy dresser, strutting around, with a stogie and a deck of cards. On television, the bookie invariably is portrayed as the cold, calculating middle-aged man, dressed in a black shirt, black tie, heavy gold chain, diamond wrist watch and rings, accompanied by another equally intimidating body-building male, with menacing attitudes, words, and behaviors. The scene may show the gambler being beaten up or in fact being killed with a bullet to the head. That is television, but it can also happen in real life. These bookies are not to be ignored or disrespected under any circumstances.

In reality, however, most bookies look and dress like everyone else: casual clothes, drive a mid-size car, and own a house with a two-car garage in a nice neighborhood. Although some bookies tend to dress in the image, wearing expensive silk suits and driving cars with blackened windows, often they do not really feel or match the fit. One compulsive gambler was relieved when he was arrested on bookmaking charges, saying "I hated to look the part of a bookie, wearing gold chains and dark glasses, going to Las Vegas, and being chauffeured in a limousine. I'm just an ordinary man, booking and working. I'm nothing special."

LEARNING THE ROPES

Bets can be made on any sport, but sports bettors usually bet first on games while in high school, advancing to betting on college and professional sports as they get older. The most popular action is betting on football games, and there is no parallel in money or numbers of gamblers when betting on the Super Bowl or betting March Madness basketball. In this particular game and also on other games, for the desperate gambler the bet may be on the line, on the team, the first touchdown, the quarterback, another athlete's accomplishment, or even an injury. There is no limit of options.

Football games are set on predetermined days and times. College games are played primarily on Saturdays, although they can also be scheduled during the week. Professional football games are scheduled usually for Mondays, Thursdays, and Sundays, except when the regular college season ends in December. At those times, some professional games may be scheduled.

Typically, a sports bettor will bet first only on football, and perhaps for several years on college and professional games. After the football season, the gambler may then start betting on basketball games, on baseball, or whatever is either appealing or in season.

The compulsive gambler throughout this time may check one line after the other through sports pages in newspapers, calling sports lines on the phone repeatedly, checking line services over the Internet, and calling the bookie with whom he's betting. Sports lines are 900 telephone numbers in which the gambler can get the latest information on the game or race, albeit this information may change repeatedly. There is a fee for this information, which is charged to the caller's telephone bill, at times costing several hundred dollars per month.

After placing the bet with the bookie, the gambler may watch the game at the stadium, on television with some friends, making it a social event, or watching the TV alone, yelling at the players after a bad play. "I always yelled at the players, convinced they could hear me. At other times, I was so nervous, I was just pacing up and down, and couldn't watch the game. Either that or I was watching one game after the other, every Saturday and Sunday afternoon and evening. It was completely time-consuming. The rest of the world didn't exist, and if someone tried to talk to me, I would yell back at them to shut up. I even yelled at my kid, and he was only five years old. I don't know how I could have done that. It really eats me up."

BETTING WITH THE BOOKIE

There are standard guidelines for bookmaking. If the gambler wants to bet on sports, the first step is to find a bookie. If he knows the bookie, most likely they are on friendly terms, knows where the bookie lives, works or goes to school, and his name. If the gambler does not know any bookies, he will express an interest to someone who may know one. That someone will vouch for the gambler, and the bookie may make some additional inquiries about the future prospect, not the least of which is to be certain that the gambler is not someone from law enforcement. The gambler then is assigned a number and the bookie is given a name: "Twenty-three" betting with "Joe." All transactions are paid in cash: no checks or credit cards to trace back to the bookie.

Bookmaking has its own language and procedures. A nickel is five hundred dollars, a dime is a thousand dollars. "I want some action" means I want to bet and I want to bet now. Some compulsive gamblers feel they are "in action" when they are getting the line. "The momentum and the excitement escalate every minute with each call," according to one sports bettor.

Compulsive gamblers constantly get an update on the line before placing the bet with the bookie at the very last moment. All bets are made on credit. The game is played, the gambler either won or lost, and they settle up in cash, usually at the end of the week. If the gambler cannot settle up at that time, the bookie may charge additional vigorish and also limit the betting activity until the debt is paid off. Being cut off by the bookie is the compulsive gambler's worst nightmare.

THE STUDENT'S BOOKIE

Betting on sports adds another dimension of excitement to the avid sports fan, whether betting on the line or the number of points over or under the actual score, while the friendlier type of wager is simply betting on the winning team: will it be Ohio State or Auburn?

Most teenage boys typically first gamble on baseball cards, then poker games with classmates during or after school. This may later set the stage for betting on football games with a bookie, who most often is a senior or recent graduate, or on rarer occasions, with a coach or math teacher. Young adults may start betting with their neighborhood bar bookies, who tend to be "small-time" and who ply their trade rather openly. College students usually bet with a classmate, fraternity brother, a senior, or a recent graduate. Some college students may not actually resort to bookmaking, but instead serve as the go-between the gambler and the bookie. They deliver the bets and money to the bookie and take the winnings to the gambler. Unfortunately, many of these "runners" are unaware that their activities are considered to be part of an illegal bookmaking operation and they could face legal charges as well as suspension or dismissal from school.

On occasion, a college student who is a compulsive gambler may become the bookie himself or may become part of the bookmaking operation in order to pay off his own debts. Some college students also start booking "just for the fun of it and for the quick money." These actions, of course, are done surreptitiously because bookmaking is illegal and is not allowed on campus or elsewhere for that matter.

The National Collegiate Athletic Association (NCAA) this past decade was deeply concerned about gambling on sports by student athletes, regardless of whether the bet was on their own team or the opposing team, on their own sport or another sport. In 2002, it undertook research of 23,000 student athletes and their gambling behaviors, and found the results to be shocking. Students, both male and female, bet on all sports, and some admitted they had been approached by bookies to shave points or throw a game for a substantial amount of money to pay off the bookie or face exposure. An immediate Task Force was formed, instituting a zero-tolerance edict hoping to curb student athlete gambling on sports. Strict guidelines and consequences for violations were implemented. The amount of the bet was not at issue, it could for as little as a dollar or the team's t-shirt: the assumption was made that the coach or player would have information that might affect the integrity and outcome of the game.

The NCAA was also concerned about the health and welfare of student athletes, and indeed, some respondents to the survey could be identified as possibly being a problem or compulsive gambler. The NCAA's hope was that coaches and other staffers would be able to help these athletes; however, without a confidential hotline, restricted to athletes, they did not avail themselves of this help, fearing the consequences if they were identified.

THE NEIGHBORHOOD BOOKIE

In one small town in Tennessee, it was a standing joke that if you want a bookie, go to your neighbor. This neighbor may live next door, at the end of the block, be the supermarket clerk, or the local delivery truck driver. Friendly guys who take small bets: a $500 bet would most likely be their limit. Bets were made, taken, and paid off. It was social gambling, even if it was illegal.

However, if the gambler wanted to wager an amount above the bookie's ability to handle, the bookie would "lay off" the bet to a bookmaker operating on a larger scale. These bookies more often have their own legitimate business and book bets on the side. For some unknown reason, often local automobile dealership owners or managers tend to be prominent in this role, although one such dealer suggested it might be to stimulate some excitement due to the long hours of downtime among the sales associates when there were no customers.

THE PROFESSIONAL BOOKIE

Professional bookmakers are those bookies who earn their livelihood from booking and who most likely are part of a larger group of bookies. Their action may be from hundreds of gamblers betting several games at one time, with hundreds of thousands of dollars. They have little respect for compulsive gamblers and refer to them as degenerate gamblers. These bookmakers and their operations are of special interest to law enforcement because they may be connected with or actually be part of an organized crime syndicate.

Professional bookies also have close connections with money lenders: the loan sharks or shylocks who will lend money to the desperate compulsive gambler at an exorbitant rate. A loan of $500 is expected to be repaid at $600 within one week. One such mobster spoke anonymously to a group of Baltimore high school students who had formed a club, Students Against Gambling Addiction, after a number of their classmates were found to have gambling problems. Asked by one of the students, "What happens if you can't pay the bookie?" The mobster, deliberately dressed in black clothes and gold chains for the occasion, responded in an angry, fierce voice, "There's no such thing as not paying the bookie."

THE GAMBLER'S NUMBER ONE FEAR: BEING CUT OFF

Social gamblers may bet on one or two football games, but the compulsive gambler will bet anywhere from five to ten or more games. If the compulsive gambler has lost and owes the bookie a substantial amount, the bookie may cut off the gambler until the debt is paid. In the compulsive gambler's mind, being cut off from gambling is the worst possible thing to happen and becomes virtually terrifying.

Attempts then to bet with other bookies are futile because the gambler will quickly be labeled as a stiff. To avoid being cut off becomes all-consuming acts of desperation.

The compulsive gambler typically resorts to a finely tuned skill to overcome and control this dilemma: verbal manipulation. An actual dialogue between a compulsive gambler and a bookie was recorded by a law enforcement agency which had been seeking evidence against the bookie for several months. In this instance, the gambler had bet with the bookie for nearly ten years and now owed him thousands of dollars. The bookie was refusing to accept any more bets until he was paid in full. (B=bookie, G=gambler)

> Bookie: You know how much you owe me?
> Gambler: Well, I can't pay you all that money now, I told you that.
> B: I know, but every time you wanna bet you always say you're gonna pay, but I never get paid.
> G: I never was not gonna pay...I just put up $3,500, now that should give me the right to bet when I want.
> B: Tomorrow, when you pay off, you can bet...
> G: No, I wanna bet tonight. It's as simple as that.
> B: You gotta pay me first.
> G: If I ask you to place a bet for me, you should place it for me.

B: You gotta pay me first.

G: I promise, on the Bible, I will be there with the money, tomorrow morning.

B: Fine, then we'll play.

G: I want to play tonight, now. You can come over and cut off my xxxx if I don't bring you that money tomorrow.

B: Boy, you're putting me in a jam, boy.

G: No, I'm not. In another week I'll be a millionaire. I mean, I'm gonna have the status of a millionaire.

B: Well, I'm not gonna be a millionaire.

G: But you're gonna be my best friend. That's just as close to a million dollars as you can possibly get without having it.

B: Yup.

G: You know I'd walk through hot coals for you, because that's how you've been with me.

B: But you'll settle up with me tomorrow?

G: I'll settle up tomorrow, but I want to be able to bet what I want tonight.

B: OK, I'll get the line.

G: OK, and then come to my house for dinner."

The gambler then placed ten bets, all over a thousand dollars, and lost most of it. The bookie was arrested for running an illegal gambling operation and was sentenced to jail. The gambler continued to bet with another bookie and eventually was also sentenced to jail for crimes he committed to support his addiction.

THE GAMBLER'S NUMBER TWO FEAR: EXPOSURE

Bookies want their money, and as amateur psychologists, they know how to attack the gambler's second greatest area of vulnerability: a sense of honor. "We had a deal. I always paid you. You want me to tell your boss?"

Fear Number Two is being exposed by the bookie. High school students are afraid the teachers will find out, leading to meetings with parents and the principal, and possibly facing suspension. College students' greatest fear is that parents learn that tuition, book money, and allowances have been lost on betting, that they now owe ten thousand dollars to the bookie, and several thousand more on credit cards that the parents did not know about. "I'd rather get beaten up by the bookie than tell my father."

Parents may know little about bookmaking, other than that bookies are known to harm the gambler and his family. After all, they have seen this on television shows many times. Thus, they will pay off the bookie, usually the full amount, on the gambler's convincing promise never to gamble again. At the time the gambler's intent is sincere, but realistically, the gambler has received a bail-out, the pressure is off, and he will return to betting with the bookie as soon as possible.

"You want me to come over to your house?" Dad will find out, be disappointed, and critical. This counters the gambler's constant efforts at meeting Dad's approval, which is the underlying fear of being seen as incompetent or worthless. Or a wife will find out, rave, and rant, sometimes for many days, and threaten to leave. This then compounds the gambler's long-time fear of being rejected.

Compulsive gamblers who are especially vulnerable are those working in a financial setting, such as a bank manager, a bookkeeper handling escrow accounts for a law firm, or an accountant of a large company. In the gambler's mind, which is worse: having the bookie come to the office, or "borrowing" the money to pay the bookie, who threatens "I know where you work." The gambler's immediate emotional response is one of anxiety, the fear of being discovered for potential or actual mismanagement of funds and being fired.

THE GAMBLER'S NUMBER THREE FEAR: PHYSICAL HARM

Bookies at times may also make comments hinting at physical harm. "I saw your little girl go to school this morning. She looked really pretty in her blue dress." The implied threat clearly is that harm will come to the little girl if the debt is not paid, at once. "You want to pay me. Now." Said in a tone of anger, this implies, "Do it or else." It can be very intimidating.

In one case, the bookie's two enforcers appeared at the gambler's dorm at college, pounding on each door, yelling for him, wanting their money. Security personnel responded, and all students were immediately moved to another dorm or sent home where they were safe.

In some more coercive instances, personal property was damaged: car windows were smashed, plants around the house were uprooted, company trucks were stolen, and bricks were hurled through store windows. The threats of physical harm to the gambler were clearly implied. In these instances, the gambler and the bookie need to come to an immediate agreement about payment and future gambling.

However, when threat is no longer implied but is specifically spelled out, then the gambler indeed needs to take protective action. A threat such as, "Pay or I'll kill you" is a real threat of harm. In fact, one bookie put a gun in the gambler's mouth. In another instance, the bookie's two enforcers confronted the gambler and left him badly beaten, next to a garbage dump. The compulsive gambler at this point has no alternative but to contact the local FBI office for protection.

NEGOTIATING WITH THE BOOKIE

There are different approaches to resolving the issue of money owed to the bookie, ranging from paying nothing, ever, to paying the full amount at once. Bookies know their business is illegal, which can result in their arrest and incarceration. They want their money, but not at the price of losing tax-free income or freedom. The compulsive gambler, on the other hand, is usually a law-abiding, honorable person, who wants to be fair and "do the right thing," and not suffer physical harm.

Before dealing with the bookie, the gambler is wise to consider several issues with a therapist, an attorney, or a law enforcement officer.

1. Who is the bookie: a colleague at work, the boss, a local businessman, a fellow student or teacher, a neighbor, a part-time bookie or a professional bookie, someone who may be connected with the mob?
2. Overall, during the time that the bookie was taking the gambler's bets, who has profited from the relationship in actual dollar amounts? Most likely, if the betting has occurred for more than a few months, the bookie has profited from the gambler's losses. But how much?
3. How much money does the gambler owe the bookie?
4. What are the implied threats of harm or the actual threats of violence?

Next, what are the options open to the compulsive gambler in addressing these issues? Payment in full today is one extreme, even if it means to beg, borrow, or steal the money. The other extreme is to pay nothing whatsoever, be banned from all further betting with this bookie and most likely some of his cohorts, and taking a chance on possibly some retaliation from the bookie. Some things to consider are:

1. Beg, borrow, or steal the money and pay off the bookie in full. This has some obvious unacceptable consequences, the worst being that the bookie will continue to take the gambler's bets. Also, if the money is borrowed, is

it a bail-out? If the money is stolen, what are the legal consequences? The gambler's real motive for full payment to the bookie must be explored and challenged.

2. When is the full amount to be paid off? In a month, a year? Is the amount to be paid reasonable or may it lead to further stress, gambling, and illegal acts?

3. Negotiate with the bookie to pay a percentage on the dollar, at once or over time. The bookie will want as much money as quickly as possible. This will relieve both of them of certain stressors. Bookies know their business is illegal and they do not want to go to jail; thus, if the threats do not work and the gambler is definitely a degenerate, the bookie will take as much as he can squeeze out of the gambler. It may be only forty percent, but forty percent is better than nothing or going to jail and losing everything.

4. Another option is to pay nothing. This most certainly will result in a negative and explosive reaction from the bookie, especially if the amount owed is substantial. However, the bookie knows he has taken a chance by conducting an illegal enterprise and is quick to figure out the overall play: how much has he won from this degenerate over the years? The gambler can negotiate the terms, "I don't tell and you don't take action from me."

The gambler may confront the bookie with the issue, alone in person, or by phone. A second option is to negotiate together with a member of Gamblers Anonymous, again in person or over the phone. A third choice, and one that is advisable if the amount of money owed is substantial or could lead to harmful consequences, such as being terminated from a banking job, the gambler's lawyer may contact the bookie with a simple message: "As an officer of the court, I am advising you that my client will make no further payments, there will be no further contact from my client to you, and no further contact by you or your associates, to my client, or law enforcement will be notified accordingly." Again, any of these contacts with the bookie can be in person, over the phone, or letter. Each situation is unique and must be negotiated accordingly.

It is critical that these options be addressed in detail with the gambler and therapist, GA participant, or lawyer, looking at all benefits and unacceptable outcomes, until a plan is developed. This plan, obviously, must also be shared with close family members, such as a spouse or parent. The lawyer should be informed of the overall situation, and if necessary, a restraining order may be served against the bookie.

Regardless of the option taken, the bookie must be informed of the gambler's addiction, that he is attending Gamblers Anonymous, is undergoing treatment, and will no longer be gambling on sports or any other form of gambling. Most bookies will respect this approach.

It is incumbent for the therapist to recognize the special relationship that develops between the gambler and his bookie. Betting with a bookie is personal and very different from putting a coin in a slot machine or handing money to a teller at the race track. It is also important for the therapist to recognize and address this termination of betting with a bookie as a loss, the loss of a "friend" and the loss of gambling. Grief counseling is important in helping the gambler overcome whatever emotional reactions may occur, and there will be many.

Finally, what is the relationship between the bookie and the gambler, and how strong is it? In the case of a college student undergoing counseling, the the student spotted the bookie's enforcers after his therapy session a short distance from the therapist's office. Terrified, the gambler stole money he owed the bookie, was arrested, and committed suicide rather than go to jail.

LOAN SHARKS

If the amount of money owed to the bookie is substantial, and payment cannot be made within a reasonable length of time, the bookie may turn the debt to another bookie or to a loan shark. Loan sharks lend the money, in cash, and at a usurious rate of interest. Interest gets paid first. Always. For example, a compulsive gambler made monthly payments on interest, and at the end of the year owed the same amount that was borrowed.

Loan sharks can be found everywhere. Most often, they work with bookies, although they have also been known to operate alone at race tracks and at casinos. They are to be feared. The fear is warranted. Almost all are dangerous. Loan sharks often are affiliated with groups given to violence. The loan shark will threaten actual violence if he is not reimbursed, in full, at the time agreed upon. The violence may be against the compulsive gambler himself or against a family member. Threats of violence made by bookies and loan sharks are not to be taken lightly.

In cases such as these, the gambler is wise to immediately contact the local FBI's Organized Crime Unit. Any information given to the FBI is confidential and the FBI will arrange for protection, if necessary. Contacting local police is not advisable, since on occasion someone within the department may be a bookie. "I called the police and then found out the chief himself was a bookie."

The Dead Fish

Yesterday, Mr. Sam brought Dad a fish wrapped in a
newspaper.
He said it was for the family.
Dad looked kinda scared. Real scared.
Now why would anyone be scared of a dead fish?
Or of Mr. Sam?

CHAPTER 15
THE CRIMES, THE COURTS,
AND THE JAILS

INTRODUCTION

Compulsive gamblers will use myriad means to find the money needed to pay off debts. Eventually, they will acquire it illegally, although given their sense of integrity, moral conduct, and law-abiding behavior prior to developing a gambling addiction, it seems inconceivable to them and others that they would do anything in violation of their standards or those of the law. Yet it is impossible to stop in the midst of a financial addiction simply because there are no more options left to acquire money legally. The next step inevitably is to borrow the monies they need, not just to pay bills and replace the money that they "borrowed" but also to continue gambling. Their reasons to continue gambling are at least three-fold: to recoup overall losses to pay off long-overdue bills, to maintain that sense of competitiveness of being a winner rather than a loser, and to maintain the emotions of action or escape that gambling offers.

There is another important motivation for gambling that is reported frequently by them, many with similar themes. For instance, the gambler has lost $10,000 and now is in a desperate state to recoup that money. The gambler may win back $8,500 and knows, however briefly, that this is the time to stop, collect the money, and pay at least some of the bills. However, the frequent large wins, mixed in with losses, give the gambler a false sense of control, believing without reflection that the next bet will be a winning one and the entire $10,000 will be recouped; instead, only to lose it all once again. The gambler's desperate needs, his personality characteristics, and the process of variable ratio render the gambler unable to think rationally and also unable to stop. This is the pathology of gambling.

Many tears and outbursts of anger occur when the gambler's children discover that money is missing from their savings accounts or piggy banks. Discovery that college tuition has been secretly withdrawn and used for gambling will result in strained relationships that might last for years. How can children respect or feel safe with a parent who has stolen and lied to them? To them, it is the ultimate betrayal and breach of trust.

Compulsive gamblers almost always will sell a family member's belongings. Family heirlooms are "misplaced" and disappear. One wife who had collected over 100 original German Hummel figurines discovered one day that half the collection was missing. The maid was blamed. Expensive Tiffany glass vases were "broken" and the spouse was "too upset so I threw the broken pieces in the trash." A spouse's jewelry was "stolen" during a burglary. A "loose prong" was responsible for the missing diamond in a ring. These technically are all thefts, but which spouse, child, or parent will press legal charges against the compulsive gambler once the truth comes out? The guilt and shame is sure to follow. In the meantime, the gambler has gotten the money for the stolen item and usually the insurance money as well.

Most questionable practices committed to obtain money start at home (see crimes by adolescents at the end of this section). The adult gambler initially may write checks on a joint checking account and "balance" the checking account statement each month (many spouses turn this job over to the gambler even before the addiction) by writing a check from the back of the book to avoid detection of shortages. The gambler may also write checks for the same purpose despite knowing the account is overdrawn. Too many NSF checks may result in the bank closing the account, but the gambler continues writing checks on this closed account to bide for time. Another common practice is to forge a spouse's signature on a restricted joint savings account or on any item requiring the spouse's signature.

Thefts from a family-owned business is even more disturbing for family members. Who will have a son arrested, knowing that incarceration is sure to follow? The entire family will be in an uproar. In one case, the compulsive gambler admitted during therapy that he had embezzled over $200,000 from his father's automobile dealership. The father negotiated loan payments with the bank for the son to make restitution without facing criminal charges. The other members of the family begrudged the entire incident, and it required many sessions of therapy to restore cohesion within the family and the family business.

Thefts from an employer very often are not reported. This is especially true of law firms when an associate or partner has misappropriated funds, usually from clients' escrow accounts. The firms will replace the misappropriated monies to the clients and the gambler will sign a demand loan and other legal documents prior to termination. At other times, the firm may allow the gambler to continue working for the firm until all monies are repaid and then terminate the offender. Law firms do not want the negative press that is likely to follow with the filing of a police report or be subject to other public exposure.

Scams against colleagues or friends are common. "I desperately need the money to meet payroll. I'll pay it back in two weeks when the account receivables come in. I'll give you two checks in advance now for repayment." Unfortunately, both checks will be returned NSF, with more lies. One salesman convinced a colleague to invest in a new product and then fled to Las Vegas with the money. A favorite one for college or professional athletes is to promise tickets for a big game and receive the money, but they never had the tickets from the onset of the scam.

The first and most frequent crime perpetrated against strangers is writing bad checks. These may be checks that are drawn against insufficient funds, on a closed account, on another person's account, kiting a check, floating a check, or any variation thereof. One compulsive gambler wrote a bad check to a supermarket, usually under $50, in every county in his state. Although he paid off each check before going to court, eventually one judge looked at the entire criminal record and sentenced him to two years of incarceration. Ultimately, the state was responsible for the costs of a public defender, incarceration, medical expenses, lost business, lost taxes, and lost job. The son had to work to prevent foreclosure and was unable to continue his academic studies. In sum, even a "small-time" gambler can cause considerable damage and costs.

The most frequent federal crimes committed by compulsive gamblers are fraud, forgery, embezzlement, and money laundering. One employee repeatedly submitted fraudulent insurance claims, writing her name on the claims checks. The auditors did not discover it until two years later when a customer filed a complaint and the account records were investigated. The thefts were not discovered until the auditor did a more thorough review by screening the actual cancelled checks. Each had been forged. A branch bank manager issued false loans to himself and took the money to Las Vegas. Since the gambler was an authorized signatory, the casinos did not refuse the checks until one of them was written for $500,000. The total count of "customer loans" exceeded three million dollars. Business owners or executives file fraudulent financial statements to increase loan equity or avoid paying taxes. Sales executives on expense accounts use company credit cards for gambling expenses. IRS tax returns are either false or not filed at all, sometimes for years.

Occasionally, a family member may be an unwitting accomplice. A wife of a sports bettor, turned bookmaker without her knowledge, innocently cashed checks for her husband while she was working at her boutique, only to be arrested, along with her husband, for money laundering. She served two years in federal prison and promptly divorced him upon her release. He served another five years. A "dumb and dumber" compulsive gambler called his bookie from his prison cell, even though knowing that his calls were being monitored for similar offenses. It earned him one month in solitary confinement.

On occasion, a bank is robbed. Guns without bullets, without a firing pin, and a toy gun have been used. A favorite story among prison inmates is about a compulsive gambler who used a water pistol to rob a female bank teller. "Where were you aiming?" He became the laughing stock in prison. Another anecdotal but true account is about the gambler who robbed a bank and rode away on his bicycle. An innovative gambler drove up to a bank teller's window, shook a box filled with his children's Lego blocks, and convinced the teller it was a bomb. He then drove off in his car, filled it up with gas before returning home, and was greeted by the police. Then there was the gambler who robbed a bank of $400, walked around the block, and returned the money. Yet another gambler, a police detective assigned to investigate bank robberies, stole money from the same bank's ATM machine that he was investigating.

While these and similar bank robberies are surprising and are committed almost always without a functional weapon, they are nevertheless robberies that endanger everyone in the bank and could result in violence or shootings by bank guards or police, customers or employees, as well as being emotionally traumatizing for the employees and customers.

As stated previously, the profile of a compulsive gambler has changed over the past two decades with the rapid expansion of legalized gambling and the greater access to gambling sites, especially the Internet, by many diverse groups of adults and adolescents. Today, a larger variety of crimes are being perpetrated by compulsive gamblers, many of them violent in nature. These include robberies and burglaries. Another violent crime emerging is that of selling drugs, and a few cases have been reported of attempted or actual homicide. One gambler purposely damaged the tires on his wife's car, hoping for an accident and getting double indemnity from the insurance company. Extortion has occurred occasionally. A man sent a note printed out of newspaper letters to his neighbor, writing, "You don't want to know what will happen to your daughter if you don't give me $100,000. Leave it in a bag under the second seat of the bus to Toledo. And don't call the police." Needless to say, the gambler was met by special agents of the FBI holding the bag.

Two new groups of compulsive gamblers have emerged in the past decade: adolescents and seniors. Each has its own unique criminal behaviors.

Adolescents and young adults at the onset of their gambling use their pocket money, allowances, and other spending money from parents, stashed money, or whatever is in a savings account. They will do odd jobs, work part-time after school, or find other means to obtain funds. Their gambling may have started many years ago when they were in elementary school, pitching pennies, playing nickel dominoes or card games with family members, and as they grew older, started playing poker in school and betting on the Super Bowl game. This was at the social level of gambling, affordable, fun, and part of rites of passage for teenage boys.

However, as the gambling escalates, that is, more frequently and with larger amounts, the legal money is used up and acquisition comes to the second level, yet still legal and all belonging to the gambler himself. This money might be obtained by borrowing, pawning or selling personal items of value, or getting cash back from a returned gift. This is gradually heading toward gambling abuse or problem gambling.

One college freshman reported he was a sports bettor who became rather enterprising during the escalation of his gambling. In his freshman year at school, he made new friends and joined a fraternity. His frat brothers played poker regularly and bet on sports with a classmate who was the runner for the bookie. It was convenient for him and his fraternity brothers to place bets and collect winnings through this runner. Early on, finding himself losing more than he had intended and being short of cash, the freshman opened a charge account at a computer store and bought a laptop. He made regular payments, opened a charge account at a second department store, and in the process, established his own good credit rating. Within a few months, he had charge accounts at three stores, was regularly buying and selling merchandise, and soon owed two thousand dollars. He took a part-time job to make the additional payments, but found that his grades were beginning to slip because of stress and lack of sleep.

Soon, this problem gambler came to the realization that more money was lost than won and that repayment of borrowed money or retrieving a pawned item was impossible unless he could find a new source of money. During spring break and between semesters, he convinced himself that Mom or Dad wouldn't mind if he "borrowed" some of their money left on a dresser or in a purse and also used their credit cards. When the father discovered the debts and thefts, he beat his son until the boy needed medical attention. The student did not stop betting on sports; rather, he found new ways to hide his gambling from his father (the father was threatened with being reported to Child Protective Services if the abuse did not stop immediately and forever).

Teenagers find creative means of supporting their compulsive gambling. One student pawned his mother's ring and another sold off the sterling silver flatware, one spoon or fork at a time. Another teen saw a credit card application sent to his grandmother. He filled in the information, received the credit card, which he used for cash advances, and made regular payments until the credit card company's security called the grandmother, questioning the frequent cash advances. She, of course, had no knowledge of the card, it was reported as fraud, and shortly thereafter, the teenager was arrested by the Secret Service. Mom and Dad paid for the defense attorney and repaid the credit card company.

It is often common practice for credit card companies to send applications to college students to open an account. Within one year, this same student who was beaten by his father had maxed out five credit cards and was ten thousand dollars in debt plus owed $500 to the bookie classmate. "Hey, man, you're going to get me in trouble if you don't give me the money. I told the bookie you were good for it. Now he's after me. I trusted you. You can't do this to me. I can't believe you would do this to me." He feared another beating from his father but was even more afraid of his fraternity brothers. If they found out he stiffed the bookie, all of them would get in trouble, but even worse, he was convinced they would kick him out of the fraternity. It was only after he attempted to commit suicide by overdosing on drugs mixed with six-packs of beer that the parents recognized he was suffering from a psychiatric disorder and had their son hospitalized.

College students have other sources of money, such as college expenses. Parents tend to give the student money for tuition, books, and other expenses, all of which is eventually used for gambling. Some students also get a full-time job, which then interferes with their studies. Tuition, scholarships and grants, salaries, loans, selling valuables, and cash advances are all sources of money to be used for gambling with a bookie, or a runner from the bookie's organization, as well as for poker or trips to casinos.

At this time, most adolescent compulsive gamblers are boys. However, this changed as physical education classes in schools offered more sports to female students, such as field hockey and basketball. Teenage girls followed the path of boys and, not surprisingly, themselves became problem gamblers.

It must be noted that college-age gambling abuse can be equated with alcohol abuse, especially on campus, although most of these drinkers and gamblers return to social drinking and gambling as they graduate and mature. Nevertheless, some of them will become alcoholics or compulsive gamblers. Various epidemiological surveys estimate there are over 500,000 adolescent problem gamblers in the United States and it is predictable that there will be an increase in crime to support their addiction, although these crimes often are not reported.

Seniors follow a somewhat different pattern of getting money for gambling. They, too, use their cash on hand, bank accounts, charge the maximum amount on their old and new credit cards, and eventually use their retirement funds and Social Security benefits. Since, most often, their home mortgages are fully paid off, they may obtain a new mortgage or equity loan, which is then quickly spent at the casino, in slots parlors, bingo halls, or card clubs.

It is becoming more frequent among seniors for husband and wife to visit gambling sites with both of them becoming gambling addicts or one of them becoming an alcoholic. Their options are even more limited: they have no money for food or medical expenses, they may be forced to sell their home, and some have been known to even sell their household goods including furniture, dishes, and clothes. They are less likely to commit thefts, but if they do, it is usually from the family rather than strangers or financial institutions. They no longer work so they cannot steal from an employer. While it is not illegal, many find that bankruptcy is their only viable financial option, other than moving in with their children.

CIVIL ACTIONS AND VIOLATIONS

Motor vehicle violations, such as unpaid parking tickets, speeding or reckless driving, failure to carry auto insurance, having outdated vehicle inspections or tags, driving with suspended or cancelled licenses, poor brakes, worn tires, and failure to pass emission tests are common among populations of active compulsive gamblers.

Today, more young female adults have jobs, their own money, and independence and are less likely than their older counterparts to stay in a disruptive marriage. They tend to divorce, which may lead to child custody battles. In the past, most courts awarded custody to the non-gambling parent; however, in more recent court rulings, the courts granted custody to the gambling father, considering this to be in the best interest of the child.

Child custody cases and non-payment of child support are on the rise and conceivably will continue to escalate, especially since many new gambling sites, such as casinos, are opened. Similarly, alimony payments could be on the increase since gambling environments often are becoming the norm in today's communities.

Another consequence of compulsive gambling-related civil violations or other misconduct is that of losing a professional license. Lawyers and real estate sales agents rank highest among these professionals, and only rarely is a license restored; an exception may be made when the gambler has completed a period of suspension for five years or more and has proof of rehabilitation. Only rare cases are reported of lawyers regaining their license, especially after having been incarcerated. A wiser course of action for lawyers and other licensed professionals is to resign before their license is suspended or revoked although there are relatively few cases of compulsive gamblers seeking this course of action. Typically, a reason for disbarment, even if restitution has been made to the victims through the lawyers Grievance Fund, the gambler must repay those monies to this fund. Unfortunately, many disbarred lawyers now earn less and reimbursement is virtually impossible. "Even if I had the money to pay back, I wouldn't want to practice law again. Who would hire me? Besides, it would be too embarrassing."

CRIMES AGAINST THE FAMILY

A frequent complaint is voiced by wives who are now facing an "empty nest" and find solace in playing cards with friends, going to bingo, or playing slots at local casinos and race tracks. "I was lonely, I was bored, I just wanted us to go out for dinner with friends or go on a vacation. He thought it was a waste of money, and I really resented him for that, so I started taking a dollar or two and bought lottery tickets. I won occasionally, but then I lost more."

After twenty years of marriage, a wife wanted to replace the bedroom furniture her parents had given them to set up housekeeping. She felt it "was ugly and worn out." The husband opined, "Why spend the money? No one sees the bedroom anyway" and refused to give her the money for it. She started playing slots at a nearby racino, hoping to win the money. She didn't. Instead, she played longer and spent more money, dipped into their savings account until it was empty, and then altered the weekly check her husband gave her to run the household. When her husband finally found out, she had lost over eight thousand dollars. He reacted by threatening to throw her out of the house, yelling at her in anger, and then not talking to her for days at a time. Sunday dinners with the children and grandchildren became a nightmare. He would berate her, saying, "Did you know your mother is a liar and a thief?" The daughter stopped coming over because she did not want her children to witness this abuse. The verbal and psychological abuse continued until the wife attempted suicide and the entire family sought therapy.

These and other cases are illustrative of the progression from social to problem gambling, in which initial fun and repeated winnings turn into repeated losses. The money used during this period is money taken from the home or family. It rarely ends up in legal action. It also is not reported in research studies, thus crime statistics are low and inaccurate.

PAWNING

A family item, such as a dad's watch, mom's rings, or a brother's television, hoping to win at gambling and redeem the items before it is sold. The same ring might be pawned and recovered several times before its loss is discovered. "The last time my mom got it out of hock. I'll never forget the hurt look in her eyes."

TAKING KID'S MONEY

Nothing will anger a son or daughter more than to learn that the compulsive gambler, be it either Mom or Dad, has taken that child's savings account or tuition money. "All you had to do was ask, you didn't have to steal it from me." It is the ultimate violation in a parent/child relationship.

LYING-AROUND MONEY

What a temptation for the adolescent gambler. He's lost the money for school expenses, owes the bookie or debts that haven't been paid, and there's Dad's wallet on the dresser or Mom's purse on the kitchen table. Quick, remove $20, they'll never notice, and this continues until Mom or Dad do notice there is a thief in the house. Anger and tears lead to promises to repay what was taken, but too often the emphasis is on the missing money, not on its cause, compulsive gambling.

WEDDING MONEY

"We were both full-time students when we got married. I got a full-time job, and a year later, she got pregnant. I was really good at poker, so I played in the casino tournaments and won. That helped, but on the last hand, with a big jackpot, I folded instead of doubling the bet. There was no way I would let my wife or dad find out what happened, so I started going into our savings account where we had our wedding money. Five months later, the savings account was empty."

TUITION

Many parents will entrust a credit card to their children for college expenses. Instead, students who are compulsive gamblers use the credit cards for gambling.

As pressures escalate, they usually tap into their tuition money, taking fewer classes or dropping out entirely. What follows is a charade of deceptions to parents, lying about classes and exams. "My roommate was also the runner for the bookie and he was after me day after day to pay up. We were both scared of the bookie too, not knowing what he would do. You feel so guilty, you just want to end it all."

INSURANCE CASH VALUE OR REFUNDS

A favorite source of money which can be tapped into quite easily is the cash value on a life insurance policy or to cancel a health insurance policy and use that money for gambling. This can be done secretly without a spouse finding out about it until months or years after the fact. "I went to the doctor for my tension headaches, and he told me that my health insurance was dropped two months ago. I was shocked. Then my husband came home, bragging that he had won $500 in a poker game. I got suspicious, and he finally admitted that he took $2,000 from his life insurance. My tension headache got so bad, I started vomiting."

SUPPORT CHECKS

Another method is to cash in unemployment checks, disability payments, welfare checks, child support payments, and pension checks, to name just a few examples. The justification in the gambler's mind is, "I earned it, it's mine to spend, they'll never know it." Family members will disagree, especially since these monies are regular weekly or monthly payments that families depend upon for daily living, and thus failure to get these monies impacts negatively on all of them.

SELLING FAMILY POSSESSIONS

For whatever reasons, spouses or children of compulsive gamblers do not notice what should be obvious. One wife stated, "I was barely functional, I was so doped up on depression medication that I just started blocking things out. I never noticed the first-edition antique books were missing. I thought I was going crazy. My daughter told me that her dad sold them, one by one and took the money to the track. Her dad made her promise not to tell me. It's no wonder her grades dropped. We were all sick."

BANK AND OTHER LOANS

Compulsive gamblers are often referred to as con artists, and it isn't at all difficult for them to get a bank loan even though both spouses are required to cosign. "He's in Europe for a sales meeting. I'll have him sign the loan as soon as he gets back." Or easier yet, the wife may have already signed a blank loan agreement, never imagining that the proceeds would be used for gambling.

FLOATING CHECKS

This is a favorite method used by individuals who have a business and a personal checking account over which they have exclusive responsibility. One such owner, who was a race track gambler, wrote a personal check for $1,000, deposited it in the business account, knowing it would not clear for three days. He then wrote a check on the business account and deposited it in the personal account, again hoping to avoid either check from being returned NSF. He kept this up for two years, ultimately driving over fifty miles per day, involving five banks, and owing nearly $100,000, until he dropped from exhaustion and found himself facing numerous legal charges in federal court.

ALTERED CHECKS

Altering a check is a preferred form of bad checks perpetrated by the traditional housewife who earns no income. "He works, it's his money" is the underlying culture of this family system, and any spending money she may want has to be requested. She feels demeaned and trapped: the joy has been taken out of her life because she can't go out for lunch or buy a new dress without her husband's tacit disapproval or criticism.

A figure of four hundred dollars can easily be altered to eight hundred or a check can be altered by adding a new number. This is not discovered until the income earner tries to verify the checking account statement or if a check has been returned by the bank.

CLOSED ACCOUNT

Both male and female gamblers write checks on closed accounts. They try to make them good, but this embarrassment for the family adds additional pressure on the gambler, which leads to an escalation of gambling and family turmoil. "Dad's not only a liar, he's also a crook."

UTTERANCE

This method of check writing tends to be more popular with the casino high rollers. They may win ten thousand dollars or fifty thousand and put it in a checking account for future gambling or to cover overdrafts. They know that any withdrawal of $10,000 must be reported by the bank to the Comptroller of the Treasury. However, in one case, the bank notified the FBI and since there were over a dozen of such deposits and withdrawals, it was viewed as a scam or drug-related activity.

FRAUD

One enterprising mail-carrier urgently needed to replace gambling losses so that his son could attend summer camp. The mail carrier recognized envelopes which held welfare checks and IRS checks. He simply took these checks, fraudulently signed them over to himself, and cashed them. He hid the envelopes and other mail in the trunk of his car. He did this for two years. Since these were US Treasury checks, he was sentenced to serve three years in a federal prison. His wife and children refused to visit him in jail. Thousands of customers did not receive their mail for two years.

OTHER NONVIOLENT ILLEGAL ACTS

Gamblers resort to other crimes of a nonviolent financial nature, regardless of the type of gambling or uniqueness of the individual.

THEFT

Seeing money lying around often becomes "a crime of opportunity"; the crime was not planned beforehand, but rather is a consequence of the gambler's impulsive behavior. As many have admitted, "I never in my life stole any money. If I was overpaid at the store or if I saw someone dropped a dollar bill, I always made it a point to return it immediately. And now I'm facing criminal charges because I stole money from a neighbor. I can't believe it. Can you imagine how my kids feel about that? I would rather die than deliberately hurt my kids ever. My neighbor didn't press charges, but my actions ended our friendship. Their kids aren't allowed to play with my kids anymore. And all because of me and my gambling."

Not too many years ago a highly decorated state trooper was suffering from post-traumatic stress disorder and turned to casino gambling to temporarily avoid the ongoing terrors, nightmares, and startle responses. While performing his duties, he intercepted a vehicle with drug dealers and found sixty thousand dollars in drug money hidden under the seat. He kept some of the money and falsified the evidence report. His actions were discovered. The officers he worked with seized his home computer and records in front of his children, he was fired from the job, beaten up in prison, and the only job he was able to find thereafter was to work in a fast-food restaurant. Only the intervention by the police chaplain saved him from an intended suicide with his own weapon.

FORGERY

Forging a signature on a check payable to someone else is not that difficult for an employee. When one bookkeeper was questioned why the boss's name was written all over her desk calendar, she responded that she was simply doodling while being on hold on the phone. Three months later, the boss discovered that twelve thousand dollars was missing from the company checking account. The bookkeeper was a slot machine addict and gambled away the company money at a local racino. In another instance, the accountant typed a letter which gave the accountant authority to have checks cashed at a nearby check-cashing store and forged the boss's signature.

Government checks, such as tax refunds, Social Security checks, unemployment checks, disability checks, and welfare checks are too often stolen from the recipient's mailbox or forged by the gambler.

INSURANCE FRAUD

Health insurance company checks are easy to cash at local banks. The companies are reputable, and the bank may know the customer to whom the checks are endorsed. What the bank may not know, however, is that the insurance check should be endorsed over to the physician or out-of-network health provider instead of to the subscriber. In essence, the medical provider is paying the gambler for treatment services instead of the gambler paying the provider.

Another insurance scam developed into a seemingly fine art is that of a faked accident, claiming the car was damaged or vandalized by persons unknown, when in fact the compulsive gambler caused the damage, seeing this as a means of getting insurance reimbursement. The braver compulsive gambler may resort to yet another form of insurance fraud, that of claiming personal injury. The injury is self-inflicted by deliberately stepping in front of a car and getting bumped or by slamming on the brakes, resulting in a minor rear-end collision and claiming a painful soft-tissue injury. Such claims are quickly settled for five or ten thousand dollars, an amount too small to merit a costly fraud investigation and legal costs.

STEALING FROM THE EMPLOYER

Bank managers or loan officers can easily create a phantom loan and keep the proceeds. They will do this repeatedly, with larger and larger amounts to cover gambling debts, stealing several million dollars, until the phony loans are finally detected. Banks by law must report such cases to the authorities and cannot settle the theft within their own institution. Expenses are borne by the federal government.

Money laundering often requires a mandatory prison sentence. One family was completely disrupted when the father, who owned a retail business, turned to bookmaking to support his own addiction. He took checks paid by his bettors, had a friend cash them and lost the money the race track. Both the bookie/compulsive gambler and the friend were sentenced to jail, leaving the older son to run the business and take care of the younger siblings.

Military members may be suspected of selling military secrets, but more likely, they will alter a travel voucher or charge the maximum on their government credit card and are then unable to pay it off. One particularly sad case involved an army sergeant who was given custody of his physically disabled six-year-old daughter after the mother deserted the family. The divorce caused serious financial hardship. He went to a nearby slots parlor in hopes of winning money to pay for medical bills. Two years later, he was facing a court martial and given the choice between an immediate discharge or serving two years in the Ft. Leavenworth military prison. A discharge meant he would lose his health benefits; prison meant leaving his daughter in a group home. He hanged himself so that his daughter would not lose her medical benefits.

On an aside, the base post exchange sold gambling games, such as hand-held slot machines, marked for children ages six and over, and it held regular bingo nights. It had no compulsive gambling education or prevention program.

VIOLENT CRIMES

With the greater diversity of gamblers as a consequence of the growth of the gambling industry, the easy access to the myriad forms of gambling, as well as to money, it is not surprising that now there is also a change in the types of crimes committed by compulsive gamblers. To date, compulsive gamblers tend to refrain from running a gambling operation on cock fights or pit bull fights, and they have been known to pass out when faced with a needle for a blood test. Nevertheless, it is realistic to predict there will be an increase in these and other forms of gambling and crimes to support that gambling.

ARMED ROBBERY

Perhaps the most frequent type of "violent" crime as opposed to "nonviolent" crime committed by compulsive gamblers is that of robbery. A military officer parked his car on the base and robbed the convenience store. He was identified through his name tag, which was prominently displayed on his uniform. A police officer robbed a woman while he was pushing his two-year-old daughter in her stroller. To date, few of these types of violent crimes have been reported; however, that may change as compulsive gamblers come to reflect a greater population diversity.

BREAKING AND ENTERING

Again, one of the newer forms of crimes committed by compulsive gamblers is that of breaking and entering. In several cases, the door to the house of a neighbor or friend was left ajar or unlocked. Most often, cash is stolen instead of items such as televisions or computers. It is rare for the gambler to use a weapon, other than a hand tool to gain entry into the house.

EXTORTION

Extortion is a rare form of theft committed by compulsive gamblers, although conceivably this type of criminal activity will also increase as legal gambling spreads across the country and attracts a gambling population more inclined to such criminal acts.

SELLING OR DISTRIBUTING DRUGS

Compulsive gamblers typically do not use drugs. They may have experimented with some, but more often if drugs are used, it tends to be as an adult, using marijuana to feel relaxed or cocaine to stay awake at the casino blackjack table. Occasionally, a gambler may use amphetamines, but again, this is the exception rather than the rule. Gamblers have an inordinate need "to be in control of all things at all times" and deliberately succumbing to mood altering states through the use of hardcore drugs, such as heroin, is rare. Alcohol as a first form of abuse and later during heavier gambling is fairly common. As much as thirty percent of gamblers entering inpatient treatment programs are also treated for their alcoholism.

Selling drugs, however, is becoming a more frequent form of crime. If the gambler has access to drugs, such as being a bartender in a local bar where drugs are sold, that gambler is likely to venture into buying and selling drugs, albeit not necessarily using the drugs. This drug dealing is simply a crime of opportunity which can be repeated until the gambler is caught or hits bottom.

DOMESTIC VIOLENCE

Domestic violence, in the form of verbal and physical abuse, unfortunately is not uncommon, especially if the compulsive gambler is a male. Research shows that about two out of three men will verbally abuse the wife by demanding money, yelling in anger, or nagging her for hours on end until she gives in. It is estimated that about one in five men turn to physical abuse, such as pushing or shoving and occasionally hitting the female partner. Physical abuse is almost always limited to the gambler's desperate need for money and rarely happens in the absence of gambling. Verbal abuse and some physical abuse by the non-gambling parent was first documented in 1978 (Lorenz, V. C. *Pathological gambling: Its characteristics of the gambler, its impact upon the family, and the effectiveness of Gam-Anon*. Master's thesis, The Pennsylvania State University) and apparently is on the increase.

CHILD ENDANGERMENT, CHILD NEGLECT

A most disturbing form of criminal behavior is violence against the gambler's own children. Mothers and fathers have been arrested for leaving their infants and toddlers locked in their cars for several hours at a time, unattended while they were gambling. As a result, some children died of heat exhaustion or were found frozen to death. Casinos, racinos, race tracks, and bingo halls now have security guards patrolling their parking lots, inspecting each car to save these young victims. Other parents have been known to leave an infant or young child in a crib, intending to return within an hour and instead gambling at a casino for one or two days before returning home. They feel inordinately guilty and promise themselves and others to never leave the child alone again, which they won't—until the next gambling spree a week or two later. Children of compulsive gamblers also report having been taken by their mothers to illegal card rooms when they were young, having to sit under the card table for hours or overnight, while the mothers gambled.

HOMICIDE

While homicide, most often the husband killing the wife, is extremely rare, it has been identified more frequently in the past decade. In one case, an Asian woman was forced by her loan shark to hand over all of her family's antiques and jewelry. It was an act which she felt brought great shame upon her and her family. When she had nothing of value left, the loan shark insisted on a sexual relationship with her and also forcing her into prostitution. She shot and killed him.

In another incident, a female compulsive gambler was paid to care for an elderly man in her home, which included cashing his Social Security payments, pension checks, and handling his finances. Sinking deeper into debt because of her gambling, she suffocated him and hid his body in the trunk of a car, which she later abandoned in another state. She continued to cash his checks for several years until the fraud was discovered, which then lead to solving the homicide. She was sentenced to a life term in prison.

THE JUDICIAL SYSTEM

ARRESTS AND THE FAMILY

An arrest is shocking and frightening to family members, especially to the children of all ages, since none have ever been exposed to such an event and have no frame of reference on how to react or cope with it. Fortunately for the family, most compulsive gamblers know they have committed crimes, the same ones repeatedly for months or even years, and know that eventually they will either admit to the crimes on their own or their crimes will be discovered at work. In such cases, a traumatic police arrest at work or home can be prevented—the gambler and his attorney report to the police or prosecuting attorney, acknowledging the crime. Many times, the gamblers will sigh with relief: "I'm glad it's over, I feel like a piano was taken off my back. I wanted to stop but couldn't do it by myself."

One owner of a medium-sized business with approximately 100 employees was a big-time Las Vegas gambler. He was wealthy and at the onset of his gambling used his own money and blackjack winnings to support his gambling. Eventually, his losses increased drastically, and he signed marker after marker while gambling. Unable to redeem them, he used company funds to avoid legal charges. Confronted by the company's accountant, he protested that it was his company and therefore his money. Two months later, he was unable to make payroll, his company was on the verge of collapse, and all employees were at risk of losing their jobs. Only through negotiations by the company accountant and lawyers was he able to secure bank financing and save the company from ruin. To protect the company from further embezzlement, a new accounting system was set up and the gambler no longer had access to any company checks, income, or disbursements. When his wife learned of his actions, she filed for divorce. "I never thought I would be married to a felon."

In another instance, an insurance agent signed claims checks over to herself and embezzled $200,000 before her crimes were discovered. She was a long-term trusted employee with an excellent work history when she became addicted to slots at a nearby racino. Based on her past work performance and having no prior history of any legal entanglements, not even a motor vehicle violation, her public defender was able to negotiate home monitoring, lengthy probation, and restitution. She found employment with a similar company, continued to gamble, stole another $100,000, and FBI agents arrested her a second time. Prosecutors and defense attorneys were dumbfounded when her new crimes came to light. This time, she was sentenced to jail. She had never joined Gamblers Anonymous nor had she sought professional treatment after the first arrest.

In a frightening case, a sports bettor owed several thousand dollars to a loan shark and could not pay. The loan shark went to the sports bettor's house and pointed a gun at the young wife who screamed in terror and tried to hide her young children. Desperate, the sports bettor broke into his neighbor's house, stole what he could, and one day came home to find his house surrounded by police, cruisers with emergency lights on, and neighbors milling around. The children witnessed their father being arrested and led away in handcuffs. It took months of psychotherapy before the children were able sleep without nightmares and stop hiding whenever they saw a police car.

DEFENSE ATTORNEYS AND PROSECUTORS

Most compulsive gamblers have no prior criminal history of entanglements with the law, although many have civil violations, mostly motor vehicle violations, such as unpaid parking tickets. They do have a history of being high achievers at school and work, avoiding illegal drugs, and want nothing more than a "normal family with three kids and a backyard." Contrary to common beliefs, they do not see themselves as great spenders living in lavish houses, with gleaming sports cars, and going on expensive vacations. As one accountant turned bookie said, "I was just an ordinary guy."

That's not to say that the flashiness doesn't happen, it does, but this is the exception rather than the rule. Certainly, there are many compulsive gamblers who earn a substantial income, thus the larger house and new car are understandable. And yes, when gamblers win big at the casino, they do live in a temporary "big shot" image, whooping it up at the craps table, tipping dealers generously, and spending lavishly on their friends and family. These spenders and high rollers are the action gamblers, who, as part of their big shot image, must be bigger than big. This behavior is rarely demonstrated by escape gamblers.

Compulsive gamblers know they have committed crimes and are relieved when their criminal activities are discovered. Almost always, they will plead guilty and await sentencing, rather than pleading not guilty and facing a trial by judge or jury. If the crimes were committed against a company, such as a salesman misusing a company credit card and charging casino hotel bills, the company's accountant will sort through the issues, make arrangements for restitution, usually demand treatment, and the employee is likely to be terminated. If the once-valued salesman is allowed to remain with the company, then arrangements are made to prevent him from having access to any credit cards or advance payments.

If, on the other hand, a company has been defrauded of a substantial amount or is obligated by virtue of state or federal law to report the crime, the police are contacted and an arrest is made. A thorough investigation is undertaken by the prosecutor's office to determine the exact amounts misappropriated, which may take several months.

If the employee has stolen money from a business, there may be dispute between the gambler and the company regarding the amount stolen. The gambler most frequently is in disbelief when the larger figure is proven. In a recent case, a book keeper for a small business thought she had stolen $34,000 until she was shown the account books and saw that she had, in fact, stolen $51,000.

DEFENSE ATTORNEY

Compulsive gamblers have not only stolen monies and properties, but they are also in great debt and without any financial resources. Most assuredly, they do not have the thousands of dollars necessary to pay for a private defense attorney, nor are their families generally willing or able to hire an attorney. They require the services of a state or federal public defender.

There seems to be considerable differences in funding between state and federal public defenders offices. State public defenders are overburdened with cases, do not have sufficient monies for support staff, investigations or witnesses. Offices tend to be overcrowded and in less desirable buildings or locations. In most instances, a state public defender may be contacted at the time of arrest but will not actually be able to work the case until shortly before the pleading and sentencing. In the case previously mentioned involving multiple bad check charges in which the defendant had repaid all checks, the defense attorney did not meet with the gambler until they were actually in the courtroom, at sentencing. This is not an unusual case.

Federal public defenders, although also handling a large caseload, may have considerably more time to work their cases, tend to have sufficient attorneys and support staff, equipment, and reasonable financial support for investigations and witnesses. As a general rule, their offices are more comfortable and pleasant and are located closer to the federal courthouse, if not actually inside the federal building. They often also have more contact with probation and parole officers and more time to negotiate with prosecutors. Thus, in most instances, a federal public defender can offer more services than the state counterpart.

Federal and state prosecutors at times face similar issues. If a case is high profile, some prosecutors have been known to be overzealous in their public stance, claiming "sixty-nine charges," which during negotiations between prosecutor and defense counselor may be collapsed to three. Other prosecutors may see a case of public interest as an opportunity for career enhancement. In one federal case involving embezzlement of nearly one million dollars, the federal prosecutor was accompanied by two assistants and three FBI agents in the courtroom, sitting at the same table. Prosecution was well-prepared with findings from investigations, reports, and witnesses. The gambler sat at the defense table with his court-appointed defense counselor, without a paralegal assistant or expert witness.

On occasion, prosecutors and judges step over the line of civility. One state judge referred to the public defender as, as "you're not a real lawyer, are you?" and then made a reference to the expert witness as "psychologists and all that ilk." A federal prosecutor was particularly abrasive toward an expert witness in a high profile case and then apologized to the witness when they were in the courthouse elevator. "I was just doing my job." Others may resort to grandstanding during court proceedings or when questioned by the media.

Although the above are just a few selected instances, these behaviors can terrify a compulsive gambler who has had no prior experience or knowledge of the criminal justice system. Not surprisingly, these first offenders who are now facing prison, seriously consider or actually attempt to commit suicide.

THE JUDGE

Judges are elected officials and as such are keenly aware of the impact any crime may have, especially a crime with profound impact on the community. A bank robbery or a multi-million dollar insurance fraud are types of crimes that a compulsive gambler might commit that would alarm or outrage the community.

Judges are obligated to consider several factors in sentencing an offender:

1 – Punishment to reflect the seriousness of the offense;
2 – Deterrence of future criminal conduct by the gambler and the public;
3 – Protection of the community;
4 – Restitution to any victims of the offense; and
5 – Providing for the rehabilitation of the offender.

Some judges are considered "hard." They tend to mete out severe sentences for relatively minor crimes, while others are considered "soft" and are more lenient. All judges are expected to be knowledgeable of the law and to rule accordingly; nevertheless, judges have a certain amount of discretion in sentencing and may also follow their own personal convictions and experiences.

Congress set the standards for federal guidelines when it enacted the Sentencing Reform Act of 1984. The act created a federal sentencing commission, which took discretion of sentencing out of the hands of federal trial judges. Judges were now required to follow strict formulas to determine the range of a sentence. The Federal Sentencing Guidelines further created a somewhat complicated point system for determining the range of a prison sentence. It attempted to take into account every relevant factor that could conceivably be connected with the crime, such as the gambler's voluntarily admission of guilt, prior criminal history, cooperation with prosecution, nature and extent of economic crimes, and amount of money involved. A serious shortcoming is the amount stolen – a bank teller may steal three thousand dollars, a bank loan officer could steal three hundred thousand dollars. Both are compulsive gamblers committing crimes, but their access to funds differ, and the amount of their theft.

In its *Application Note*, the Federal Sentencing Guidelines state:

> For purposes of this policy – Significantly reduced mental
> capacity means the defendant, although convicted, has
> a significantly impaired ability to (a) understand the
> wrongfulness of the behavior comprising the offense or to
> exercise the power of reason; or (b) control behavior that
> the defendant knows is wrongful.

Thus judges have guidelines for using diminished capacity
at sentencing. These guidelines were used successfully in a
number of important precedent-setting rulings; unfortunately,
Congress reduced the diminished capacity option in favor of
aberrant behavior, which is somewhat more difficult to apply to a
compulsive gambler, most particularly one who has been out of
control for many years. The behavior therefore is deemed to be
normal or customary, rather than aberrant.

There is considerable discrepancy between sentencing in state
courts and federal courts. There is even more discrepancy between
state courts and within state and county courts. For example, some
states may have a mandatory sentence of life in prison without
parole for a homicide, whereas another state court may sentence
the offender to six years of confinement. Punishment can range
from severe or mandatory periods of incarceration, to a waiver of
all or part of the incarceration sentence, or probation. A state court
sentence of incarceration generally must be served for two-thirds
of the sentence before the offender is eligible for parole, whereas
the entire sentence must be served in a federal jurisdiction. More
recently, some reduction of incarceration is valid, on the basis
of good behavior, and also because of overcrowding in state and
federal correctional institutions.

Frequently, the gambler's defense attorney may seek to have
the gambler's case steted or submit a plea of nolo contendere. A
stet or nolo contendere ruling requires that there be no further

infractions for a period of one year, after which the case will be dismissed. A violation of the stet ruling will result in both cases being prosecuted.

Several years ago a momentous event occurred. Judge Mark Farrell established a gambling court, similar to drug courts. (Amherst, NY). Criminal defendants, identified to having a gambling problem, have their cases heard in this court. They can also be referred to treatment.

PROBATION/PAROLE OFFICERS

After having been charged with infractions of the law, an arrest summons may be mailed or hand-delivered to the gambler. In other cases, the gambler may be arrested, booked, and held in custody until bail is set or the gambler is released on his/her own recognizance. This occurs when the charge does not represent a serious or violent criminal act, or the offender is not a flight risk. If bail is set, the gambler will need to pay the entire amount in cash, ten percent to a bail bondsman, or remain in jail until such time bail can be paid or the case is heard in court; however, more typically, compulsive gamblers are released on their own recognizance.

The next appearance in court after the bail hearing is the status hearing, at which time the gambler must enter a plea of guilty, not guilty, not guilty by reason of insanity, or an Alford plea. The Alford plea is used only in state courts and is infrequently used by compulsive gamblers. It says basically that the person pleads not guilty but acknowledges that there is enough evidence to secure a finding of guilt. The insanity defense is rarely valid; rather, a defense of diminished capacity or aberrant behavior is presented at sentencing.

After the status hearing, the compulsive gambler is assigned to a pre-trial probation officer who conducts an extensive, detailed, and verified background check on the gambler. This includes specific information about family of origin and marital family, education, work history, health, prior criminal and civil charges, and other pertinent information, such as suffering from compulsive gambling. The higher the number of points, the greater the punishment and likelihood of incarceration. The pre-sentence investigation report includes recommendations to the judge. The report also indicates if the gambler had any prior offenses, acknowledged the criminal behavior, cooperated with prosecution, and assisted in other means, with each factor assigned a pre-determined number of points. These points may be moved up or down or remain intact, based on prosecutor's and defense attorney's arguments. Prosecutors tend to demand a higher punishment with a longer period of incarceration while the defense attorney will claim extenuating and mitigating circumstances leading to a lower sentence.

Whereas the pre-sentence investigation is factual, it does not include emotional impact or behavioral aspects. The report will contain specific information about the father, such as age, education, and employment, without indicating that the father was physically, verbally, and psychologically abusive, which left emotional and developmental scars on the compulsive gambler. It may state that the paternal grandmother died at age 65, but does not indicate the emotional closeness between the grandmother and the six-year-old child, the unresolved grief leading to a dysthymic depression and emotional withdrawal. Nor does it identify the critical adverse life events in childhood, adult life, and during a two-year period immediately prior to out-of-control gambling, and how these contributed to the desperate gambling and subsequent offenses.

Nevertheless, the entire process, from crime committed, to arrest, and going through the legal and judicial systems is alien to virtually all compulsive gamblers, who typically have no history of prior criminal offenses. Even those serving in the law enforcement, legal, and judicial fields, and who may be thoroughly familiar with the process, are overwhelmed and often terrified when they themselves face the legal consequences of their crimes.

THE JAILS

The majority of compulsive gamblers serve in minimum security camps, which are referred to as "country clubs." These camps do not have prison walls with razor wire, such as found in medium or maximum secure facilities. Some are located on military bases. In camps, the inmates have greater freedom of movement than they would have in any penitentiary or higher level of security; nevertheless, the boundaries are clearly defined and any steps outside of these boundaries are considered prison breach and will result in consequences.

Most compulsive gamblers are sentenced to federal prison, which in the past almost always housed nonviolent inmates; however, today, these prisons house offenders who often are drug dealers with a history of violence. Compulsive gamblers are convinced that all prisons are like maximum security state penitentiaries in which inmates are raped, severely beaten, stabbed, or killed, as depicted on television, and which does occur in real-life situations. It has been found helpful for compulsive gamblers to become familiar with federal prisons, perhaps even drive past them to view the prison site. Without exception, this will reduce the acute anxiety level suffered by these compulsive gamblers and will also lessen the potential for suicide.

Exceptions exist and occur. Whereas physical harm from other inmates is infrequent in federal camps and prisons, on occasion, a prison guard uses excessive force or has a personal vendetta against an inmate. One compulsive gambler who was a lawyer reported such incidents of beatings upon his release, and took appropriate actions against the guard. He recognized that it would have been imprudent for him to do anything while he was still in custody.

After an offender has been sentenced, the case is turned over to the Designator's Officer, who reviews myriad factors to determine which facility is most in compliance with the court's sentence and the needs of the offender. Some of the considerations are the length of the sentence, closeness to the offender's home, medical needs, specific requirements in the court order, and space availability. The compulsive gambler is usually ordered to report to jail in two weeks, enough time to settle personal and business matters.

Family members should learn as much as possible about the prison system. A caveat: today's county jails are rarely "drunk tanks" or ten-cell jails; rather, many consist of tiers of barred cells, concrete floors, hundreds of inmates, heavily armed guards patrolling the walkways. Today's county jails can be intimidating even in their design, size, and mix of inmate population.

Incarcerated offenders are allowed to write and receive letters but not packages; they can make collect phone calls but cannot accept any calls from outsiders. Inmates must designate visitors and an application must be completed by the visitor. Approval of the application to be added onto the inmate's visitor's list generally is completed within two to three weeks. Inmates meet their visitors in a large lounge, noisy and without privacy or in a small windowless, cell-like room, separated by a glass partition and speak to the visitor by phone. Attorneys and their staff have ready access to inmates and usually these visits are held in private cubicles or, on occasion, inside a cell.

Inmates need spending money for personal items, i.e. thirty dollars per month for deodorant or such, which they receive from family members and friends. Inmates can also perform various prison maintenance functions for which they earn a nominal amount of money, usually sufficient to meet their monthly needs. Both state and federal prisons try to accommodate inmates who have religious constraints, such as observance of holidays and serving kosher food.

SUMMARY

Legalization of many forms of gambling throughout the United States, and, indeed, the world, has introduced a whole, new, diverse population of gamblers and compulsive gamblers. They now cross the spectrum of people: young and old, single and couples, of all socio-economic classes, races, ethnicities, religions, and cultures; who are independent, and those who are self-sufficient or cared for by others; those who are healthy and those who are addicts or suffer from other psychiatric, behavioral, mental, and medical disorders. Gambling today is universal, available, and easily accessible. The latest estimates by private and governmental-funded studies indicate that the number of compulsive gamblers in the United States varies from one percent to five percent of the gambling population, from three to five million gamblers.

Money is the abused substance of gambling addiction. Virtually all compulsive gamblers will commit crimes or civil violations, whether these become public or not. These crimes in the past were of a nonviolent financial nature. However, the greater diversity of gambling addicts has also led to a greater diversity of criminal and civil violations. Presently, the majority of crimes fall under the federal criminal code. It is estimated that twenty-five percent of these addicts are arrested, and fifteen percent are incarcerated.

Typically, compulsive gamblers have no prior criminal history of entanglement with the law. Many do, however, have been charged with civil cases, such as motor vehicle violations or domestic issues. Nevertheless, the entire law enforcement, criminal, and judicial processes are unknown and terrifying for them and their families. Education and prevention programs, research and treatment are needed to combat "the addiction of the nineties."

Valerie C. Lorenz, Ph.D.

THE FAILURE OF AMERICAN JUSTICE, 1999: JAILS AS SUBSTITUTES FOR HOSPITALS THE CRIME OF PUNISHMENT THE DEATH OF COMPASSION

by Valerie C. Lorenz, Ph.D.

Compulsive Gambling is the name
Horses, slots – whatever's the game.
"A mental illness." Can it be so?

Saul's diagnosis: Gambling Addiction
"I can win" was his conviction.
A mental illness does not show.

Saul lost his money, every penny
And yet his friends still lent him money.
They hoped, but did not know.

At last, through anger, fear and sorrow,
They realized that he'd always borrow
And not a soul would lend him more.

He turned to crime to pay his debts
But used the funds to place more bets.
The "Big Win" was his goal to score.

The prosecution saw a chance
To take a loud and public stance:
The legal system did not know.

"It's greed, he's guilty," and sought
conviction.
"Don't tell us about addiction.
The place for him is prison."

The doctors rallied, pled their case,
The mighty judge just turned his face.
Why would he not listen?

The doctors pleaded, "Jail can't cure.
We can treat, thus heal his mind.
Let our justice not be blind."

"To deter others, to punish all,
To keep the city safe from Saul."
The judge's voice was firm.

His mother cried, "Where did I fail?
She begged, "Don't send my son to jail."
She was old, her health was frail.

To care for Mom had been Saul's mission.
With heavy heart he left for prison.
Was there no other way?

He sat in jail, day after day,
To help his heart he turned to pray.
The doctor's help was far away.

At last his prison time was done,
Saul hurried home to see his mom.
"I'm back to care for you."

He found his mother on the floor:
She'd left this world an hour before.
And Saul screamed out–in vain.

"Mom," he cried, his pain so great.
He held her in his arms, afraid
To let her be alone again.

"Compulsive gambling is the name
That broke my mind and broke your heart.
No more will it keep us apart."

And put a bullet through his head.
(CR.A. No. 1:97 CR00-106-001, (LON)
Camden)

CHAPTER 16
THE PEER COUNSELOR

The peer counselor of a compulsive gambling treatment program has a unique, integral role in a comprehensive treatment team. This peer counselor is an individual who is in recovery from compulsive gambling, who is committed to the philosophy and principles of the 12-Step Gamblers Anonymous program. This team member assists the compulsive gamblers/clients who are seeking to overcome their gambling addiction and the devastation they have caused.

There is a financial distinction: peer counselors working in professional treatment settings earn a salary, Gamblers Anonymous members do not. The twelfth step of their recovery program is a voluntary activity of "giving back." This financial distinction can create tension and conflict between the peer counselor and GA members.

In the past, peer counselors serving in clinical settings did not need any credentials other than abstinence, recovery, and a desire to teach the 12-Step program. This has changed in recent years, and this role is now being professionalized. Currently, in most states, a State Professional Board certifying and licensing alcohol and drug abuse counselors requires them to have a master's degree in counseling or psychology with specialized training in substance addictions. Similar steps are being taken in the compulsive gambling arena. Certified compulsive gambling counselors are defined as Level I, peer counselors without academic training or licensure, but who completed a compulsive gambling training program. Level II compulsive gambling counselors are those with training in addiction or mental health counseling, who have academic credentials at the master's level in counseling, who are certified or licensed by their state professional licensing boards, and who have completed a specialized compulsive gambling training program, usually consisting of sixty hours of classroom training, a specified number of treatment sessions with gamblers, and supervision. Thus their state code accreditation might read, "Masters in psychology with specialized training in compulsive gambling." Each state has its own criteria for this designation. "Compulsive gambling counselor" itself is not a designation which meets standards for state licensure.

THE PAID PEER COUNSELOR'S ISSUES

There are a number of issues which confront the peer counselor who becomes a member of a professional treatment team.

VIOLATION OF ANONYMITY

The peer counselor, by the very nature of its function, plays a dual role: one as John Smith, paid counselor in a mental health setting, and the other as John S., member of Gamblers Anonymous. The mental health setting will use the peer counselor's full name on legal materials, i.e., paychecks, clinical notes, legal documents, and program certification documents. Gamblers Anonymous does not. It espouses anonymity and instead refers to the peer counselor as John S. — the first name and initial of the last name.

This creates some immediate complications for the outside community and the peer. Prisons and jails, for instance, find it useful to have a 12-step program in their institutions to serve in conjunction with their drug treatment programs. Members of GA see this as an extension of their own program, the twelfth step of giving back to others. However, in order to enter a prison, the individual must undergo screening and a background check, which requires full disclosure of name, address, and photograph identification. Even the GA member who is on the inmate's visitors list undergoes such screening. Thus, disclosure of personal identity, i.e., full name, is in violation of the principles of Gamblers Anonymous.

CONFLICTS BETWEEN PROFESSIONALS AND PEERS

Aside from administrative complications, there are also personal issues between professionals and the peer. Often professionals view the peer as uneducated and unskilled in professional therapy and thereby do not accept the peer as a valued member of the treatment team. The peer, on the other hand, may view the professionals as lacking in knowledge about compulsive gambling and understanding the compulsive gambler's needs and behaviors. This mutual distrust can be harmful to all: the professional, the peer, and especially the client.

Further, peer counselors may start using clinical terms, which more often than not are incorrect or which give a false impression of the peer's qualifications. They may use terms such as "personality disorder" or "affective disorder" or "misplaced anger." It is not the role of a peer to be a professional. The peer's function on a clinical team should remain "peer" rather than "professional."

DIFFERENCES IN APPROACHES

An example of this is when the client owes money to his bookie. Professionals view bookmaking as an illegal activity and are apt to promote the position of, "Don't pay the bookie." Gamblers

Anonymous generally views this approach as a bail-out, less than honest, and prefers to work out a payment plan with the bookie. It can become very troublesome if the clinician and the peer voice these differences in the same clinical session. It shows a lack of teamwork and philosophy of the treatment program and also lessens the trust and confidence the client may have in the clinician or the peer or both. It is incumbent upon both the professional and the peer to remain in their roles and to work together, the key to which is regular communication between the two.

CONFLICTS WITHIN THE GA GROUP

Gamblers Anonymous tends to have a high drop-out rate and longevity of membership is often a defining factor within the group. Thus it is not surprising if a GA member with more years of abstinence than the peer counselor voices feelings of being rejected and being more qualified to become a paid member of the clinical team. This becomes an ego issue of "character defects" and "humility." Being paid is also a money issue; after all, gambling is about money. These differences can lead to tension within the GA group and with members taking sides. Such conflicts must be addressed immediately to prevent emotional injury to the group and the peer.

FROM COUNSELOR TO SPONSOR

Another ethical issue confronting the peer counselor begs the question: "What is the role of peer counselor for the client who completed the treatment program?" During treatment, the peer counselor and the client tend to bond and develop a therapeutic relationship. Does this role terminate after a client's discharge from professional treatment or is the peer counselor then expected to become a GA sponsor for the client? If the client lives out of state, that may not be an issue; the client can be referred to a counselor and local GA chapter. However, if the client lives close to the peer, is it feasible for both to attend the same meeting? The peer counselor may have some personal issues for which he seeks help from GA, but this may lessen the respect from the former client. The peer is deprived of the support and fellowship from the GA group.

Conversely, is it ethical for the peer counselor to serve as a sponsor for the former client if the client requests this, or is this another dual role which is likely to cause friction? Failure to serve as sponsor may lead to feelings of rejection. Is this a trigger for a potential relapse? Additionally, if the peer counselor serves as a sponsor for one discharged client, will other former or future clients expect that same attention and support? Once again, this can become troublesome for the peer, the ex-client, and the GA group. Added to this confusion, what distinctions are made if a client was discharged from the program prior to the peer's inclusion in the treatment team. What are the limits and expectations of either GA member? These issues, ethical and legal concerns, must be addressed, repeatedly, to avoid undesirable consequences.

Clarification of the peer's roles, that of wearing "two hats," becomes critical if bad feelings, uncertainty and tension are to be prevented. As with any interpersonal issues, this needs to be done on a one-on-one basis and then with the group.

THE GAMBLERS ANONYMOUS PROGRAM

Gamblers Anonymous is without doubt the most effective support for compulsive gamblers trying to recover from their addiction. However, there are some differences between Gamblers Anonymous, in program and in practice, and between other twelve-step programs, which must be understood in order to reap the full benefits of what GA has to offer.

This 12-Step program is based on the principles of the Alcoholics Anonymous (AA) program. Started in 1957 in Los Angeles by two recovering alcoholics, Gamblers Anonymous (GA) now has chapters in most states and many foreign countries, including Europe, South America, and Africa. There are approximately 1,500 chapters in the US. Not surprisingly, Nevada has the largest number of meetings, over 150 per week, a dozen states have less than ten, and some states have none. States receiving state-funding for treatment and prevention tend to have fifty or more.

The majority of GA meetings are closed, meaning membership and attendance is restricted to compulsive gamblers or individuals who are uncertain of their addiction. There are some meetings which are held jointly with Gam-Anon, the twelve-step program for friends and family of the compulsive gambler. Some GA meetings are open to the public. GA also has special meetings: for women only, for beginners, and for Spanish-speaking members.

Although much of the GA literature is the same as that of AA, in practice, the two programs differ in some areas. These variations may be due to the lack of knowledge or experience by GA members, lack of resources, or differences in the personalities of the gambler and that of other types of addicts.

LONERS

A basic difference between GA members and those of other 12-Step meetings is that of relationships. Gamblers have a lifetime history of being loners and therefore have difficulty accepting a concept of fellowship. This is especially true of action gamblers who seek attention and approval, in contrast to escape gamblers who feel more confident in themselves and prefer to be left alone. Yet reaching out to others is virtually alien to both and they feel vulnerable. They need someone to approach them. Unfortunately, in most GA meetings, the new member is given a phone list of other members in the group. The new member will rarely initiate a plea for help, especially from strangers.

LACK OF SPONSORS

The retention rate of GA members is low, between three to five percent, in contrast to AA and other 12-Step programs which have many members with twenty or thirty years of active membership and sobriety. In addition, not many GA chapters have members with more than five years of recovery: many gamblers drop out of the program within the first year. Thus not all chapters of GA have members who can or are willing to serve as a sponsor for the new member.

COMPETITIVENESS

Another difference between GA and other 12-Step programs is the competitive nature of the gambler. The action gamblers tend to have narcissistic features, and too many narcissistic members in one group leads to dictators rather than fellowship, resulting in a struggle between being a leader or dictator versus being a "trusted servant."

Humility, a characteristics often absent among compulsive gamblers, does not mean thinking less of one's self, but rather thinking of oneself in relation to others.

MONEY

Money is the substance of compulsive gambling. Twelve-step guidelines teach the addict to become responsible, such as handling finances responsibly. In contrast, the GA wisdom is that the gambler should not handle money or have access to money. Ever. Indeed, GA offers a financial pressure relief group in which a designated person in the gambler's family takes control of the finances. If not conducted cooperatively, this can lead to a resentment of having to ask for money or of having money being doled out to them, especially if the gambler was accustomed to carrying large sums of cash and several credit cards. They find this new way of managing money demeaning, and this can become a powerful trigger for relapsing. It is a conflict between ego and humility. This is not an issue within other 12-Step programs.

CONTROL

Compulsive gamblers also have a strong need to be in control and to be the best of the best. These entrenched beliefs make it difficult for them to accept the first and second steps of the program, "We admitted we were powerless over gambling—that our lives had become unmanageable" and "Came to believe that a power greater than ourselves could restore us to a normal way of thinking and living." Compulsive gamblers abhor being powerless and believe in themselves and their own capabilities rather than others or a higher power.

INVENTORIES

The most frequent complaint by new members of GA after having attended meetings for three or four months is, "It's nothing but war stories, over and over. After a few meetings I can tell you exactly what their story is." Another complaint is that of interaction. "When I have a problem, I like for the members to give me some feedback. Instead, they clap and go on to the next guy." "Miss a few weeks and there will be a whole new group of guys. The older ones are gone." "Inventory? They're great at taking your inventory. Who needs it? I come for support, not to be judged." "Sponsorship means they give you a list of phone numbers. I'm messed up enough, I don't need some stranger to tell me what to do. Besides, what if that guy doesn't want to be bothered with me or my problems?"

AVAILABILITY

Other problems are those of availability. "Ninety meetings in ninety days—that's AA, not GA." Fifteen states have less than 10 GA meetings per week, some have only one meeting. Many meetings have fewer than ten members. New members, in the depth of debts and lack of money, may not have a car or money for gas to get to a meeting. Most meetings are held in the evening, from 8 to10 p.m., but many women or the elderly prefer not to drive at night, or to drive alone.

EXPOSURE

Many GA members handle money in the course of their work—lawyers, accountants, bankers, businessmen, cashiers, sales associates—which puts them at greater risk of losing their jobs than if they had an alcohol or some other medical problem. "Have an alcohol problem and your boss sends you to rehab for a month. Have a gambling problem, you can bet on being terminated. Can you imagine going to an accountant or stock broker who has a gambling addiction? Your money is safer under your mattress. There is no way that I can join GA." In these cases, a professional counselor might encourage the client to attend AA meetings. Even though the client may not suffer from alcoholism, many members of AA also have a gambling addiction. Another alternative is to attend a professionals meeting, which is usually an AA or NA meeting but invites all addicts who serve in a profession that demands greater anonymity and confidentiality.

CHANGES WITHIN GA

With the introduction and expansion of legalized gambling in forty-eight states, slot machine gamblers and lottery players are now accepted as compulsive gamblers and are no longer viewed as "not real gamblers." Membership has changed from middle-aged white males, to include young adults and seniors, males and females, small-time gamblers and casino whales, and from all racial, ethnic and socioeconomic backgrounds.

LITERATURE

Although literature is sparse, it is anticipated that the GA International Service Office will develop more, just as the public arena and academia are now researching and writing more about this disorder. As compulsive gambling becomes better known, understood, and accepted by the outside community, there will be more compulsive gamblers who will practice the twelve steps and share their experiences with others, and as the availability and accessibility of legal gambling increases, so will the number of compulsive gamblers, and therefore more GA meetings, more members with longevity, more sponsors, and more literature. The number of state-wide, multi-state, and regional conferences is also growing, and therefore more members with greater diversity will need, learn, and incorporate new methods and variations in their meetings.

GAM-ANON

There are far fewer Gam-Anon meetings in the country, and Gam-Ateen is virtually non-existent, thus limiting the support for the gambler's family. It is more important now than ever before to expand treatment within a professional treatment program, to include family therapy and to offer Gam-Anon attendance. A Gam-Anon member could also serve as a peer counselor.

THE TWENTY QUESTIONS
OF GAMBLERS ANONYMOUS

Currently, in most GA meetings, a newcomer is taken aside and responds to the Twenty Questions of Gamblers Anonymous. Some newcomers may minimize the extent of their gambling and the consequences. This is quite true of those who attend GA at the demand of someone else, usually a spouse, rather than being self-motivated. Others, those who are in a severe state of depression or who have had suicidal thoughts, may attend because they recognize that they have lost control over their lives and are willing to reach out for help, and thus are prone to give more accurate responses.

Compulsive gamblers tend to have a poor or fair level of insight (the ability to be aware of internal and external realities) into themselves and their behaviors, thus denial of the seriousness of their addiction may last for months or years, before they hit the proverbial "bottom" at which time they are emotionally exhausted and can no longer deny the evident.

Those who are in denial of their problematic gambling virtually always respond Yes to Question 4 (guilt), 5 (get money), 7 (chasing), 9 (last dollar), 10 (borrow), 15 (escape), 16 (crime) and 20 (self-destruction), yet even those responses may be minimized, or trivialized with comments such as, "well, only one time" or "not that much." Family members would often respond quite differently to the Twenty Questions if they were asked to respond for the gambler.

1. *Did you ever lose time from work or school due to gambling?*
    Many compulsive gamblers will respond NO, rationalizing that they were physically at their work site or in school. That is a concrete interpretation of the question. The question implies any distraction due to gambling, resulting in poor performance at work or school.

2. *Has gambling ever made your home life unhappy?*
   YES and NO. While many gamblers will admit to this, others believe they have successfully manipulated their finances and gambling behaviors and thus avoided detection.

3. *Did gambling affect your reputation?*
   Many times compulsive gamblers will minimize the answer to this question.

4. *Have you ever felt remorse (or guilt) after gambling?*
   A YES response is almost universal. Their feelings of guilt lead to many other behaviors in order to assuage the guilt, such as gambling to escape these painful thoughts and feelings, more desperate efforts to win back losses, and ultimately even to thoughts of suicide.

5. *Did you ever gamble to get money with which to pay debts or otherwise solve financial problems?*
   YES, gambling invariably is seen as a quick means of getting the money they need, for whatever reason. The need for money is perhaps the most severe trigger to gamble, in spite of all obstacles or intentions to remain abstinent.

6. *Did gambling cause a decrease in your ambition or efficiency?*
   YES and NO. In most instances the gambler's state of depression or desperation to recoup losses inhibits the gambler's ability for efficiency and inhibits any motivation to do well at work or school. In contrast, some compulsive gamblers are able to completely compartmentalize their addiction and become hyper-focused on their work, to the exclusion of all other distractions.

7. *After losing, did you feel you must return as soon as possible and win back your losses? (chasing)*

   YES, chasing after losses is the hallmark of gambling addiction.

8. *After a win did you have a strong urge to return and win more?*

   YES, a win is viewed as another opportunity to gamble, to win money to pay overdue bills, to repeat the sense of action, or to emotionally escape a troubling reality.

9. *Did you often gamble until your last dollar was gone?*

   YES, with the very rare exception, the answer to this question is always YES.

10. *Did you ever borrow to finance your gambling?*

    YES, this is typically the first indication that social gambling has become problematic, especially when the "borrowing" is stealing.

11. *Have you ever sold (or pawned) anything to finance your gambling?*

    YES, this starts in the earlier stage of compulsive gambling. The items sold or pawned belong to the gambler or to a close family member rather than someone outside of the family.

12. *Were you reluctant to use "gambling money" for normal expenditures?*

    YES and NO. Compulsive gamblers talk of having two pockets, one for gambling and the other for debts and expenses. When the "gambling pocket" is empty, the gambler will take money from "the other pocket" or seek money from alternative sources, legal or illegal.

13. *Did gambling make you careless of the welfare of your family?*

NO and Yes. More often than not the gambler will protest that financial family needs were met, not realizing that many items, such as medical care and social activities, have been curtailed.

14. *Did you ever gamble longer than you planned?*

YES, gamblers lose track of time when gambling, spending many hours in front of a computer, two to three days at the blackjack table, ten or more hours playing slots, or from noon till midnight at the OTB watching horse races.

15. *Have you ever gambled to escape worry or trouble?*

YES, although in many instances this is denied, often due to a lack of insight into their actions, or their rationalizations that they gamble "for the action," "because I like it," or "she made me so angry."

16. *Have you ever committed, or considered committing, an illegal act to finance gambling?*

YES and NO, nearly 99% of compulsive gamblers resort to some form of illegal activities to obtain money due to gambling losses or to continue gambling. Most often illegal activities start with thefts from the family, yet they do not consider selling a family item or taking out a credit card in a family member's name as illegal or stealing. Virtually all illegal acquisition of funds, regardless of method, amount, or frequency, is viewed as "borrowing," with the sincere intention of replacing the item or the money after the Big Win, which is sure to be the next bet.

17. *Did gambling cause you to have difficulty in sleeping?*

YES, all forms of sleep problems may occur, such as insomnia, early morning awakening, intermittent sleep disruption, bad dreams and nightmares.

18. *Do arguments, disappointments or frustrations create within you an urge to gamble?*

YES, in many cases, although some will insist they gamble for the action, high, or rush. Slots gamblers in particular gamble to escape troubles and bad feelings, and will play two or three slot machines at a time to intensify that sense of peace and hypnotic trance.

19. *Did you ever have an urge to celebrate any good fortune by a few hours of gambling?*

YES, assuming that the good fortune means having an unexpected source of money which can then be used for gambling.

20. *Have you ever considered self-destruction as a result of your gambling?*

YES and NO. Many compulsive gamblers report having been obsessed with thoughts of suicide for weeks before they "hit bottom." Some do attempt suicide, most often by causing an auto accident, although if unsuccessful, they will deny that the accident was a suicide attempt. If carefully probed, however, they will admit that the "accident" was a suicide attempt.

Gamblers Anonymous espouses that *"Most compulsive gamblers will answer Yes to at least Seven of the 20 Questions."* In clinical settings, YES responses more typically range between 14 to 20.

The peer counselor is perhaps the most effective person to help the gambler in working Steps 4 (honesty), 5 (courage), and 6 (willingness) of the program, taking an inventory of their character defects and being willing to change them. This ideally is a two-person process initially before being addressed in a group meeting in a professional setting or of Gamblers Anonymous. Self-deception is best recognized and confronted, in a supportive manner.

Equally difficult for the gamblers in recovery is to acknowledge the emotional and financial damage they have caused and to make appropriate amends. The peer counselor can be an invaluable guide in these efforts.

INTERVENTION

Denial is a common reaction from people upon being told they have a serious medical or mental health illness. This is equally true of compulsive gamblers. "It's not that bad, I can afford it, I can stop anytime, I need time for relaxation," are just a few of the more common protests. In conjunction with this denial by the gambler is the reaction by the spouse or family member. "It's my fault, I make him angry, he'll stop because he loves me, he has to want treatment, etc." Denial, codependency, and enabling are all associated with substance and behavioral addiction, such as drinking, drugging, smoking, shopping, Internet games, and, of course, gambling.

The alcoholism field was the first to respond to the need for help and developed an Intervention program, which usually requires six or more training sessions with family members and significant others. Each member of the group writes a letter to the alcoholic in which they express their feelings and concerns about the drinking, and how that has impacted them. They insist the alcoholic attend AA meetings, enter professional treatment, or both, and present a list of consequences of these demands are not met. This process usually leads to breaking down the alcoholic's denial and the alcoholic is then taken immediately to a treatment facility or an AA meeting. The entire process is one of caring and concern, presented in a loving, supportive manner.

Seemingly such an intervention would also be effective with compulsive gamblers, but generally speaking this tends not to be the case. The gambler will immediately confront the members of the intervention group, manipulating them with outrage and emotional blackmail. It is a "fight to the death" for the gambler, whose competitive personality, need for control, and fear of being labeled a loser overshadow the intent and success of the intervention. The gambler will simply leave the room—very likely to head straight to the casino or race track. If, on the other hand and after strong persuasion, the gambler agrees to abide by the members' demands, it may still be with reservations and bartering, such as "I'll need a few days to get things in order" or "I'll go when I finish the project at work" or "I have to go to xxx, I already paid for the ticket." In such responses the gambler will rarely follow through with the demands of the group to enter treatment or attend GA.

Compulsive gamblers fear going for counseling, which in many minds means being "locked up in the looney bin, with crazies," being given medication which will turn them into zombies, or some similar horror. An effective approach is to speak with the gambler in a calm manner, showing proof of the progression and damage of the compulsive gambling, and, most importantly, explaining to the gambler how mental health counseling sessions are conducted.

"No, you will not be doped up with pills, you will not be told what to do, but rather you and the counselor will talk about what is happening in your life and what can be done to rid you of all that stress and make you feel better. Most of your sessions will be one-on-one with your counselor and there will also be sessions with your family, so that they can overcome their anger or fears. You will not be judged or ordered to do what you can or cannot do. You set your treatment goals and your counselors will help you to achieve them by talking out what's troubling you." This overcomes fear and resistance, and also strengthens motivation for healing.

Gentle confrontation and information can help to "bring the bottom up." The gambler does not need to be at the end stage of financial ruin, facing jail, or on the verge of committing suicide. This smaller variation of intervention process, then, is helpful not only to the gambler but also to the family members who have led their own lives of despair. The peer counselor serves in a most important capacity, from the first meeting until the client's discharge and later.

RECOVERY FOR THE GAMBLER AND FAMILY

If the professional treatment program offers family therapy, it could also have a Gam-Anon member on its staff who would serve as the peer counselor for the family. The peer counselor's role, then, is to introduce the Gam-Anon program to the spouse, parents, or other family members of the client in the treatment program, so that the family can begin to understand the turmoil within the gambler, how gambling served initially as an escape and then ultimately led to more turmoil and desperation. Introduction to Gam-Anon is an essential component of the treatment program.

These educational sessions are quite revealing for family members, as they realize how they themselves have coped, often in ineffective or unacceptable behaviors, in order to survive the chaos and financial fears. Some have become hysterical hyenas, as one spouse described herself, while others become the victim who seeks reassurance for her suffering self, or the Mother Superior who takes charge over household and family to the extreme, leaving little room for individual space or growth. Others turn a deaf ear to the situation to avoid having to admit the obvious, and many themselves become depressed and think of suicide. The gamblers, in turn, almost always recognize what is happening, even though there is no overt acknowledgement of it. Nevertheless, the guilt, fear, anxiety and anger lead to cravings to escape into gambling, oblivion, depression and possible suicide attempt.

The children become the victim of both parents' troublesome behaviors. Dad (if Dad is the gambler) tends to neglect them, while Mom vents her disturbing emotions on the children, becoming verbally abusive, psychologically neglecting or rejecting them, and at times also becoming physically abusive (Lorenz, 1978). The children's emotional development is truncated, they become fearful and depressed, do not learn coping skills, turn their emotions inward, all leading to low self-esteem. Acting-out behavior or developing their own addiction is predictable.

The gambler, spouse, children, parents, grandparents, siblings, and others all need help and support, ideally from professional treatment providers knowledgeable and experienced in treating gamblers and their families, and supported by Gamblers Anonymous and Gam-Anon peer counselors.

Finally, the peer counselor can answer questions such as "Can I ever gamble normally again?" or "Why can't I just use will power to stop?" "Why can't I just read GA literature or medical books?" "Isn't this just a financial problem?" "How can GA help me and what if others find out I'm in GA?" These are just a few of the many questions that newcomers can ask the peer counselor, the person "who's been there."

Perhaps one way to describe the compulsive gambler nearing final stage, hitting bottom, is through the following poem, slightly edited.

Please Hear What I'm Not Saying
Author Unknown

Don't be fooled by me,
Don't be fooled by the face I wear,
For I wear a mask. I wear a thousand masks,
Masks that I'm afraid to take off.
And none of them are me.
Pretending is an art that is second nature to me,
But don't be fooled, for God's sake, don't be fooled.

I give you the impression that I'm secure,
That all is sunny and unruffled with me,
Within as well as without.
That confidence is my name and coolness is my game,
That the water's calm and I'm in command,
And that I need no one.
But don't believe me. Please.

My surface may seem smooth, but my surface is my mask,
My ever-varying and ever-concealing mask.
Beneath lies no smugness, no complacence,
Beneath dwells the real me – in confusion, in fear, in
   aloneness.
But I hide this.
I don't want anybody to know it.

I panic at the thought of my weakness and fear of being exposed.
That's why I frantically create a mask to hide behind.
A nonchalant, sophisticated façade, to help me pretend
To shield me from the glance that knows.

I'm afraid your glance will not be followed
By acceptance and love.
I'm afraid you'll think less of me, that you'll laugh.
And your laugh would kill me.

I'm afraid that deep-down I'm nothing, that I'm just no good
And that you will see this and reject me.
So I play my game, my desperate pretending game
With a façade of assurance without,
And a trembling child within.

Please listen carefully and try to hear what I'm not saying,
What I'd like to be able to say,
What for survival I need to say,
But I can't say it.
I dislike hiding. Honestly.

You've got to help me.
You've got to hold out your hand,
Even when that's the last thing
I seem to want or need.

You alone can break down the wall behind which I tremble,
You alone can remove my mask.
You alone can release me from my shadow-world of
Panic and uncertainty, from my lonely prison.

So do not pass me by. Please do not pass me by.
It will not be easy for you.
A long conviction of worthlessness builds strong walls,
It's irrational, but despite what the books say about man,
I am irrational.

I fight against the very thing that I cry out for,
And in this lies my hope.
My only hope.

Please try to beat down those walls with firm hands,
But with gentle hands.

(Edited, Author unknown)

CHAPTER 17
THE PRIVATE PRACTITIONER

This chapter will focus on outpatient private practice guidelines which have been found to be essential, effective, and informative for both the therapist and the client. It includes some standard federal, state and local laws which are mandatory or recommended. It is addressed to you, "Dr. Jones" and the ABC Gambling Treatment Agency."

INITIAL CONTACTS

In the majority of cases, the initial contact is made over the telephone by a close family member of the compulsive gambler. It is usually the spouse or significant other, the husband or a wife. Typically, this person is very upset, perhaps angry, afraid, or crying, and talking very rapidly, as though there is not enough time to tell all. On other occasions, considerably less so, the caller is virtually numb, subdued, and sounds worn out emotionally, and a quick mood assessment becomes essential because often the non-gambler is depressed to the point of being suicidal. One case is illustrative. A neighbor phoned a national compulsive gambling hotline about her concern. She stated that her neighbor was baking a batch of cookies, "So the kids will remember me baking cookies for them." It was an implied threat of suicide. The neighbor was told to call 911 immediately for assistance, and then to go over to speak with this suicidal mother. The mother broke down, sobbing, "I just can't handle his gambling anymore."

On occasion, both the gambler and the spouse need immediate attention. You, Dr. Jones, the therapist must remain calm, be supportive, while also offering information and assistance. A caveat: At this stage, the compulsive gambler may have had thoughts of suicide for several weeks, and with additional pressures and losses piling up, sees no alternative but to stop hurting the family. Unable to tolerate any more guilt, may act on those feelings of suicide which have escalated with each day.

If the caller/gambler conveys what may be suggestive of a suicidal plan, again immediate action must be taken. You must take control of the situation: call 911, be empathic, get pertinent contact information, find out if the caller is alone or someone else is nearby, and determine what means the caller intends to use, and if possible, suggest that anyone else nearby remove any weapon, pills, and car keys to prevent the suicide. In most instances, the suicide can be prevented by being supportive to the person in distress. It is very rare for the gambler to endanger the caller's life; however, even a remote possibility must be taken seriously.

In some instances, the gambler may be near the caller, listening to what is being said. Encourage the caller to speak openly, directly, and factually, avoiding any hint of conspiracy or criticism. Often a gentle nudge will help in getting the gambler to speak on the phone or speaker phone as well.

A calm, gentle opening statement to the gambler may be, "Hello, Joe, this is Dr. Jones. I'm a psychologist specializing in the treatment of compulsive gambling. Your wife seems to be upset about your gambling. Can you tell me what is troubling her?" Several points are noted here: (1) Dr. Jones knows something about compulsive gambling, (2) has worked with other gamblers,

(3) is not judgmental, and (4) is asking Joe for his input. This can be the start of bonding and developing into a therapeutic relationship between the gambler and Dr. Jones. In the course of the conversation, Dr. Jones can also explain the process of mental health counseling.

If "Joe" insists the wife "is crazy, doesn't know what she's talking about" or some similar resistance, Dr. Jones should neither dispute nor agree with these comments. Instead, encourage him to bring his wife in for an appointment, so that the three of you can have a better understanding of the circumstances. If he insists he does not have a problem, then Dr. Jones can encourage him to come in so that the two of you can help his wife. This gives the gambler a sense of safety and belief that he is in control of the situation.

Caveat: Many compulsive gamblers have a rather distorted view of mental health treatment. They view treatment as being necessary only "for crazies." They fear that by being in treatment they will lose control, and that the therapist will tell them what to do. Clarify this. "No, Joe, we will just look at issues from all possibilities and think of ways that might work better for you. We can consider these options, but only you can make the decision on what steps to take. It's all up to you."

If Joe insists he does not want to take any pills and become "a zombie," inform him there are no pills to treat compulsive gambling, but medication may be helpful for people who are depressed or feeling overly anxious. "If I believe an antidepressant will help you, I can refer you to our psychiatrist or your family doctor. If they agree, you still have the choice of taking the medication or not. Again, it's up to you."

By this time, generally both husband and wife have calmed down and become more agreeable to seeing you. Suggest a meeting time, tell them about your fees, and get their insurance information. Inform them that the initial evaluation will take two hours and to call you if any emergency occurs prior to their appointment.

THE INITIAL EVALUATION

You, Dr. Jones, should should be aware that both may present with very different strong moods. The wife may be angry, the gambler may feel guilty or very depressed. Let the gambler know that most sessions will be individual, but at times, it may be helpful if a spouse or others participate in a session.

Now is the time to briefly speak about yourself, training and experience, and perhaps give them your brief vita. Consent forms need to be signed. Give the gambler the Intake Form and highlight certain areas: front page, what help he is seeking, and fill in the rest of the form. Some gamblers complete the form very quickly, often because they don't want to be left out of the conversation. Others are very slow, most likely because of their depressed mood. In either case, consider this as a guideline for future sessions.

Be clear about the consents given, explain that only general information is shared, such as attendance, unless the gambler specifies otherwise. That information should be included in the clinical chart, as well as all information regarding the suicidal intentions and any other crisis.

If appropriate, a Suicide Prevention Contract should also be filled in, which will have on it your name and phone numbers, as well as others to call and their phone numbers. One signed by the therapist is given to the gambler; another signed by the gambler is placed in the clinical chart. A follow-up phone call from the therapist is particularly meaningful, and recommended.

The substance abused in compulsive gambling is money. Some preliminary guidelines are helpful: the fee is paid at each session, a check should be signed by the spouse to limit the gambler's access to money, a session longer than one hour is billed accordingly. Compulsive gamblers will attempt to manipulate these fees: forgot to bring the check, my spouse didn't write one, etc. As one compulsive gambler stated, "You've got to be a fool to extend credit to a gambler."

TREATMENT SESSIONS

The following sessions are fairly standard: let the gambler set the goals, using Motivational Interviews or Harm Reduction techniques. Prioritize the goals, set strategies, be flexible only when new situations occur, suggest the anticipated length of treatment, who else may participate (always include a family member), etc. Each session should start with a focus on gambling: was the client tempted to gamble during the past week, did the client in fact gamble since the last session, what were the circumstances, losses and effects on others, reasons for not calling the therapist, what was the source of money (be prepared that more money may have been stolen), and similar discussions. One therapist encouraged the gambler to "Call me anytime, but not at three in the morning." It was said jokingly, but it gave the gambler a sense of security, prevented him from gambling, and he felt proud of himself for having overcome the urge to gamble. It showed him he could do it. He never did find it necessary to call the therapist; just knowing she would take his call was enough.

One anxiety-provoking incident that occurs almost always in early treatment is that of dreams. The gambler may for one or more nights have exhilarating dreams of wins and excitement of gambling. This is normal, and the gambler must be reassured about this phenomenon.

After several weeks of outpatient care, it is wise to implement the Compulsive Gambling 'Action' Inventory (see Chapter 9). The spouse, parents and other important members should participate. This discussion is very helpful for them in understanding the gambler's thought processes, and also helps the gambler understand his own actions and how they affected others.

As in any other therapy relationship, the gambler must agree to contact the therapist prior to terminating the treatment, and be encouraged to contact the therapist again as troublesome situations arise. It is not unusual for a gambler who has finished or terminated treatment prematurely to have a slip within the year, to prove that gambling can be controlled. Seeing the therapist for even one session can have very positive results.

PSYCHOMETRIC AND PROJECTIVE TESTING

Psychological testing is always encouraged. The MMPI should not be administered for several weeks after the first session. Emotional stability is important. The Beck Depression Inventory could be given at the first session to measure the level of depression, and then several times thereafter so that the gambler is aware of the improvement. The Millon Clinical Multi-Phasic Inventory (MCMI) has been found to be especially helpful for both the gambler and the therapist. Only one administration is necessary.

All tests must be thoroughly discussed with the gambler, identifying various scales and their meanings. The MMPI should be administered again, several months later or closer to termination of treatment. Although the MMPI has been considered to be stable over time, there is evidence that elevated scales become lowered, much to the gambler's relief. Gamblers are visual individuals who relate well to numbers—these and other tests, such as biofeedback, can have amazing results in identifying and reducing stressors. It shows success, always the compulsive gambler's goal.

Art therapy has been found to be exceptionally useful with compulsive gamblers. Initially they are apprehensive about this form of therapy, fearing ridicule because of poor drawing abilities, but this is rapidly overcome when clients learn how much of them is revealed through drawings, especially sexual abuse, dysfunctional family life, and the focus on money. Drawings also reflect their growth in recovery. Art therapy is effective with the compulsive gambler in individual, family, and group sessions.

The Twenty Questions of Gamblers Anonymous should be administered during the first or second session. This may be the first contact or awareness of the 12-Step program. If possible, also give the gambler a list of GA meetings, and information how to access the GA website.

CRITICAL LIFE EVENTS

Critical life events, especially those in early years, and post-traumatic stressors must be addressed, but only after stability in mood, cessation of gambling, financial issues, and legal issues have been achieved. Often, it is necessary to refer the gambler also to other support groups, such as rape crisis centers or AA. In one instance, after several weeks of art therapy which clearly suggested sexual trauma, the client was able to tell his father about having been raped by a priest when he was twelve years old. The father was a police officer who worked sex crime cases for several years and never suspected his son had been molested. In this instance, treatment was not only for the client, but also for the father, who felt exceedingly guilty. They both also needed to concur on what legal and civil actions were to be taken, without creating more emotional harm.

As with any addiction, a suitable substitute will fill in the time formerly used in gambling or gambling-related activities. Action gamblers seem to prefer some sort of physical activity, such as working out, coaching Little League, or joining a local sports team. Many prefer to play golf; however, it must be clearly established that any wager is considered gambling, no matter how small the wager may be. Escape gamblers tend to prefer family meetings and socializing with friends, resuming old hobbies, and cultivating new interests.

AFTER CARE AND RELAPSE PREVENTION

In all treatment of addictions, after care and relapse prevention are critical to recovery. A four- or six-week treatment program can certainly identify and address any number of troubling issues in a client's life; however, not all issues are identified and treated, nor are all of these issues treated to the extent that may be required for recovery. Two examples come to mind immediately: that of posttraumatic stress of rape victims and of warriors returning from the battle front. Short-term residential and outpatient care and intensive outpatient treatment can be helpful, it can also lead to more troubling events in a client's life if the treatment is neither appropriate nor sufficient. These complexities are even greater for private practitioners whose clients have not had the benefit of prior intensive care. Whenever expedient, referrals should be made to a rape crisis center, domestic violence shelter, and post traumatic stress program to complement ongoing therapy. Note: Not all locales offer rape crisis or domestic violence programs, nor do all local communities offer Veterans Administration treatment and support.

The need for lengthy and ongoing care is epitomized by 12-step programs for friends and families of addicts, such as Gam-Anon. AlAnon. ACoA (adult children of alcoholics). This is problematic for Gam-Anon, which has very few chapters throughout the nation. Maryland, for instance, has eighteen chapters of Gamblers Anonymous, and only two chapters of Gam-Anon, in which attendance often consists of less than ten members.

Additionally, not all private practitioners are trained or experienced in relapse prevention care. This, like compulsive gambling, is a specialty within the mental health treatment community; it requires training and experience to be effective. Relapse prevention must be viewed as an integral part of any addictions treatment program.

In sum, compulsive action gamblers present with a complex and diffuse history, escape gamblers less so, but with the appropriate and sufficient treatment both action and escape gamblers can recover from their gambling addiction and other illnesses and lead productive, fulfilling lives.

Susan G. Jones, Ph.D.
Licensed Clinical Psychologist, MD #1234
Street, City, State ZIP
Phone – Fax – Cell - E-Mail – Web page

Private Practice Treatment Guidelines

Thank you for choosing me to provide mental health services for you and your family. To avoid confusion, I would like to inform you of a number of guidelines and standards that pertain to my practice and to therapy procedures with which you may not be familiar. The more common ones are listed below. Please ask me about any other concerns you may have.

Therapeutic Relationship

A trusting relationship is essential to good psychotherapy. This requires full honesty no matter how difficult or embarrassing something may be for you. Many very personal issues may be raised in the course of treatment – know that what you say will be kept confidential between you and me, and that I will not judge you for your thoughts or your behaviors. My role is to help you. Mutual trust is accompanied with respect.

Forms and Clinical Chart

You will need to fill in a number of forms. Several of these are consent forms, such as Consent to Treat, Consent to Give Information - to designated individuals, such as certain family members, lawyer, or doctors. Consent forms are generally valid for six months, but may be withdrawn in writing prior to that, or may be extended. Some Consent forms may concern the use of clinical data or art therapy for educational purposes only. There will be no identifying information on these materials.

You will also need to fill in a Client Intake form, giving details about your family and your life, such as your education, illnesses, jobs, and relationships. If you believe you have a gambling problem, you will be asked to also fill in a 4-page gambling-specific questionnaire. for that. There is also a one-page substance use questionnaire which may be required.

All forms and clinical notes will be kept in your clinical chart. The chart is kept in a locked file and no one other than me, or my staff, have access to it.

In the event that your clinical chart is subpoenaed, every effort will be made to prevent disclosure of any or all information in your chart. If this is not possible, all identifying information will be blacked out to protect you and others mentioned in the chart. You will be fully apprised and involved in this process.

Psychometric and Projective Testing

New clients usually suffer from a number of strong negative emotions which may interfere with good daily functioning. You may be given several tests to measure the level of your depression, anxiety and anger. It may also be advisable to conduct more psychological testing after several sessions, such as the MMPI and the MCMI, or projective testing (art therapy). All test results will be discussed with you in detail.

Initial Sessions

The first session typically lasts two hours. Ideally, a close family member, such as a spouse or parent will accompany you, to give additional information and to share another viewpoint. The session will focus on the problems for which you are seeking help. Psychotherapy involves treating all of you, not just the presenting problem, so we will be including your parents, grandparents and/or other family members in this session, if appropriate.

I will arrive at a diagnostic impression and discuss this with you – the meaning of the diagnosis and what type of treatment is recommended. The next session will start with setting treatment goals – what we hope to accomplish, how to do that, others who may participate, and how much treatment may be recommended to meet your goals.

Clinical Hours and Billing

Therapy sessions typically last 45-50 minutes. This is considered one "clinical hour." Thus a session which lasts 90-100 minutes, which is 1 ½ hours in "real" time, is considered two hours in "clinical hour" time. Sessions are billed according to time, not by the number of family members or others (a boss or lawyer) who may be participating in the session.

Family members and others may participate in sessions with you or without you. You may also participate in group sessions. Billing is based on time, who participates, and the type of services rendered.

Outpatient therapy sessions typically are one clinical hour per week, preferably at a set day and time; however, if appropriate, this can be increased or decreased. If you have completed intensive or residential treatment elsewhere, your aftercare sessions most likely will be more frequent in the first month, and then taper off as your recovery progresses.

Telephone Sessions

Feel free to phone me if you need to, between appointments. There is no charge for brief calls (15 minutes or less). Telephonic sessions are limited to emergency cases, in the instance of extremely bad weather, or some other reason, such as moving or distance and not being able to come to the office.

Cancellations and Missed Appointments

If you must cancel an appointment, please let me know at least 24 hours in advance to avoid being billed for the session. A family member may fill in for you, if that person is part of your overall treatment plan. Inclement weather generally is not sufficient reason for canceling without notice. I will contact you if a session needs to be cancelled.

Fees and Health Insurance

My fee is $xxx per hour and $xxx for the initial session, which typically lasts over two clinical hours. If I am a participating provider with your health insurance company, I am required to file the insurance claim myself and there is no fee for you, other than possibly a co-pay, as determined by your policy. The co-pay has to be paid prior to each session.

If I do not participate in your plan, I will fill out your insurance forms and provide you with whatever assistance I can in helping you receive the reimbursement benefits to which you are entitled; however, you are responsible for full payment of my fees at the time services are rendered. If your policy requires pre-authorization, I will need a signed consent form from you to call your insurance company.

It is important for you to have a copy of your insurance benefits and read the section that describes behavioral health benefits. Be aware that behavioral health benefits differ substantially from medical benefits – reimbursement tends to be considerably lower.

Unpaid Bills

Every effort will be made between you and me to resolve unpaid fees for services rendered. In the event this is not possible, your bill may be sent for collection to the Small Claims Court. Please be aware that certain information will no longer be confidential, such as your name, contact, and non-clinical information, and the amount of the bill. You will be responsible for all court costs and related fees.

Medication

On occasion it may be advisable for you to take medication. In that event, I will refer you to a psychiatrist or your family doctor. I will need a signed consent form from you to discuss my findings and recommendations with this professional.

Danger to Self or Others

I am, by law, required to breach confidentiality if I sense that you are at risk of doing harm to yourself or others. This means I may call 911 for an ambulance or police, a family member, friend or neighbor, or even a stranger, based upon the immediacy of the situation. Danger to others includes child or elder abuse, sexual abuse, or physical abuse. Your anonymity is important, but your safety and that of others is more important and takes priority.

Final Session

If you feel at any time that you no longer need to participate in treatment, or you want to continue with another therapist,, please bring that to my attention so that we can review or clear up any remaining issues, and I can refer you to another therapist.

Keep in Touch

Please also note that you are always welcome – and encouraged – to contact me on occasion and let me know how you are doing. Drop me a note, e-mail or give me a call.

Thank you

Susan G. Jones, Ph.D.
Licensed Clinical Psychologist, MD License #xxx
Address
Phone, Cell, Fax numbers, E-mail

Exceptions to Rules of Confidentiality

All written and verbal counseling information is considered confidential. It cannot be released without the client's written consent. However, there are some legal exceptions:

Duty to Warn and Protect

When a client discloses intentions or a plan to harm another person, my staff and I are required to warn the intended victim and to report this information to legal, health, and other appropriate authorities.

When a client implies or discloses a plan for self-injury, my staff and I are required to take reasonable precautions, contact 911 for assistance, notify the client's indicated emergency contact or other family member, and notify others deemed to be necessary.

Abuse of Child and Vulnerable Adult

If a client discloses an intent to abuse or neglect a child or vulnerable adult, or have recently abused or neglected a child or vulnerable adult, my staff and I are required to report this information to an appropriate family member, the client's emergency contact, social services and/or legal authorities.

Client's Death

In the event of a client's death, the spouse or parents, or the client's attorney has a right to access the client's records.

Court Orders

I am required to release a client's records when a court order has been placed; however, all attorney contacts and clinical chart documentation is privileged and all references to non-clients will be deleted or blackened out unless otherwise authorized by the client. Court records are public information - your chart will not be submitted unless no other recourse is available.

Health Insurance Companies

Insurance companies are given limited information of treatment services and the client's treatment needs for authorization and reimbursement of services.

Other

_____

_____

I have been informed of the above conditions which require the release of information about me and all or portions of my clinical chart.

Date	Printed Name	Signature

ABC Gambling Treatment Agency

Client Intake Form

The purpose of this form is to obtain preliminary information about you, your background, and some of the more important events in your life. All information on this form and other notes will be kept in your clinical chart. Case records are strictly confidential. Disclosure of any part or all of your file requires your written consent. Please fill in the form as much as possible, and use the back of the page, if necessary. Print or write legibly. Thank you.

Day/Date_____

GENERAL INFORMATION

Full Name_____ Soc.Sec.#_____

Home Address_____

City, State, ZIP_____

Home Phone_____ Cell_____ E-mail_____

Date of Birth_____ Place of Birth_____ Grew up in_____

Religion_____ Active? Y N Ethnic Origin/Race_____

Current Marital Status: ___Single ___Married ___SigOther ___Separated ___ Divorced ___Widowed

Employer_____ Supervisor_____
(If currently unemployed, list most recent employer)

Address_____

You job Title_____ Phone_____
                                                                          Extension?

Your Annual Income $_____ Total Family Income $_____

Please list two Emergency Contacts

Name_____ Name _____

Address_____ Address_____

H-Phone_____ H-Phone_____

W/C Phone_____ W/CPhone_____

Relationship_____ Relationship_____

If you are presently incarcerated, what is your # and address_____

Attorney_____

Your Education
Highest grade completed_____ College/Major_____

Sports or academic awards_____

Negative events_____

Military Service
Branch_____ Entered_____ Discharged_____ Type_____

Rank at Discharge_____ Combat Zone_____

Actions, Medals_____

Work History
List your jobs, your age, title or type of work, why you left and any other special circumstances about them:

Age from/ to	Job title/Type of work	Why did you leave there?
_____	_____	_____
_____	_____	_____
_____	_____	_____
_____	_____	_____

Your Medical History

Height_____ Weight_____ Overall health_____ Allergies_____ Last physical_____

Please list below all major illnesses, operations, accidents, broken bones, injuries, disabilities, your age and, impact on you

_____

_____

_____

_____

What medications are you now taking? Why_____

_____

Mental Health Problems – List all past/current problems, therapy, rehab, age, meds you are taking now & why

_____

_____

Your Suicidal History –Thoughts/attempts

Past attempts, how/age _____

Current thoughts/plans/why_____

Relationship and Marital History
Please give us some information about your significant partners/spouses, starting with your first "great love."

Partner's First name. your age, how long were you together, why you split up

_____ ____ _____

_____ ____ _____

_____ ____ _____

_____ ____ _____

Children, Step-children   **Siblings**
Name, age, what is special about this person   Name, age, what is special about this person

_____   _____

_____   _____

_____   _____

_____   _____

_____   _____

Father: Age_____ Education_____ Occupation_____

His Problems: Alcohol____ Gambling____ Drugs____ Health_____ Anger___ Focus on $____

Dad's age at time of death_____ Your age_____ Cause of death_____

Describe your father_____

_____

Mother: Age_____ Education_____ Occupation_____

Her Problems: Alcohol____ Gambling____ Drugs____ Health_____ Anger____ Focus on $____

Mom's age at time of death_____ Your age_____ Cause of death_____

Describe your mother_____

_____

How did they get along_____ Divorced_____ Your age_____

Whom did you live with_____

What is special about your grandparents or other adults in your life that you would like us to know about?

_____

BIG "OUCHIES"

Describe any unusual or traumatic events, losses, deaths, or other stressors, or BIG OUCHIES in your life that left their mark on you, still leave you with bad feelings, or still trouble you, your age at that time. Or write: Will tell you later

What issues are troubling you for which you are seeking our help?

What else would you like us to know?

Is there anyone who should participate in your care with us and why?

Gambling History

My favorite forms of gambling are _____

Please give us some general information about your gambling. Where did you gamble, alone or with others, your ages, and add comments.

Form of Gambling	Age	Comment	
Asian games			
Baccarat			
Bingo			
Blackjack			
Dominoes			
Dice			
Dogs			
Golf			
Horses			
Keno			
Lottery			
Numbers			
Options, stocks, trading			
Poker, other cards			
Pull tabs, punchboards			
Roulette, Big Wheel			
Slots			
Sports			
Table games, chess			
Tournaments			
Other			
Other			

What are some of your special gambling experiences – The amount of money you won or lost at one time and on what form of gambling, how old you were, how you felt or reacted, large comps, any accidents (vomiting, car, etc, , overdosing, etc.

_____

_____

_____

_____

Legal Issues

Please give us a complete history of your past legal charges, your age, and disposition. Also, please let us know what charges you are facing now or you might face in the near future.

_____
Age   Legal charge   Outcome (NG, PBJ, Jail, etc)

_____
Age   Legal charge   Outcome (NG, PBJ, Jail, etc.)

_____
Name & contact information of your attorney

_____
Address

_____
Phone #   Cell phone   FAX

_____
E-mail   Web Page

_____
Name and Contact Info of P.O.

Legal and Illegal Gambling Debts

Please list all your legal and illegal gambling debts, indicate whom you owe and how much.

Bank loans _____

Finance Co. _____

Credit Cards _____   _____

Markers _____

Employer/Co-worker_____

Family, friends_____

Bookies, Loansharks _____

IRS $_____   Court order_____

Gambling Feelings and Behaviors

Please indicate with a check mark in the appropriate column which best describes you during the worst of your gambling. Feel free to add to this list.

Type of physical or emotional response	Never - rarely	Some-times	Usually	All the time
I speed excessively when I drive to the casino, etc.				
I'm in a rush to make that next bet				
I gamble to "stay in action"				
I gamble because I desperately need the money				
I gamble because I want to beat the game or dealer				
I gamble to stop thinking about my problems				
I feel like I take on another identity (big shot, etc.)				
I feel strong, powerful, invincible when I win				
I feel like I am in a trance while gambling				
I "zone out" or "feel like my head is in a fog"				
I am convinced the next bet will be the "Big One"				
For me, gambling has become torture				
I feel like I'm hypnotized, pulled into the slot				
I'm afraid of a separation or divorce due to gambling				
I always fear being arrested				
I feel agitated, restless, anxious				
I feel angry, irritable, argumentative				
I feel depressed, hopeless				
I wish I could go to bed and not wake up				

Physical Symptoms

Below is a list of physical symptoms. Please fill in if you suffered from any of them during the months or years when you were gambling. Be specific - can't fall asleep, have bad dreams, etc.

Eating _____

Back_____

Neck, muscles_____

Hand, arm_____

Headaches_____

Heart_____

Panic attacks_____

Stomach_____

Sleep problems_____

ABC GAMBLING TREATMENT AGENCY
Baltimore

Client Contacts

Name of Client_____ Dx_____

Address_____

Phones_____ E-mail_____

Other contact_____

Evaluations $xxx   Individual or Family $xxx/hr.   Group $xxx

Date/day	Participants/Code	Hrs.	Cost	Paid	Bal. due

Name_____ Age_____ Date_____

The 20 Questions of Gamblers Anonymous

_____1 Did you ever lose time from work or school due to gambling?

_____2 Has gambling ever made your home life unhappy?

_____3 Did gambling affect your reputation?

_____4 Have you ever felt remorse (or guilt) after gambling?

_____5 Did you ever gamble to get money with which to pay debts or otherwise solve financial problems?

_____6 Did gambling cause a decrease in your ambition or efficiency?

_____7 After losing, did you feel you must return as soon as possible and win back your losses?

_____8 After a win did you have a strong urge to return and win more?

_____9 Did you often gamble until your last dollar was gone?

_____10 Did you ever borrow to finance your gambling?

_____11 Have you ever sold (or pawned) anything to finance your gambling?

_____12 Were you reluctant to use "gambling money" for normal expenditures?

_____13 Did gambling make you careless of the welfare of your family?

_____14 Did you ever gamble longer than you planned?

_____15 Have you ever gambled to escape worry or trouble?

_____16 Have you ever committed, or considered committing, an illegal act to finance gambling?

_____17 Did gambling cause you to have difficulty in sleeping?

_____18 Do arguments, disappointments or frustrations create within you an urge to gamble?

_____19 Did you ever have an urge to celebrate any good fortune by a few hours of gambling?

_____20 Have you ever considered self-destruction as a result of your gambling?

CHAPTER 18
THE COMPULSIVE GAMBLERS' VIEWS AND RESISTANCE

THE GAMBLERS' VIEWS OF PROFESSIONAL TREATMENT

It is a commonly said that the compulsive gambler will end up in jail, in a morgue or in a hospital. Unfortunately this is true for many compulsive gamblers. They commit crimes to obtain money for gambling or debts, they think about suicide for weeks or months before taking that final step, and the lucky ones enter treatment, whether this is professional or in self-help groups, willingly or after a losing struggle.

Even though they "have gone through hell and back," they still resist treatment, almost always on the basis of having to give up control or worse yet, letting someone else take control. Below are some of the common protests and resistance to treatment.

As one compulsive gambler said, "Going into a gambling rehab is like driving a car with a shattered windshield, without a steering wheel and without a brake pedal, down a steep hill."

Translation, "I am terrified that I will lose control, that you will control me, and my personality will change."

I DON'T NEED TREATMENT

How many times have family members heard this protest? Unfortunately, this kind of response may also indicate that the compulsive gambler has not yet fully realized the extent of the gambling, the financial costs and the impact on the family, and is still convinced that the next bet will be the Big One, the one that will end all the problems. Now bills will be paid, spouse and kids will no longer be angry, and the boss will reconsider a leave without pay or termination. The family recognizes the need for treatment, but the gambler is still caught up in the magical thinking of a quick fix.

An intervention type of session may be an option for the family, and the gambler may resist and attempt to control the session, but when it is clear that "the game is over," may grudgingly yield to the demands. Motivation may be lacking and a good treatment outcome is doubtful if this attitude persists.

I CAN CONTROL IT, I CAN STOP ON MY OWN

If compulsive gamblers could stop on their own, they would have done so a long time ago. Almost all of them have tried to stop, sometimes repeatedly, only to find that facing the reality and consequences of their addiction is too great to bear. They will tell themselves over and over again, I won't go tomorrow, but when tomorrow comes they'll call the bookie, buy that lottery ticket, or drive to the OTB. Even if they do not bet again, and refrain from gambling for a period—a week, two weeks, two months—their withdrawal symptoms will be so uncomfortable that they will return to gambling simply to feel better physically and emotionally. They will experience symptoms such as edginess, headaches, stomach aches, inability to sleep, irritability, short tempers, despondency, just to name a few. And yet others will relapse because a gambling buddy says "Let's go to the track" or an incident triggers an urge followed with an impulsive dash to the gambling venue.

It is true that some compulsive gamblers "just stop" but more likely they were problem gamblers rather than compulsive gamblers. It is a matter of degree of the severity and the length of loss of control over their gambling. Compulsive gamblers who Just Stop are more likely to resemble the alcoholic who has become the Dry Drunk. They no longer gamble, but without help from others they may still have unresolved deep-rooted issues and may lack the coping skills they need to live better lives and have more meaningful relationships.

JUST GIVE ME SOME PILLS

Pills work, for depression, anxiety, high blood pressure, and many other ailments. But to date no pill has been developed to stop someone from gambling. There is no Antabuse for gamblers such as there is for alcoholics. And since gambling addiction (like other addictions) has its roots in troubled relationships, possibly intensified by critical life events, and may also have a small neurological component, neither a pill nor surgery will cure the problem. Nor will a pill relieve the gambler's low self-esteem; however, Naltrexone has been found to help in relieving some of the cravings for some compulsive gamblers.

JUST HYPNOTIZE ME

In other words, give me a quick fix and one that doesn't require too much effort. Recovery from addictions isn't quite that easy. It takes time, new skills and experience to change the way one thinks, feels and acts.

There may be a bright side to this quest. Hypnosis has been tried on some compulsive gamblers in the very recent past; however, the purpose is to undercover underlying traumas and to teach relaxation, thus removing the constant stress the gambler experiences. Hypnosis alone does not stop the addiction, but the gambler is better equipped to cope with life and fight the urges and cravings which lead to relapses.

WHAT, GO INTO A LOONIE BIN? NEVER

Ask a compulsive gambler to give a description of a mental health treatment center and they will talk in obvious fear of Nurse Ratchett, zombies, lobotomies, and being locked up. Plus being labeled "crazy," which means psychos and bag ladies. This is simply way beyond the gambler's ability to cope with and accept, so resistance escalates.

This is the time for therapists to step lightly, to be empathic. "I can understand your concern, but let me explain rehabs and treatment for you…." It is important at this first step to assure the gambler that there are no pills, shots, or brain surgery for compulsive gambling and that treatment consists of talk therapy and nonverbal therapies, one-on-one, in small groups, and eventually with family members.

It is also important to explain that the gambler will be with other gamblers and not with psychotic patients, the truly insane people. Gambling programs are not alcohol and drug rehabs, and though some gamblers may also have an alcohol or drug problem, which will be addressed, the focus of treatment is on compulsive gambling and recovery.

It is equally important to inform the gambler at once that residential gambling treatment programs have an open door policy. No one is locked up. This cannot be emphasized enough, since being locked up is seen immediately as a loss of control and therefore is very scary.

IT COSTS TOO MUCH

It is most difficult for a spouse or parent to understand the gambler's concern about treatment costs when the gambler has shown such incredible disregard for money, has lost everything of value, and indeed is in debt. Treatment does cost money. Psychiatrist, psychologists, counselors and other therapists have spent many years and dollars for their education, as have other therapists, such as the art therapist, biofeedback clinician, acupuncturist, deep clinical massage therapist, and relapse prevention counselor. Treatment costs vary with the type of therapist, length of treatment, whether inpatient or outpatient, and if state governments allocate any funding for treatment.

The state of Louisiana, for instance, allocated money for treatment of its citizens. Costs for residents are minimal, costs for out-of-staters approximate five thousand dollars for a six-week stay. Treatment in a private facility may cost as much as twenty thousand dollars or more.

MY INSURANCE WON'T COVER IT

This may be true, at least in part. Insurance reimbursement depends on the type of insurance coverage, does it include mental health therapy, and what other restrictions are on the policy itself. Is there a high deductible? Does it cover only admission into a psychiatric hospital or also into a residential treatment facility? Are only a limited number of outpatient session allowed? Is the therapist or treatment facility on the insurance panel, or are they considered out of network? Many of these issues can be worked out between the billing agent and the insurance company although this may take some time.

Treatment providers therefore require payment at the time services are rendered, but will also give the patients receipts which can be submitted to the insurance company for reimbursement.

I CAN'T ASK MY FAMILY TO PAY

Here is yet another excuse for not entering treatment. This could be true but it is more likely the gambler is too embarrassed or too afraid to ask the family. The family may be so angry that they may not want anything more to do with the gambler. They will refuse to pay for treatment, convinced that this is just another one of the gambler's scams.

At this point it may be an option for the therapist to contact the family, explain the program, invite the family to visit the rehab, and discuss costs. It is very important to direct the family to make checks payable to the therapist or facility and not to the gambler. There are many examples in which the gambler was given the money for treatment, only to take a detour to the track or casino.

THEY DON'T CARE ANYWAY

More likely, the family is angry, disgusted, even fearful that the gambler will steal from them again. They care, but troubling emotions may interfere. This is just one reason of many why treatment for gambling addicts should include treatment for family members, especially the more significant ones, such as a spouse, parent, child, or sibling.

Families care, they want what is best for the gambler, but they just don't want to be hurt again.

I'LL JUST LEAVE, IT'S BETTER FOR EVERYBODY

Leaving or being separated from a spouse definitely is not on the gambler's agenda. Nothing could be worse for the gambler and is considered to be the most serious form of rejection. Similarly, most spouses do not want a separation, all they want is for the craziness to stop.

On the other hand, even in their desperate state compulsive gamblers may manipulate a situation and play on the spouse's fear of separation. A threat to leave can be just as devastating for the spouse as it is for the gambler. In family or couples therapy, the gambler can learn that running away from stressed relationships is not the solution.

I CAN'T TAKE TIME OFF FROM WORK

The first of the Twenty Questions of Gamblers Anonymous reads "Do you lose time from work due to gambling?" While there are no hard statistics on responses to this question, it is a common defense used by new members of Gamblers Anonymous. "No, I always went to work." True, the gambler may have physically been on the job, but how much work was accomplished? There are untold stories of the gambler's concerns which detract from the job: How am I going to get the money to pay the bills, to pay back what I took from the boss, what if the bookie shows up here, looking at the clock, watching the market, answering the bookie's phone calls, or being distracted in a number of ways, rather than concentrating on the job at hand—they don't start the report, they don't finish it, it is incomplete, it has many errors, it is, quite frankly, poor work productivity, yet the gambler is physically at the office or on the job site.

Taking the question a bit further, in the midst of the addiction, the gambler will arrive late for work, having been unable to sleep because of the money pressures; or may be sick on the job, with severe headaches or being sick at the stomach; or not show up at all, because missing a race or not playing the slots means losing more money; leaving early because the bookie is waiting; or not showing up at all, because the few hours allotted for casino gambling have turned into two or three days.

I CAN'T GO NOW BECAUSE...

I have to go to work. I'm a presenter at the conference, the big sales meeting is in two weeks, I have to be there. These and similar excuses tend to have one common denominator: fear of being discovered. Company money is missing, accounting books don't accurately reflect checks coming in, cashing checks, false entries, company credit cards used for gambling trips, phony loans, fraudulent financial reports, and more. As long as the gambler is at work, the "loans" and other manipulations of funds can be covered up.

Then there are also the more altruistic excuses: I have to work to pay the bills, I can't miss my son's graduation, my daughter's birthday, the team championship games. The underlying reasons, the ones not verbalized, are, "I'm afraid treatment will destroy my ability to make money, it will change my personality, they'll think I'm a failure." In cognitive therapy, this is termed negative fortune telling.

QUIT GAMBLING? FOREVER? HOW ABOUT...?

In addictions, there are many "bottoms" before the final one. In the meantime quitting forever is out of the question for the compulsive gambler, and the objections are many: I'll cut down on the amount of money I gamble, I'll gamble less often, you can go with me and handle my money. All of these objections have been tried, and failed. That is why the Gamblers Anonymous program encourages the One Day at a Time concept, stay away from your gambling buddies, don't go near or into the gambling places, ask someone to help you. It may be difficult, but it is possible, and has proven to work.

THE DOCS DON'T UNDERSTAND GAMBLING

This is yet another desperate attempt to refuse treatment, but in fact the statement has some merit. There are very few compulsive gambling treatment programs in the United States and many of the therapists are substance abuse counselors with the belief, "all addictions are the same. Treat gamblers the way you would treat alcoholics or drug addicts." The therapist needs to help the gambler overcome that "book smarts" can be helpful in treatment with a simple admission, "You're right, I haven't lived the life of a compulsive gambler but maybe you can help me understand," thus develop a cooperative relationship rather than a resistant or competitive one.

I'LL GO TO GA

This often is in resistance to going for professional treatment, which is so scary. Going to Gamblers Anonymous may appease the family, but many times the gambler, especially the one refusing to stop gambling, will drop out after attending a few meetings. This is especially true if there is no Gam-Anon meeting available.

REACTIONS AND RESISTANCE TO GAMBLERS ANONYMOUS

Even today there are many who do not truly understand alcoholism or accept it as a disease. There are the moral attitudes of "you shouldn't" and the demanding attitudes of "just stop" among others. If alcoholism has its disbelievers even after so many years of public awareness efforts and treatment, why would anyone understand compulsive gambling and Gamblers Anonymous any better? Even gambling addicts themselves have their attitudes and prejudices about GA. Some of the more frequents objections are:

THEY'RE A BUNCH OF RELIGIOUS FREAKS

This is probably the most frequent objection to attending a GA meeting. "I don't want to hear about God, I just need some money." Gamblers have difficulty accepting God. They need to be in control and turning life over to God or a higher power is way beyond the gambler's ability, especially if motivation for abstinence is minimal.

THE MEETING IS TOO FAR AWAY

There is some merit to this objection. Many states have only one or two chapters of GA, although a few others, like California, Nevada, and New Jersey have meetings at different times of the day and within a short driving distance. Nevertheless, if the gambler is truly motivated, the time or distance does not present a problem. It's the gambler's attitude that is the problem.

I DON'T HAVE ENOUGH GAS FOR THE CAR

This reason is heard again and again, and there is some truth to it. Gamblers Anonymous members are firm on this, "You had gas money to gamble, you can find gas money to come to meetings." This is viewed by the new member as criticism and rejection. Nevertheless, it is helpful if a GA sponsor or member can offer a ride. That reflects fellowship and the twelfth step, "giving back to others."

THE MEETINGS LAST TOO LONG

Alcoholics Anonymous and other 12-Step meetings generally last one hour. Most GA meetings last two hours, although that tendency is changing, with meeting time being limited to one hour. A two-hour meeting can be an obstacle for early morning or lunch meetings, and some members do not drive late at night.

MEETINGS ARE NOTHING BUT WAR STORIES

Unfortunately, this is true in many meetings. Members tend to tell their story for fifteen or twenty minutes, thus denying others from speaking. "Why go to meetings? I can tell them their own stories."

THEY NEVER HAVE OTHER TYPES OF MEETINGS

Not all meetings are war story meetings. There are some topic, open, cross-talk, and 12-Step meetings, but generally these are only in states with a large number of meetings. Attending AA meetings sometimes serves as an alternative, particularly since many of these also have members dually-addicted to compulsive gambling.

THEY CRITICIZE YOU

This objection again is heard quite often. Taking someone's inventory does happen and scares newer members away from future meetings. They do not want to be the target in a GA meeting. It also leaves the newcomer confused in trying to understand the Recovery Program.

THEY AREN'T LIKE ME

This is a common excuse for refusing to go to any GA meeting. The gambler can be encouraged to attend other meetings until the most helpful ones can be found, those meetings where the gambler feels safe and becomes part of the fellowship.

THEY'RE SLOTS PLAYERS, I BET ON THE PONIES

This attitude was prevalent in the seventies, when compulsive gamblers were mostly casino, race track and sports bettors. Only Vegas and Reno had banks of slots at that time. This has changed with the proliferation of all forms of gambling across this country and internationally. Today, many GA meetings are comprised predominantly of slots gamblers and in some cities, such as Las Vegas, more than half of GA members are female slots gamblers, very different from the older GA meetings which were comprised of male sports, race track, and casino gamblers.

THEY TAKE THE INFORMATION OUT OF THE ROOM

Unfortunately, this can happen in any 12-step meeting. Members are people with myriad problems, including a lack of humility. As one new member lamented, "I'm a professional athlete. My coach found out the next day that I had a gambling problem and had attended a GA meeting. After that, I went to AA instead." It is true that not everyone abides by the "What you hear in this room stays in this room" unity rule.

MY BOSS WILL FIND OUT

The boss may find out but on the other hand, the boss may already know about the gambling and encourage the gambler to join GA. In fact, the boss may be a member of GA as well.

I'M A BANKER, I CAN'T TAKE THE CHANCE

AA has Professionals meetings, which gives the members a greater sense of confidentiality. Members of these meetings typically are doctors and nurses who are more likely to turn to alcohol or drugs to ease their pain. Lawyers, accountants, and finance officers are more likely to become gamblers, thus hopefully GA will also have meetings for professionals in the future.

I THOUGHT THEY WOULD LEND ME THE MONEY

A bit of insanity but it does happen and the new member is not the only one with those hopes. It is simply another desperate attempt for a bail-out and quick fix. Actually, this often brings a bit of humor into the meeting: "I thought the same thing. Was I ever shocked and disappointed when I found out that GA wasn't a lending institution."

THE GAMBLERS' REACTIONS TO GAM-ANON

New members of Gamblers Anonymous learn very soon after joining GA that there are problems within Gam-Anon. Some members indeed are quite a bit opposed to Gam-Anon and pass these opinions on to newer members. New members tend to fear exposure, so it would be surprising if they did not assume the same opinions.

THEY'RE JUST A BUNCH OF ANGRY PEOPLE

Yes, it is true that Gam-Anon has members with strong emotions, usually anger. They have lived with the gambling problem too long, they need emotional support, and that is why there is a GA and a Gam-Anon. Many members of Gam-Anon may be angry initially, but in time they too can find the practical and emotional help they seek.

SHE'LL LEARN TOO MUCH ABOUT ME

The new Gam-Anon member may not learn more about the gambler, but certainly there will be a better understanding of the gambler's illness and behaviors. New members of Gam-Anon learn to take their own inventory and change those behaviors which interfere with growth and serenity.

THEY'LL TELL HER WHAT TO DO

There's a difference between telling someone and helping some-one and showing by example. The Gam-Anon program teaches its members to lead by example, not to be dictatorial.

GAM-ANON TELLS THEM TO LEAVE ME

Unfortunately, this is true at times, particularly if the new member is not yet married to the gambler. "Run as fast as you can. Why would you want to live with all those problems?" What should be leading by example turns into taking inventory and not being a trusted servant, both of which are contrary to the Gam-Anon 12-Step program.

GAM-ANON SAYS GIVE HIM A DOLLAR A DAY

No one is perfect, nor are Gam-Anon's members. GA, together with Gam-Anon, offers a financial pressure relief group. During that process, a budget is set up and a decision is made who will manage the actual monies. Ideally this is a joint decision, thus the gambler feels included instead of emasculated. Nevertheless, an angry Gam-Anon member may say something like "You gambled all the money away. Now I'm in charge. You want seven dollars a week for spending money? I'll give you a dollar a day." Not only is this likely to lead to relapse, but it also prevents the gambler and partner from making informed, joint decisions, and which is then likely to undo prior efforts at reconciliation.

THE MEETINGS ARE TOO FAR
AWAY OR ONLY AT NIGHT

Once again, this is true. Gam-Anon has far fewer chapters than GA thus the Gam-Anon member has limited opportunities to join, to learn, and to change. An alternative is to attend an AlAnon meeting which may be nearby and most likely will also have family members of a compulsive gambler in it. The Gam-Anon member could also attend the various local, state, and regional GA/Gam-Anon conferences, which typically have Gam-Anon, GA/Gam-Anon, and Open workshops.

SUMMARY

There is no doubt that some semblance of truth is in virtually every objection that the gambler might face. However, these objections most often are based on fear of exposure, fear of rejection, and loss of control. The gambler can overcome these emotional states by attending GA regularly, with strong motivation for recovery, be willing to take a "moral inventory and take the necessary steps to remove these character defects." It's all a part of the program, for both the gambler and the family, friends, and colleagues of the gambler. As is said after the Serenity Prayer: "Keep coming back."

CHAPTER 19
REGAINING FINANCIAL STABILITY

(Note: Financial stability is perhaps the most critical area in recovery from compulsive gambling and its impact on others. Therefore, this chapter will address many issues and in greater detail than in other chapters)

Money is the substance abused in gambling. This is true temporarily of problem gamblers but always true of compulsive gambling. Ultimately, compulsive gamblers will find themselves in debt, without financial resources, and in dire straits to meet basic needs. They are convinced that further gambling will solve their financial problems even though their gambling has led them to this state of pecuniary disaster. Gambling addicts, like other addicts, do not learn from experience.

Gamblers Anonymous (GA) offers a financial pressure relief group, which is usually held with two recovering gamblers, a member of Gam-Anon, the compulsive gambler and the gambler's spouse or designee (referred to as "partner" in this chapter for the sake of simplicity). Most compulsive gambling treatment programs offer similar financial pressure relief groups; however, there is a caveat: compulsive gamblers are convinced that further gambling will get them out of trouble, not in trouble. This attitude is carried through in attempting to establish financial stability, thus it can reasonably be said that any kind of financial adjustment will be met with resistance during the planning process or after the new budget system has been put in place. Or both. The peer counselor can be instrumental in breaking down this resistance.

Newly recovering gamblers invariably have three delusional objectives. The first is that of the quick fix, namely that all gambling debts be paid first, second, that all bills will be paid within one year, and third, that they themselves will handle the monies. Gamblers Anonymous dispels these demands at once, not only by developing a budget based on two lists, one made up by the compulsive gambler and the other by the partner and secondly, finding agreement on who will handle the money. The Who invariably will be the non-gambler.

THE MEANING OF MONEY

Emphasis on money has influenced the young child who eventually becomes a gambling addict. This future gambler may be part of a family that is poor, in which basic needs are met but there is little money left for extras, such as new clothes or dining out, or by growing up in poverty. Then there are those families which at one time lived in reasonable comfortable circumstances but for whatever reason may sink to a lower economic level. Ironically, a sudden increase in living standard can also contribute to the child's sense of financial vulnerability. An example is that of a family moving to a more affluent neighborhood, thus the youngster loses his friends, must change schools, and also try to fit in with the new crowd.

Community impacts can also contribute to the child's understanding of money. This may be a community in which professions—thus income—are highly valued, "My son the doctor, my son the lawyer" are examples of this. Another form of community influence is that of "closed" communities, in which the community assumes the problems of its members, which may include resolving the legal and illegal debts of its members. Thus it is important to challenge the gambler's emotional attachment to money, most importantly those of:

- Money is a measure of my worth, without money I am a loser
- I am expected to be successful and have an above-average income
- Money will guarantee me approval and acceptance

These are the most obvious and the most frequent convictions, but by no means is this list complete. Whatever they may be, it is essential that underlying emotional meanings of money and attachments be identified. They are irrational, unprovable, or unattainable. They cannot be ignored. Unless they are challenged the gambler is at risk of relapse. Disputation of these beliefs is essential so that more mature and realistic beliefs can be accepted and practiced. For instance, if money will guarantee acceptance, is the non-income earner, such as a student, traditional housewife, retired worker, or senior citizen, not acceptable if they do not earn an income? If money is a measure of the gambler's worth, will the gambler be worthless if there is a sudden decrease in income?

THE GAMBLER'S SOURCES OF INCOME

Not all gambling results in losses, there are also wins. Research and experience have identified another major contributor to developing a gambling addiction and that is an early Big Win. The Big Win may occur at the very onset of gambling or after many years of buying lottery tickets resulting in many small wins before hitting the big jackpot. Nevertheless, besides family influence, the Big Win is the precursor to compulsive gambling.

This Big Win is relative: the Big Win may be considered small to others but its impact is dependent on income. For a teenager with a weekly income of a twenty dollar allowance, a win of two hundred dollars is a Big Win. For a college student with a substantial allowance or income from a part-time job, a win of five hundred dollars or more reaches that same feeling of excitement and success.

For low or middle income gamblers the Big Win may be several hundred dollars or several thousand dollars. For high income earners a Big Win may be fifty or one hundred thousand dollar wins. The general rule is: the higher the income, the bigger the bet, the bigger the win. Lottery gamblers are the exception: the purchase of a five dollar Lotto ticket may be a multi-thousand or multi-million dollar jackpot.

Throughout the gambling period there are numerous small and larger wins and this intermittent reinforcement contributes to the addictive behaviors. "I won in the past, I know I will win again this time" is the unprovable self-talk. What is true is that the gambler's low self-esteem is temporarily raised to the Big Shot level, and that feels good.

If the compulsive gambler experiences losses and runs out of money, casinos use a method of granting *markers* to make money available while gambling. Markers are a check payable to the casino, signed in advance, with the amount left blank. It is a form of credit guaranteed by a blank check. The casino may advance a marker at its discretion, usually during a period of intense gambling. Casinos determine when the marker is to be cashed, usually when a substantial amount has been granted. Casinos usually allow the gambler forty-five days to clear this marker. If the check is returned for insufficient funds (which is a regular occurrence), the casino will use various means to collect the payment. There may be a threat of legal action and jail. The casino may choose to work out an installment payment arrangement. These payments may be made for several months, a year, or longer, but during this time the casino will not allow any further markers or gambling on credit. However, the host continues to interact with the gambler, offering words of encouragement, such as "you're almost finished paying off, I'll have a limo ready for you."

Other forms of gambling on credit are made over the Internet or those from bookmakers, albeit these are illegal in most states. Sports betting is betting on credit, the payoff occurs only after the game is over. Example. The gambler tells the bookie he wants to "bet a dime" or one thousand dollars on the Ohio/Penn State game. If the gambler wins the bet, the bookie pays the full amount won on the bet, i.e., one thousand dollars. If the gambler loses, the gambler pays the full amount of the bet plus "vigorish" or interest. This is an additional ten percent, or one thousand and one hundred dollars. This loss of the bet plus vigorish lifts the competitive spirit of the compulsive gambler and the chasing continues, i.e., more bets, larger amounts, and more frequently to recoup the losses.

But before any kind of goal of financial stability can be reached, it is incumbent upon the leader of the pressure relief group, whether it is the GA member, the peer counselor, or a professional financial counselor, to know the sources of money that the gambler has used and abused. A partial list of legal sources is:

- Pocket money
- Monies taken from checking accounts through checks, debit cards, and ATMs
- Salaries and earnings
- Small loans from friends or colleagues
- Withdrawals from savings account
- Working overtime, getting advances on paychecks
- Part-time job to supplement full-time job income
- Other incomes, such as Social Security, stocks, trust fund, royalties

- Cash advances on credit cards
- Obtaining additional credit cards
- Cashing in life insurance cash values
- Pawning or selling personal items of value, such as jewelry, baseball card or Tiffany lamp collection, stocks
- Cashing in or taking loans against retirement plan
- New bank loans, consolidating loans
- New home equity loan, refinancing, or second mortgage
- Taking income instead of vacation time at work.

Another method is to reduce spending, often at the family's expense, such as denying the family what once were basic expenditures. These include:

- Failing to purchase necessities, such as clothing, school supplies
- Avoiding social activities, canceling club memberships
- Delaying or non-payment of utility bills
- Delaying or avoiding health care, such as doctor or dentist visits
- Delaying repairs on house, car, or other items
- Canceling health, life, car, or others types of insurance
- Late or non-payments on mortgage
- Reducing or eliminating debts through bankruptcy.

The gambling addict does not simply stop gambling because there are no more legal funds; rather, the gambling addict will now enter a course of "borrowing." Borrowing is the rationalization of "I will take only as much as I need right now and pay it back tomorrow." This period is truly "borrowing" in the gambler's mind, since it will be repaid almost immediately. Initially, these "borrowed" monies are repaid the next day. Unfortunately, the borrowing continues repeatedly, in ever-increasing amounts. At some point the compulsive gambler will realize that this borrowing is in fact stealing; however, the debts and need for money overpower logical thinking and the cessation of illegal acts. In legal terms this meets the criteria of "diminished capacity." Under this interpretation of the law, the gambler knows the difference between right and wrong, does not consider the consequences of these acts, and is unable to control his actions according to the law. This "borrowing" follows a fairly uniform pattern and process:

- Stealing from a family member or friend
- Selling or pawning a family member's items of value, most often jewelry, coin collection, art, or similar items
- Forging a family member's name on a checking account and savings account
- Applying for credit cards in another's name, usually a family member
- All forms of bad checks
- Falsifying financial statements, IRS returns
- Establishing phony bank loans, other bank transactions
- Falsifying reimbursement claims
- Stealing from company deposits or cash collections
- Stealing from client's escrow accounts
- Misusing a company credit card
- Credit card identity theft
- Scams, false loan guarantees, Ponzi schemes
- Money laundering, fraud, forgery
- Selling drugs
- Acts of violence: armed robberies, arson to collect insurance payments

In short, compulsive gamblers in dire financial straits will use any means, first legal and then illegal, to support their gambling addiction, whether it is to pay off the most pressing debts or to continue gambling or, more often, both. This access to extra funds reinforces delusional thinking, and leads to further indebtedness and chaos.

THE PRESSURES ON THE FINANCIAL COUNSELOR

(For this chapter, the gambler will be the husband.)

The GA member of the pressure relief group or the peer counselor of a professional treatment source must insist that the gambler attend financial pressure relief sessions with a spouse or parent, someone who is likely to know more than a little about the extent of the gambling, the debts, monthly expenses, and income. It must also be decided from the onset who will handle the finances. In this example, it will be the wife of the gambler.

WHO GETS CONTROL

Understandably, wives will want financial control to protect themselves and their family, yet their approach is not always the most desirable one in the long term. Their strong emotions underscore this thinking and attitude: anger because of the money gambled away, frustration because they were unable to stop the gambling, and fear that the gambler will return to gambling once money is available.

They want to dole out one or two dollars a day to the gambler. This does not work. Being in control is the compulsive gambler's mantra, so it is essential that confrontation and demands be avoided and to focus instead on cooperation and reconciliation. It is more effective to give and solicit from these compulsive gamblers various options so that they can choose which might work best for all, while still believing that they are in control. Thus, the financial pressure relief group considers not just the debts but also the realistic handling of monies, while meeting emotional needs of both the gambler and the designee, the person who will be handling the money.

The financial counselor must be prepared for the fact that the gambler may not remember all of the debts. This is understandable, especially since compulsive gamblers sit at a blackjack table or in front of a slot machine for many hours without interruption or while they are in the zone. They lost track of time, money won, money lost, and the markers they have written. On the other hand, the gamblers may admit to only 95% of the debts in order to keep even a small amount of control, or in the desperate hope of being able to continue gambling and have the Big Win.

SPOTTING THE LIES

Importantly, admitting to 100% of debts reinforces their sense of failure and failure is simply not acceptable to the competitive mind set of the compulsive gambler. They are convinced that others will criticize or reject them, the loser. Omissions or admitting to much less than the actual amount in debt can also be based on the conviction and fear that a spouse may leave once full disclosure is made.

Yet there are some definite clues that would suggest when someone is lying or concealing information, and it behooves the pressure relief counselor to know some of these signs. These can be grouped into three categories: facial, body, and verbal.

1. Facial clues are predominantly related to the eyes and the mouth

   a. Eyes

      - the direct eye contact is too long
      - the pupils become dilated
      - the pupils may dart to the upper right
      - increased blinking.

b. Mouth

- the smiles are untimely
- smiles are inconsistent with the mood
- smiles are crooked
- the lower lip may tense up
- the Adams' apple will start bobbing.

2. Body: there are various indicators which suggest the person is lying or concealing information:

- rapid breathing
- sweating, especially under the arms
- wringing hands, wiping them on the upper legs
- shrugging
- cracking knuckles
- fussing with clothes or jewelry
- crossing arms or legs
- movements in general are out of sync with the conversation or mood.

3. Verbal clues are the least reliable indicators of lying or concealment. This is especially true of compulsive gamblers who are adept at withholding information, exaggerating or minimizing facts, denying behaviors or events, or simply telling untruths. These verbal cues are:

- responding rapidly and without much forethought
- higher pitch of tone than normal
- more rapid speech, lengthy
- hesitation before responding
- evasive answers
- distracting, ignoring the question, and commenting on something else.

These con artists are adept in the use of words and in their ability to manipulate people and situations. They most likely will argue their positions and turn to emotional blackmail. Unless they are completely devastated, exhausted, and feeling too guilty to even speak up, they will present a host of objections to any initial attempts at budgeting. Some of the more common objections are:

> If the bookie (or loan shark) isn't paid first, he'll hurt all of us.
>
> If we don't pay the casinos off first, they will present my markers and I'll go to jail on bad check charges.
>
> If I don't pay back right now, my boss will find out and fire me.
>
> My boss will call the police.
>
> IRS will charge interest and penalties or put me in jail.
>
> It's cheaper to consolidate, we'll have only one bill instead of ten.
>
> We'll never get out of debt because of the late fees, fines, and high interest.
>
> You have the money, you can pay some of the debts.
>
> The pressure's killing me and will drive me back to gambling.
>
> I might as well kill myself.
>
> You're safer and better off without me.
>
> I'll just leave and not come back.

Some of these answers may be true, at least in the gambler's mind. Others connected with the pressure relief group may agree; however, part of the group's goal is to assist the gambler in admitting to the bookie or casino that he is a compulsive gambler and wants to work out some kind of arrangement that is mutually agreeable. The boss, in most instances, simply wants the money to be returned. If the boss, however, is a bank or federal agency, informing the police is mandatory, even if full restitution is made. The IRS may negotiate repayment, albeit with continuing interest charges, or it may be agreeable to an Offer in Settlement. The IRS can also file criminal charges, so it behooves the gambler to be accompanied by a lawyer.

"Getting out of debt" is one of the goals for the pressure relief group.

Wanting to consolidate bills may make economic sense but is also another version of the quick fix. Paying off in full one debt at a time is a form of reward and also a reminder of the debts accrued due to gambling.

Almost uniformly compulsive gamblers who are in the process of developing some sort of financial stability with their significant others also have another delusional conviction— all the bills will be paid off within one year. It is only through some very delicate probing and suggestions that the gambler will recognize that wants are not needs, and that neither can be accomplished according to their expectations. This attitude is usually accompanied by the demand that the wife get a job and also contribute to settling the gambling debts. The answer is No. The compulsive gambler created the debts, the compulsive gambler must take responsibility for the debts.

BOOKIES AND LOAN SHARKS

Bookies want the money they are owed and often are willing to negotiate terms of payment. The financial counselor needs to know the type of bookie in order to determine how, if any, payment will be made and the potential for physical harm.

Loan sharks, on the other hand, tend to be unsavory people, and many are mobsters and members of organized crime families. They most often are associated with big-time bookies and can be found in bars, casinos, race tracks or with the bookmaking operation. They threaten or actually carry out these threats of physical harm to the gambler. A general trend is the bigger the debt, the nastier the means of collecting it. Loan sharks do not charge interest at 21% per year, they charge 10% a week. They may lend the gambler $500 and want repayment of $600 within one week. Any payment is credited towards interest first, then principle. A compulsive gambler may pay a loan shark every week for a year and still owe the original amount borrowed—all payments were credited to the interest. The financial pressure relief leader must be able to distinguish among types of bookies and if there is any hint of danger should encourage the compulsive gambler to report this to the local FBI office. Their agents know about local and national loan sharks and what actions to take against them.

In developing strategies for financial stability, the gambler most often wants the bookie at the top of the list of debts to be repaid. Once again, these compulsive gamblers have a litany of reasons:

- The bookie always paid, I should do the same.
- He trusted me.
- He likes me, I'm his friend.
- He will get in trouble with his own bookie.
- He will tell my parents or wife.
- He will tell my boss.
- He will harm me or my family.
- He's not a crook just because he's a bookie, everybody bets on sports and sports betting should be legalized. He should be paid like everybody else.

The compulsive gambler and financial manager have some options in dealing with bookies:

- Let the gambler's attorney take over. The attorney can remind the bookie that bookmaking is illegal, no payment will be made, warning the bookie that if any attempt is made to collect the debt there can be legal consequences;

- The bookie will cease all contact with the gambler and in return the gambler will not contact the bookie or notify law enforcement;
- The gambler and the bookie review all wins and losses and pay the difference if, and only if, the bookie's losses are greater than the wins, and further, will be no further contact by either party;
- Pay now or over time the full amount owed;
- Pay a partial amount now or over time as agreed;
- Pay nothing but inform the bookie of this decision.

Virtually always, the bookie would rather know what decisions are made and respond accordingly. Again, bookmaking is illegal and the bookie knows that. Losing some money is better than losing the entire operation and going to jail.

BANKRUPTCY

A more frequent action taken or wanted by the gambler is to declare bankruptcy, but this is just another bail-out and is to be avoided except as a very last resort, i.e., basic needs such as food and housing are greater than the income. It costs approximately $300 to file for bankruptcy and lawyer's fees are in the neighborhood of $2,000. Bankruptcies are public records but generally no one will know a bankruptcy is filed except for the creditors who are named in the bankruptcy. Credit card companies usually will cancel a card even if there is a zero balance. Credit bureaus record all bankruptcies and the information is kept on file for ten years.

There are two personal bankruptcies, chapter 7 and chapter 13. Each has its own requirements and advantages. Bankruptcy requirements are to list all debts and assets. Bankruptcy courts will determine full or partial payment of debts or forgive all debts. Chapter 7 bankruptcy is commonly used when the debtor has no personal property except items such as clothing and furniture, and little or no money after paying basic expenses. Most of these debts are due to unemployment, large medical expenses, seriously overextended credit, marital problems, and other large unexpected expenses. Most unsecured debts can be discharged, that is, completely voided, and creditors may not contact the debtor during the process or after debts are discharged. It takes approximately four months. Spouses may or may not be affected by the gambler's bankruptcy, depending on state community property laws.

Chapter 13 is commonly used when the debtor has significant equity in a home or other property and wants to keep that property. In these cases the debtor has a regular income and can pay living expenses but cannot keep up with scheduled payments on the debts. The advantage is that the debtor can keep personal property and spread out delinquent payments over a three- to five-year period, according to an agreement reached by the debtor and bankruptcy trustee. The debtor makes a monthly payment to the trustee and has no direct contact with the creditors. Cosigners on these debts may be protected.

Debts that are not erased in a Chapter 13 bankruptcy are child support and alimony, debts for personal injury or death caused by drunk driving, income tax debt and student loans. Debts that may continue after filing for bankruptcy are those debts not listed in the filing, fines and penalties imposed for violating civil law, such as traffic fines, and court orders of criminal restitution. Some federal income taxes may be discharged under certain circumstances. Debts incurred on the basis of fraud, such as forgery or lying on a credit application, embezzlement, larceny, or breach of trust are not dischargeable, while there are special requirements on debts owed under a divorce decree or settlement. Illegal debts, such as thefts or money owed to bookies, will not be considered or forgiven by bankruptcy courts.

Some compulsive gamblers in debt may need to change careers. An example of that is the military member or federal government member who has misused government credit card payments. This is subject to possible legal action or dishonorable dismissal.

Compulsive gamblers tend to file for chapter 7 because of their huge indebtedness involving multiple loans, mortgages, credit cards, and unexpected loss of income which far exceed their income.

THINGS TO AVOID AND THINGS TO DO

There are various non-profit agencies which help the debtor resolve financial issues. Consumer Credit Counseling Services is an example. It has offices throughout the country. These agencies will negotiate with credit card companies to discharge part of the debt, which requires closing all of the credit cards. It must be noted that not all credit counseling services are free. Some of them charge as much as $1,000 up front as well as monthly fees. A gambler can also negotiate directly with credit card companies to charge off some of the debt. Charge-offs remain on a credit report for ten years. While this will impact on future credit ratings, this method has been found helpful to make a relapse more difficult since the gambler will have fewer opportunities to access cash. Below are some guidelines:

- Do not liquidate assets, such as stocks or items of value;
- Do not refinance a mortgage or take out a second mortgage;
- Do not increase a credit line or home equity loan;
- Do not borrow or take out loans from financial institutions;
- Do not allow the quick fix or the bail-out;
- Do close all credit cards and charge accounts;
- Do negotiate with credit card companies and financial institutions for lower interest rates and new repayment terms;
- Do advise and negotiate repayment terms of personal loans, i.e., from family, friends, neighbors, or colleagues.

SOME PRACTICAL STEPS
FOR THE FINANCIAL COUNSELOR

Compulsive gamblers know how to manipulate and talk about how money has been spent or should be spent. Their plans make sense to them and to others, but the counselor or GA members conducting the pressure relief group must remain in control, not the compulsive gambler. Thus, it is important that the counselor establish rapport with the gambler at once, so that they can work together. Their work will be futile if the compulsive gambler is not fully honest and does not disclose all financial information. Should the counselor suspect subterfuge, then a simple question, "I know this is uncomfortable for you, but do you want to be here again in the future?" Some of the practical steps are:

1. Set a time that fits all: While this may take some initial effort, it is essential that everyone devote the time to participate throughout the process. If someone misses a session, the gambler may see this as a rejection and could lead to other interfering emotions and behaviors. Additionally, inform all participants the projected time in hours and days this financial pressure relief may require.

2. Find a time balance: Don't try to solve all the issues in one hour or session, but be cautious about taking too long. Too little time spent can lead to poor solutions or an attitude of "He's just doing his job" or "I can con my way out of this." Too much time spent may be interpreted by the gambler as "I'm sicker than others. There's no hope."

3. Set rules: Everything is kept confidential until final agreement has been reached, avoiding all influence from outsiders. Discussions are to be kept polite and non-accusatory.

4. Expect lies: The gambler's misinformation may be deliberate. Conversely, the gambler may not remember all or some of the monies involved. It is not unusual for gamblers to believe that money stolen is one figure while investigation indicates a higher figure.

5. Watch for incongruity: The gambler may verbalize one thing but the body language implies something else, with the nonverbal messages usually being the more accurate ones. They suggest that the gambler doesn't want to be there, doesn't agree with the findings, and doesn't like the budget or solutions. "My way is better than yours," and vehemently resist. Unless they are completely beaten down or feel inordinate levels of guilt and despair, deserving of punishment, they will resist daily handouts or allowances. Be aware that these attitudes are sure to result in non-compliance of budget agreements and lead to early relapse.

6. Take time to review the process: It is helpful if the counselor and others in the relief group review progress as it is being made. "Let's see, what has been accomplished so far?" is a good question to ask occasionally.

7. Take time to review the requirements: Review all the needs, regular expenses and unexpected expenses, legal and illegal debts, as well as all income throughout the planning stage. This should also be a review of the needs versus the wants, for both the gambler and the partner, whether this be the spouse, parents, siblings, children or other relatives and significant others.

8. Demand proof of all debts: No meaningful financial plan can be achieved without full knowledge of debts, expenses and income. Full disclosure of debts can be the most troublesome. Sometimes figures are forgotten, other times they may not be known, and other times they are fabricated. Caveat: There are two kinds of lying, e.g.,

Commission is deliberately telling a lie, and Omission is intentionally omitting information that is relevant.

Get copies of credit card statements, checking and savings accounts, and from all financial institutions and insurance agencies, and reports from credit score companies.

Remember, the compulsive gambler is under emotional pressure, self-imposed and from others.

People with higher incomes or management-level positions often don't use the word "debt." Instead, they use the term "leveraged" because in the business world, the "leverage" is seen as sophisticated and intelligent borrowing. The financial counselor must be familiar with this.

9. Consider all the income: Get proof of all employment incomes and consultant fees, bonuses and commissions, as well as incomes from interest on stocks and bonds, royalties, child support, alimony, tax returns, and others. Then there is the hidden income: slot machine players earn points which can be used for purchases, and are not transferable. Compulsive gamblers are very resistant to giving up these points and may argue "Just let me go back this one more time to buy up my points." The answer is No.

10. Keep on target: Do not let the gambler distract you, so listen briefly and then simply say, "Let's get back on target."

11. Never be judgmental: Compulsive gamblers fear criticism and rejection. Statements such as "You should have known better" or "How could you be so ....?" are counterproductive. Instead, ask "What else?" "Is there anything we have overlooked?" The financial counselor must be aware of their own behaviors. Rolling eyes, shaking head, making faces or giving other nonverbal gestures of disapproval are bad and could upset the participants and, worse yet, give the gambler an excuse to walk out of the meeting.

12. Business financial management does not equal personal money management: This is not an easy concept to understand and it is often a pitfall for the financial counselor to assume that the gambler does not know how to handle money. Truths can differ from assumptions. Many gamblers are accountants, sales associates, stock brokers, bankers or work in the financial section of their companies. Many have majored in business or economics in college which includes being a graduate of the Wharton School of Finance. They know how to manage finances. It is only in their personal lives that these rules do not apply. Their attitude is "I'll spend today and pay for it tomorrow." The gambling itself creates financial disasters, monies tend to be shuffled around, and it is this financial mismanagement that leads to financial crisis and crimes.

WORKING OUT THE BUDGET

Once all the debts, incomes, fixed and unexpected expenses are known and all participants work in tandem, it is time to generate The Budget. Caveat: Experienced financial counselors avoid use of the term "The Budget" because of the knee-jerk negative connotation it evokes. Terms such as "spending plan" or "financial plan" are more acceptable and does not conjure up such negative restrictive feelings.

GA members routinely conduct financial pressure relief groups and the preferred method and forms are those of Gamblers Anonymous. Using GA forms is helpful because they are comprehensive and consider both spouses or parties. It is also a more subtle way of connecting the gambler and others to the GA and Gam-Anon 12-Step programs.

The budget must be accepted as helpful and not as too burdensome or as punishment. Budgets are generally set up on monthly plans, even though expenses and incomes may be on a daily or weekly schedule. Expenses are further specified as fixed, non-fixed and unanticipated. Annual, semi-annual and quarterly expenses should be converted into monthly payments. The totals of expenses must be equal or lower than the income and "If Plan A doesn't work, go to Plan B" – keeping in mind that throughout the process expenses and incomes are changing. Expenses include:

- Housing: rent or mortgage payment, insurance, real estate tax, condo or lot fee, interest;
- Housing operations: heat, air conditioning, all utilities, maintenance, repairs, pest control, cleaning service, gardening, installations, additions;
- Credit and loans: all credit cards, department store charge accounts, all bank and agency loans, private loans;
- Clothing: for all family members, laundry and dry cleaning, repairs, alterations;
- Food: all basic and necessary foods, non-essentials, indulgences;
- Health: medical, dental and vision insurance, office examinations, illnesses, accidents, ER and hospital stays, prosthetics, prescriptions, vitamins, supplements, mental health counseling;
- Transportation: monthly payment, repairs, gas/oil, tune-ups, tires, parts, parking fees, and fines for each car, bus/cab/train/plane fares, drivers licenses, registration;
- Personal: hair care, cosmetics, manicures, physical fitness;
- Professional: school costs and tuition, dues, conferences, continuing education, licenses, supplies, office expenses, computers;
- Family: babysitter, day care, private lessons, school events, pets, social activities, allowances;
- Voluntary miscellaneous: donations, church support, club fees, entertainment, dining out, social organization dues and expenses, media fees; restitution agreements;
- Non-voluntary: child support, alimony, court orders, garnishees.

These are the more common items to be included in the budget. No doubt other items will be identified and added to the expense or income side of the budget. All legal gambling-related debts, such as casino markers, must be included. Illegal gambling debts, such as debts to bookies or loan sharks, may or may not be included, depending on prior arrangements. A full copy of the budget must be given to the gambler and the partner to minimize any confusion or disagreement, which must then be addressed at once. The budget should clearly indicate when the first payment is to be made and the first date that any income is due.

Most importantly, who will be the manager of the funds, both income and payment of expenses? In most cases it is the spouse of the gambler. If this option does not exist, then it may be the parents, sibling, or other adult who will be in charge of the budget. On occasion, the budget manager may be an accountant or court-appointed individual.

Before the budget can be implemented, there must be an understanding of how it should be implemented. How is the income protected from the gambler? Should it be deposited into the partner's checking account? Who makes the deposit: the gambler, the partner, or is income automatically credited to an account? If automatic deposits are made, this will require a written consent from the gambler, but it can also be withdrawn without the partner's knowledge until the anticipated income is missing. A precaution is to use a limited power of attorney.

Additionally, both parties must be in agreement on the budget, rather than being forced into a financial contract. Be aware that there is a distinction between "agreement" and "acquiescence." The latter may be a trigger to relapse.

There must be a clear understanding of how, when, and how much money is given to the compulsive gambler for spending money, such as a snack or cup of coffee en route to work or extended travel. Nothing will contribute sooner to a relapse or relationship stress than for the gambler to feel demeaned by having to ask for an allowance. A simple way to overcome this is to have a set amount placed in the same place, at the same time. Keeping a daily record of expenses helps the gambler to be more aware of how money is spent or can be saved.

It is a common faulty belief that a budget or financial recovery plan is reasonably permanent over a period of time. Not true. Circumstances may change and impact the budget, so a regular review is recommended.

Finally, it is helpful to set consequences if any part of the budget is violated. For instance, what are the consequences if the gambler intercepts a paycheck and in what manner, behaviorally and emotionally, are these consequences set in place? Will the gambler's "allowance" be affected? What are the consequences for various violations of the budget contract, when will the consequences be enforced, how and by whom? Importantly, will the manager be strong enough to follow through on the agreement, consistent, and not waver even one iota. Any variation of the consequence agreement will be seen by the gambler as a win. Is the financial manager following through on the agreed consequence even if this means filing civil or criminal charges? These are difficult questions and tasks for all concerned. Thus close monitoring and a word of encouragement are strong reinforcers for adhering to the budget. These periodic rewards can be tangible, visible evidence that the gambler is succeeding even against considerable obstacles.

A word of caution about periodic rewards: they should not be costly or in any way affect the budget. Taking time out for some fun, watching a television Demand movie at home with friends, serving a favorite meal, are some examples of good periodic rewards which cost little money. In a recent case, the wife of a gambler rewarded him with a new computer. Her intent was good, the outcome was not. The gambler was confused about her chronic complaints of having no money, where did she get it, and how would this affect their budget? He felt betrayed, convinced that she was lying, and therefore he no longer had to adhere to the budget. The "reward" became a "temptation."

Note: It is a common belief that a compulsive gambler can be trusted with money once the gambling is no longer a concern. Not so. The compulsive gambler in recovery may want to handle household finances again, with the consent of the family member or others who previously handled the gambler's finances. The financial counselor must be aware that there are gambling venues and advertisements virtually everywhere. Given the combination of stressful events and other disturbing circumstances, the gambler is at risk of relapsing, no matter how strong any intention may be to refrain from further gambling. Denying access to money is an obstacle at least temporarily. This may be just enough time for the gambler to overcome the urge and craving to escape from these pressures. The cravings are powerful. The cravings become even stronger if the pressures involve money or a lack of money. The gambler has long been convinced that money will solve problems and impulsively gives in to the cravings, hoping once again for the Big Win. Needless to say some compulsive gamblers are able to control and handle finances in the future, but the caveat is "Addicts can relapse, at any time." Why put temptation in their way?

Finally, credit reports from Equifax, Experian, and TransUnion list the date an account was opened, closed, over-due payments, balance from bank loans and credit cards, as well as charge-offs, debts sent for collection, bankruptcies, liens and judgments. These listings start from ten or more years ago and negative items may be kept on the report for up to ten years. They also list any company that has requested credit informa-tion in the last two years. They include requests from a potential employer, investor or pre-approved credit grantor. The report indicates which items may be considered negative and accounts which are in good standing.

The credit report companies update these reports each month. They provide one free report per year. Additional or monthly reports can be purchased for a nominal fee.

An alert can be added, which provides security if any attempt is made for a loan or credit card. Getting a monthly credit report is an easy way to monitor financial activity, thus can protect the family and also the gambler. These reports include the credit score.

Equifax
www.investigate.equifax.com
Equifax Information Services, LLC
Atlanta GA 30348
www.Equifax.Com/fcra
This will be the full credit report with the credit score.
Phone 800-377-6568

Experian
P.O. Box 9701
Allen, TX 75013
This is a full report with credit score.–www.experian.com/
   monitor
Disputes can be called in to 800-509-8495
The VantageScore can be purchased for $7.95
Phone 888-322-5583

TransUnion
P.O. Box 2000
Chester, PA 19002-2000
Phone 800-916-8800
The full TransUnion Consumer Credit Score can be
   purchased for $7.95.

BIBLIOGRAPHY

This chapter is limited to compulsive gambling. There are too many journals with refereed articles on compulsive gambling and gamblers to cite in a book such as this one, and it is similarly unnecessary to list all the books with ethnographic and cultural references in historical or ethnographic literature or fiction. It is not intended to be a scholarly book that would be more appropriate for academia. Nevertheless, important journals, individuals and books are listed for quick access to information about this field. It is not intended to be all-inclusive.

JOURNALS

There are many articles published in refereed professional journals, such as the *Journal of Gambling Behavior*, first published in 1984, started by pioneer Henry R. Lesieur, PhD, PsyD, in the field of compulsive gambling. This journal was the hallmark of recent and current findings on compulsive gambling, leading the way to a centralized forum for clinicians and researchers. In 1991, this journal was renamed *Journal of Gambling Studies*, then *Journal of Gambling Issues*, and now *International Gambling Studies*, representing a broader view of gambling, reporting issues such as lotteries and gambling venues, as well as research on compulsive gambling.

Other refereed journals include articles on compulsive gambling. Most noteworthy are journals such as *Addictions* and *Addictive Behaviors*. These tend to focus more on alcoholism and drug addiction as a primary disorder, and which include compulsive gambling as a secondary disorder. For instance, how many alcoholics in treatment also present with a gambling disorder?

The *Journal of Psychiatry* and other psychiatric journals emphasize studies with a focus on neurological and genetic factors, and research studies on the effectiveness of various medications, such as Naltrexone.

Additionally, there are various journals from other countries, most often the United Kingdom and Australia. These countries have an exceptionally large number of gambling addicts who play the "pokies" or slot machines; thus there are also many research articles.

CLINICIANS AND RESEARCHERS

In addition to journals, a number of clinicians have contributed extensively leading to the advancement of knowledge on compulsive gambling. The most significant or prolific authors are listed below. Caveat: some of these contributors to the field have passed away, but their writings reflect seminal research which still serve as a reference to the many directions that the field has taken, whether prevalence, etiology, impact, prevention, or treatment.

Special recognition must be given to psychiatrist Richard J. Rosenthal, MD and Henry R. Lesieur, PsyD. They are both the earliest, prolific and authoritative researchers and clinicians in the field of compulsive gambling. Without their commitment and unparalleled stellar contributions, the field would still be in the dark ages. Psychiatrist Robert L. Custer, MD, and clinical psychologists Julian I. Taber, Alida Glen, and Durand F. Jacobs are the heroes of the Brecksville VA Medical Center, which opened in 1971, being the first compulsive gambling treatment program in the United States. Professor Robert R. Ladouceur follows in their footsteps with his many contributions to cognitive processes during the compulsive gambling.

There are other major contributors, including Alex P. Blaszcynski, PhD, co-morbidity and treatment; Sheila Blume, M.D., cross addictions; Robert B. Breen, PhD, video gambling machines; Jack L. Derevensky, PhD and Rina Gupta, PhD, youth gambling; Mark D. Griffiths, PhD, slot machine gambling in England; Mary Heineman, LCSW, family issues; Rena Nora, M.D. who developed the Lie-Bet Questionnaire; Nancy M. Petry, PhD, comprehensive view; Howard J. Shaffer, PhD, addictions, former editor of the *Journal of Gambling Studies*; Marvin M. Steinberg, PhD, treatment and stock market gamblers; R. D. Stinchfield, PhD, and K. C. Winters, PhD, prevalence and diagnostics; and Rachel A. Volberg, PhD, prevalence are among the many others who have contributed extensively to the field.

The author also has numerous publications and chapters in 18 books relating to compulsive gambling:

BOOKS

These are the more current books written on compulsive gambling. There are several autobiographies by gambling addicts. Only those published more recently are included.

Adamec-Collins, Christine. (2010). *Pathological gambling*. New York: Facts on File.

American Gaming Association. (1996). *Responsible gaming resource guide*. Washington, DC: American Gaming Association.

American Psychiatric Association. (2013). *Diagnostic and statistical manual of mental disorders* (fifth edition). Washington, DC: Author.

Barthelme, F. & Balthelme, S. (1999). *Double Down*. San Diego: A Harvest Book.

Beattie, Melodie. (1987). *Codependent no more.* New York: Harper/Hazelden.

Beck, A. (1976). *Cognitive therapy and the emotional disorders.* New York: International Universities Press.

Bergler, E. (1958). *The psychology of gambling.* London: Bernard Hanison.

Berman, Linda & Siegal, Mary-Ellie. (2000). *Behind the 8-Ball: A recovery guide for the families of compulsive gamblers.* New York: Simon & Schuster.

Borrell, Jennifer. (2008). *Understanding problem gambling: The interaction of personal and structured processes.* Germany: VDM Verlag.

Borreson, Michael G. (2007). *The free drink: The gambling addiction epidemic.* West Conshohocken, PA: Infinity Publishing.

Burke, Michael J. (2009*). Never enough: One lawyer's true story of how he gambled his career away.*

Castellani, Brian. (2000). *Pathological gambling: Making of a medical problem.* New York: State University of New York Press.

Chafetz, H. (1960). *Play the devil: A history of gambling in the U.S. from 1492 to 1955.* New York: Clarkson N. Potter.

Chamberlain, Linda L. & McGoverns, William G. (2000). *Best possible odds: Contemporary treatment strategies for gambling disorders.* New York: Wiley and Sons, Inc.

Ciarrocchi, Joseph W. (2002). *Counseling problem gamblers: A self-regulatory manual for individual and family therapy.* San Diego: Academic Press.

Chin, John. (2000). *A way to quit gambling.* Writer's Digest Books. iUniversity, Inc.

Clotfelter, C.T. & Cook, P.J. (1989). *Selling hope: State lotteries in America.* Cambridge, MA: Harvard University Press.

Commission on the Review of the National Policy Toward Gambling. (1976). *Gambling in America.* Washington, DC: U.S. Government PrintingOffice.

Cornish, D. B. (1978). *Gambling: A review of the literature and its implications for policy and research.* London: Her Majesty's Stationery Office.

Corwin, Mary Sojourner. (2011). *She bets her life: A true story of gambling addiction.* ReadHowYouWant.com, Ltd.

Curtis, Mike. (2009). *Slaying the devil: One man's fight to risk a gambling problem into touch.* Author House Publishing.

Custer, Robert L. & Milt, H. (1985). *When luck runs out: Help for compulsive gamblers and their families.* New York: Facts on File.

Davis, Diane Rae. (2009). *Taking back your life: Women and problem gambling.* Center City, MN: Hazelden Information and Educational Services.

Dement, J.W. (1998). *Going for broke: The depiction of compulsive gambling in film.* Lanham, MD: The Scarecrow Press, Inc.

Derevensky, Jeffrey L. & Gupta, Rina. (2004). *Problem gambling in Youth: Theoretical and applied perspectives.* New York: Springer Publishing.

Derevensky, Jeffrey, Shaek, Daniel, Merrick, & Noav (eds.). (2011). *Youth gambling: The hidden addiction.* Berlin, Germany: Walter de Gruyter and Company.

Dickerson, M. (1984*). Compulsive gamblers.* London: Penguin Books.

Eades, J.M. (1994). *Gambling addiction, the problem, the pain, and the pathways to recovery.* Publisher: The author.

Eadington, W. R. (ed.) (1996). *The gambling studies proceedings of the 6th National Conference on Gambling and Risk-taking.* Reno: Institute for the Study of Gambling & Commercial Gaming, University of Nevada.

Eadington, W., R. (ed.) (1998). *Gambling research: Proceedings of the 7th International Conference on Gambling and Risk-taking.* Reno: Institute for the Study of Gambling & Commercial Gambling, University of Nevada.

Eadington, W.R. (ed.). (1990) *Indian gaming and the law.* Reno: Institute for the Study of Gambling & Risk Taking. University of Nevada.

Eadington, W.R. & J.D. Cornelius (eds.) (1993) *Gambling behavior and problem gambling.* Reno: Institute for the Study of Gambling & Commercial Gaming, University of Nevada.

Ellis, A. (1983). *Rational-emotive therapy and cognitive behavior therapy.* New York: Springer.

Estes, K. & Brubaker, M. (1994). *Deadly odds: Recovery from compulsive gambling.* Garden City, NY: Simon & Schuster.

Galski, T. (ed.). (1987). *Handbook on pathological gambling.* Springfield, IL: Charles C. Thomas.

Gamblers Anonymous. (1984). *Sharing recovery through Gamblers Anonymous.* Los Angeles: Gamblers Anonymous Publications.

Goodman, Robert. (1995). *The luck business: The devastating consequences and broken promises of America's gambling explosion.* Garden City, NY: Simon & Schuster

Gowan, W. (1988). *Early signs of compulsive gambling.* Center City, MN: Hazelden Educational Materials.

Griffiths, M.D. (1995). *Adolescent gambling.* London: Routledge.

Grinols, Earl. (1988). *Gambling in America: Costs and benefits.* Press Syndicate of the University of Cambridge: Cambridge, UK

Halliday, J. & Fuller, P. (1974). *The psychology of gambling.* London: Allen Lane.

Haubrich-Casperson, J. with Doug Van Nispen. (1993). *Coping with teen gambling.* New York: The Rosen Publishing Group.

Hautman, Peter. (1998). *Stone cold: Young adult problem gambling.* New York: Simon and Schuster Children's Publishing.

Heineman, Mary. (1988). *Sharing recovery, overcoming roadblocks.* Center City, MN: Hazelden Educational Materials. Pamphlet.

Heineman, Mary. (1988). *When Someone you love gambles.* Center City, MN: Hazelden Educational Materials. Pamphlet.

Heineman, Mary. (1991*). Losing your $hirt: Recovery for compulsive gamblers and their families.* Center City, MN; Hazelden Press.

Herman, R. D. (1976). *Gamblers and gambling*. Lexington: Lexington Books.

Icon Health Publications. (2004). *Compulsive gambling: A medical dictionary, bibliography, and Internet references*. Icon Health Publications.

J., Bill. (2012). *Betting Man: A personal battle with gambling addiction*. Virtualbookworm.com Publishing, Incorporated.

Kallick, M., Suits, D., Dielman, T., & Hybels, J. (1976). *Survey of American gambling attitudes and behaviors*. Washington, DC: US Government Printing Office.

Kindt, John & Kindt, J. (eds.). 2012. *The gambling threat to homeland security: Internet gambling*. Buffalo, NY: William S. Hein and Company, Inc.

Kindt, J, & Kindt, J. (eds.). (2010). *The gambling threat to economics and financial systems*. Buffalo, NY: William S. Hein and Company, Inc.

Korsi, Elisa R. (2005). *Gambling: America's latest addiction. Our story:* Mountain Valley Publishing, LLC.

Ladouceur, Robert & Lachance, Stella. (2007). *Overcoming pathological gambling*. New York: Oxford Press.

Ladouceur, Robert & Lachance, Stella. (2007). *Overcoming pathological gambling: The therapist's guide*. New York: Oxford Press.

Ladouceur, Robert, Sylvain, C., Boutin, C., & Doucet, C. (2002). *Understanding and treating pathological gamblers*. London, Wiley.

Lesieur, Henry R. (1984). *The Chase: Career of the compulsive gambler*. Cambridge, MA: Schenkman Books.

Lesieur, Henry. (1988) *Understanding compulsive gambling*. Center City, MN: Hazelden Educational Materials. Pamphlet.

Livingston, J. (1974). *Compulsive Gamblers: Observations on action and abstinence*. New York: Harper Torchbooks.

Lorenz, Valerie C. (1978). *Pathological gambling: Characteristics of the gambler, its impact upon the family, and the effectiveness of Gam-Anon*. The Pennsylvania State University, Capitol Campus: Middletown, PA.

Lorenz, Valerie C. (1983). *An annotated bibliography on pathological gambling behavior of students from the University of Nevada at Las Vegas and Georgia State University in Atlanta*. Ann Arbor, MI: University Microfilms International.

Lorenz, Valerie. (1988). *Standing up to fear*. Center City, MN: Hazelden Educational Materials. Pamphlet.

Lorenz, Valerie. (1998*). Releasing guilt*. Center City, MN: Hazelden Educational Press. Pamphlet.

Lorenz, Valerie & Politzer, Robert (eds.). (1990). *Final report: Task force on gambling addiction*. Baltimore, MD: Maryland Department of Health and Mental Hygiene.

Mansood, Zangeneh, Blaszczynski, Alex, & Turner, Nigel E. (2007). *In the pursuit of winning: Problem gambling theory, research and treatment*. New York: Springer.

Marotta, Jeffrey J., Cornelius, Judy A., & Eadington, William R. (eds.). (2002). *The Downside: Problem and pathological gambling*. Reno: University of Nevada.

Martinez, Tomas M. (1983). *The gambling scene: Why people gamble*. Springfield, IL: Charles C. Thomas Publisher

McGovern, William G., & Howatt, William A. (2007). *Treating gambling problems.* New York: Wiley Series of Treating Addictions.

Mawer, Philip. (2010). *Overcoming gambling: A guide for problem and compulsive gambling.* London: Sheldon Press.

McGurrin, M.C. (1992). *Pathological gambling: Conceptual, diagnostic, and treatment issues.* Sarasota, FL: Professional Resource Press

Meyer, Gerhard, Hayer, Tobian, & Griffiths, Mark (eds.). (2008). *Gambling in Europe:* Berlin, Germany: Springer Verlag.

Meyer, G., Althoff, M., & Stadler, M.A. (1998). *Gambling and delinquency.* Frankfurt/Main: Peter Lang Verlag.

National Gambling Impact Study Commission. (1999). *Final report.* Washington, DC: U.S. Government Printing Office.

National Research Council. (1999). *Pathological gambling: A critical review.* Washington, DC: National Academy Press.

Offitt, Sidney (1995). *Memoirs of a bookie's son.* New York: St. Martin's Press.

Perkinson, Robert R. (2003). *The gambling addict: Patient workbook.* New York: SAGE Publications.

Petry, Nancy M. (2004). *Pathological gambling: Etiology, comorbidity, and treatment.* Washington, DC: American Psychological Association.

Politzer, Robert & Lorenz, Valerie C. (1990). *Final report: Gambling addiction in Maryland.* Baltimore: Maryland Department of Health & Mental Hygiene.

Public Independence Educational Publishing Co. *Overcoming compulsive gambling.* UK: Constable and Robinson.

Quirke, M. (1996). *Women gambling on poker machines: A way of coping?* National Association of Gambling Studies, Glenelg, South Australia.

Rose, I. Nelson. (1986). *Gambling and the law.* Whittier, CA

Rosecrance, J. (1988). *Gambling without guilt: the legitimation of an American pastime.* CA: Brooks/Cole Publishing Company.

Schull, Natasha Dow. (2012). *Addiction by design: Machine gambling in Las Vegas.* Princeton University Press.

Shaffer, Howard J. (2012). *Change your gambling, change your life: Strategies for managing your gambling and improving your finances, relationships and health.* New York: John Wiley and Sons, Ltd.

Shaffer, Howard J., Hall, M.N., & Vander Bilt, J. (1997). *Estimating the prevalence of disordered gambling behavior in the United States and Canada: A meta-analysis.* Boston: Harvard Medical School, Division on Addictions.

Shaffer, H., Stein, S., Gambino, B. & Cummings, T. *Compulsive gambling: Theory, research and practice.* Lexington, MA: Lexington Books.

Skolnik, Sam. (2011). *High stakes: The rising cost of America's gambling addiction.* Ypsilanty, MI: Beacon Press.

Sojourner, Mary. (2010). *She bets her life: A true story of gambling addiction.* Berkeley, CA: Seal Press.

Steenbergh, Timothy, Whelan, James P. & Andrew W. (2007*)*. *Problem and pathological gambling advances in psychotherapy: Evidence-based.* Practice Series, Vol. 8. Hogrefe Publishing.

Taber, Julian (2001). *In the shadow of chance: The pathological gambler.* Bluffton, SC: ExGambler Services.

Taber, Julian. (2008). *Addictions Anonymous: Outgrowing addiction through a universal, secular program of self-development: A comprehensive text for recovering addicts and counselors.* Whidbey Island, WA: Ingersoll Literary Productions.

Tepperman, Lorne. (2009). *Betting their lives: The close relations of problem gamblers.* New York: Oxford University Press.

Ustok, Lisa & Hughes, Joanna. *First steps out of problem gambling.* Oxford, UK: Lion Hudson Pic.

Volberg, Rachel A. (2001). *When the chips are down: Problem gambling in America.* A Century Foundation Report.

Wagenaar, W. A. (1988). *Paradoxes of gambling behavior.* Hove, UK: Lawrence Erlbaum Associates.

Walker, M.B. (1992). *The psychology of gambling.* New York: Pergamon Press, Inc.

Wanda, G., Foxman, J. (1971). *Games compulsive gamblers, wives and families play.* Downey, CA: Gam-Anon Inc. Pamphlet.

APPENDIX 1
THE ABCs OF GAMBLING

WITH A FOCUS ON COMPULSIVE GAMBLING

The world of gambling has a verbiage all its own. Some of the words below pertain to gambling in general, others more exclusively to the field of problem and compulsive gambling.

Abuse by a family member: non-gambling parents, usually the mother, may verbally abuse their children in trying to cope with the chaos created by the compulsive gambler.

Abuse suffered by the gambler: virtually all action compulsive gamblers grow up in an abusive family of origin in which they are subjected to verbal abuse ("don't you ever do anything right?"), psychological abuse (rejection), and physical abuse (often at the hands of the father, against the mother and/or the gambler).

Abuse by the gambler: compulsive gamblers are infrequently physically abusive, although most become verbally abusive and threatening when they are in a desperate need for money.

Access to gambling: is possible in person, through the Internet, phones, or mail.

Accident: death by automobile accident is the preferred form of committing suicide by male compulsive gamblers. A deliberate auto crash can easily be disguised as an accident and is not likely to be considered a suicide. The gambler's belief is that the family will receive insurance benefits which can be used for bills and living expenses.

Action: also referred to as In Action, it is associated with euphoria or the expectation of euphoria, experienced by Action gamblers. Its onset may be during a particular activity, such driving past a particular race track or while actually gambling.

Action gamblers: a term used for compulsive gamblers who seek the fast pace and excitement of gambling, such as shooting dice, betting on sports, and horse racing. They gamble for the money, attention, and a sense of being the "big shot."

Addiction: compulsive gambling is considered a psychological or process addiction, as opposed to being a substance addiction.

ADHD: in recent years, clinicians and researchers have found that some Action gamblers are also suffering from Attention Deficit Hyperactive Disorder.

Affect: an external expression of an internal emotional state. Affect is described as flat, blunted, or normal. Compulsive gamblers often exhibit a flat affect when they first present for treatment or attend Gamblers Anonymous.

Aftercare: aftercare follows completion of treatment in a residential facility, rehabilitation program, or psychiatric hospital. Aftercare sessions include such issues as re-entry into the family system, work or school, stabilization of finances, and relapse prevention training.

After-hours club: a location in which illegal gambling is conducted. This may be in a legal gambling site after closing hours or a property used by an organized crime syndicate.

Alcohol and gambling: alcohol dependence is found in perhaps thirty percent of compulsive gamblers, either as a cross-addiction or a co-addiction. Compulsive gamblers avoid alcohol during active gambling in order to maintain clarity of mind.

Antisocial: an activity violating the law. It is also a personality disorder suffered by some compulsive gamblers, especially those who tend to have a history of repeated illegal activities due to their gambling addiction.

American Gaming Association, founded in 1995 to "create a better understanding of gaming." It represents commercial casinos, provides funds for research, and supports the Responsible Gaming program.

American Psychiatric Association (APA): the official body (including the World Health Organization, WHO) which defines and sets criteria for Pathological Gambling, in its *Diagnostic and Statistical Manual of Mental Disorders (DSM)*. It first included Pathological Gambling in its third edition, 1980, under Impulsive Control Disorder, Section 312.31. The DSWM 5 lists it under Addiction and Related Disorders.

Anxiety: an emotional state based on thoughts predicting future negative events and consequences. The anxiety becomes intense as gambling losses increase.

Art therapy: a form of expressive therapy which is especially helpful in diagnosing and treating compulsive gamblers. It minimizes the effectiveness of the gambler's verbal manipulation and overcomes the gambler's fear of expressing thoughts and feelings.

Assertiveness: many compulsive gamblers lack the ability to be appropriately assertive, fearing ridicule, criticism and rejection.

Athletes: most compulsive gamblers, especially the Action gamblers, have a history of being outstanding athletes, due in part to their competitive nature and determination to be the best. Some professional athletes and other personnel have ruined their careers due to compulsive gambling, including NBA players Charles Bradley and Antoine Walker, Major League Baseball player Pete Rose, NFL quarterback Art Schlichter, referee Tim Conaghy, and Chet Forte, of Monday Night Football.

Atlantic City: the mecca of casino gambling in the East Coast of the United States.

ATM machine: bank machines, often located in casinos and racinos, allowing the gambler quick access to cash.

Attitudes: social attitudes towards gambling continue to change, with proponents favoring the legalization of gambling to create jobs and add revenues to state budgets. Opponents view gambling as sinful, immoral, or as poor economics, leading to addiction, bankruptcy and crime.

Availability: today gambling is ubiquitous, found in traditional sites such as race tracks and casinos, and also in schools, businesses, at home, in churches and jails, on the Internet, and throughout the world.

Avoidance: compulsive gamblers tend to repress their emotions and avoid conflict, because of their sense of vulnerability, fear of exposure, criticism, and rejection if their true feelings are expressed.

Avoidant Personality Disorder: a psychiatric disorder often observed in Escape gamblers. It is treatable.

Bail-out: a plea by the compulsive gambler for someone to pay off a gambling debt, accompanied with a well-intentioned or manipulated promise to abstain from further gambling. The bail-out offers the gambler temporary relief from debts and stress; however, it generally enables further gambling.

Bankruptcy: a form of bail-out often preferred by compulsive gamblers, but discouraged by Gamblers Anonymous and mental health therapists.

Baseball cards: collected by teenage boys who purchase a pack of eight cards, hoping to find the special card needed to complete their collection. Buying a pack of cards while not knowing which cards may be in it is considered gambling. Trading or buying a specific card is considered collecting, not gambling, since there is no risk involved.

Bet: a term more commonly used than "wager."

Benefits of gambling for the family: the family may be the recipient of monies won by the gambler, or of casino comps, such as free meals, transportation, or expensive gifts.

Benefits for the gambler: the gambler may win money or points; experience euphoria and the self-image of being a superior gambler; and the momentary relief from emotional pain and stress.

Big Win: a major trigger leading to problem and compulsive gambling. During later stages of the gambling addiction, a Big Win is seen as the only hope for paying off gambling debts. The amount of money defining a Big Win is relative to the gambler's financial state.

Bingo: a game in which the object is to match the numbers drawn at random on a card with 25 numbers. Social gamblers may play three or four cards, compulsive gamblers tend to use twelve or more cards. Many bingo players use fetishes and other objects of superstition. Bingo has a long history of being a fundraiser, legally or illegally, for churches, schools and other non-profit organizations. Bingo traditionally is seen as a form of family recreation, preferred by women and seniors, but legislative actions in recent decades led to the opening of bingo parlors which can accommodate hundreds of male and female gamblers at each sitting of two hours.

Bipolar Disorder: a physical/psychiatric disorder which requires pharmaceutical intervention, in which moods vacillate between periods of manic behaviors and depression, lasting for days or weeks. In recent years more compulsive gamblers are being dually diagnosed as also suffering from bi-polar disorder.

Blackjack: a card game, also known as "21" preferred by Action gamblers. In casinos, blackjack may be played as a table game with live dealers and pit bosses or on an electronic slot machine.

Blaming others for one's own gambling: a rationalization and outburst of anger which gives the gambler an excuse to gamble. Co-dependents feel guilty and responsible for the gambler's accusations, then blame themselves.

Bookie or bookmaker: the person who accepts a bet, usually on sports or horse racing, with a built-in advantage for profit. There are many types of bookies and levels of bookmaking, ranging from classmates to organized crime members. Most states have laws which define bookmaking as an illegal activity, subject to prosecution.

Books on gambling: of which there are many, which describe betting strategies. They tend to explain many forms of gambling, together with social customs and descriptions of the gambling paraphernalia.

Books on compulsive gambling: of which there are few. In the past decade, some books have been published, most often in English, Spanish or German, which are autobiographical; others focus on psychological issues of gambling.

Break even: a gambling addict's oft-used description to minimize gambling losses.

Casino: a gambling site of various models: Las Vegas destinations, Indian reservations, land-based, or cruise ships, of varying sizes. Casinos offer slots, card games, dice, roulette wheels, Asian games, and simulcasts of races, keno, or sports. Slot parlors are also called slots casinos. Casinos may be legal or illegal. State laws also permit charitable casinos as a temporary fundraiser for schools, churches, and charitable organizations.

Card clubs: a gambling venue, legal in California, limiting gambling opportunities to card games.

Cards: a very popular form of gambling in many cultures and societies, throughout history. The most popular gambling card games in casinos and card clubs in the US are blackjack and poker. Card games are popular with all segments of a population, as a recreational activity or for gambling.

Charitable gambling: an organized gambling activity operated as a fundraiser by a not-for-profit charitable agency, following strict codes of state regulations.

Chasing: the urgent need to continue gambling in order to recoup monies from lost bets. The term "chasing" was coined by Henry Lesieur.

Cheats: individuals who use deceptive means to increase their likelihood of winning, using marked cards, crooked dice, or dishonest methods, gaffing carnival games, or sleight of hand tricks either singly or with accomplices.

Checks: typically the compulsive gambler's first illegal method of obtaining money for gambling or to pay off gambling bills.

Child abuse: the most frequent type of child neglect or child endangerment, i.e., leaving a young child at home unattended for many hours or in a locked car exposed to severe weather. It also consists of physical or emotional abuse.

Chips: an alternative to paper currency, of different monetary values. The color of the chip determines it value, i.e., a black chip is worth $100. Casinos offer chips of much larger denominations.

Community awareness: an attempt by advocates, local groups or state-funded programs to increase the knowledge and awareness of compulsive gambling as a preventable and treatable psychiatric/behavioral disorder.

Competitive: a personality characteristic essential to compulsive gambling. Compulsive gamblers are highly competitive.

Comps: compensation offered by casinos to gamblers, based on the customer's gambling habits, in an effort to develop loyalty to the specific casino.

Compulsive: the same acts repeated over an extended period of time, often associated with loss of control.

Compulsive gambling: a layman's term for the clinically correct term of Pathological Gambling. It a psychiatric disorder, progressive in nature, in which the gambler is driven by overwhelming, uncontrollable cravings to gamble, and loses control over the gambling behavior, resulting in serious consequences regarding finances, relationships, employment, health, crime and suicide. The disorder is treatable and according to Gamblers Anonymous, can be arrested but never cured. Compulsive gambling is considered by clinicians to be a psychological addiction, in which the substance, money, is abused but not ingested. The DSM5 version lists it as an addiction and has renamed it to "gambling disorder."

Consequences: the results of unacceptable actions which typically are ignored by addicts. For ex.: compulsive gamblers may steal, but they do not consider the consequences of their acts, even if this means possible incarceration or losing a job or occupational license.

Consumer Credit Counseling Agency: a non-profit agency to help debtors budget their finances and to clear up their debts.

Contributing factors: the issues or incidents which lead an individual to develop a gambling disorder. Among Action gamblers, contributing factors are a dysfunctional family of origin, family emphasis on money, personality characteristics, availability and accessibility to gambling, and response to critical or traumatic incidents. Contributing factors among Escape gamblers tend to be troubled marital or family relationships and sudden financial expenses or reversals and other critical life events.

Co-occurring or co-morbidity: a term used in the medical/mental health field and health insurance industry indicating multiple diagnoses. Co-occurring disorders with compulsive gambling may be another addiction, affective disorders, such as depression or anxiety, and personality disorders.

Coping: the ability to tolerate stress in a positive manner. Compulsive gamblers tend to have poor coping skills.

Craps: a fast-action dice game popular with Action gamblers.

Cravings: stronger than an urge, cravings can become critical triggers for relapses.

Credit: used by gambling venues as a means of providing money to a gambler. Casinos extend credit through the use of markers—checks which are not submitted for collection until 45 days after the marker is signed. Sports betting is also done on credit. State lotteries are prohibited from extending credit to gamblers.

Credit cards: compulsive gamblers typically have six or more credit cards as a consequence of their gambling, which may be acquired legally or illegally, and which are charged to the maximum amount allowed.

Crime: illegal acts by which compulsive gamblers will obtain money to pay bills, other gambling-related debts, and to continue gambling. The crimes may be violent or non-violent. Non-violent financial crimes tend to be committed dozens of times, until the thefts are discovered, or the gambler has hit bottom.

Criticism: a compulsive gambler's worst fear, believing criticism to be an indication of failure, thus leading to rejection.

Cut-off notice: a frequent occurrence during the latter stages of compulsive gambling, due to failure to pay utilities and other household bills.

Day trading: a potentially destructive financial way of gambling with stocks due to the nature of high stakes and fast action.

Debt: a compulsive gambler's nightmare, which triggers an increase in gambling.

Degenerate: a term used most often by a bookie or loan shark in referring to a compulsive gambler.

Delusion: magical thinking, most frequently a conviction that the next bet will be the *Big One.*

Denial: an internal or external refusal to accept that the gambling has become problematic or addictive.

Depression: various forms of a depressed emotional states suffered by Action and Escape gamblers. It may be a dysthymic disorder, major depression, manic-depression, or other forms of depression. Most Action gamblers have an underlying dysthymic depression. A major depression almost invariably occurs during the Desperation Stage and Exhaustion Stage of compulsive gambling.

Desperation: the near-end stage of compulsive gambling during which the gambler will resort to many aberrant means, including illegal acts, to obtain money to repay debts.

Dice: or craps, a form of gambling which pre-dates written history, and which is one of several favorite forms of gambling for the Action gambler. Betting on dice, or shooting craps, is favored by males. Cheats often use crooked dice., those that are shaved, weighted, have wrong numbers, etc.

Diminished capacity: a legal term used in criminal court sentencing, describing a state of behavior in which the gambler knows the difference between right and wrong, does not consider the consequences of his actions, and has lost the ability to control his behavior. Diminished capacity can lead to downward departure in federal sentencing cases. Clinically, it is less severe than insanity.

Don't Bet On It: a slogan used by the NCAA to warn collegiate athletes and related personnel of its zero tolerance for gambling on sports.

Dreams: a system used in which a number seen in a dream is believed to be the winning one. Dreams and dream books are common in the African-American culture.

Drugs: the most common drug used by gamblers is alcohol, and to a lesser extent marijuana or cocaine. In more recent years, compulsive gamblers have sold but not used drugs to support their gambling addiction.

Drug of choice: an expression: "gambling is my drug of choice."

Dual diagnosis: a term popularized by the health insurance industry to diagnose an individual with an addiction and a mental health disorder.

Dual personality: compulsive gamblers are described as Dr. Jekyll/Mr. Hyde, in which one is the "real" person and the other is the monster.

Dysfunctional family of origin: often a major contributing factor in Action gamblers, in which a child is denied healthy role modeling, emotional nurturance, guidance, and coping skills, is often exposed to various forms of abuse, most often by an alcoholic parent, and inconsistent parenting, leading to low self-esteem. This, plus the family's strong emphasis on money, sets the groundwork for potential development of compulsive gambling.

Dysthymia: a low-grade level of depression, typically with an onset during childhood, especially prominent among Action gamblers.

Effective communication: usually lacking in compulsive gamblers, whose style of communication tends to be superficial and manipulative.

Enabling: actions performed by family members and others which allow the person to continue gambling, such as providing money or covering up for the gambler.

Escape Gambler: compulsive gamblers who seek to avoid people and problems by immersing themselves into a solitary form of gambling, such as slots or gambling over the Internet. They describe themselves as "being pulled into the machine" and seek the numbing effect of gambling, rather than the exhilaration and excitement experienced by Action gamblers.

Experience, or not learning from experience: one of the hallmarks of addiction. "Only an addict will do the same thing, over and over again, expecting a different outcome."

Family of origin: the family into which the gambler is born and raised. Action gamblers are usually exposed to dysfunctional family life and describe their childhood as troubled and unhappy, whereas Escape gamblers typically describe their childhood as happy and supportive.

Feelings: an emotional state brought on by a person's thoughts, beliefs, and experiences, leading to various behaviors. Compulsive gamblers admit that Guilt during and after their gambling is their most intense feeling.

Financial sense: gamblers are able to understand and manage finances for others, but during gambling leave their own financial matters in a state of chaos and indebtedness. Compulsive gamblers also tend to think in terms of "spend now, pay later."

Football: sports bettors usually start betting on football games, which becomes the entrée to gambling on other sports, such as baseball and basketball.

Fun cards: another word for "players cards," a means used by casinos and slots vendors to monitor a player's gambling. These plastic cards, set with computer microchips, resemble a credit card and are inserted into a slot machine in place of coins or currency.

Gam-Anon: a fellowship of family and friends of the compulsive gambler, seeking through the 12-Step recovery program to understand and cope with the chaos brought on by compulsive gambling. The free program is based on anonymity and confidentiality.

Gambling: made up of three criteria, whether legal or illegal, (1) betting something of value (usually money), (2) on a game predominantly chance, (3) hoping for a greater reward. Without Value or Chance, the activity would be considered skill or gaming, rather than gambling.

Gamblers Anonymous: a fellowship started in 1957 by compulsive gamblers sharing their experiences and following the 12-Steps Recovery Program. It is free, based on anonymity and confidentiality.

Gambler's Prayer: a desperate gambler's plea to a higher power or Lady Luck, to win "just this one more time."

Gambling Disorder: a term coined by the American Psychiatric Association in the DSM5 which came into use in 2013, preferred to "pathological gambling."

Game of chance: a formal description of gambling, often used within the legal, legislative or law enforcement arena.

Game of skill: a game which does not meet the three criteria for gambling, i.e. value, chance and reward. PacMan and pinball machines are a game of skill, slot machines are a game of chance. The card game, poker, is gambling, although there is a strong factor of skill, such as knowing the laws of probability, money management, bluffing, practice and experience, which give the player greater odds of winning.

Gaming: the industry's word for its activities – gaming industry. The act of betting is considered "gambling."

Gaming industry: a commercial enterprise providing legal gambling opportunities and its related activities, such as manufacturing equipment.

Golf: a sport which compulsive gamblers state they enjoy not only to win, but also because if offers "complete silence, away from the world." Recovering compulsive gambler frequently protest, inaccurately, that betting for "only one dollar" on golf does not represent real gambling since the amount is too small.

Government addicted: a frequent criticism against state legislatures which legalize gambling in order to raise revenues and create jobs: "The government has become addicted to gambling."

Guilt: the strongest and longest feeling suffered by compulsive gamblers. The gambler's sense of guilt becomes all-encompassing and overpowering, leading to depression and acts of desperation, ultimately also to suicidal obsessions. Approximately twenty percent act on their suicidal intentions. Compulsive gamblers may suffer from feelings of guilt for many years after abstinence.

Habitual gambler: another word for compulsive gambler, used in the past and most frequently in England.

Health: the years of compulsive gambling, stress, anxiety and depression contribute to the gambler's poor health—chronic headaches, upper and lower back pain, wrist and elbow pain, muscle stiffness, substance abuse, gastrointestinal disturbances, sleep irregularities, poor dental health, etc.

Health insurance: many health insurance companies and managed care companies deny reimbursement for "gambling." Often a "doc-to-doc" consultation is necessary to clarify the difference between "gambling" and "pathological gambling" as defined in the DSM. The gambler's insistence of "I have good health insurance" may be true for medical treatment but generally not for mental health or behavioral care, thus limiting access to treatment and reimbursement.

Help: "help" from the gambler's standpoint typically means a bail-out, whereas at the end stage of the addiction also refers to treatment. The family, in contrast, wants help in understanding and coping with the disorder.

High rollers: a term used by casinos to describe their patrons who gamble with large amounts of money.

Horse racing: a form of gambling popular with males since the founding of the US. Compulsive gamblers almost always state they were introduced to horse racing by a male figure, such as a family member or close family friend, while they were still in their teens. Horse race gamblers are considered to be Action gamblers.

Hotline: various state governments give financial support for a state-wide problem gambling hotline, providing crisis intervention, information and referral. At this time there are no state hotlines using a universal intake form, referral system, or data collection.

Immaturity: Action gamblers tend to be emotionally immature and function at an early teen age emotional level. Escape gamblers have more advanced emotional development but often also suffer from low self-esteem and vulnerabilities similar to action gamblers.

Impact: compulsive gambling affects the gambler, families, employers, and communities, leading to financial instability, loss of work productivity, poor health, increase in crimes, broken homes, and suicide.

Impulse Control Disorder: a recurrent loss of control over impulsive behavior. Since 1980, Pathological Gambling has been listed under Disorders of Impulse Control in the American Psychiatric Association's *Diagnostic and Statistical Manual of Mental Disorders*, Section 312.31. The DSM5 lists it under a general category of addictions.

In action: the intense feeling and behaviors of Action gamblers, describing themselves while gambling, or desiring to gamble, reaching euphoric or dissociative states.

Incarceration: approximately one in four of compulsive gamblers are charged with criminal acts, leading to a period of incarceration for many of them. The length of sentence is based on the crime, amount of money stolen, history of criminal acts, acceptance of responsibility, and cooperation with law enforcement. Incarceration has been found to be an ineffective means of preventing further gambling.

Inpatient treatment: treatment in a psychiatric hospital in which the patient is housed under secure conditions. There are very few facilities which offer inpatient treatment for compulsive gamblers.

Insight: compulsive gamblers tend to be lacking in the ability to be aware of internal and external realities.

Intelligence: research and clinical experience has determined that compulsive gamblers are above average in intelligence, especially in the area of mathematical abilities.

Internet gambling: a computer-based location which has become a popular gambling site. It is considered highly addictive due to the solitary form of gambling, availability, and the ease with which gambling can be hidden or disguised. Money is cabled, charged against credit cards or sent via Western Union, and the forms of gambling are similar to land-based gambling—horse racing, card games, sports, bingo, etc.

Intervention: a process by which family members and friends in a supportive manner confront the addict's unacceptable behaviors and then encourage the individual to attend professional treatment and/or a 12-Step program. Compulsive gamblers tend to resist this approach and often turn the intervention into a battle of the wills.

In the jackpot: an expression used by gamblers to describe being in debt due to gambling.

Irrational beliefs: psychologist Albert Ellis developed a treatment modality based on overcoming irrational beliefs held by clients. Compulsive gamblers have many, most often: "I must be in control of all things at all times," "Criticism is an indication of failure," "Rejection is awful and must be avoided at all costs," "Money will solve all my problems," and "I must be liked by everyone at all times," etc.

Isolation: Action gamblers learn in early childhood that they can avoid vulnerability by isolating themselves emotionally and physically from others.

Judgment: a reaction to a particular situation, usually Poor among gamblers. In legal arenas, it also refers to actions of the judge in sentencing the offender, as in "It is the judgment of the court…"

Jury: compulsive gamblers tend to plead guilty, thus avoiding a trial by jury.

Jinxed: a series of gambling losses, also termed by race track gamblers as "a bad beat."

Jackpot: the gambler's description of a Big Win—"I hit the jackpot." Being "in the jackpot" means the gambler has lost considerable amounts of money and is in debt.

Keno: a game consisting of 80 numbers, similar to bingo, offered by state lotteries and casinos. It has very poor odds of winning.

Kiting: a form of a bad check writing frequently used by compulsive gamblers in desperate need of money.

Knowledge: compulsive gamblers tend to study, practice and develop their own system to elevate their knowledge and skill, thus improving the odds of winning bets.

King: "I feel like a king with an inferiority complex" is an expression frequently uttered by casino Action gamblers.

Lady Luck: the gambler's fervent hope for godly intervention to win the bet.

Lazy: gamblers appear to be lazy, when in fact they might be suffering from major depression.

Legal problems: virtually all compulsive gamblers commit crimes in the latter stages of their addiction and at least 25% have legal charges brought against them.

Line: Determined by the bookie, in which a point spread may determine a win even if the team lost the game.

Loan shark: loan sharks lend money at usury rate of interest and demand prompt repayment with interest being paid first. Failure to repay so may result in violence.

Losses: the compulsive gambler's nemesis which leads to "chasing" in order to recoup monies they have lost.

Losing phase: the middle stage of compulsive gambling, leading from social gambling to desperate gambling, and ultimately hitting bottom.

Lottery: a game of chance, usually operated by a state government or charitable agency, in which tickets with self-selected or machine-selected numbers are sold, and in which winning is based on matching randomly drawn numbers. Power Ball and MegaMillions are multi-state lotteries with prizes in the millions of dollars.

Magical thinking: delusional thinking during intense gambling in which the gambler is convinced of a winning outcome.

Mah jong: a gambling game of Chinese origin played with 144 dominoes.

Mail fraud: one of many non-violent financial "paper" crimes committed by gamblers, it is a federal offense usually leading to incarceration.

Manipulation: a form of communication by gamblers who are noted for their outstanding ability to verbally control a situation through guilt-inducing techniques in an effort to obtain money or as an excuse for gambling. "I never knew this wasn't normal talking."

Marker: a casino's temporary loan secured by a blank check which usually needs to be repaid in 45 days or result in legal charges if it is not honored.

Memory: compulsive gamblers have an uncanny memory of past athletic events, being able to recall which athlete played in which game, how many times at bat, who scored in which inning, etc. Their memory tends to be either highly accurate or exceedingly inaccurate in terms of monies gambled, lost and stolen.

Mind-reading: an irrational belief, a la Albert Ellis, in which gamblers (and many others) are convinced they know what another person is thinking.

Myths: stories and beliefs with a minor element of truth in them. There are many myths regarding compulsive gamblers.

Narcissistic Personality Disorder: a psychiatric condition frequently observed in Action gamblers, having a sense of grandiosity and entitlement.

National Center for Responsible Gaming (NCRG) is the AGA's affiliated charity. It funds research to "increase understanding of pathological gambling."

National Coalition Against Gambling Expansion (NCAGE): a 501(c)4 non-profit public action committee to influence specific legislation

National Coalition Against Legalized Gambling - NCALG: a 501(c)3 educational group which educates the public about detrimental effects of gambling

National Council on Problem Gambling (formerly National Council on Compulsive Gambling), founded in 1972 to be an advocate for problem gamblers and their families. "It maintains a neutral stance regarding the legalization of gambling."

Numb: the emotional state experienced by Escape gamblers during the final stages of their addiction, most often associated gambling on slot machines.

Numbers: an illegal form of lottery prominent among African-Americans and which is closely tied to their customs and social interactions.

Neurological testing: new studies suggest there may be neurological factors involved in compulsive gambling.

Occupation: compulsive gamblers typically work in occupations involving money.

Odds: gamblers will study, practice, and handicap to improve their chances of winning.

Off-shore betting sites: illegal Internet gambling sites in the Caribbean Islands.

OTB: off-track betting parlors which feature horse and dog races.

Outpatient care: treatment for a patient who is neither hospitalized nor receiving treatment in a residential treatment program.

Pachinko: a variation of a Japanese pinball machine favored by Asian gamblers.

Paddlewheel: also known as pusher or bull-dozer, an enclosed gambling machine with one or more levels of coins, usually quarters, in which the player drops a coin in the shooter, forcing the coins on the ledge to move. Illegal in most states, it gives the delusion of an impending win.

Pathological gambling: the clinically correct term for what is commonly referred to as "compulsive gambling" and more recently "gambling disorder."

Peer counselor: a recovering compulsive gambler who teaches newcomers the Gamblers Anonymous program and counsels them on gambling-specific issues. Peer counselors are not licensed but may be paid employees in treatment programs.

Personality disorders: compulsive gamblers may suffer from traits, features, or full-fledged personality disorders. Action gamblers are more likely to have narcissistic features, whereas Escape gamblers are more likely to have dependent or avoidant features.

Player card: a plastic card similar to a credit card used for slot machine gambling, which is computerized to monitor all of the owner's gambling activities and allocating points accordingly. Points can be redeemed for gambling store items. The card may not be transferred.

Player profile: the financial value of the gambler's wins and losses which casinos use to determine compensations.

Pokemon: a popular card game among children typically 7-14 of age, developed in Japan in the early 2000s, similar to baseball cards. The collector buys packets of Pokemon cards hoping to get that special one needed to complete the collection. It is considered gambling but has lost its popularity.

Poker: a popular card game, generally considered a man's game although during the 1800s some female gamblers were notorious for their histrionic antics and daring to violate social norms. Poker Alice was a heroine among gamblers. Poker is often considered a game of skill, but is actually a game of chance.

Poker machine: an electronic version of a slot machine which became popular in the 1970s displaying card games, sports and other gambling games rather than the more traditional cherries and Sevens depicted in manual slot machines. Poker machines have three or five electronic reels, with multiple winning lines.

Problem gambling: a level of gambling between controlled and compulsive gambling.

Process addiction: non-ingested, behavioral addictions. Compulsive Gambling is considered to be a process addiction.

Procrastination: it has jokingly been said that "procrastination is the compulsive gambler's middle name."

Public defender: an attorney paid by the federal or state government who represents the compulsive gambler unable to pay for a private attorney.

Pull-tabs: a form of instant lottery in which the gambler pulls tabs or slips from a card. They are popular in fraternal clubs and bars. Variations of pull-tabs include pickle jars and tip-boards. Most are illegal.

Quick fix: the gambler's need for a bail-out. "Quick gain, long-term pain" is a description of the Quick Fix.

Racino: a word coined in the late 1990s, defining a combination of race tracks and casino.

Recovery: being in recovery is defined as not only abstinence from gambling but also changing one's attitudes and behaviors.

Relationships: gamblers tend to avoid intimate relationships, feeling vulnerable to criticism and rejection, yet their gambling invariably harms the relationship.

Rejection: the ultimate fear held by compulsive gamblers, which signifies being a failure in life and unworthy of association with others. Abandonment is a severe form of rejection.

Relapse: a relapse occurs when triggers, urges and cravings are ignored. A one-time incident of gambling may be considered "a slip" whereas continuous gambling is considered a relapse.

Relapse prevention: an educational program which identifies triggers, urges and cravings, which lead to slips and relapses. The relapse prevention therapist and gambler determine a strategy for preventing them. Certified Relapse Prevention Therapists are addiction counselors who receive special training in relapse prevention.

Remorse: a relatively infrequent feeling among compulsive gamblers, who are more inclined to feelings of guilt, which then requires punishment by self or others. Remorse suggests recognizing unacceptable behaviors, learning from them, and a determination to correct such unacceptable behaviors in the future.

Residential treatment: a treatment program, usually 4-6 weeks, in an "open" housing location, as in a drug and alcohol rehab, rather than a locked unit in a psychiatric hospital.

Responsible gaming: a program developed by the private gaming industry and state lotteries in response to public outcry of gambling addiction. It refers to social and problem gambling, not compulsive gambling.

Restitution: developing a financial strategy for repaying monies that were owed, borrowed, or stolen. It is part of the GA 12-Step program of recovery and mandatory when court-ordered.

Risk: as different from Chance, in which individuals expose themselves to harm, such as a soldier risking his life in battle.

Roulette wheel: a gambling game in which players bet on the spin of the wheel, found in casinos and at fund-raisers. The odds of winning are low.

Self-defeating: a personality disorder or behaviors which defy a more rational, productive outcome. Self-defeating thoughts are "Yes, I should, but…"

Self-esteem: a state of mind in which individuals compare themselves to others, thus describing themselves as "having low self-esteem." Many compulsive gamblers score their self-esteem to be twenty, on a scale of 1 – 100 percent.

Seniors: individuals who start gambling in late adult age.

Sex: prior to the 1960s, most compulsive gamblers were males. The vast expansion of legal gambling has nearly equalized male and female compulsive gamblers. In Las Vegas, Gamblers Anonymous chapters tend to have 70% female membership.

Serenity Prayer: the Serenity Prayer is spoken at the end of every 12-Step meeting:

> God grant me the Serenity
> To Accept the things I cannot change
> Courage to change the things I can,
> And Wisdom to know the difference.

Shaving points: deliberately changing the outcome of a sport.

Signs: although compulsive gambling is often described as a "silent" addiction, there are many signs of gambling, most frequently changes in financial stability, attitudes, behaviors, appearance, and mood swings.

Simulcasting: televising all horse or dog races, running continuously from noon to midnight, in OTBs (off-track betting parlors), racinos, and casinos.

Slots: a mechanical or electronic gambling machine, in which coins, currency or a plastic players card is inserted, leading to the spin of wheels, and coming to rest on symbols. The amount of money and the number of reels bet determines the payout. Slots offer various initial amounts: pennies, nickels, up to $100, for one to five reels. Ratios of payouts are determined by state law or Native American regulations.

Smoking: smoking increases dramatically during the out of control stage of gambling. "I never smoked more than half a pack a day, but when I'm at the casino I smoke three or more packs." When in treatment, gamblers may protest, "I can't quit everything at one time, I just want to stop gambling." Nevertheless, their smoking tends to decrease or stop once they are in treatment and their stress level is reduced.

Social gambling: the frequency, length of time and the amount of money to spend serve as guidelines for social gambling. This level of gambling does not interfere with finances, family, work, health, or social pursuits. Social gambling may vary from an annual outing to the Preakness with friends, a trip to a casino with colleagues, or the daily purchase of a lottery ticket. Heavy social gambling is dictated by the amounts of money wagered and is consistent with income and the ability to afford it.

Sports betting: making wagers on high school, college or professional sports. Sports betting is favored by male gamblers.

Stop Predatory Gambling: a 501(c)3 not-profit organization, which evolved from NCAGE and NCALG, which educates the community about the detriments of legalized gambling on the family and community.

Stressors: gambling is one method of avoiding or coping with life stressors, although problem gambling can lead to an increase in stressors.

Sweepstakes: a form of legal gambling, similar to international lotteries, operated by a government, such as the Irish Sweepstakes.

Suicide: viewed by many compulsive gamblers as the only way out of the relationship and financial mess they have created. Suicide methods vary: race track and casino gamblers prefer automobile accidents while driving to and from the gambling site, females prefer using prescription pills, while hunters, military and law enforcement members are more likely to use a gun.

Sure thing: a gambler's conviction that the next bet will be the winning bet.

Telephone: The bookie's tool in trade for accepting bets, and the family's nemesis, fearing calls from creditors. The telephone is often the first household utility to be turned off for non-payment of bills.

Throwing the game: a term used in sports in which an athlete deliberately makes a false move to effect the integrity and outcome of the game. Throwing the game results in life-time ouster from collegiate and professional sports.

Urges: urges last for only a few minutes but can occur throughout the gambler's lifetime. Urges can develop into cravings, easily advancing to a slip or full-fledged relapse.

V-Chart of Compulsive Gambling: a graphic description of the Winning, Losing, and Desperation Stage of compulsive gambling, ultimately ending in Hitting Bottom, which then continues into the Critical, Rebuilding and Growth stages of recovery. It was developed by Robert L. Custer, MD, while he was serving as Chief of Psychiatry at the VA Medical Center in Brecksville (Cleveland), Ohio in 1972.

V-Chart of the Effects of Compulsive Gambling on the Spouse (and Family): a companion graphic description similar to Dr. Custer's V-Chart, developed by Gam-Anon member and addictions counselor, Sheila Wexler, of New Jersey. It depicts the downward progression of the Denial, Stress, and Exhaustion Phase, ending in Hopelessness, and continuing into the Critical, Rebuilding, and Growing Phases of recovery.

Value: paper currency loses its value and is viewed by compulsive gamblers only as a means to continue gambling, not as currency. "It's just paper."

Valuables taken: items of value taken illegally by the compulsive gambler from a family member, which is then pawned or sold. Pawned articles tend to be redeemed by the family member, which technically is a bail-out.

Video gambling devices: electronic versions of slot machines, in which buttons are pushed, and which depict lines or symbols on each reel. These machines may be legal, according to state law, or illegal due to lack vague state law. The latter are termed "grey-area" machines. These machines can be converted electronically to depict games of skill, such as PacMan, when the site is under investigation by law enforcement.

Vigorish: or vig, the term used in bookmaking, defining the interest rate.

Violent crimes: In more recent years, compulsive gamblers have also commited violent crimes — crimes with the use of a weapon, bank robbery, breaking and entering, domestic violence, prostitution, child abuse and neglect, selling drugs, and occasionally also homicide.

Wagers: another word for bets, which is more frequently used in reference to horse racing, as "What's your wager?" The term also tends to be used in formal language and by law enforcement.

Waves of gambling: described by gaming specialist, attorney J. Nelson Rose, in his book *Gambling and the Law*, in which he discusses the three strong movements of pro- and anti-gambling in the United States. The gaming industry and Stop Predatory Gambling represent opposing views.

Western Union: Internet gambling is paid through Western Union money grams, if payment cannot be made via credit cards.

Whale: description of a casino gambler who surpasses a High Roller in the amount of money bet. Whales are highly treasured, thus pampered by casinos through a multitude of services and generous gifts.

Work productivity: during the desperation phase, the gambler's work becomes sloppy, inconsistent, inaccurate, or incomplete, which leads to reprimands, suspensions and being fired. A similar pattern is true of students who perform poorly in class, leading to failing grades, suspensions, or dismissal from school.

Youth: youthful compulsive gamblers have increased consistently with the growth of legalized gambling.

APPENDIX 2
THE GAMBLERS ANONYMOUS PROGRAM

Note: The information of this chapter is taken directly from printed materials of Gamblers Anonymous (printed in 11/02).

HISTORY

The fellowship of Gamblers Anonymous is the outgrowth of a chance meeting between two men during the month of January in 1957. These men had a truly baffling history of trouble and misery due to an obsession to gamble. They began to meet regularly and as the months passed neither had returned to gambling.

They concluded from their discussions that in order to prevent a relapse it was necessary to bring about certain character changes within themselves. To accomplish this, they used for a guide certain spiritual principles which had been utilized by thousands of people who were recovering from other addictions. The word *spiritual* can be said to describe those characteristics of the human mind that represent the highest and finest qualities such as kindness, generosity, honesty and humility. Also, in order to maintain their own abstinence, they felt that it was vitally important that they carry the message of hope to other compulsive gamblers.

As a result of favorable publicity by a prominent newspaper columnist and TV commentator, the first group meeting of Gamblers Anonymous was held on Friday, September 13, 1957, in Los Angeles, California. Since that time, the fellowship has grown steadily and groups are forming throughout the world.

GAMBLERS ANONYMOUS PROGRAM

"Gamblers Anonymous is a fellowship of men and women who share their experience, strength and hope with each other that they may solve their common problem and help others to recover from a gambling problem.

The only requirement for membership is a desire to stop gambling. There are no dues or fees for Gamblers Anonymous membership; we are self-supporting through our own contributions. Gamblers Anonymous is not allied with any sect, denomination, politics, organization or institution; does not wish to engage in any controversy; neither endorses nor opposes any cause. Our primary purpose is to stop gambling and to help other compulsive gamblers do the same.

Most of us have been unwilling to admit we were real problem gamblers. No one likes to think they are different from their fellows. Therefore, it is not surprising that our gambling careers have been characterized by countless vain attempts to prove we could gamble like other people. The idea that somehow, someday, we will control our gambling is the great obsession of every compulsive gambler. The persistence of this illusion is astonishing. Many pursue it into the gates of prison, insanity or death.

We learned we had to concede fully to our innermost selves that we are compulsive gamblers. This is the first step in our recovery. With reference to gambling, the delusion that we are like other people, or presently may be, has to be smashed.

We have lost the ability to control our gambling. We know that no real compulsive gambler ever regains control. All of us felt at times we were regaining control, but such intervals—usually brief—were inevitably followed by still less control, which led in time to pitiful and incomprehensible demoralization. We are convinced that gamblers of our type are in the grip of a progressive illness. Over any considerable period of time we get worse, never better.

Therefore, in order to lead normal happy lives, we try to practice to the best of our ability, certain principles in our daily affairs ".

THE RECOVERY PROGRAM
(ALSO KNOWN AS THE 12-STEPS OF GA)

1. We admitted we were powerless over gambling, that our lives had become unmanageable.
2. Came to believe that a Power greater than ourselves could restore us to a normal way of thinking and living.
3. Made a decision to turn our will and our lives over to the care of this Power of our own understanding.
4. Made a searching and fearless moral and financial inventory of ourselves.
5. Admitted to ourselves and to another human being the exact nature of our wrongs.
6. Were entirely ready to have these defects of character removed.
7. Humbly asked God (of our understanding) to remove our shortcomings.
8. Made a list of all persons we had harmed and became willing to make amends to them all.
9. Made direct amends to such people wherever possible, except when to do so would injure them or others.

10. Continued to take personal inventory and when we were wrong, promptly admitted it.
11. Sought through prayer and meditation to improve our conscious contact with God as we understood Him, praying only for knowledge of His will for us and the power to carry that out.
12. Having made an effort to practice these principles in all our affairs, we tried to carry this message to other compulsive gamblers.

THE UNITY PROGRAM

1. Our common welfare should come first; personal recovery depends upon group unity.
2. Our leaders are but trusted servants; they do not govern.
3. The only requirement for Gamblers Anonymous membership is a desire to stop gambling.
4. Each group should be self-governing except in matters affecting other groups or Gamblers Anonymous as a whole.
5. Gamblers Anonymous has but one primary purpose: to carry its message to the compulsive gambler who still suffers.
6. Gamblers Anonymous ought never endorse, finance or lend the Gamblers Anonymous name to any related facility or outside enterprise, lest problems of money, property and prestige divert us from our primary purpose.
7. Every Gamblers Anonymous group ought to be fully self-supporting, declining outside contributions.
8. Gamblers Anonymous should remain forever non-professional, but our service centers may employ special workers.
9. Gamblers Anonymous, as such, ought never be organized; but we may create service boards or committees directly responsible to those they serve.

10. Gamblers Anonymous has no opinion on outside issues; hence the Gamblers Anonymous name ought never be drawn into public controversy.
11. Our public relations policy is based on attraction rather than promotion; we need always maintain personal anonymity at the level of press, radio, films and television.
12. Anonymity is the spiritual foundation of the Gamblers Anonymous program, ever reminding us to place principles before personalities.

Gamblers Anonymous International Service Office
P. O. Box 17173
Los Angeles, CA 90017
Phone 626-960-3500
Fax 626-960-3501
www.isogamblersaonymous.org

THE TWENTY QUESTIONS

_____1. Did you ever lose time from work or school due to gambling?

_____2. Has gambling ever made your home life unhappy?

_____3. Did gambling affect your reputation?

_____4. Have you ever felt remorse (or guilt) after gambling?

_____5. Did you ever gamble to get money with which to pay debts or otherwise solve financial problems?

_____6. Did gambling cause a decrease in your ambition or efficiency?

_____7. After losing, did you feel you must return as soon as possible and win back your losses?

_____8. After a win did you have a strong urge to return and win more?

_____9. Did you often gamble until your last dollar was gone?

_____10. Did you ever borrow to finance your gambling?

_____11. Have you ever sold (or pawned) anything to finance your gambling?

_____12. Were you reluctant to use "gambling money" for normal expenditures?

_____13. Did gambling make you careless of the welfare of your family?

_____14. Did you ever gamble longer than you planned?

_____15. Have you ever gambled to escape worry or trouble?

_____16. Have you ever committed, or considered committing, an illegal act to finance gambling?

_____17. Did gambling cause you to have difficulty in sleeping?

_____18. Do arguments, disappointments or frustrations create within you an urge to gamble?

_____19. Did you ever have an urge to celebrate any good fortune by a few hours of gambling?

_____20. Have you ever considered self-destruction as a result of your gambling?

Most compulsive gamblers will answer yes to at least seven of these questions.

VOICES FROM THE MEMBERS OF GAMBLERS ANONYMOUS

Gamblers Anonymous holds conferences throughout the year, all across the nation. Many chapters hold statewide annual one-day conferences, others hold conferences for two or three days, which include GA chapters from various nearby states. There are also regional and national conferences.

These conferences generally have a speaker of some important to the gambling field—it may be a member of the GA program, for instance, the Director of the International Service Office of Gamblers Anonymous, or a "professional" — someone who has conducted research on compulsive gambling or who is the head of a compulsive gambling treatment program, or a legislator or administration representative.

The conferences tend to have sessions for GA members alone, Gam-Anon alone, GA/Gam-Anon joint, or open sessions. They tend to be educational and spiritually powerful. They are a forum in which members of GA and Gam-Anon can give their testimonials of how these programs changed their lives. Some of the GA responses are:

When I gamble I can't think, I can't feel, I can't live right. I die.

When I was gambling, I was a child. When I accepted GA, I became a man.

When I went to GA I didn't want to be there. They talked about hope – I wanted hope.

I couldn't Do until I learned to Feel

My wife said You get well and We'll take care of this. I got well at once because now I had hope and support.

GA gave me hope.

I always knew I had a problem, but I never knew I had a gambling problem.

The first year of gambling is all about the big score. The last year of gambling is all about suicide.

GA gave me hope at the lowest point in my life.

It's a revelation that no one in GA is ashamed of me.

When I joined GA I waited for the day I could bust out again. Seven months later I saw Step 2, a Power could restore us to a normal way of thinking and living – and it all made sense.

When I joined GA I thought I would learn how to gamble.

God is grace. Gambling is a crisis.

My ego would not let me admit there's a power greater than myself.

If I'm happy, I did it. If I'm unhappy, she did it.

In GA I saw people who were enjoying life. I saw hope.

I used to think religion is weak, and I didn't want to be weak.

All my life I felt negative emotions about everyone, till I came to GA.

There's no reason ever big enough to go back to the life of misery.

GA helps me think right and act right.

I was so sick I was ready to commit suicide, except I was too much of a coward. Then I was gonna run away but only after I borrowed from the shylock.

Even a moron can do one day at a time.

When the woman of the house is happy, it's like a ray of sunshine. When I gamble, I have to hide in my cubbyhole.

When I went to GA, I had a lobotomy of the mind.

I thought everybody felt good except me.

I thought money was the problem. I thought gambling was the cure-all.

When I started GA, I was comparing. Now I am relating.

When I started GA, I kept wondering "What do you want from me?"

Gambling addiction robbed me of choices.

I thought I had a fear of failure. I was an expert on failure.

Without strokes you get strikes.

The opposite of Love is not Hate, it is Fear.

Compulsive gamblers are like little children, hiding the hurt inside.

APPENDIX 3
THE GAM-ANON PROGRAM

Gam-Anon is a fellowship, whose function is to support the family and friends of the compulsive gambler. It has chapters throughout the world, its own groups and structure, and although separate from Gamblers Anonymous, has many joint programs, including regional, national, and international conferences. It has its own literature, either free of charge or available at a nominal cost. The following information is taken directly from two of its booklets, *The Gam-Anon Way of Life: A Gam-Anon Handbook* (59 pages) and *Games Compulsive Gamblers and We Play* (27 pages).

The Gam-Anon Way of Life describes the Gam-Anon program. It includes six chapters: 1) Welcome to Gam-Anon; 2) Suggestions for Recovery; 3) Tools of the Program; 4) How Gam-Anon Functions; 5) Gam-Anon International Service Office; and 6) Inspirational Thoughts.

The writings below are taken directly from these two booklets, with permission by the Gam-Anon International Service Organization, Inc.

THE GAM-ANON WAY OF LIFE:
A GAM-ANON HANDBOOK

GAM-ANON

Gam-Anon is a fellowship of men and women who have been affected by the gambling problem. If you are seeking a solution for living with this problem, we would like you to feel that we understand, as perhaps few can. We, too, are familiar with worry and sleepless nights and promises made only to be broken. Our thinking had become confused, and many of us had become nervous, irritable, bitter and unreasonable.

We come into the group feeling alone, frightened, desperate, and ashamed. We hesitate to share our problems and failures, fearing no one could understand. The Gam-Anon group is warmly accepting, and it offers its members identification. The message we receive is: Come join with us, we too were alone, afraid, and unable to cope with the problem; we will share with you a new and fulfilling way of life.

Living with the effects of someone else's gambling is too devastating for most people to bear without help. In Gam-Anon we learn we are not responsible for another person's disease or for their recovery from it. We let go of our focus on the gambler's behavior and begin to lead happier and more manageable lives for ourselves. This "detachment" does not imply a judgment or condemnation of the gambler. It is simply a means of allowing us to separate ourselves from the adverse effects that gambling can have on our lives. We look at our situation realistically and objectively, thereby making intelligent decisions possible.

The Twelve Steps of Gam-Anon, which we follow, are not easy. At first we may think that some of them are unnecessary, but we soon discover that they apply to us as well as to the compulsive gambler. The benefits to be derived from a strict and constant observance of them can be limitless. We believe that a change in our attitudes is of boundless help to us as well as to our gamblers.

Gam-Anon, a worldwide organization, offers self-help recovery whether or not the gambler seeks help or even recognizes the existence of a gambling problem, though recovery is enhanced when the gambler and Gam-Anon member seek help jointly.

Gam-Anon is not a religious organization or a counseling agency. It is not a treatment center nor is it allied with any other organization offering such services. Gam-Anon family groups neither express opinions on outside issues nor endorse outside enterprises. No dues or fees are required. Membership is voluntary, requiring only that one's own life has been affected by someone else's gambling problem.

THE PURPOSE OF GAM-ANON

A. To grow spiritually through living by the twelve steps of Gam-Anon.
B. To learn to understand the gambling problem and its impact on our lives.
C. To give encouragement and understanding to the compulsive gambler.
D. To welcome and give assistance and comfort to those affected by the gambling problem.

EXPLANATION OF COMPULSIVE GAMBLING

We have learned that compulsive gambling is an illness, not a moral issue. The disease of gambling is twofold: an obsession of the mind, coupled with a spiritual emptiness. It can be arrested but never cured.

Only complete abstinence from the first bet of any kind can arrest this illness. No one, not the psychiatrist, neither clergy, nor the family can do this for the gambler.

We have found that compulsive gambling does not indicate a lack of affection for the family. It is not a matter of love, but of illness. The gambler has lost the power of choice in the matter of gambling. Even knowing what can happen when that first bet is made, the gambler will do so anyway. This is the "insanity" we speak of in regard to this illness.

When we fully understand, and accept the fact that compulsive gambling is a disease, that it is a mental obsession, and that we are powerless over it, we become ready to learn a better way to live.

SUGGESTIONS FOR RECOVERY

(This chapter lists each step and gives a brief synopsis explaining that step.)

1. We admitted we were powerless over the problem in our family.
2. Came to believe that a Power greater than ourselves could restore us to a way of thinking and living.
3. Made a decision to turn our will and our lives over to the care of the Power of our own understanding.
4. Made a searching and fearless moral inventory of ourselves.
5. Admitted to ourselves and to another human being the exact nature of our wrongs.
6. Were entirely ready to have these defects of character removed.
7. Humbly asked God (of our understanding) to remove our shortcomings.
8. Made a list of all persons we had harmed and became willing to make amends to them all.
9. Made direct amends to such people whenever possible, except when to do so would injure them or others.
10. Continued to take personal inventory and when we were wrong promptly admitted it.

11. Sought, through prayer and meditation, to improve our conscious contact with God, as we understood Him, praying only for knowledge of His will for us, and the power to carry that out.
12. Having made an effort to practice these principles in all our affairs, we tried to carry this message to others.

HOW GAM-ANON FUNCTIONS

In order to maintain unity, all Gam-Anon meetings follow the Unity Steps. *(Thirteen pages are devoted to explaining in detail each of these Unity Steps.)*

GAM-ANON UNITY PROGRAM

In order to maintain unity, our experience has shown that:

1. Our common welfare should come first; personal serenity depends upon Gam-Anon unity.
2. Our leaders are but trusted servants; they do not govern.
3. The only requirement for Gam-Anon membership is that there be a gambling problem in the family.
4. Each group should be self-governing except in matters affecting other groups or Gam-Anon as a whole.
5. Gam-Anon has but one primary purpose: to carry its message to the family of the compulsive gambler.
6. Gam-Anon ought never endorse, finance or lend the Gam-Anon name to any related facility or outside enterprise, lest problems of money, property and prestige divert us from our primary purpose.
7. Every Gam-Anon group ought to be fully self-supporting, declining outside contributions.
8. Gam-Anon should remain forever non-professional, but our service centers may employ special workers.

9. Gam-Anon, as such, ought never be organized; but we may create service boards or committees directly responsible to those they serve.
10. Gam-Anon has no opinion on outside issues; hence the Gam-Anon name ought never be drawn into public controversy.
11. Our public relations policy is based on attraction rather than promotion; we need always maintain personal anonymity at the level of press, radio, films and television.
12. Anonymity is the spiritual foundation of the Gam-Anon program, ever reminding us to place principles before personalities.

EACH KNOT FROM OUR GAM-ANON SYMBOL

REPRESENTS ONE THING LEARNED FROM GAM-ANON

1. **Admission** – Admit our need for help. – God and Gam-Anon.
2. **Higher Power** – Our need for God – Someone or something greater than ourselves.
3. **Help** – Be supportive of the gambler and other members of Gam-Anon.
4. **Humility** – Remember that we too can be wrong.
5. **Let Go** – Let go of the gambler. Let him or her face the consequences of gambling. Let go and let God.
6. **Live** – Just for today, one day at a time, allow time for reflection, meditation, and family fun.
7. **Thankfulness** – Count your blessings. Do not blame all problems on the gambling problem.
8. **Happiness**–Smile often. Happiness is contagious.
9. **Acceptance** – Take life as it comes. Do not try to change people and things to your way.

EACH LITTLE KNOT IS
A STEP TOWARD A BETTER LIFE.
INSPIRATIONAL THOUGHTS
(ONLY SELECTED PASSAGES ARE COPIED)
YESTERDAY, TODAY, AND TOMORROW

There are two days in every week about which we should not worry; two days which should be kept free from **fear** and **apprehension.**

One of these days is **yesterday** with its mistakes and cares, its faults and blunders, its aches and pains. All the money in the world cannot bring back **yesterday. Yesterday** has passed forever beyond our control. We cannot undo a single act we performed. We cannot ease a single word we said. **Yesterday** is gone.

The other day we should not worry about is **tomorrow** with its possible adversities, its burdens, its large promise or poor performance. **Tomorrow** is also beyond our immediate control.

Tomorrow's sun will rise, whether it is in splendor or behind a mask of clouds...but it will rise. Until it does, we have no stake in **tomorrow**, for it is yet unborn.

This leaves only one day...**TODAY.** Any person can fight the battles of just one day. It is only when you and I add the burdens of these two awful eternities—**yesterday** and **tomorrow**—that we break down.

It is not the experience of **today** that drives people mad— it is the remorse or bitterness of something which happened **yesterday** and the dread of what **tomorrow** may bring.

Let us, therefore, **LIVE BUT ONE DAY AT A TIME.**

GAMES COMPULSIVE GAMBLERS AND WE PLAY

This booklet was published in 2012 by the Gam-Anon International Service Office, Inc. It provides information explaining the impact of compulsive gambling on the gambler, the spouse/loved one, the gambler's parents, and the children. It presents a brief explanation of the progression of compulsive gambling.)

PREFACE

Compulsive gambling is an emotional illness. This is, perhaps, the most difficult premise for someone close to a compulsive gambler to believe and understand. It can affect anyone: women as well as men, young as well as old. Cultural background also does not determine the likelihood of falling prey to the disease.

Because of the games that gamblers play, those close to them often come to believe that the issues and problems they must deal with are actually their fault. This is the ultimate goal of the gamblers' games – to shift the blame and avoid the consequences. It is essential for anyone dealing with gamblers to understand this first very basic fact – that compulsive gamblers are master manipulators. They are the ultimate "gamers."

Life for active compulsive gamblers and their loved ones may be seen as such a game. The gamblers must manipulate situations and people in order to maintain their gambling activities. Those who love the gamblers can be easily manipulated and can never win playing the gamblers' games. The gamblers know each person's weaknesses and the moves that will be made before they do.

THE GAMES

Fifteen pages are devoted to describe various "games" that others play while attempting to cope with the impact of compulsive gambling. Sections of this booklet are copied below. Some of the games played by the gambler and non-gamblers are the *Catch Me if You Can* game; *Deny and Lie* game; *Promise/Trust Me* game; *Pick a Fight* game, the *Silent Treatment* game, and others. It concludes with suggestions on how loved ones can stop playing these games.

Some of the suggestions are:

- When the gamblers lie, tell the gamblers you don't believe the lie.

- When the gamblers ask for money, say NO, no matter what the gamblers say will happen if they don't get the money.

- Don't pay the gamblers' debts.

Regina K., Executive Secretary
Gam-Anon International Service Office, Inc.
P.O. Box 570157
Whitestone, NY 11357-0157
Phone: 718-352-1671
Fax 718-746-2571
Website gam-anon.org
E-mail Gam-Anonoffice@gam-anon.org

SOME VOICES FROM MEMBERS OF GAM-ANON

(Taken directly from the research thesis by the author, Valerie C. Lorenz, for the MPsSc degree in Community Psychology, The Pennsylvania State University, 1978).

> *Having been separated only three months, I am hopeful, one day at a time, that God's will be that my husband returns to GA and recovery.*

> *My life is Gam-Anon! Thank God!*

> *How can I get my husband to come?*

My experience in AlAnon helped me not only with his drinking problem, but with the gambling as well.

Thank God I had an open mind and put everything into action.

Heartless man, headless woman.

Living the GA and Gam-Anon life is the kind of life and marriage that can be happy and meaningful.

Excellent—most meaningful involvement in my life.

I don't think I would have made all these improvements if not for joining Gam-Anon and learning a new way of life, because my spouse was a secretive gambler – and I didn't understand.

I am more outgoing and loving toward others today. I even look better physically because I think better.

Still no communication. Our sex life is a complete zero. My gambler cannot give of himself to me or our children, he doesn't know how and he's afraid to reveal his feelings.

I've been in Gam-Anon only three months and am still angry and resentful.

I have learned to let other people be what they are and not mold everyone into what I want them to be.

I have learned that a person's feelings are neither right nor wrong— they just are.

If it wasn't for Gam-Anon I don't know where I would be.

Gam-Anon is my life line. I learned there was plenty wrong with me and am really trying to change.

I have been in the program only a short time but I do feel it is a program that can help any human being to grow.

I have a general feeling of well-being—serenity—which is very new to me.

APPENDIX 4

THE EARLY WARNING SYSTEM THAT FAILED

The Early Warning System That Failed:
A Personal Account

Paul William Ottinger

The author, a criminal lawyer and judge, writes from prison about his views of compulsive gambling, incarceration, the road to recovery, and the special burden placed on sentencing judges when a member of the bar stands before them.

It was summer. I was five years old. The corn which grew up to the back yard, where I was playing with my three-year-old brother, was not "as high as an elephant's eye" (the red clay of eastern Tennessee was not as productive as the alluvial loam of Oklahoma); but it was tall enough to conceal my father as he crept up to the back of the house.

I ran in to tell my mother that father was home. Mother and her cousin were adjusting their clothing.

Father divorced mother. In those good old days (1920) adultery was considered such a stain on a woman's character (but not on a man's), that the custody of me and my brother was given to Father without argument. He did not want us, but he did want revenge. He was later charged with child neglect but acquitted when he gave us back to our mother, temporarily.

We thought she did not want us, either.

Editor's Comment: The Honorable Judge Ottinger, 73, who graduated Magna Cum Laude and Order of the Coif from law school, practiced criminal law for forty years, served four terms as District Magistrate, and two terms as Circuit Court Judge in the state of Maryland. He lost control over his gambling affliction at age sixty-nine. He is attending a self-help group in prison.

Address reprint requests to Paul Ottinger, J.D., P.O. Box 600, Dorm #4, Eglin AFB, FL 32542.

Journal of Gambling Behavior Vol. 4(4), Winter 1988
© 1988 Human Sciences Press

309

Valerie C. Lorenz, Ph.D.

How does one become a compulsive gambler? With this kind of a background, it doesn't seem to be hard.

When I was 15 years old, I lost all my paper route money in my first poker game. I was so annoyed with my lack of self-control, that I promised myself that I would never gamble again; and I didn't, until I attended baby judges' school in Reno 43 years later, when I lost all my extra money in the slot machines.

Again I made the same promise. I kept it for fifteen years. By then I was so heavily in debt (a divorce and remarriage, two families to support, three children to put through college, a contested double campaign, an inadequate judicial salary), with my judgment impaired by alcohol, that I tried to recoup by gambling. There were three state lotteries and two race tracks within easy reach; and there were numerous accommodating poker playing friends. Winning was exhilarating; losing was hell. After a while I was gambling to get the rush, like a runner's high, which accompanies the gambling itself, regardless of winning or losing.

Of course I knew that using the money of others was wrong, but I could not seem to stop. There came a Friday when I knew I would have to produce $50,000 on Monday. I did not have it and I could not get it.

I disappeared for three months.

I was arrested in April 1987 and have been in jail ever since. In federal court my crimes were called mail fraud. In the state court the same incidents were labelled forgery and larceny.

The feds are fond of saying that the honest admission of your error is the first step in your rehabilitation. No doubt. Getting off the booze also helps. But it is still necessary to reshape one's attitudes, one's distorted thinking.

After a great deal of sober reflection (I stopped drinking entirely seven weeks before I was incarcerated), I have concluded that compulsive gambling is an illness (or a disease, as lawyers prefer), just as alcoholism and drug dependency are illnesses.

Is incarceration useful under these circumstances? For a short time, perhaps. Something drastic must be done, no doubt, to break the addictive habit patterns, but jail for more than a few months is a waste of public funds and the talent of the defendant.

Everybody in the penal system knows that prisons do not rehabilitate. They don't even try. It would have made more sense in my case to restrict my activities (half-way house, house arrest) and sentence me to community service and therapy.

The problem seems to be that sentencing judges are targets of severe criticism from numerous segments of the community if they appear to be lenient. Nobody believes that I am a danger to the community or to myself; and nobody believes that I am being rehabilitated. I am in jail to frighten other people who might be similarly tempted.

The question that is so difficult is, "How is the compulsive gambler to know that he is mentally ill?"

A compulsive gambler—at least this one—suffers from a false sense of beliefs. A terrible sense of inadequacy seems to cause overcompensation—working too much, smoking too much, eating too much, drinking too much, gambling too much. The reaction to the inability to be perfect results in a hopeless depression which further distorts one's thinking.

When I read *Feeling Good* (Burns, 1980), I was astounded that a man who had never seen me could describe me so accurately. Sometimes one has to live a long, hard life before one realizes the universality of experience and the brotherhood of man.

When I took various psychological tests, they indicated that I needed professional treatment. I never knew I was sick. I thought that's the way life is.

The road back is not a straight line; but, with counseling, I am slowly realizing that it is all right to forgive myself for being less than perfect; that an imperfect decision is better than no decision; that most people are not nearly as critical as I have always assumed them to be; that I can survive even if they are critical; that most people are much more concerned about themselves than they are about me; that I will continue to fail regularly, but that such failures will not be disastrous; that most of the disastrous things which I anticipate probably will not happen and, even if they do, I can cope, on the average, not perfectly, but as well as most others.

Every day I tried to be perfect, and every day I thought I had failed. I felt the pain of inadequacy, of imagined criticism and rejection. But now I am learning I no longer need to drink or gamble or think the way I once did. Now I can be Me.

REFERENCES

Burns, D.M. (1980). *Feeling good. The new mood therapy.* New York: William Morrow and Company.

CPSIA information can be obtained at www.ICGtesting.com
Printed in the USA
LVOW10s1459160615

442682LV00015B/806/P